POLITICS

POLITICS

An Introduction to Democratic Government

THIRD EDITION

Munroe Eagles

broadview press

Broadview Press

is an independent, international publishing house, incorporated in 1985. Broadview believes in shared ownership, both with its employees and with the general public; since the year 2000 Broadview shares have traded publicly on the Toronto Venture Exchange under the symbol BDP.

We welcome comments and suggestions regarding any aspect of our publications—please feel free to contact us at the addresses below or at broadview@broadviewpress.com

NORTH AMERICA
Post Office Box 1243
Peterborough, Ontario
Canada K9J 7H5
Tel: (705) 743-8990
Fax: (705) 743-8353
customerservice@broadviewpress.com

2215 Kenmore Ave.
Buffalo, NY
USA 14207

**UK, IRELAND, AND
CONTINENTAL EUROPE**
NBN International
Estover Road
Plymouth PL6 7PY
UK
Tel: 44 (0) 1752 202300
Fax: 44 (0) 1752 202330
enquiries@nbninternational.com

AUSTRALIA AND NEW ZEALAND
UNIREPS
University of New South Wales
Sydney, NSW, Australia 2052
Tel: + 61 2 9664 0999
Fax: + 61 2 9664 5420
info.press@unsw.edu.au

www.broadviewpress.com

Library and Archives Canada Cataloguing in Publication

Eagles, Munroe, 1956–
    Politics : an introduction to democratic government / D. Munroe Eagles.—3rd ed.

Includes bibliographical references and index.
ISBN 978-1-55111-858-1

    1. Democracy—Textbooks.   2. Comparative government—Textbooks.   3. Political science—Textbooks.   I. Title.

JA66.E34 2008   321.8   C2008-900802-2

Copy-edited by Betsy Struthers.

Book designed and typeset by Zack Taylor, design@zacktaylor.com.

This book is printed on paper containing 100% post-consumer fibre.

Printed in Canada

CONTENTS

PART TWO Ideas   75

PREFACE

It is said that "May you live in interesting times" is a Chinese curse. If so, we are in some respects cursed, because our political world has never been more interesting. Following the events of 9/11 in Washington, DC, and New York City, we have been engaged in a costly and difficult "war on terror." While we have successfully avoided further terrorist attacks, progress in democratizing Afghanistan and Iraq has proven to be elusive. Climate change, world poverty, and the economic dislocation associated with globalization are among the many causes for concern as we approach the end of the first decade of our new millennium. These developments point to the extraordinary and growing interdependence of peoples. We cannot be indifferent to injustices or exploitation or environmental degradation anywhere in the world. Humanitarian values are aligned with our self-interest as we work towards solutions to our pressing problems.

Here is one of the most important reasons for turning to the study of politics. It will be collective (political) action that holds the key to addressing the troubles of our times. As the world draws more tightly together to form a global village, it will be increasingly helpful for us to appreciate how others live. The incredible diversity of political life and the broad differences in the institutional configuration of this life will be of growing value to global citizenship. We offer this introduction to the study of politics and to the fundamental ideas, institutions, processes, and policies that make up politics in the spirit of contributing to the cultivation of a new generation of global citizens.

If the world of politics is tumultuous, so too is the state of political science. Debates about how the subject of politics should be studied and disagreements on the relative merits of a scientific as opposed to a more humanistic approach continue to rage within the discipline. As a result, the field of political science as a discipline is replete with debate and intellectual ferment. Students coming in to the discipline should be made aware of these intellectual currents. The lack of closure on such basic questions makes the study of politics not only challenging but also an exciting and diverse enterprise.

Writing this text has been a genuinely collaborative project in the sense that a number of people have made significant contributions to the finished product. The book began as a collaborative project with Larry Johnston, and in the second edition we included Chris Holoman who contributed an important chapter on the international dimension of politics, which appears again here in a revised and updated form. In this substantially revised third edition, by mutual agreement, we decided to shift the focus somewhat to include more discussion of empirical research in political science. With this development, and due to the pressure of other commitments, Larry Johnston decided to focus his research and writing efforts on other projects. We would like to express sincere appreciation to Larry for his contribution to this book, and to say publicly that is has been a great pleasure working with him on earlier editions. Thus, while Eagles has taken the lead in most of the revisions that appear in this edition (except for Chris Holoman's revisions in Chapter 14), this book remains very much a joint project.

We have been gratified by the warm reception given to the first two editions of our text. We have continued to refine our presentation in this third edition. In addition to thoroughly updating the tables and examples (and if a week is a long time in politics, the five years that have intervened since we published the second edition seems like an eternity), we have expanded upon the introduction to the role of empirical methods in the study of politics. By developing—if only briefly—the underlying logic of empirical analysis, we hope that students will feel empowered to try their own hand at designing and completing their own empirical work, that is, to test their own theoretical ideas by measuring correlation and drawing their own causal inferences.

Secondly, we have consolidated two aspects of our earlier discussion. In this edition, we combine the important discussion of the origins of democracy with considerations of conceptualization and definition. Similarly, we have consolidated our discussion of the liberal democratic state with our introduction to its two main institutional variations, presidential and parliamentary government. The result, we hope, is a tighter and more streamlined overview of these two important topics. These changes are reflected in the fact that this edition contains two fewer chapters, something that will align the book more squarely with a standard college semester-long course.

In other respects, we have attempted to preserve our original vision for the text while improving its exposition and accessibility. Our philosophy in the first two editions was expressed in four principles or convictions that we still endorse.

First, we write in the conviction that everyone can benefit from a basic knowledge of the political world he and she inhabits. Within the liberal democratic tradition, political education—like political participation—is voluntary, but within all societies, liberal democratic or otherwise, one cannot escape the consequences of political decisions. Somewhat paradoxically, in a world where more and more countries are democratic (at least formally), the political sophistication of citizens does not necessarily keep pace. This lack of depth to our everyday knowledge of the political world is compounded by the degree to which we depend on media like television or tabloid-style newspapers for political information. In short, this text is written for students who will be citizens in a modern world and in the expectation that those who go on to a more intense study of politics will remain the minority.

Second, in the knowledge that our students live in a liberal democracy, and in the expectation that most will spend their lives in one or another of the world's advanced industrial states, this book reflects no attempt to deal adequately with the problems and prospects of the developing world. Despite the manifest significance to all of us of the struggles of developing countries and peoples, these issues are too complex to be covered adequately in an introductory text such as this. However, our discussion of the ideas, institutions, and processes of liberal democracies will stimulate students to inquire further into—and perhaps to take courses in—the politics of the developing world. In any attempt to understand the world of politics, we must start somewhere, and it makes sense to locate the beginning of this process close to home.

Third, as the goal of this book is to impart to students a basic understanding of their political surroundings and the preliminary tools for more in-depth study of the political world, should they be so inclined, it bears no claim to present the complete and final word on any topic. Insofar as it is written for first-year students, it does not attempt to cover the vast literature on each subject, although indications of further sources of reading at the end of each chapter are intended to serve as an entry to the broader scholarship that is available in each case. Every attempt has been made to avoid that trap into which too many texts fall: namely, to write for the audience least likely to read the book from cover to cover—the instructors who assign it.

Finally, the approach taken here is avowedly eclectic, giving privilege to no particular school of ideology or methodology. In a modest way, we hope that this book demonstrates the value of appropriating from a variety of approaches, perspectives, and even disciplines in our attempts to make sense of political phenomena. This is not intended to be an introductory overview of the world of politics but an introduction to the study of the political world.

We have organized the material into six sections, although cross-referencing within the text indicates that these should not be regarded as "watertight compartments." Part One (The Study of Politics) introduces students to the language, methods, and historical contexts that form the background for studying politics in contemporary liberal democracies. Similarly, Part Two (Ideas) offers the principal themes and substantive issues that have occupied normative political discourse and that continue to animate discussion of the purposes and ends of power and authority. Part Three (Institutions) introduces and explains the common institutional components of the liberal democratic state (e.g., the executive, legislature, and judiciary) and explains the principal variations in how these institutions are structured, organized, and coordinated.

In Part Four (The Political Process), the popular foundation of liberal democratic government is explained, compared in its various institutional forms, and assessed with regard to the degree it satisfies democratic principles. Accordingly, Part Five (The Political Process in Liberal Democracies) continues with an examination of the contribution of institutions of the state to actual government, and thus it closes the loop by exploring what the state returns to the populace. A brief examination of the dynamics of public policy-making is followed by a study of the rise and fall of the welfare state in the second half of the twentieth century. The final Part Six (Governing) provides a brief introduction to the sub-field of

International Relations, focusing particularly on the new dynamic of globalization.

We wish to express thanks to Michael Harrison and Greg Yantz of Broadview Press for their continued encouragement and support of this project. We are also grateful to Brian Nottingham, a PhD candidate at the University at Buffalo and graduate assistant on this project. Brian put together the supplemental material for use by instructors and in the course of that work made a number of important contributions to the text itself. Munroe Eagles would like to thank his students and colleagues at the University at Buffalo-The State University of New York for providing such a stimulating and supportive place to teach and write, and to Deb for her constant enthusiasm and encouragement in this as in all projects. Chris Holoman thanks his students and colleagues at Hilbert College for providing an environment so supportive of teaching; and Allie, Fran, and especially Connie for their constant and indispensable love and support.

PART ONE | getting started

ONE | Foundations of Politics

"Man is by nature a political animal."
— Aristotle, *The Politics*, 384–322 BC

"Government is a contrivance of human wisdom to provide for human wants. Men have a right that these wants should be provided for by this wisdom."
— Edmund Burke; *Reflections on the Revolution in France*, 1790

W e inhabit a political world. We may choose to study politics or not or, having studied politics, decide that we will do so no more, but *we cannot opt out of the political world*. Politics is as inevitable an aspect of the political world we live in as weather is a part of our natural environment. Just as the sky rains upon us regardless of whether we understand why it rains, so, too, no matter how well or poorly we understand political events, however much or little we choose to participate in political activities, our lives are shaped by political circumstances, changed by political decisions, and limited by the political possibilities left to us and others. Indeed, some of the most critical questions facing us as humans—justice, peace, liberty, security, etc.—are determined by the political process.

This text aims to introduce you to two main things. First, we wish to provide an overview of what we know of the key ideas and principles, institutions, and processes in our world. Not only is politics pervasive, but it is also diverse. Over time, and across geographic space, humans have identified different political goals and have found a wide variety of ways to pursue and realize these goals through political practice. Second, we want to introduce you to the discipline of political science. In doing this, we ask you to consider how we can best observe the political world and the ways in which we can acquire valid, reliable, and precise knowledge of

1.1 Politics: An Initial Definition

that world. Permeated as our lives are by politics, a basic knowledge of the foundations of political life and the ability to acquire new and specific knowledge for oneself are essential if we are to be equipped to take effective part in the democratic process.

Understanding the political realities we confront is no guarantee that we can alter them, no more than understanding tornadoes allows us to prevent them. Still, making sense of the political dimension of our lives may help us to influence their future course. When the Greek philosopher Aristotle began his *Politics* by observing that humans are "political animals," he was claiming not only that we live in political societies but also that it is in our nature to be active in the politics of our community. Such an idea underpins our belief in the value of democracy. Often, though, our stance is passive rather than active; others take political action, and we cope, one way or another, with the consequences. Indeed, our experience of politics is, more often than not, gained at the receiving end of things.

Our world is inevitably political because we share space with others. Our lives are essentially and not accidentally social: we live in neighborhoods and communities; we work and play and communicate with others. Our collective activity requires some degree of predictability, regularity, or order; otherwise, there is inefficiency, miscommunication, or even chaos. Regularity and the way it is maintained are at the heart of the political dimension of our social existence. Not surprisingly, many definitions of politics begin by talking about **POWER** (i.e., control). We, too, will find it useful to talk not only about power but also about **AUTHORITY**; there is a fundamental political distinction to make here. But, regardless of whether we understand power and/or authority, we rarely escape their domain.

Does the presence of power or authority in itself define politics? Perhaps, as one political scientist has argued, politics is "any mixture of conflict and cooperation" (Laver, 1983: 1; see also Figure 1.1). It is hard to know what kinds of human interaction would be excluded by such a definition, and while there may be a political dimension to all our relationships, to say that doesn't get us very far. Our initial definition of politics is this:

> Politics concerns the formulation and execution of decisions that are binding upon the population of a society and the relationships between those who make or implement such decisions and those who are affected by them.

FIGURE 1.1
Definitions of Politics

"Politics involves the authoritative allocation of values for a society."
— Easton, 1953

"Politics: who gets what, when, how."
— Lasswell, 1936

"The activity by which decisions are arrived at and implemented in and for a community."
— Bogdanor, 1987

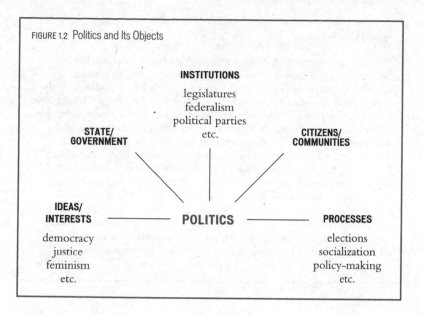

FIGURE 1.2 Politics and Its Objects

This definition attempts to be comprehensive without including all human activity in the class of things political:

- it allows us to recognize politics where there is neither a "state" nor a "government";
- it reminds us that politics is usually about social wholes (community, society) and the way they are organized or ordered; and
- it also recognizes the common (almost inevitable?) division of a society or community into those who make the rules and those who are ruled, and it asks about the kinds of interaction that occur between these two groups.

In the course of investigating the relationships between the state, government, and the people, the objects of our political study will include **INSTITUTIONS**, **PROCESSES**, and **IDEAS** (see Figure 1.2). For example, Congress is an example of a type of institution known as a legislature. Legislatures employ a legislative process to make law (another type of institution). When it is possible to trace the use of public power or authority back to laws, a normative idea—the "rule of law"—is satisfied. Conversely, the rule of law is institutionalized in part by the creation of impartial courts, due process, and other related aspects of the justice system.

FIGURE 1.3 On Institutions

We will not attempt to define institutions here beyond noting that
they embody recognized patterns of behavior organized to accomplish
identifiable purposes. For example, the university is an institution, as is the
court, the marketplace, the church/mosque/synagogue/temple. What comes
to mind with each of these may be a building, but the physical entity is not
what matters. The institution is found in the roles played by those whose
behavior follows the rules necessary to achieve the purpose for which
the institution exists: what makes a university is not its bricks and mortar,
but the organization of the people within—professors and students—to
achieve a set of purposes broadly known as "education." Certain routines
are central to this institution (e.g., the division of pupils into classes,
assigning and grading essays and projects) that would seem inappropriate
in another institution (e.g., a hospital, a library). Just as any discussion of
education would be incomplete without any mention of schools, so too,
our introduction to the study of politics requires attention to political
institutions.

1.2
Community and Society

If humans are naturally sociable, there are many ways in which
their social environments can differ. **COMMUNITY** and **SOCIETY** are
terms used to describe the social whole within which individual
life is experienced. All human life occurs within such wholes—
something which exceptions serve only to confirm. Robinson
Crusoe, for example, is interesting not just because he is an individual removed from his accustomed environment but also because his
behavior in his new setting so clearly identifies him as a product of
a certain (in this case, European) society. Similarly, the individuals
involved in the *Survivor* series are very obviously products of the
society from which they have been drawn. Although "community"
and "society" are often used interchangeably, the former can indicate a specific type of society or, more accurately, identify something that may characterize a society to a lesser or greater extent.

Communities are marked by homogeneity and cohesion;
their members share language, culture, and beliefs of a moral and
religious nature; and their lives are governed by common norms
and customs. A particular way of life, such as farming or fishing,
may also be shared. Membership is more or less total (one belongs
or one doesn't) and often requires a commitment, some participation or performance of duty. Communities are conservative in the
sense of attempting to maintain the integrity of what is held in
common and collective, given that the welfare of each member is
of interest to others. These characteristics suggest that community
is like family, only on a larger scale. Like families, communities can

be nurturing and supportive; they can also be dysfunctional and destructive to individuals within them. Like families, too, communities are formed involuntarily. One is born into a community, and although one may repudiate it, one is unlikely ever fully to escape its influence.

Evidence indicates that from the start, humans lived in communities, or, to put it another way, the first human societies were characterized by a strong degree of community. As societies expand to become less homogeneous and more differentiated, they lose the cohesiveness of community. The more that the members of the society come to differ in their values and beliefs, the sense of a common life in which all participate may lose its meaning. Societies without community are more like collections of individuals; you may choose to live in a society in a way that is not possible to live as a member of a community (also, the community may refuse to have you, while a society is less likely to do so). If belonging to a community is analogous to membership in a family, then living in a society without community is more like participating in a voluntary association, like a campus club, the auto league, or an Internet chat line.

To talk about communities on the one hand and societies without community on the other is to make an *analytic distinction*, something that is useful for clarifying our thinking but may not hold up in practice. It is more accurate to talk about varying degrees of community within societies. Clearly, as communities become larger, cohesiveness and homogeneity are more difficult to maintain. But it is not just that community dissolves as societies grow and change; sometimes societies fragment into (or are constructed from) distinct, even hostile communities. For any one of several reasons, two or more communities may be forced to share the same **TERRITORY**. To the degree that most contemporary societies no longer have the characteristics of community (or have them weakly), it is sometimes difficult to appreciate fully the distinction we are making. This is because community is typically associated with conditions less likely to be encountered today. Community is more likely or possible in societies that are small (both in population and extent) and in societies of lesser rather than greater complexity. Modern societies generally are extensive, populous, pluralistic, and complex in their organization or structure. They may often contain the remnants of several communities. One analogy might be the difference between life in a rural village and in an urban metropolis. The former is likely a community where everyone knows everyone; the latter is a place where most people are strangers.

The big city may be home to many smaller communities, but that multiplicity only serves to dissolve the exclusivity of each. On a very basic level, the difference that matters is that community is personal and familiar, while society is impersonal and, in a curious way, invisible. Members of a community, for example, can usually articulate what their community is and why it is important to them; each of us is in many ways the product of the society in which we have lived, but often we fail to recognize the ways in which this is so. At the risk of making too broad a generalization, the sweep of human history has been a movement from simple communities to complex pluralistic societies.

This distinction between community and society, with the corresponding observation that community is often weak in contemporary society, has considerable political significance. For example, Laver suggests that we need government when community fails (1983: 46). The more cohesive and homogeneous a people, and the more united they are in their beliefs and committed to them, the greater the likelihood that their beliefs will effectively guide their actions and thus provide order and regularity. Conduct will be regulated by customs, tradition, and religious beliefs, all of which exist as part of what the people hold in common. In societies where community is strongest, politics will be very much bound up with religion, moral beliefs, customs, taboos, etc. In rare instances, one may not even encounter specifically political institutions like law or government. Where community is weaker or fragmented, the political realm may be more detached from religious or ethical spheres, and, correspondingly, the division between public and private spheres is more obvious. Conversely, the separation of the political from the religious or moral realm allows a society to accommodate communities that dispute or differ on religious or moral questions. As noted, the effect of history and of social and technological change has not been simply to dissolve community but sometimes to bring communities together or to fragment one community into several. At the time of the American Revolution in 1776, the country was much less heterogeneous in religious and cultural terms than it is today. Centuries of immigration have resulted in the establishment of a broader range of communities in the United States today than in almost any other nation-state. Such observations prompt a question at least as old as the Roman Empire but no less relevant today: how does one accommodate diverse communities within a single political society? To anticipate a point yet to be made (see Chapter 9 on *cleavages*), the most difficult diversity to contain peacefully is a two-fold division, as history has demonstrated time and again (e.g., Israeli/Palestinian; Catholic/Protestant; Hindu/Muslim; Afrikaner/Zulu).

At some stage in human social development something we call the state emerges to organize the collective experience of the community. So, too, in a similar and not unrelated way, human communities come to identify with a specific domain and attempt to enforce a title to it. This is the beginning of territoriality. From this develops a variety of relationships between peoples and territories and their governments. One result is a rather confusing vocabulary in which common terms are used to refer to quite distinct entities (see Figure 1.4). The terms **NATION** and **STATE**, for example, are sometimes used interchangeably but should be considered distinct political concepts:

> *Nation*: a people whose collective identity is based on common descent, language, religion, sense of history, customs, and traditions, who usually (but do not always) inhabit a contiguous territory.

> *State*: a structure of power and authority organizing the political community that inhabits a given territory.

A state may include within it several nations or parts of several nations: Belgium comprises the Flemish and the Walloons; Zimbabwe the Shona and Ndebele. Within Canada the Québécois claim to be a "distinct society" or nation, just as in Spain the Basque and Catalonians express nationalist aspirations. Or, a nation may be spread through several states. The Kurds, a homogeneous people who regard themselves as a nation, occupy an area that includes parts of Iraq, Iran, Turkey, and Syria.

Interestingly, just as politics puts us at the intersection of people, territory, and authority/power, each of these has also served as the basis for political conflicts. A people with a strong identity may fight for independence from a dominant or foreign power, seeking their own autonomous territory and state. Within states, the struggle between nations for power and/or territory has often led to civil war. Between states, competing claims of jurisdiction over territory may lead to tensions, conflict, and even war. The geographic boundaries left after armies have decamped, peace treaties have been signed, or de-colonization has taken place have rarely coincided with the territory where the peoples of real nations are situated.

1.3
Nation and State

FIGURE 1.4 Clarifying Terms

NATION refers to a people united by a collective identity, and

is distinct from

STATE, which indicates the ongoing institutions of government for a particular territory, and

is distinct from

JURISDICTION, which defines the people and territory over which a state has authority, as well as the nature of that authority, and

is distinct from

COUNTRY OR NATION-STATE, which indicates the conjunction of a particular state, territory, and people, and may be referred to by some political scientists as a **POLITY**.

1.4
Power and Authority

Just as nation and state are seemingly interchangeable words marking two distinct realities, so also are two very useful terms: power and authority. All social existence requires the maintenance of some minimal degree of order and regularity; authority and power refer to ways decisions are made and enforced within a society or community. The difference between them is crucial to the politics of societies. In this book, power is used primarily to refer to *the implementation of decisions through force*, which ultimately involves physical coercion (though often merely the threat of force is sufficient to obtain compliance). Exercising power means imposing decisions upon people who might not otherwise accept or obey them by threatening sanctions or penalties for disobedience. Those who are subject to power face real consequences of an unpleasant or painful nature (such as imprisonment, loss of property, or even death). For this reason, to wield power requires possessing the means of **COERCION**, without which power cannot be said to exist.

By contrast, authority is said to imply **CONSENT**. Decisions that are implemented with authority do not involve force and therefore are not imposed upon people. When people willingly obey or accept a decision we say that they recognize the authority of whoever has issued the command or order. This does not necessarily mean that people agree with the order or are happy with what it commands them to do, but that for some reason or another they see the command as "right" or as one that the author has a "right" to demand of them. The reasons why people grant or recognize the authority of a person or group of persons are various, and we shall consider several of them shortly.

Power is attractive because, as long as the necessary means of coercion are available, one is sure to get one's way. With power we do not have to convince or persuade others or gain their consent; we merely impose our will upon them. On the other hand, power is expensive, because it not only requires possession of the means with which to force others (such as police, courts, military, secret police, jails, and money to pay for all of this) but also might require their ongoing employment. If we must be forced to do something in the first place, we are likely to stop doing it once we can safely get away with it. In the absence of force or evidence that force is close at hand, compliance may no longer be forthcoming.

The advantage of authority, then, is that once established it does not require a constant expenditure of means. Authority has its way not once but continually. Our present consent to a direction is likely to entail our future consent, all things being equal. This advantage of authority over power means that governments will seek, wherever possible, to establish authority rather than simply to employ power. Power invites opposition in an expensive way that authority does not. If the inefficiency of power is the expenditure of means it requires for enforcement, the challenge for authority is that it must establish and maintain consent. Thus, in cases where governments cannot maintain authority, or are unwilling to take the necessary steps to establish it, they frequently resort to power. Although power is expensive to exercise, and relatively inefficient because it uses resources that could be employed much more productively elsewhere, it is in some ways or in some cases more expedient than authority.

At this point, it may have become clear that the politics of societies is always a mixture of power and authority. To rely solely upon authority, a regime would have to be a perfect (or complete) community—all would agree about what each should do, and each would do his or her part. In the real world, power remains necessary in order to enforce rules upon those who fail to acknowledge authority or are otherwise tempted to do what they may very well know is illegal or wrong. Most of us abstain from driving while under the influence of alcohol because we accept the law as a legitimate rule, *not* because we are afraid of the punishment for disobedience. At the same time, we want our government to have the power necessary to punish those who do not recognize the authority of the state to make such rules or who are willing to flaunt them. Without power to enforce rules, those who recognize authority are often at the mercy of those who do not.

Similarly, it is just as unlikely for us to encounter a regime that rests solely on power or pure coercion. Even the most brutal dictators rely on a core of supporters who carry out their commands and often do so for some reason other than fear or greed. At the same time, those regimes that ultimately rely on power are nonetheless concerned to establish authority to whatever degree this is possible and, by doing so, minimize the actual expenditure of force they must make. What they claim, and hope to establish, is the legitimacy of their actions.

O**BLIGATION** and **LEGITIMACY** are two sides of the same coin: if you recognize the legitimacy of government, then you are obliged to obey it. Conversely, if you feel obliged to obey, then you have conceded legitimacy. "Obligation" is a statement about what you *ought* to do, but it is a special sense of the word "ought."

1.5
Obligation and Legitimacy

Suppose, for example, the penalty for petty theft is the loss of a hand; this is a strong incentive not to steal. Here the "ought" is tied to a punishment; if the penalty for petty theft were a very small fine, you might well calculate that what is gained by the theft is worth the risk of being caught and punished. Obligation, by contrast, indicates that you have a good reason not to steal, regardless of the magnitude of the penalty. When one is obliged, one has concluded, for one reason or another, that the rule (whatever its content) is a legitimate one. We have said that authority implies consent. In other words, authority requires a foundation of obligation: for some reason or another people accept the legitimacy of the decision or of the decision-maker. Conversely, where judgments of obligation are lacking, or legitimacy is denied, power—the implementation of force—is required.

One way to understand institutions is as organized systems of "offices" that employ differing degrees and types of authority. A key difference between types of regimes is the route(s) by which individuals come to occupy an office legitimately. For example, in a hereditary monarchy, the office of being king or queen is inherited according to local rules of succession (i.e., who is "next in line"). In an absolute monarchy or dictatorship, many of those holding subordinate offices will have been chosen for their position personally by the monarch or dictator according to his or her own whims and agendas. In a legal-rational system, individuals will be elected to some offices; others who are appointed may be subject to a public process of scrutiny and approval; and the majority of public servants will be hired on the basis of open competitions, often involving examinations (i.e., a demonstration of "merit"). In short, where authority is sanctioned by its basis in law and assumed through a rule-governed process, such as an election, its legitimacy is legal-rational.

Authority in modern states can be characterized by specific terms more readily recognizable to citizens. Neither those who govern nor those governed talk very much about the "legal-rational" basis of the state. Today, most rulers claim two things about their state or government: that its decisions are "just" and that the will of the people is reflected in its decisions or by the composition of the government in power. In short, within most legal-rational states today, justification of authority rests on two concepts: **JUSTICE** and **POPULAR SOVEREIGNTY**.

The authority generally exercised within contemporary states is of the legal–rational type (see Figure 1.5). Traditional authority is most appropriate within relatively static (unchanging) communities, while the fluid, pluralistic nature of contemporary societies means they are commonly not characterized by a high degree of community. Another way of saying this is to note that most of us live in a world inhabited by strangers. In the past, for most humans, this wasn't the case. Similarly, the rise of universal literacy and

1.6
Justice and Democracy

FIGURE 1.5 Max Weber's Ideal-Typical Sources of Legitimate Authority

The noted political sociologist Max Weber (1864–1920) identified three distinct *ideal types* of legitimate authority based on the nature of their source. Ideal types are intellectual constructs that refer to artificially pure forms of phenomena that are present in different measures in many settings, though they do not occur naturally in such a pure form. In political science, ideal types are analogous to the distilled and purified chemicals used in labs to isolate chemical relationships that may be distorted by impurities in the real world.

The first type is **TRADITIONAL AUTHORITY**: rule that is justified on the basis of its long history and a "habitual orientation to conform" (Weber, 1958: 79). In other words, it is custom and the weight of history ("But we've always done it this way ...") that makes things right with traditional legitimacy. Hereditary monarchy is frequently cited as a political example of traditional authority, but even within modern democracies attachment to some institutions or symbols (the constitution, the flag, a particular electoral system) may be as much about tradition as anything else.

Second is **CHARISMATIC AUTHORITY**, where it is believed that the ruler possesses extraordinary personal qualities which justify his or her rule. This is more than the view that those in charge are gifted; it is the claim that they are *uniquely* gifted. Those who have been able to convince others that they were chosen by God have been among the most successful charismatic leaders. Most importantly, Weber's use of charismatic here is not at all what is usually meant today when a politician is identified as "charismatic," often because he or she is a capable media performer or a polished public speaker able to ignite public emotion. Thus, while many Americans regarded John F. Kennedy, Ronald Reagan, or Bill Clinton as charismatic figures, they owed their authority to a legal-rational process—democratic election.

Finally, Weber spoke of **LEGAL-RATIONAL AUTHORITY**, where legitimacy derives from "belief in the validity of legal statute and functional 'competence' based on rationally created rules" (1958: 79). One of the major transformations carried out (but not perfectly) in the development of modern liberal democracy was the de-personalization of power/authority. The ability to govern comes to be associated with an office such as president or prime minister, and an individual employs that ability only so long as he or she properly occupies that office. According to Weber, the prevalence of legal-rational authority claims was one of the hallmarks of political modernity.

public education means that people cannot be relied upon to accept things simply because "that's how they've always been done." Finally, the role of religion in attributing charismatic (and some forms of traditional) authority means that these avenues for securing political legitimacy are generally closed in secular societies. (By contrast, the few contemporary examples of "charismatic" authority can be found within religious communities or in societies where religious fundamentalism is entrenched.)

Justice means different things to many people; here it refers to norms describing the way authority is or should be exercised. Within many contemporary states, justice is embodied in three ideas or norms: the **RULE OF LAW**, individual or group **RIGHTS**, and **EQUALITY**. To take just the first of these, the rule of law is a set of norms concerned with the proper use of law as an instrument of authority and with the ways law is made, interpreted, and administered. Justice rooted in the rule of law may find expression in notions such as *constitutionalism* (the belief that the ultimate power/ authority of the state is based on fundamental rules that are difficult to change and are typically articulated in a constitution) or may stress concepts such as the "presumption of innocence" or "due process." One of the most successful television series ever—*Law and Order*—may be seen as an extended treatise on the idea of the "rule of law." Of course, justice is not *only* about law, but much of the discussion of justice in contemporary states concerns law and who is responsible for it. (For a further discussion of justice, see Chapter 12.)

Popular sovereignty, as a norm, claims that the ultimate source of any legitimate authority exercised by the state or government is the people. That is, governments are legitimate because (or to the extent that) they have the public's consent. This is clearly incompatible with the view that time or custom confers authority or that only some individuals are divinely chosen or endowed with special gifts that entitle them to rule. The form of popular sovereignty with which most of us are likely familiar is **DEMOCRACY**. Although popular sovereignty is not confined to democracy, our discussion will focus upon various models and institutions of democracy, examining the degree to which they actually deliver popular sovereignty.

Thus, within legal-rational states, when the question is asked "what makes authority legitimate?" part of the answer is provided by the concept of popular sovereignty—it is legitimate because it is exercised by individuals the public has chosen or given its consent to—and part is provided by the concept of justice—it is legitimate because it is exercised according to the rule of law, respecting rights, etc. These are powerful arguments for the legitimacy of government; if one accepts that authority is just and something to which one has consented, it is difficult to imagine a place from which one might consistently challenge that authority. Conversely, the legitimacy of the state will remain unchallenged only as long as its actions are seen to be just and to reflect the public will. One problem, as we shall see below, is that most expressions of the public will are at best indirect and open to considerable interpretation. Another is competing notions of what justice or democracy entails. Nonetheless, justice and democracy are very powerful concepts that rulers use to try to secure legitimacy for their power (thus establishing their authority) and which critics use to argue for change or reform in the politics of a society.

We noted earlier that human history has witnessed a move from familiar communities to increasingly impersonal societies, something reflected in Weber's successive categories of legitimacy: from traditional to charismatic to legal-rational. As societies become larger and more complex, power and authority become increasingly depersonalized. Modern societies are governed by something we have been calling the state, by which we mean the permanent institutions and structures of authority, distinct from the actual individuals who control or populate them. For example, Congress is, on the one hand, an institution in which certain processes (such as making law) are carried out and, on the other hand, a collection of individuals who perform the function of legislator. Congress endures while hundreds of Members of Congress, for a comparatively short time, occupy a seat there. Similarly, the office of the president is distinct from the particular individual who happens to occupy or "hold" that office. The depersonalization of the form of government known as the state means that power or authority are more properly seen to be properties of institutions rather than belonging to the individuals who occupy those institutions or exercise their powers. The institutions continue to exist and function as individuals come and go.

In order to be clear about whether we are talking about the institutions or the individuals, it is useful to distinguish clearly between state and government. State will be used generally to refer to *the enduring complex of institutions and processes by means of which authority and power are exercised in a society.* This complex of authority and power is impersonal and relatively permanent. By contrast,

1.7

State and Government

Acropolis Pillars

GOVERNMENT refers collectively to *the individuals entitled to employ the power and authority of the state.* In the broadest sense, power and authority are exercised not only by elected officials but also by public servants and officers of the judiciary in their work of carrying out or implementing policies and programs established by present and past governments.

So, to say that modern societies are characterized by legal-rational authority is to indicate two things:

1. that the state is justified in terms of its legality (that is to say, its grounding in and use of *law* as the primary instrument of authority) and

2. that the government is chosen by a legal, rule-governed process such as an election.

We can go further and note that where governments are determined by popular political processes, such as elections, the state endures while governments come and go. An election is a device that allows the public to challenge the legitimacy of the (current) government while respecting the legitimacy of the state.

We can now expand on the earlier suggestion that *justice* and *popular sovereignty* are modern measures of legitimacy, which is challenged whenever decisions are seen to be "unjust" or contrary to the "popular will." To claim that the *state* (rather than the government) is unjust or undemocratic is to argue that the *institutions* and/or rule-governed *processes* by which authority is gained and/or exercised are in some way inadequate. Such a challenge calls for the reform or elimination of institutions or for the creation of new ones. A challenge to the legitimacy of the state is thus a call for constitutional change or reform (see Chapter 6). The tremendous changes in Eastern Europe and the former Soviet Union since 1990 (at the end of the "Cold War") may be seen as responses to challenges of this kind. Challenges of constitutional legitimacy question the *way* authority or power is exercised.

Sometimes, however, what is questioned is not the way authority or power has been used, but *what* has been done. In other words, it is not the means that is problematic but the end or the *substance* of what has been done. In these cases the specific use that the government has made of the authority of the state is being challenged rather than the existence or make-up of that authority. What is distinct about the kind of legal-rational state we know as liberal democracy is that these kinds of challenges to the government are usually pursued in one of two ways. One is to claim that the government's actions exceed or offend some existing definition of the state's power, as found in a constitution. Here the claim is made that the government's action has exceeded the proper authority of the state. This is not to challenge the constitutional legitimacy of the state but a claim that the government has acted unconstitutionally (beyond the authority that the constitution grants the state). In some states it is possible for citizens to use the courts to challenge the government's exercise of authority. This represents a specific (and especially serious) kind of claim that the government's actions are *unjust*—unjust because it is acting beyond the authority granted by the constitution.

In most cases, though, when government policies or actions are challenged as unjust, there is no doubt that they are fully legal and constitutional. This may seem strange—the idea that something could be legal *and* unjust; however, it can happen, in part because there are limits on what can be specified in constitutions, in part because justice is broader than the rule of law or rights, and in part because in any given society there may be a plurality of notions about what is "just." A good example concerns taxation. On one view of what justice requires, taxes should be progressive; that is, the tax burden should be directly proportional to the taxpayer's ability to bear that burden (i.e., as income rises, the tax *rate* also rises). A sales tax, for example, is regressive, because its burden falls most heavily on those whose income is most committed to expenditures, i.e., those with the least income. (The impact of such taxes can be minimized by providing tax credits for low-income families and/or exempting certain basic items—such as groceries—from the tax.) On the other hand, some people believe that progressive taxation "unfairly penalizes" those with higher incomes and call for the application of a flat rate of tax to all income. Some even believe that all taxation is unjust (i.e., not just bothersome). To take a non-economic example of differing ideas of justice, while many citizens believe that a law outlawing abortion would be unjust, many others believe a law permitting choice in this matter is wrong. In either case, a finding by the courts that the law permitting (or forbidding) abortion is constitutional would not likely change the beliefs of most people who feel strongly about the issue. Finally, the manner in which an electoral system (such as the single-member plurality model used in the House of Representatives and the British House of Commons) distributes seats in the legislature may be regarded as unjust, for reasons we will examine more closely in Chapter 9. Nonetheless, few of these critics calling for electoral reform would claim that the existing set-up is unconstitutional.

In situations where the government is acting constitutionally, but citizens believe it is acting *unjustly*, the principal avenue of action is the **POLITICAL PROCESS** (see Part Four). Here, individuals or groups attempt to persuade the government to take a different course of action. An important element in this process is the communication of information, but, alternatively, the principal means of persuasion is the withdrawal (or the threat of withdrawal) of support. Citizens who cannot change the government's policies will attempt to change the government. It is not the state that is under suspicion but those who are exercising its authority. The most important function of electoral democracy is to provide citizens with a regular, peaceful opportunity to replace the government of the day.

The political process generally, and elections specifically, are means by which citizens express their political will. Indeed, the political process is not only a means of challenging the claim of government to be acting justly but also (and perhaps principally) a means of challenging its more general claim to be carrying out the popular will through the policies it implements. We should be clear that these are often distinct concerns. While the public may protest the legitimacy of government actions on the basis of norms of justice about which the constitution remains silent or neutral, it may also express a discontent neither conceived nor presented in terms of justice. Elections have often been fought over any number of key issues—free trade, tax cuts, participation in war—that the electorate has not approached as issues of "justice."

To summarize, then, within the framework of modern conceptions of authority, contemporary problems of legitimacy may apply to either the state or the government and may be primarily framed in terms of justice/injustice or democracy/non-democracy. Challenges to the legitimacy of the state amount to demands for constitutional change, that is, for a redefinition of the institutions by which authority and power are exercised and of any limits confining this exercise. Challenges to the legitimacy of the government, on the other hand, accept the existing constitutional order and proceed in one of two ways. One is to claim that the government has violated the constitutional definition of its authority. In some polities at least, this claim can proceed by way of legal challenge through the courts. The second route of challenge operates through the political process, where citizens work to replace the current administration with a government more representative of, or responsive to, their will.

The discussion to this point might well prompt some further questions, such as:

- What is the relationship between democracy and justice?
- Can one have a state that is just but not democratic (or vice versa)?
- Would such a state be legitimate?

This book is informed by the belief that legitimacy requires *both* justice and democracy but recognizes that many may dispute this. History confirms that justice has often been conceived as something independent of (if not, at times, in tension with) democracy. This is less problematic where there is widespread agreement on what is and what is not just. Where community is strong it may well be that justice is possible without democracy: rulers and ruled alike will agree on the appropriate norms and follow them. In modern pluralistic societies with competing notions of what is just, which or whose conception of justice should prevail? That which is more "rational?" Who would determine this? Should it be decided by at least a majority of the people? Or, can a majority sometimes fail to understand what justice requires? Answering these questions leads us back to the notion that democracy may be an important means of identifying and securing justice in modern societies. Certainly the proposition informing this book is that, in a society where democracy flourishes (see Chapter 6), justice has better prospects than in a society without democracy.

1.8
The State and Civil Society

In all political systems, a considerable sphere of privatized public activity falls outside the authority of the state. This is the realm of **CIVIL SOCIETY**, which could be defined as those areas of our social life where the state is absent. Considered carefully and critically, "civil society" is a rather slippery notion. Consider, for example, the antithesis of civil society, the totalitarian state ("**TOTALITARIANISM**"), which, in theory, recognizes no limits to the reach of its power: "in theory," because no state has the will, let alone the means, to govern everything its citizens do all the time. In totalitarian (and authoritarian)[1] states, there are often elements of unregulated activity, like black markets or underground religious congregations, but the boundaries are uncertain and insecure. This suggests that what matters is not the mere existence of areas of life where the state is absent (*that* is inevitable) but the official withdrawal or abstention of the state from specific areas of social interaction. In states with effective constitutions, the boundaries of civil society may be more clearly drawn and the existence of civil society be so much taken for granted that even to talk about it seems strange. In these countries an expectation of civil society is implicit in the political culture.

Comparing states reveals that what falls within civil society can vary widely. In many so-called Western countries, a separation of church and state places religion and its institutions (the church, the synagogue, the temple, the mosque) within civil society. In other words, the state neither enforces nor do its policies reflect the precepts of any particular religion. (Again, this may be truer in theory than it turns out to be in practice.) The rise of the Taliban to power in Afghanistan illustrated how civil society is greatly diminished in a theocratic state (i.e., one where church and state are united or very closely entwined): edicts governing matters as simple as growing facial hair were strictly enforced by the state. Wearing a beard (or not) ceased to be a personal decision. The future course of Iraqi society will depend as much on the ability of its various Islamic populations (Shiite, Sunni, Kurdish) to accommodate each

1 An authoritarian state is any in which an individual or a group is more or less permanently in control of the government and cannot easily or peacefully be removed. A totalitarian regime is an extreme example of an authoritarian state, one in which there are no effective limits to the exercise of political power and therefore no guaranteed realm of privacy for citizens.

other, as it will on the withdrawal of Western military forces and the delivery of economic aid. The well-known opposition of a substantial number of American citizens to any form of gun control reflects a view that gun ownership is a question to be answered by civil society. The proposition that this division between state and civil society is contained in the Second Amendment of the American Constitution continues to attract serious debate.[2]

Examples in the previous paragraph illustrate the paradoxical nature of the relationship between the state and civil society. Suppose that the 'American judiciary were to decide that the Second Amendment to the American Constitution effectively limits the state's ability to regulate gun ownership. Ultimately, this is playing one part of the state (the judiciary) against another (the legislature). Moreover, the Second Amendment is a change that was made to the American Constitution that could—however unlikely it might seem—be "un-made." The freedom to worship that we identify with religious pluralism would not exist had not states come to enforce laws of tolerance and/or protect the religious rights of minorities. If the state had remained completely neutral and on the sidelines concerning religious questions, persecution of religious minorities by majority sects would have been even more prevalent in human history. This points to two important features of the relationship between the state and civil society:

1. First, the state can shape the nature of civil society. The constitution and ordinary laws are very much instruments that map the terrain that civil society occupies.

2. Second, there is considerable power within civil society. In fact, any adequate definition of civil society needs to give recognition to the significant forces of private (non-governmental) power that operate within its sphere.

A good example of both these points is provided by the economy. The market economy underpins developed world democracies and is regarded as a central institution of civil society in such states. As we will see much later (Chapter 13), the market economy has two fundamental features: the private ownership of property and primary reliance on the market (transactions between buyers and sellers) as a mechanism of distributing goods and labor. A sustained look at human experience reveals that neither private property nor a market economy "just happens." Each presupposes a fundamental framework of laws, protections, supports, and sanctions

2 See the website called GunCite at <http://www.guncite.com/>.

that requires the willing exercise of authority by the state. Perhaps the old adage that "possession is nine-tenths of the law" should be amended to "possession is *only* nine-tenths of the law" (if *that* much). Possession notes what I occupy or hold; property indicates my *entitlement* to what I possess, and this means at least two things: recognition by others of the legitimacy of my possession and a body willing to protect me against those who would usurp (i.e., take) my property. In history, protection of property has been one of the primary functions of the state.

In much of the so-called developed world, the economy is the source of considerable, even formidable, forces of private power; for this reason, the banking system, financial markets, and other elements of a market economy may be seen as institutions of civil society. Somewhat paradoxically, as an institution of civil society, "the economy" rests on a foundation of supportive public policies *as well as* maintaining a considerable degree of autonomy from the exercise of public power by the government/state.

The family is the third principal institution of civil society, and logically it precedes both religion and the market. Obviously, the family is also circumscribed to various degrees by regulations of the state. The rules of marriage and divorce, family support, child welfare, and education are all subject to laws, and violation of these can lead to state intervention. The last 100 years has witnessed a tremendous transformation in the nature of the family: from the extended multi-generational family, to the urban/suburban nuclear family (two parents with children), to fluid, segmented multi-parented, single-parented, and same-sex partnered/parented families, as well as many families without children. The shifting character of institutions of civil society such as the family, religion, and the economy have tended to be more seriously studied by sociologists and anthropologists as political scientists have concentrated on public rather than private power. As the last few paragraphs have attempted to demonstrate, there is sometimes a great degree of artificiality to these distinctions.

In any human community we can expect to find a kinship structure, a process for sharing or allocating scarce resources, and a central belief system—i.e., family, economy, religion. In such settings, the maintenance of well-being depends entirely on the systems of distribution and redistribution, the family, and religion. In one sense, then, we are tempted to say that in such pre-political communities there is only civil society; another view might argue that it is anachronistic to speak of civil society before the emergence of a "political regime" (i.e., the state and government) with which civil society can be contrasted.

At any rate, it should be clear that the distinction between civil society and the state is not a simple one between where or when we are free and where or when we are not. Our existence as social beings is always constrained, even if it is only by the values and customs of our culture. Within the family, or as members of a religious community, or by occupying a place within a particular economic system, we are subject to rules, remain limited in our choices, and must accommodate the interests and desires of others. Such is life. What distinguishes the institutions of civil society is that they do not have at their disposal the same range of coercive sanctions that the state can ultimately draw upon to enforce its laws. Perhaps it is the case that the state emerges at that point in a society's development when its non-political means of control are no longer adequate.

Just as importantly, civil society is not just another means by which our behavior is regulated; it is also where we are cared for and receive support, love, encouragement, and assistance. This is particularly the function of institutions like the family and the church (or synagogue, temple, or mosque) and of countless clubs, associations, fraternal organizations, etc. And just as our social being must always endure regulation, we are rarely so self-sufficient that our welfare has no need of others.

We noted earlier Laver's observation that "we need government when community fails." In part, the tremendous growth of the state in the twentieth century was a response to the inadequacy, decline, or changing character of the institutions of civil society. Consider the great changes that the forces of modernization have made to that very central element of civil society—the family. We noted above the overall trend towards a fragmentation (or "desegmentation") of "the family." When elderly family members can no longer rely on children or grandchildren to care for them in their declining years, the existence and level of pensions or income supplements become significant, as do the numbers of retirement homes and long-term care facilities. When parents cannot afford to withdraw from the labor force and have neither parents nor siblings who can look after their children, the availability and quality of child care becomes critical. Into the late nineteenth century, churches and benevolent organizations provided the bulk of assistance to the economically unfortunate or to those disabled in one way or another. Combine the decline of the church with the growth of egalitarian expectations that all have a right to a minimum standard of well-being, and the increasing inability of private charity to meet these demands is not surprising, particularly during periods of prolonged widespread destitution, as in the Depression of the 1930s or as has persisted in under-resourced areas of North America, both rural and urban. On any number of fronts, the state, generally in the form of what has been called the **WELFARE STATE**, took up the slack. Apart from the large military budgets of some states (particularly the United States) in the Cold War era, the major expenditures of governments since 1950 have been on health, education, and social assistance. This highlights that the activity of the state is not only about regulating our behavior but may also be about providing us with some very essential goods and services.

We will reflect on the relationship between the state and civil society often in this text. At this point, though, two propositions are worth pondering. One, popularized by Robert Putnam (1994), is that a sustainable, healthy democracy requires a healthy civil society. Put generally, the idea is that people bring to the political realm the habits, behaviors, values, and skills that they have acquired and use in the non-political spheres of public life. Democracy is not simply about the existence of free elections; it is about working with others, being able to compromise, learning realistic expectations of efficacy (i.e., what one can expect to accomplish by participating), accepting defeat, seeing beyond one's own interests most narrowly defined, developing a sense of obligation to participate or take responsibility even when it is inconvenient or fails to be "fun," etc. These life skills are often imparted through the activities and institutions of civil society—in school and church groups, clubs and associations, the workplace, the labor organization, the boardroom, and yes, the family. Acquiring these facilities and transferring them to the political realm are what make us citizens and not simply subjects (those who are ruled). Passive, solitary activities such as watching television or surfing the Internet are less likely to teach us how to be citizens.

On one level this is just so much common sense: why would we expect someone who has never had the opportunity to share in decision-making to be a citizen rather than a subject? Few of us would expect to step on the golf course for the first time and shoot par or bowl a 180 average on our initial visit to the alley. (Similar beliefs about cause and effect inform the skepticism that one can overthrow a long-running dictatorship and within months put an effective democratic government in its place.)

More generally, theories such as Putnam's recognize that the political realm cannot be treated in isolation from the larger social context. Whether variables such as a people's history, culture, education, and level of development make a particular type of politics and government possible or whether a type of political regime is likely to encourage or sustain social and economic development is less important than recognizing the necessary connections between them. It is almost universally accepted today that a free and democratic society cannot be sustained or flourish without a competitive mass media that is free from political pressure, from concentration of ownership within a small elite, or from both. (Hence the concern expressed in Italy several years ago under the government of former Prime Minister Silvio Berlusconi, who was estimated to have control over 90 per cent of national television—direct control over three private networks and indirect control over the state-owned channel.[3]) Since 1990, the experience of republics and other subnational political units that were once part of the quasi-totalitarian Soviet Union has been illustrative. The absence of adequately developed institutions and practices of civil society has meant environments in which organized crime has flourished (Russia), personal dictatorships have arisen and persisted (for example, until his death in December 2006, Turkmenistan had been ruled by a President for Life), or stagnation and civil unrest have persisted (Chechnya or Moldova, for example). Latterly, it has been known from the outset that the real challenge in Afghanistan and Iraq was not achieving a military victory by the American-led coalition forces but creating a viable civil society and stable government *after* conflict ceases. That such a government might resemble representative democracy seems still rather dubious, even after years of effort and bloodshed.

The other proposition, more relevant to post-industrial democracies, is that civil society no longer possesses the resources to ensure the well-being of all within the community. Whether or not this is true is critical in light of the effort in the last 25 years to scale back the welfare state created in the 30 years after World War II. In Chapter 13 we trace in greater detail the social and political reasons for the rise of the welfare state and the economic conditions that caused governments of almost every political stripe in the 1990s (and after) to seek to bring about a smaller, more efficient state. Strong ideological currents have also fueled these developments. But if one basis for the growth of the state in the middle part of this century was to compensate for the inability of civil society to provide those things that we cannot provide for ourselves, such as education, health care, and social security, how well-equipped is civil society to resume responsibility for these public goods? Interestingly, many of those who advocate a smaller role for the state with respect to these social welfare functions would turn to

3 Crispian Balmer, "Does Berlusconi Threaten Italian Democracy?" (August 2003), PBS website at <http: www.pbs. org/wnet/wideangle/shows/ berlusconi>.

FIGURE 1.6 Office of Faith-Based and Community Initiatives

One of President George W. Bush's first official acts in his first term as President was
to create the White House Office of Faith-Based and Community Initiatives. The
Office was tasked at its inception with leading a "determined attack on need" by
strengthening and expanding the role of faith-based and community organizations
in addressing the nation's social problems. The President envisioned a faith-friendly
public square where faith-based organizations can compete equally with other groups
to provide government or privately funded services.

President Bush also created Centers for Faith-Based and Community Initiatives
in seven cabinet departments—the Departments of Justice, Agriculture, Labor, Health
and Human Services, Housing and Urban Development, and Education, as well as
the Agency for International Development—to promote the initiative.

The mission of the Office and the ten Centers is to empower faith-based
and other community organizations to apply for federal social service grants. The
Office does not administer any grant programs or participate in funding decisions.
Likewise, the Centers supply information and training to faith-based and community
organizations, but they do not make the decisions about which groups will be
funded. The agencies make those decisions through procedures established by each
grant program, generally involving a competitive process. No grant funding is set
aside for faith-based organizations. Instead, the Faith-Based and Community Initiative
creates a level-playing field for faith-based as well as other community organizations
so that they can work with the government to meet the needs of communities in the
United States. See the website at <http://www.whitehouse.gov/government/fbci/mission.html>.

institutions and organizations in civil society (such as churches and
charities) for help in meeting public needs. Many advocates of a
smaller state see a larger role for the private economy here, a more
promising direction perhaps than turning to the family and the
church, which show little sign of recapturing their once central
position in society. On the other hand, the George W. Bush Administration's Office of Faith-Based and Community Initiatives (see
Figure 1.6) may reflect the relative strength of religion in American
civil society. Not surprisingly, then, we hear much more discussion
today than previously about charter schools, private health care, and
other market-based approaches to social policy.

Critics of this approach suggest that, because a market economy distributes wealth unevenly (see Chapter 13), turning to
MARKET-BASED SOLUTIONS for social policy issues raises the possibility of an unequal access to (or access to an unequal quality of) social
goods such as education, health care, and income security. Students
need only to reflect on the impact of reductions in the level of
state funding for higher education on tuition fees and student debt
levels. Public opinion surveys reveal that many of the same citizens who want smaller government and lower taxes continue to

expect adequate state funding for public goods such as defense and education.

The appropriate balance of roles for the state and for civil society, and the compatibility of that balance with values such as equality, fairness, and democracy, will continue to inform political debate over the coming years.

The discussion so far—as in most of what follows—has been about what transpires within the state, the nation, or the union of these two in the modern nation-state. The reason for this is simple: politics is about the regulation of our interactions with others, and for most of us, most of our relationships are with our fellow citizens. In other words, most politics is *intra*-national.

There has long been a discipline within political science called **INTERNATIONAL RELATIONS**, which is concerned with world politics, or what some call "geopolitics," in which the primary actors are countries. International relations studies the conflicts between nation-states, the alliances they form, and their diplomatic and military manoeuvres—what is commonly known as "foreign policy." The study of international relations is no less important in today's world, with almost 200 countries, than it was 100 years ago when there were less than 80. We will have more to say about this important subdiscipline of political science at several points in this book.

Phenomena such as the **GLOBALIZATION** of trade, culture, and communications are somewhat different than the relations between states, for here the forces are *trans*-national rather than intra- *or* international. In today's world, citizens expect their governments to tackle problems that do not recognize borders on topics such as the economy, the environment, public health, regulation of the Internet, and the preservation of human rights. This means that the modern state must be concerned not just with what happens within its territory but also about how its own policies affect the well-being and activities of its citizens in the wider world. Similarly, globalization means that the citizens of any given country are increasingly affected by decisions made somewhere outside the direct control of their own state. Will enacting tougher environmental protection laws increase the costs of goods and services for consumers or make it difficult for domestic firms to compete in the global marketplace? Will higher taxation rates cause companies to relocate to less restrictive regimes, or will they provide the state with the means to deliver good social programs and sound infrastructure, which in turn might attract investment from abroad?

1.9
Beyond the State

In a world of freer trade, international finance, and transnational corporations, an increasing array of subjects invites response from multinational bodies, international organizations, or countries acting together. Internal conflicts that threaten to disrupt the global economy or send streams of refugees abroad cannot be regarded simply as civil wars. The state is *not* (as some would have it) becoming less relevant in the era of globalization, but as its challenges change, so, too, must its responses.

Interestingly, it might be argued that globalization will exert pressure on all countries to adopt at least formally democratic political systems. This poses the greatest challenge in those states where authoritarian rulers show little inclination to surrender power. In newly democratized countries, where political practice and political culture have not been democratic, the immediate task is to consolidate popular sovereignty by developing the institutions and habits that make democracy work (see Chapter 6). In all democracies, even the most "advanced," the challenge is to ensure that citizens have the knowledge, the tools, and the will to keep government representative and accountable. In the age of globalization, democracy is threatened by the fact that our lives are increasingly shaped by forces, institutions, and actors over which or whom we have, at best, a very indirect measure of control.

**1.10
Conclusion**

This chapter has introduced some of the concepts and ideas most basic to the study of politics. What they share is a concern with the development and exercise of power and authority within the various kinds of community and society that humans inhabit. The foundational character of these ideas means that we will have occasion to refer to them repeatedly in the chapters that follow.

To look ahead at what is to come in this book, the next chapter will provide an initiation to the contemporary discipline of political science, underscoring the tension between normative and empirical traditions. In Part Two, Chapters Three and Four explore the important role of ideas in animating political life, first in terms of the philosophical foundations of political thinking and their embodiment in major political ideologies. Chapter Five extends our consideration of ideas in political life by examining the concept of political culture. In Part Three the particular character of liberal democracy will be situated within its historical and intellectual context. Part Four focuses on the distinctive institutional configurations and variations that are characteristic of contemporary liberal democracies. Our focus here will be primarily on the

American and British experiences. In Part Five we look at some of the factors affecting the inputs to the political process. Finally, Part Six will provide an overview of the institutions and processes associated with the outputs (policies and laws) of liberal democracies and will discuss the globalization of contemporary political forces.

References and Suggested Readings

Benn, S.I., and R.S. Peters. 1959. *Social Principles and Democratic State.* London: Unwin.

Crick, Bernard. 1964. *In Defence of Politics.* New York: Penguin.

Danziger, James N. 1991. *Understanding the Political World.* New York: Addison-Wesley.

Habermas, Jurgen. 1975. *Legitimation Crisis.* Boston: Beacon Press.

Johnson, Nevil. 1989. *The Limits of Political Science.* New York: Oxford University Press.

Laver, Michael. 1983. *Invitation to Politics.* Oxford: Basil Blackwell.

Ponton, Geoffrey, and Peter Gill. 1982. *Introduction to Politics.* Oxford: Basil Blackwell.

Redekop, John, ed. 1983. *Approaches to Canadian Politics*, 2nd ed. Toronto: Prentice Hall.

Weber, Max. 1958. "Politics as a Vocation." In H.W. Gerth and C. Wright Mills, eds. *From Max Weber: Essays in Sociology.* New York: Oxford University Press.

Key Terms

authority
charismatic authority
civil society
coercion
community
consent
country
democracy
equality
globalization
government
ideas
institutions
international relations
jurisdiction
justice
legal-rational authority
legitimacy
market-based solutions
nation
nation-state
obligation
political process
politics
polity
popular sovereignty
power
processes
rights
rule of law
society
state
territory
totalitarianism
traditional authority
welfare state

TWO | Contemporary Political Science: Methods And Approaches

"Politics is not a science ... but an art."
—Bismarck, 1884

"Strive to know the political world: Engage your passions, check them with reason and evidence, and push ahead with the work. When you do that, you do political science."
—Zuckerman, 1991

2.1 Introduction

While many people are interested in politics, relatively few actually nurture and refine this interest by taking courses in the subject. Yet, the study of politics presents a rich variety of challenges. Responding to these, political thinkers and researchers have developed a wide variety of approaches and perspectives, most of which survive today. Contemporary political **SCIENCE**, then, is characterized by great diversity. Not only does the discipline pursue a wide variety of subjects and approaches, but no two political science departments in colleges or universities will represent the discipline in precisely the same way. Rather, faculty who teach in each university department represent and embody different and unique combinations of expertise and approach, reflecting in different ways the traditions and developments in understanding that have accumulated over centuries of research and writing. A good way to sample the discipline's breadth and scope, while at the same time appreciating its local embodiment, is to visit the web page of your university's political science department. Look specifically at the faculty's research statements and publications. How would you describe the mix of subjects and approaches? For political science majors, getting to know your faculty members is your entry point to the discipline and to a world of learning.

To assist you in this process of exploration and initiation, we seek in this chapter to acquaint you with some background information on the study of politics as it has developed over the past several thousand years. First, we draw a broad distinction between political **PHILOSOPHY** and empirical political science. Second, we ask whether empirical research into political phenomena can be conducted scientifically. Third, we look at some of the main currents in political thinking and research that have taken place over the last 2,500 years. We then focus on the nature of contemporary political science and describe the main subdisciplinary foci characteristic of our discipline. Finally, we offer some observations on a long-standing debate among those who study political life. On the one hand, there are those who feel that the need for objectivity in our research necessitates abstention from the practice of politics. In other words, these individuals contend that if we ourselves get involved in political life, we lose our ability to understand it dispassionately. Others, however, do not believe that political engagement necessarily diminishes our ability to understand political life.

What sets a "political scientist" apart from individuals with an interest in politics, political ambitions, or perhaps even political experience is therefore partly attitude and commitment, partly training and knowledge. In terms of attitude and commitment, a political scientist appreciates the contributions of different approaches and techniques towards understanding the political world and seeks to employ the most appropriate approaches to answering particular political questions. Similarly, the political scientist is likely to be more committed to the development of general understanding and **EXPLANATION** than others who have a casual or untrained interest in politics. Finally, the political scientist is someone who, by virtue of training and interests, has cultivated a specialized body of knowledge about the political world as it is found here in the United States and elsewhere. Over the years political science has accumulated a formidable body of concepts—such as the political system, political culture, democracy, and so on—with specialized (if often contested) meanings. These concepts facilitate communication among political scientists by standardizing meanings and thereby facilitating efficient communication and accumulation of empirical knowledge. In writing this text, we hope to encourage you to make the transition from someone with an interest in politics to someone with the sensibility of a political scientist.

To the student being introduced to the study of politics, it is useful to have an overview of some of the central concepts, information, approaches, and theories that have been advanced to help

US Capitol

us understand the political world. Empirically, it makes sense to draw illustrations of general concepts from the American political system. However, it is also helpful to help place American politics in a broader theoretical and empirical context by pointing out the many ways in which other political systems do things differently. This is the approach we have adopted here. Many comparativists who specialize in the study of cross-national variations in political phenomena operate on the assumptions (a) that a political system performs specific functions within a society or community, (b) that this is generally true of the political systems of all societies, and (c) that the more societies are alike the more similar their political systems and the functions these systems perform will be. We will talk below at greater length about the kinds of functions which governments and **STATES** are seen to play within societies and about the way institutions provide the structures to perform these functions. It is also clear, though, that every political system and every society is in significant respects unique, respects often bound up with a history, a culture, traditions, and customs. For this reason, part of the politics of each society will resist explanation in terms of functions or institutions that are common to other societies and will be best explained in terms of the mix of cultural factors unique to that society.

It is perhaps useful to keep in mind that while political scientists (like other academics, intellectuals, or scientists) often engage in primary research of one kind or another, students of political science (and often their teachers too) are mainly involved in *reading about* the primary research done by others. Chances are that you will not perform a sophisticated study of voting behavior or a cross-national comparison of electoral systems but will read instead the published reports of such studies or comparisons. To be able to understand and critically assess the work of political scientists, it is useful to know something about their methods and approaches, even if they are not methods and approaches we directly employ ourselves.

We can meet Bismarck half way and say that the study of politics is *both* a science and an art, because it is a discipline with two dimensions: the **NORMATIVE** and the **EMPIRICAL** (see Figure 2.1). This is one basis on which political study has diverged in its methods, political philosophy in particular focusing upon the normative dimension of the subject matter, political science being more directed to the empirical puzzles of political reality. This distinction begs further explanation.

2.2
Politics as Philosophy

A century ago, to study politics involved specializing in a branch of moral philosophy, a method of study reflecting the normative dimension of politics. Moral philosophy presents systematic reasoning and argumentation about *what ought to be*: the normative dimension of politics engages beliefs about what ought to be the case regarding political objects and interests. This does not mean that all moral theory is political nor even that the normative dimension of politics requires us to become moral philosophers. Nonetheless, the study of politics has traditionally engaged questions that were once studied under the heading of moral philosophy. Many of the authors studied by students of politics are philosophers who dealt with politics in their investigation of moral theory (see below, Chapter Three). This close association of politics with normative discourse is not an historical accident or a matter of preference but an inescapable feature of the study of politics.

FIGURE 2.1 Empirical versus Normative

EMPIRICAL refers to the data of experience, meaning that which happens and is subject to observation and sometimes to measurement. For example, the existence and operation of institutions; the behavior of political actors; the existence of ideas, attitudes, and values—all this is empirical, and the empirical dimension of political inquiry seeks to explain such phenomena.

NORMATIVE refers to beliefs we hold or judgments we make about what the political world should be like or, conversely, about how the existing political world falls short of that ideal. What is the good life for humans, the best kind of state or government, or the relative weight of equality and liberty in the scales of justice—these issues (and many others) are normative, and normative discourse seeks to justify a state of affairs or present a case for its reform.

The distinction between empirical and normative should not be mistakenly identified with the distinction between fact and theory. *Both* empirical and normative inquiry are theory-laden, and necessarily so. To deal with "just the facts" in the absence of theory would be like trying to talk about objects or people without using names for them. Facts may be the raw data of experience, but to describe, record, or make sense of facts (phenomena), we need concepts, and a theory is an organized body of concepts. All knowledge has an essentially theoretical component.

Normative discourse involves critical, rational debate about the ends of human life, these ends viewed as goals or states of being to which humans (ought to) aspire, and about the means of achieving such goals. Statements or **PROPOSITIONS** about the end(s) of human life are often based on appeals to our understanding of what human nature is, should be, or could become. In this way, claims about the good life seek a foundation in our experience of human life or in expectations of what that experience suggests is possible in human life. Our beliefs about the lives humans ought to spend and about human nature carry implications for the politics of the societies in which we live and for the policies of governments exercising authority.

Aristotle is famous for the proposition that man is a specifically political animal. The word "political" is derived from the Greek word "*polis*," which refers to the community in which one is a citizen. In saying that man is a political animal, Aristotle may be saying simply that all humans live and take part in the life of a community, that this is what it means to be human. But it is also possible that Aristotle means that man is an animal governed not by instinct but by politics. That is, our actions are not simply responses to ingrained biological imperatives but are consciously regulated. This is a consequence of saying that humans have free will, the ability to choose, or, in more technical language, that human behavior is *intentional*. Not only does this mean that our actions are deliberate but also that the regulation or prohibition of actions is deliberate, done by means of rules or laws rather than automatic instinctive checks. Rules or laws are specifically human devices that presuppose matters such as language and culture—in short, the community life that humans share. They also represent decisions made by someone about what is or is not to be done. When we discuss, debate, or deliberate about such decisions, we engage in normative discourse. Since politics is concerned with decisions to regulate human behavior, it is inescapably normative in character. As discussed earlier, many contemporary states are societies containing more than one community or are no longer communities in any meaningful sense; that is, there is no longer a shared set of values, norms, or beliefs that unites all members. In these societies, normative debate is necessarily persistent, as various groups, communities, and subcultures attempt to influence decision-makers about the right choices for society at large.

Whatever else they do, governments make decisions and enforce them upon populations; in this way governments address ends. Certain views about the good life for man, or about what it means to be human, are logically tied to certain kinds of government or to specific government policies. For example, the belief that all individuals are basically rational, self-interested actors more readily disposed us towards democratic government than the belief that there is a natural hierarchy of rulers and ruled. Similarly, the priority attached to certain views of liberty or security, respectively, may lead to opposition or support for gun control policies. The reverse is also true; certain actions or decisions by governments presuppose beliefs about the good life (mandatory childhood education) or about what is proper for humans (anti-discrimination legislation). Just as our actions always have consequences, regardless of whether or not we foresee those consequences, government decisions, because they are binding on a society, entail a view about what is proper for the members of that community. Government decisions always have normative consequences; that is, they always affect the kinds of ends humans may pursue and what kinds of human life it is possible to have. Politics (and society) is inevitably about norms and normative outcomes, which require selection by some means from the normative options available.

To be sure, not everyone will want to study the body of normative discourse that comprises political philosophy from Plato to the philosophers of our own day. It is nonetheless important that all students of political science understand the normative character of their discipline *and* have a basic familiarity with the normative problems and issues that underlie the institutions and structures of government today. Consider terms like *liberty, equality, rights, sovereignty, justice, democracy, the common good, opportunity, fairness, welfare, authority, and power.* It is hard to imagine a sustained political discussion or inquiry that did not make reference at some point to one or more of these terms. They are so imbedded in our understanding of political life that even those who have never studied politics use at least some of them quite regularly. Each has a normative component—that is, it involves beliefs about what is right or proper —and each is difficult to use without implying a statement about what is right or proper. Most certainly, when we wish to make a statement about what ought to be, we will use one or more of these terms or words like them. It is also the case that each of these terms has several possible meanings. For one person, freedom may mean the *absence* of a law or restraint upon their behavior. For another, freedom may very well *require* the presence of laws and restraints for protection from other individuals. For a third person, freedom may mean participating in making the laws to which one is subject. Accordingly, when a political candidate promises to reform government on behalf of individual freedom, we may well want to ask "what kind of freedom or whose freedom do you mean?"

The flexibility and ubiquity of normative terms—the impossibility of avoiding them—require that before we proceed very far we have to clarify or explain them. This means taking terms that in everyday use are very general and making them more specific. Instead of ambiguity, we look for precise, definite meanings. When we become more specific about our understanding of these terms, we often find contradictions or inconsistencies. We might find, for example, that our understanding of liberty conflicts with our understanding of equality or that we have defined justice in a way that tolerates certain situations we would normally regard as unjust. The rules of good reasoning and of clear communication ask us to try to resolve contradictions or remove inconsistency.

As political scientists, but as educated citizens too, we use the critical faculties of our reason and the analytic skills they allow us to develop in order to increase our understanding of each other. We seek precision, coherence, and consistency in the use of normative terms like freedom or justice so that we will understand the normative outcomes involved in their use, whether this is to promote a political position, advance a policy decision, or propose legislation that will bind each of us. The better we understand what is at stake in these matters, the better we will be able to judge if they are consistent with our interests or with our conception of "what ought to be."

2.3
Politics as Social Science

What does it mean to be scientific in the study of politics? Indeed, can politics—or other aspects of human behavior—be profitably studied scientifically? This question still provokes a divergent response from political thinkers and researchers. While we have our own opinions on this topic, we also acknowledge that reasonable people might arrive at different conclusions. We believe, however, that serious students of politics ought to reflect carefully on the activity of studying politics. We think that knowing something about the nature of scientific knowledge and activity will help

---

FIGURE 2.2 The Progress of Scientific Knowledge

Most of us probably have an ill-defined and reasonably simple notion of scientific progress that suggests that it is a gradual process whereby knowledge simply accumulates by building on and refining rather straightforwardly what we already know. Progress may be slow or rapid, but it is likely one-directional and cumulative. Thomas Kuhn is a historian of science who has studied the phenomena of "scientific revolutions" and offers a less sanguine interpretation of scientific progress. According to Kuhn, most scientists engage in "normal scientific" inquiry, that is, work that is based upon some fundamental and widely held conception of reality and the scientific problems it poses (this shared view he calls a "paradigm"). Over time, "normal scientific" activity uncovers things that are impossible to explain, given the assumptions of the prevailing paradigm. What is remarkable to Kuhn is the ability of the scientific community to simply ignore these "anomalies"—or instances in which reality has violated the shared scientific paradigm. However, the anomalies tend to accumulate and build up, until such time as someone turns from her or his "normal scientific" inquiry (work that falls squarely within the established paradigm) and focuses instead on the anomalies. In some cases, these "scientific outsiders," whose work is not based on the paradigmatic assumptions of normal science, can make a fundamental discovery that completely revolutionizes the way we look at reality. Such "scientific revolutions," if successful, generate a new paradigm that provides a whole new direction for "normal scientific" activity. Scientific progress, in Kuhn's view, depends not so much on the methodical application of normal scientific principles but rather on the critical imagination and intuition of pioneers who may not even enjoy much of a reputation among their peers. Scientific progress, for Kuhn, is hardly a smooth or one-directional process!

students of politics to come to their own view on the appropriate role of science in political research.

The *Oxford English Dictionary* (*OED*) defines a "science" as (among other things): "A branch of study which is concerned either with a connected body of demonstrated truths or with observed facts systematically classified and more or less colligated by being brought under general laws, and which includes trustworthy methods for the discovery of new truth within its own domain." As a science, then, political inquiry is concerned with the careful **OBSERVATION**, measurement, and explanation of the objects of political experience. The *OED* definition says little about the *content* of scientific knowledge, other than that it must be based on observation ("observed facts"), the results of which must be organized ("systematically classified and more or less colligated"). Nothing in this definition precludes a science of politics, any more than it would a science of weather or astronomy, for example. The definition does include a reference to the need for "trustworthy methods through which to discover new truth." Scientific knowledge, then, results from the application of the **SCIENTIFIC METHOD**. And the scientific method is actually a series of steps that, if followed, should generate trustworthy knowledge.

Applying the scientific method to the study of politics involves five steps:

1. Begin by observing some aspect of political life.
2. Develop, or identify, a theory that is consistent with what you have observed.
3. Use the theory to make predictions.
4. Test those predictions by experiments or further observations.
5. Modify the theory in the light of your results.

It is the responsibility of individual scientists to share the results of their work with others, and to provide sufficiently detailed information on the methods they employed so that other scholars may *replicate* (or repeat for the purposes of confirming the validity of the results) the work. Testing and validating scientific knowledge is, therefore, a responsibility of the entire scientific community. And in this respect, it is important to note that the simple application of this method does not guarantee consensus among scientists. Virtually all scientific communities, whether in the natural or the **SOCIAL SCIENCES**, are embroiled at one time or another in heated debate and disagreement. In some cases this disagreement culminates in a "scientific revolution." In these rare but important events, the scientific community rejects one set of understandings of its subject matter for a new, more powerful, or more accurate way of approaching their subject. The advancement of science, then, depends not only on the achievements of individual scientists but also on the willingness of the scientific community to verify or falsify the validity of the claims of scientists.

The clearest goal of the scientific approach to politics is to be able to make accurate observations and reliable **GENERALIZATIONS** about political phenomena. In this quest, accuracy of observations is dependent upon the development of clear and agreed-upon concepts as well as on valid, reliable, and precise measures that can be employed to describe variation in them across the units of observation. It is essential to the accumulation and efficient transmission of scientific knowledge that practitioners share an explicit understanding of the concepts they wish to observe and an awareness of the measurement strategies employed to observe them. Like all sciences, then, political scientists devote time and energy to developing useful and explicit conceptualizations of phenomena and to training and cultivating measurement skills among students.

Good measures are precise, reliable, and accurate **DESCRIPTIONS** of the variation in some phenomenon of interest. Different scientists observing the same variation should in principle be able to agree on measures describing that variation. We refer to these measures as **VARIABLES** since they express observed variations across the units of observation (these could be individuals, groups, institutions, electoral districts, countries, etc.) on some phenomena of interest. Once measures have been collected for both the political phenomena of interest and their hypothesized causes, political scientists are in a position to assess the extent to which variation in the measures of, say, political participation seems to be empirically related to variation in some other factor, say, educational attainment. In doing this, political scientists are attempting to determine whether two phenomena of interest (voter turnout and educational attainment) **CO-VARY**, such that high levels of one are associated with high levels of the other (positive co-variation) or high levels of one are associated with low levels of the other (negative co-variation). In much of empirical political research, this process involves hypothesizing a causal relationship between two or more variables, where the cause is represented by an **INDEPENDENT VARIABLE** and the effect is referred to as the **DEPENDENT VARIABLE** (because its values depend on some other variable).

Let's work through this logic with a simple and fictitious analysis. Suppose, for example, that we are interested in determining whether higher levels of education cause greater political participation among individuals. Suppose further that we have information from ten people about their level of political participation (measured by summing the number of participatory acts engaged in over the past year, with 0 representing the lowest possible level of participation, to 10, representing the highest level). Suppose that we also had information from the same ten people on the number of years of formal education (ranging from six years at the lowest level to 18 at the highest end). These example data are arranged according to individuals' level of education in Table 2.1 below.

Assuming that both these measures are valid, accurate, and reliable indicators of the underlying concepts we wish to study, we could use them to explore the relationship—if there is any at all—between the level of formal education and the level of political participation among these ten individuals. We might begin by hypothesizing that those with higher educational levels would be more participatory than those with lower education. This might be because their greater educational exposure would instill more participatory values or perhaps because their experience with education has nurtured greater skill and confidence to take part in the political process. A look at the table suggests that there is some such relationship, in that on balance those with higher levels of formal education generally appear to be more participative in politics. Another way of exploring this is to plot the scores of individuals on each measure (formal education and political participation) in a two-dimensional plot (sometimes called a "scatterplot"). Each point in the scatter represents an individual, based on their scores on the two measures.

TABLE 2.1 Example Data for 10 Hypothetical Persons

	# PARTICIPATORY ACTS PER YEAR (RANGE = 0–10)	# YEARS OF FORMAL EDUCATION
Individual 1	2	6
Individual 2	6	8
Individual 3	6	12
Individual 4	8	12
Individual 5	7	12
Individual 6	8	14
Individual 7	10	16
Individual 8	8	16
Individual 9	9	16
Individual 10	10	18

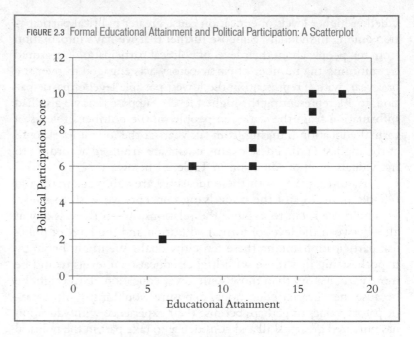

FIGURE 2.3 Formal Educational Attainment and Political Participation: A Scatterplot

Looking at the scatter, it is quickly apparent that the two measures "co-vary" such that individuals with higher educational attainment tend to be more politically participative. Visually, this is manifested by the upward skew in the plotted points from the lower left to the top right of the plot. Based on this visual inspection, we can say that formal educational attainment and political participation are "co-related." We could go on to explore mathematically how strongly and powerfully formal educational attainment levels are correlated with levels of political participation. We could add other variables to the analysis, representing additional hypothesized causes of variation in political participation. However, we will leave these refinements for the moment. For now, it is enough to appreciate the basic logic that underlies empirical political research.

While this is obviously a trivial illustration, in that we don't know how representative these ten imaginary individuals are of the larger population and there are many possible alternative factors be-sides education that may influence an individual's level of political participation, most empirical research in political science follows the same general logic. We begin with measures of variation in political phenomena of interest and explore whether the supposed causes of political variation co-vary with the hypothesized effects. Political scientists have developed a wide range of statistical proced-ures to assess co-variation and **CORRELATION** between and among variables. But there is no deep mystery to the scientific enterprise in political science. Even the most sophisticated statistical analyses can be reduced in terms of their logic to simple foundations in the measurement of co-variation and correlation.

Establishing and measuring the strength of correlations and co-variation among variables is what empirical research can accomplish. While it can show that two variables may be closely connected, the techniques of empirical analysis cannot demonstrate that one variable causes the other. For example, while our hypothetical example above showed that education and political participation were co-related, even armed with this information we cannot claim that the variations in the level of educational attainment across the ten individuals determines or causes the observed differences in their levels of political participation. There may be some unmeasured third factor that actually explains the correlation we have observed. Or it could be that the ten individuals we have studied are wildly unrepresentative in some ways. Another sample might show different results. For all these reasons, it is very important for empirical researchers to realize that causation—the claim that variation in one factor explains variation in another—will always be an **INFERENCE** that we, as investigators, draw from an inspection of patterns in the empirical world. We may infer that educational differences cause differences in participatory behavior, but on the basis of our analysis we are not in a position to claim to have "proven" this relationship. Of course, our sample exercise was over-simple, but even the most rigorous and elaborate program of research in the world could still only hope to strengthen the inference that educational differences cause different levels of political participation. Empirical researchers are continually working to try to strengthen inferences of causality. They do this by repeating investigations in different settings, at different times, and with different individuals. They develop multiple measures of underlying concepts and see if they produce consistent results. They develop different **RESEARCH DESIGNS** to explore a variety of approaches to the underlying relationships of interest. Clearly, the development and refinement of understandings of empirical relationships that we can identify in the empirical world is a challenging and on-going endeavor.

The most enthusiastic supporters of a scientific approach to politics have argued that to some extent these phenomena are subject to laws, rather as physical phenomena are subject to the laws of thermodynamics or gravity. Critics of the application of scientific methods in political research raise a number of potential objections. First, they raise the practical objection that the political world is beyond the control of the scientist, making it impossible to devise experiments or to eliminate possible rival explanations. With a complex and dynamic subject matter, their observations could be contaminated by the unmeasured influence of unobserved factors. Other critics contend that political phenomena are often over-determined; that is to say, there is such a multiplicity of causes involved in the creation of each outcome, and it is so difficult (if not impossible) to isolate causal factors, that very few law-like generalizations have been successfully demonstrated. Still others believe that the capacity of humans to choose (free will) makes it inappropriate to search for scientific laws (analogous to the "law of gravity," for example) since such laws could be violated at any moment by an individual exercising her free will or simply wanting to defy a known law. Perhaps it was these considerations that led the Noble Prize-winning physicist Albert Einstein to opine that "politics was more difficult than physics."

Today, it is less important to choose between scientific and non-scientific approaches to the study of politics than to know that these are distinct but related enterprises. Instead of seeing them as competing views of how the subject ought to be studied, they are instead best seen as complementary approaches, each capable of contributing its own insight, and both collectively necessary for a full understanding. Yet, as we will see, the discipline of political science is today—as it has been at several points in the past—locked in an intense debate about the proper place of scientific methods (and particularly statistical methods) in political research. While some might find this uncertainty and disagreement frustrating in a field that has been studied for as long as politics has been, we believe that this intellectual ferment is a healthy sign. As students of politics you will not be "inducted" into some closed and settled intellectual universe. Rather, you will be challenged to form your own opinions about the most profitable way of studying politics. In this, your own values and intellectual convictions can be your guide. You will not be left adrift in this quest, however. There are a wide range of well-defined standards and procedures that the discipline has developed over the centuries, which you can use to evaluate the work of others and to shape your own voice as a political scientist. From our point of view, students of political science should be concerned with acquiring an accurate representation and understanding of political reality, whether this arises from a quantitative or a qualitative research design. Nonetheless, positing a more modest goal, such as explaining political phenomena through the identification of **CAUSAL TENDENCIES**, is reasonable and realistic.

Canadian Parliament

Empirical accuracy remains central to good political study, and in this sense politics is legitimately a social *science*.

Politics has been a subject of study since the time of Plato and Aristotle in ancient Greece. As we will see in the next chapter, such questions as how politics could contribute to "the good life," how political power should be exercised, and by whom were of enormous importance to the Greeks. If Plato was the first political philosopher, then Aristotle broadened the intellectual terrain of political research by being the first "political scientist." One of his innovations was to attempt to bring some conceptual order to the diversity of the political world that he observed around him by developing elaborate classification schemes. He did this by simplifying and classifying this political diversity in much the same way as he had when his attention was on the diversity of life forms in biology by distinguishing separate genus, species, and so on. As he put it: "... governments differ in kind ... As in other departments of science, so in politics, the compound should always be resolved into

**2.4
The Emergence of
Political Science**

61

the simple elements or least parts of the whole. We must therefore look at the elements of which the state is composed, in order that we may see in what the different kinds of rule differ from one another, and whether any scientific result can be attained about each one of them" (Aristotle, *The Politics, Book 1, Part 1*). We will return to a discussion of Aristotle's political science in the next chapter.

It is clear that normative and empirical research traditions have coexisted in political research from the outset. Since then, however, the relative weight of each tradition in the body of political writing has changed in line with the larger currents in our intellectual history. In the roughly thousand years after the decline of Greek civilization, political writing was dominated by theologians who were primarily concerned with the realization on earth of God's will. For many centuries, then, political thought was subordinate to theology, and empirical political research languished. It wasn't until the Renaissance resurrected humanism, with its emphasis on the importance of human life in the secular world rather than life after death, that empirical political arrangements began to attract the attention of researchers and thinkers once more. This is exemplified by the publication by Niccolo Machiavelli of *The Prince* in 1515. In this brief work, Machiavelli tried to ingratiate himself to the locally ruling Medici family by offering them a series of principles that he believed would help them perpetuate their hold on political power. The book is striking for its amoral tone—there is no consideration of the proper ends of political power but rather an exclusive focus on how it could be retained. As an early work of "statecraft," Machiavelli's premise is that government is something that serves human ends (whatever they may be defined to be), and as such, it can be done well or badly. His work was intended to help the Medici rule effectively and enduringly.

The Enlightenment, with its optimism grounded in belief in human reason and progress, saw a flowering of empirical research designed to uncover the "laws" of human progress. Although best known to Americans as a source of the "separation of powers" doctrine in American constitutionalism, Montesquieu's *The Spirit of the Laws*, published originally in 1752, is a very "modern" work in its application of the scientific method to the study of political arrangements. The emergence of democratic reforms and constitutional regimes in the Americas and Europe gave both political philosophers and empirical researchers much to reflect upon in their work. By the middle of the nineteenth century, the wide spread in political reform processes around Europe and in the Americas—coupled perhaps with the threat of revolution—combined to convince a

FIGURE 2.4 An Example of Enlightenment Reasoning: The Inevitable Perfectibility of Humankind, Marquis de Condorcet (1795)

If man can predict, almost with certainty, those appearances of which he understands the laws; if, even when the laws are unknown to him, experience or the past enables him to foresee, with considerable probability, future appearances, why should we suppose it a chimerical undertaking to delineate, with some degree of truth, the picture of the future destiny of mankind from the results of its history? The only foundation of faith in the natural sciences is the principle that the general laws, known or unknown, which regulate the phenomena of the universe, are regular and constant; and why should this principle, applicable to the other operations of nature, be less true when applied to the development of the intellectual and moral faculties of man? In short, as opinions formed from experience, relative to the same class of objects, are the only rule by which men of soundest understanding are governed in their conduct, why should the philosopher be proscribed from supporting his conjectures upon a similar basis, provided he attribute to them no greater certainty than the number, the consistency, and the accuracy of actual observations shall authorize? ...

In fine, may it not be expected that the human race will be meliorated by new discoveries in the sciences and the arts, and, as an unavoidable consequence, in the means of individual and general prosperity; by farther progress in the principles of conduct, and in moral practice; and lastly, by the real improvement of our faculties, moral, intellectual and physical, which may be the result either of the improvement of the instruments which increase the power and direct the exercise of those faculties, or of the improvement of our natural organization itself?

... [W]e shall find the strongest reasons to believe, from past experience, from observation of the progress which the sciences and civilization have hitherto made, and from the analysis of the march of the human understanding, and the development of its faculties, that nature has fixed no limits to our hopes ...

The advantages that must result from the state of improvement, of which I have proved we may almost entertain the certain hope, can have no limit but the absolute perfection of the human species, since, in proportion as different kinds of equality shall be established as to the various means of providing for our wants, as to a more universal instruction, and a more entire liberty, the more real will be this equality, and the nearer will it approach towards embracing every thing truly important to the happiness of mankind.

Excerpted from Condorcet, "The Tenth Epoch, Future Progress of Mankind," *Outlines of an Historical View of the Progress of the Human Mind*, (1795); available at: <http://oll.libertyfund.org/Home3/HTML.php?recordID=0878#hd_lf0878_head_013>.

growing body of university-based intellectuals to specialize in the study of politics. Prior to this, political philosophers tended to be privately wealthy aristocrats pursing a hobby or occupying faculty positions in history or philosophy departments. Empirical researchers interested in politics were government employees or acting politicians (Edmund Burke or Thomas Paine, for example), or they were employed in universities as professors of political economy or constitutional history. Gradually, as the nineteenth century drew to a close, these individuals achieved a "critical mass" sufficient to convince universities that a separate, specialized discipline focused on political life was justifiable. The birth of a discipline in academe is recognition that there exists a distinctive subject matter that requires its own specialized focus, methods, and approaches.

In the latter decades of the 1800s, then, departments and schools of political science began to emerge. A century ago, the

FIGURE 2.5 A Law of Politics? Michels's "Iron Law of Oligarchy"

A German political sociologist named Roberto Michels claims to have proven that democracy and organization are incompatible, and that therefore, since modern society is highly organized, democracy itself is impossible under contemporary conditions. "It is organization which gives birth to the domination of the elected over the electors, of the mandataries over the mandators, of the delegates over the delegators. Who says organization says oligarchy." Published originally in 1911, his generalization is one of the closest examples we have in political research to a law in the physical sciences. Michels's empirical focus was primarily on the Social Democratic Party of Germany—a precursor of the same SPD that governs in coalition with the Green Party in Germany today. A former party member, Michels became disillusioned with what he saw to be the betrayal of the socialist ideology in the party, a process that he attributed to the emergence of a clique of leaders who essentially "sold out" the rank and file membership. For a variety of reasons he analyzed, the party's internal democratic structure had failed to render the party leadership accountable. Arguing that as a party more deeply committed to internal democracy and to furthering democratic reforms in Germany at large than any other organization, the failure of democracy in this "most likely" setting meant that the prospect for democracy in less congenial environments was doomed. In other words, if viable democracy was impossible even in a party like the SPD, it was highly unlikely for it to take hold anywhere else. In this respect, it is perhaps ironic that the current SPD is governing with a party that was explicitly and self-consciously organized in the 1980s in Germany to defy the "iron law of oligarchy"—the German Greens. We encourage you to look into this party and its brief history to draw your own conclusion about whether it was successful. Can you think of any organization that defies Michels by successfully maintaining a democratic internal organization?

discipline crossed a significant threshold when the American Political Science Association (APSA), a professional organization representing the common interests of those studying politics, was established with 214 original members. By 1906 the number of members had about doubled. Today, the APSA is the world's largest professional organization of political scientists with a total of more than 15,000 members residing in more than 80 countries. From the handful of political science departments existing in 1903, an estimate in 1988 was that of the roughly 2,000 colleges and universities in the United States, approximately 760 had departments of political science. In 2003–04, the Department of Education reported that 35,581 students graduated with a Bachelors degree in political science. A further 1,869 earned Masters of Arts and 618 doctoral degrees in the field during that year. Today, studying political science at university is a common (and in our view, an excellent!) choice for American students.

The past century has seen a sharpening and deepening of the debate over appropriate methods and approaches for the study of politics. Arthur Bentley and Charles Merriam were among those political scientists in the early decades of the 1900s to argue that the new discipline should embrace the scientific method. A confluence of events through the 1930s and 1940s combined to create a spirit of disillusionment in the political science community in the post-World War II period. The inability of the League of Nations, which was championed by American President (and political scientist) Woodrow Wilson after World War I as the institutional solution to world conflict, to prevent World War II was one such contributing factor. Similarly, the fall of the Weimar Republic to Hitler's Nazis in the 1930s also shook the political science community's faith in their institutional prescriptions, since the Republic had been designed in 1919 with substantial input from political scientists. The looming specter of nuclear holocaust and the beginning of the Cold War were also factors that weighed heavily on the hearts and minds of political scientists. David Easton, a 1940s doctoral graduate of Harvard University, captured some of the disquiet of the political science community in 1953 when he wrote the following in a chapter of *The Political System* entitled "Mood and Method":

> From the days of Aristotle, political science has been known as the master science. Although political scientists today might be accused of being overambitious or imperialistic if they were thus to cast their net so broadly, their subject matter is nevertheless central to the solution of our present social crisis ... Yet, in light of what society demands from them, and of what is in fact possible for political science, they would be compelled in equal honesty to set all pride aside and confess that in its achievement in research American political science has grave difficulty in measuring up to the tasks imposed upon it ... Many cogent reasons could be offered for the disappointing results of a discipline already 2,500 years old. It is the burden of this study that among these reasons and at the forefront we must place the constant reluctance in American political science to *adopt and teach seriously the standards of valid thinking, observation, and description that today we are prone to associate with something vaguely called scientific method*. [Emphasis in the original.]

In the context of the postwar period, these sentiments resonated with a growing number of political scientists, particularly among the younger practitioners who felt that the traditional approaches of institutional analysis and philosophy had been discredited. The **BEHAVIORAL REVOLUTION**, as it has become known, involved the widespread support for the adoption of scientific methods in political research. The characteristics of "behavioral research" during this period included:

1. an attempt to separate facts and value judgments in research, with emphasis being placed on the observable;
2. careful attention to measurement in observation, including a commitment to quantify in order to add precision to these observations;
3. a concern for the careful and systematic development of empirical theory and generalizations based on the identification of regularities in the political world; and
4. a concern for the development of "basic science" and a desire to ensure that the discipline's research agenda not be dictated by the events and crises of the day.

The rapid expansion of universities in the 1950s and 1960s in the United States ensured that there were plenty of jobs for the young graduates of behavioral political science programs. The movement reached its apex quickly, and by the middle 1960s its proponents had become the "establishment." David Easton became the president of the APSA in 1969.

Despite its importance in the discipline of political science, the behavioral revolution does not occupy a prominent position in the popular culture of the 1960s. That decade is more commonly remembered as a period of protest (civil rights and Vietnam), urban unrest and riots, and "drugs, sex, and rock and roll." In those heady times, students were drawn to political science courses out of a concern for the human condition and often out of a desire to improve it. Many were unwilling to follow the advice of their behaviorally trained professors and leave their values at the classroom door, to study statistics, and to follow the other principles of science in their work. They wanted not only to understand the political world but also to change it. Increasingly, young university students came to view the behavioralists on university faculties, themselves seen as "revolutionaries" in the 1950s, as indistinguishable from "the Establishment" against which they were protesting in the streets. In the search for quantifiable theory of regularities in political life, behavioralists were depicted as apologists for the status quo in politics. Revolution of behavioralism gave birth to a counter-revolution that became known simply as "**POST-BEHAVIORALISM**."

Within the discipline, the "Caucus for a New Political Science" emerged within the APSA to focus and mobilize this discontent. Support for the post-behavioralists came from a surprising quarter. In his presidential address to the 65th annual meeting of the APSA at its conference in 1969 in New York, David Easton himself argued that the behavioral revolution had been carried too far, that the discipline had grown too distant from the pressing political concerns of the day, and that it was necessary to combine scientific approaches and the development of basic theory in political science with a concern for the relevance and usefulness of political research. He articulated a "credo of relevance" that embraced most of the main demands of the critics of behavioralism. Essentially, Easton recommended that subjects of political research should be chosen for their substantive or practical importance, not because they can be easily measured using quantitative methods. He argued that scientific or behavioral research was implicitly "conservative," since it focused attention on what "is" (what can be scientifically observed) rather than encourage people to think about what "ought to be" or what "could be." He urged political scientists to exercise their professional responsibility to share their knowledge with those involved in political life in order to help improve the human condition.

Easton's intervention did not settle matters. In many respects political science as a discipline still wrestles with the issues that the behavioral revolution and the backlash of post-behavioralism crystallized. Most recently, in the fall of 2000 an anonymous political scientist, who adopted the pseudonym "Mr. **PERESTROIKA**" (after the reform movement associated with Michail Gorbachev that led to the demise of the Soviet Union in the 1990s), circulated an e-mail (see Figure 2.6) that criticized the dominance of mathematics and abstract applications of "rational choice theory" in the discipline and the lack of democracy in the governance of the APSA. Singled out for particular criticism was the APSA's flagship journal (*The American Political Science Review*, or *APSR*) for its role in strengthening the dominance of "scientific research." Supporters of "perestroika" have subsequently organized, and their efforts have produced a number of significant reforms to the APSA as an organization and to its offerings. For example, in 2003 the APSA introduced a new journal that would accompany the *APSR* in being circulated to all its members. Called *Perspectives on Politics*, it aims to reach a broader audience than the more technical and specialized *APSR*, enabling non-specialists and general readers to benefit from the accumulation of knowledge in the discipline. The result of these currents has been to encourage students of politics to reflect anew on the question of appropriate techniques and methods in the conduct of political inquiry.

FIGURE 2.6 Excerpts from Original Text of "Mr. Perestroika" E-mail

On the Irrelevence [sic] of the APSA and APSR!
Please spread this Letter as widely as Possible
Let them know we Exist
TO: The Editor of *PS* and *APSR* [*American Political Science Review*]
October 15, 2000
On Globalization of the *APSA* and *APSR*: A Political Science Manifesto

Questions to ponder over:

1. Why do people like Benedict Anderson and James C. Scott find the APSA and the *APSR* irrelevant? These are probably the most famous political scientists in the world. They are equally famous abroad and in other disciplines compared to the "stars" of Political Science ...
2. Related to above is the question: Why do a majority of political scientists who do comparative politics ignore *APSA* and *APSR* and go to their regional meetings and read regional association journals, e.g., such as those associated with East Asia, Latin America, Hispanic Studies, etc.
3. Why does a "coterie" of faculty dominate and control *APSA* and the editorial board of APSR? I scratch your back, you scratch mine. I give an award to your student from Harvard and you give mine from Duke or Columbia. In short, why do the "East Coast Brahmins" control *APSA*?
4. Why are a few men who make poor game-theorists and who cannot for the life-of-me compete with a third grade Economics graduate student, WHY are these men allowed to represent the diversity of methodologies and areas of the world that *APSA* "purports" to represent?
   ...
8. Why are the overwhelming majority of Presidents of *APSA* or editorial board members of *APSR* WHITE and MALE? ...
9. Why are all the articles of *APSR* from the same methodology—statistics or game theory ...?
   ...
   Lastly, ...
   I hope this anonymous letter leads to a dismantling of the Orwellian system that we have in *APSA* and that we will see a true Perestroika in the discipline.

Mr. Perestroika

Source: Monroe, 2005: 9-11.

Contemporary political science is, then, in a state of seemingly perpetual intellectual ferment. Students coming in to the discipline should be aware of these intellectual currents but not be alarmed by them. The subject matter of political research is complex, dynamic, and pressing in its importance. There is ample room for a variety of approaches and convictions about how best to go about advancing understanding and improving our political life. The challenge for political scientists is to discover their own "voice" in the discipline and to strike an accommodation for themselves with the tensions inherent in the need to develop rigorous and reliable knowledge about a subject matter that is inherently and necessarily value-laden and contested. However you feel about the current intellectual debates, it is clear that as a result of both the centuries of political analysis and the broad variety of political phenomena at home and abroad, political science today is a diverse, eclectic, and exciting discipline. Clearly, the study of politics is unlikely to be dull and boring!

2.5 Studying Political Science Today: Five Subdisciplines

From the materials we have presented in this chapter, it may appear as though the discipline of political science is fragmented, lacking in a clear identity and fundamental agreement on many important matters. In some important respects, that is true (though it is no more true of political science than of many other social sciences). The interdependence of politics with other aspects of societies encourages political scientists to borrow intellectually from other social science (and humanities) disciplines. The divisions within political science with respect to the personal political positions of scholars, which follow from their chosen approach to political understanding (philosophical or empirical) and their specialized interests in one or more of the discipline's subdivisions, combine to create a surface impression of a lack of coherence and integration within the discipline. Reflecting this, commentators have described political science as "cacophonous" (Katznelson and Milner, 2002: 1) or "a discipline divided" (Almond, 1990).

What, then, is the current state of political science? A beginning student has a right to know what kind of discipline she is getting involved in from the outset in terms of intellectual commitments. A good undergraduate education in political science will expose students to the full diversity of the discipline and encourage them to explore controversial and challenging issues in both the empirical and normative aspects of political life. Frequently, undergraduate programs will seek to accomplish this by encouraging (or requiring) course work in each of the subdisciplines commonly recognized in political science. To give you a sense of the relative size of these specializations, the list below shows the percentage of members of the APSA who reported in 2005-06 an interest in each subfield; the numbers do not total 100 per cent since some members select more than one subfield:

- Political philosophy (ethical and moral questions): 19 per cent
- American politics (study of national and subnational politics at home): 35 per cent
- Comparative politics (study of political systems other than your own): 40 per cent
- Methodology (study of research designs, and techniques of measurement and analysis): 12 per cent
- Public policy (study of forces shaping the design, implementation, and success of political interventions): 21 per cent
- International politics: 35 per cent

While the first obviously deals directly with normative issues, the remaining five subfields are all concerned, to greater or lesser extents, with empirical inquiry. The subfield of political methodology, in particular, focuses on the ways in which our understanding of the empirical political world can be made more reliable, valid, and accurate. The study of public policy represents a distinctive combination of normative and empirical research. Public policies represent the attempt to achieve certain normatively desirable outcomes through some authoritative intervention as efficiently and effectively as possible. Therefore, the study of public policy involves judgments concerning what is prudent and useful, given certain ends.

Many who are drawn to study politics at university do so as the result of long-standing interests in public affairs or perhaps in the hopes of cultivating a political career. While these motivations are justifiable, it is worth drawing attention to some key differences separating "political scientists" from all others who are simply "interested in" politics. At the same time, it should be noted that university courses in political science are not typically where one learns how to become a politician, or how to win an election, or how to wield power or authority. The student whose interest in politics is *immediately* practical—wanting to *be* a politician or political strategist—is best directed to become politically active: to join a party; to work in a political campaign; to make political friends, allies, or contacts; and to gain the experience that only comes from doing. There is no denying that the study of politics as we are introducing it and as the discipline pursues it could be beneficial to someone seeking a political career. But this course of study will not by itself lead to such a career, nor will the desire to hold political office give one the aptitude for studying politics. The difference is that the study of politics should lead to an *understanding* of political institutions, processes, and behavior, without providing a *training* in the specific activities that characterize the elected politician or governmental official.

FIGURE 2.7 The Political System

An application of general systems theory, with an emphasis on the idea of a general equilibrium, David Easton's model of the political system has been adapted and refined by numerous political scientists and teachers, who, without any commitment to Easton's propositions about this system or its functioning, have found it a useful way of visualizing and thinking about the political world. A typical simplified model of the political system might look as follows:

INPUTS	THE STATE/GOVERNMENT	OUTPUTS (POLICY)
Demands (voting, lobbying)	Legislature	Laws
	Executive/bureaucracy	Programs
	The Courts	Decisions
Support (legitimacy, compliance)		

THE POLITICAL PROCESS → GOVERNING →

THE ENVIRONMENT ←

A final word on the relationship between the study and the practice of politics. Because politics is normative and because it often involves a clash of competing interests, many political positions are controversial and may lead to heated discussions or emotional discourse. Political scientists are as likely as anyone (and more likely than most) to feel passionately about politics and to harbor intense political commitments and beliefs. Two things follow from this. First, there is an understandable tendency in the discipline—reinforced by liberal ideas of tolerance—to urge respect for the opinions of others and in this way defuse the potentially explosive atmosphere of politics (like religion or ethics). In some cases, different assumptions about what is good, just, or prudent will lead equally reasonable people to draw different conclusions. In other cases, however, positions may depend upon faulty information or ignorance. One virtue of remembering that politics is also a social science is the reminder that there is a dimension to the political world that is not merely "opinion," that there *are* matters here about which it is possible to be right or wrong. The functioning of electoral systems, or the review of legislation by the courts, or the role of bureaucrats in implementing public policy—these are not just matters about which one can have opinions, they are also subjects about which one can acquire knowledge. And most citizens are probably as ignorant about vast areas of the political world as they are about the activity of enzymes or the relationships between subatomic particles. By

2.6
Politics and Commitment

analogy, just as we understand that the weather is ultimately explicable in terms of basic laws of chemistry and physics, so too the outcomes and effects of government are explicable in terms of the behavior of political actors and the functioning of institutions.

Secondly, while it is essential that the conclusions of political analysis not be determined by the personal convictions of the analyst, it is neither necessary nor desirable for students of politics to purge themselves of their political convictions. In an age of ascendant political cynicism, the passion and conviction that leads many students to focus their studies on political life is an important resource for communities. These should be cultivated and nurtured. However, as Max Weber admonished earlier in this century (Weber, 1958), the roles of political scientist and political activist are distinct and require different kinds of talents and orientations. While the same individuals can perform both roles, neither is performed well if the differences separating them are blurred or ignored. As political scientists, each of us must attempt to locate the line where passion and value commitments end and where dispassionate, disciplined inquiry begins. In closing, we recommend taking Alan Zuckerman's advice (see the opening quotes for this chapter) to engage your passions and your analytic capacities in your work and to have fun exploring the political world.

References and Suggested Readings

Almond, Gabriel. 1990. *A Discipline Divided: Schools and Sects in Political Science.* Newbury Park, CA: Sage.

Aristotle. 1962, reprinted 1992. *The Politics*, T.A. Sinclair, trans. London: Penguin Books.

Dahl, Robert A. 1971. *Polyarchy: Participation and Opposition.* New Haven, CT: Yale University Press.

———. 1991. *Modern Political Analysis*, 5th ed. Englewood Cliffs, NJ: Prentice Hall.

Easton, David. 1965 [1953, 1971]. *The Political System: An Inquiry into the State of Political Science.* New York: Knopf.

———. 1969. "The New Revolution in Political Science." *American Political Science Review* 63,4 (December): 1051-61.

Katznelson, Ira, and Helen V. Milner, eds. 2002. *Political Science: The State of the Discipline.* New York: W.W. Norton and the APSA.

Monroe, Kristen Renwick, ed. 2005. *Perestroika!: The Raucus Rebellion in Political Science.* New Haven, CT: Yale University Press.

Parenti, Michael. 1978. *Power and the Powerless.* New York: St. Martin's Press.

Raphael, D.D. 1976. *Problems of Political Philosophy.* Rev. ed. London: Macmillan.

Ricci, David M. 1984. *The Tragedy of Political Science: Politics, Scholarship, and Democracy.* New Haven, CT: Yale University Press.

Weber, Max. 1958. "Politics as a Vocation," and "Science as a Vocation," in H.W. Gerth and C. Wright Mills, eds., *From Max Weber: Essays in Sociology.* New York: Oxford University Press.

Zuckerman, Alan S. 1991. *Doing Political Science: An Introduction to Political Analysis.* Boulder, CO: Westview Press.

Key Terms

behavioralism/behavioral revolution
causal tendencies
correlation
co-vary
dependent variables
description
empirical
explanation
generalization
independent and dependent variables
inference
normative
observation
perestroika
philosophy
post-behavioralism
propositions
research design
science
scientific method
social science
states
variable

PART TWO | ideas

THREE | Foundations of Political Philosophy

"We have laid it down that the excellence of the full citizen who shares in the government is the same as that of the good man. We have also assumed that the man who begins by being a subject must ultimately share in the government. It follows on this that the legislator must labor to ensure that his citizens become good men. He must therefore know what institutions will produce this result, and what is the end or aim to which a good life is directed."

—Aristotle, *The Politics*, VII, xiv, § 8

"The philosophers have only *interpreted* the world, in various ways; the point, however, is to *change* it."

—Marx, Theses on Feuerbach

In a song released in 1971, the late John Lennon invited us to imagine a world of perfect harmony and consensus—a world without conflict, competition, or animosity (*Rolling Stone* magazine voted "Imagine" as the "third greatest song of all time" in November 2004). In this imaginary world there would be no war. Everyone would agree on a distribution of the wealth produced by society. Everyone would presumably agree to a set of procedures and outcomes regarding their collective lives. Everyone would get what they needed and give what they could spare and, according to their abilities, share equitably in the bounty of the earth. No one would harm anyone else. Good will and fellowship would prevail. Prisons, judicial systems, and the military could all be dismantled. Resources and energies could be devoted to tackling persistent challenges such as disease and disasters. To paraphrase Karl Marx (another visionary thinker), "the institutions of the state would wither away."

"You may say that I'm a dreamer," Lennon sang, but he understood the power of ideas in motivating people and in generating action. With the happy image conjured by his song in mind, reflect back to the definitions of politics offered in the first chapter. Think for a moment about what "politics" would look like under Lennon's visionary society. Not only would there be no countries,

3.1 Introduction: The Power of Ideas

but with perfect agreement prevailing on all subjects, and a completely legitimate and agreed-upon allocation mechanism handling the distribution of all public and private goods, there would seem to be very little need for politics. In such a utopian state, politicians and political scientists alike would be out of work.

Unfortunately (or fortunately, as the case may be), neither the practitioners nor the students of politics need to worry about their careers for the foreseeable future at least. In the face of daily news stories chronicling the bloodshed and strife that afflicts so many corners of the world and the persistence of discord here at home, it is difficult to maintain Lennon's optimism that such a beautiful and peaceful world could ever be achieved. Rather than embrace a single consensual vision, people seem to disagree on almost everything. From moral values and religious beliefs to considerations about what is just and equitable—or even possible—discord and disagreement are more common than consensus. There is probably disagreement about whether Lennon's utopian vision is even desirable or not, even if it were practical to realize it in reality. People disagree on the means and the ends of collective life. They disagree on what institutions and processes are best suited for structuring politics and arriving at decisions, and they disagree about what the proper policies ought to be. A moment's reflection on the state of the world is enough to support this conclusion. Disagreement and difference are everywhere to be found in the political world, and it is in the clash of ideas about all these matters that we find the animus that motivates political life. Politics can be seen as one response to disagreements about ideas. Political institutions and processes provide mechanisms whereby some ideas are actualized in decisions while others are set aside.

In this part of the text we explore some of the basic formulations of foundational political ideas, first in the realms of political philosophy, then as they are gathered in ideologies, and finally as they are embodied in political culture. Whether we know it or not, we all are bearers of political ideas and orientations. Some of us are quite sophisticated in our political thinking, spending a great deal of time and energy thinking through our personal political convictions. Most of us are not that concerned about politics. In either case, however well or ill-informed and considered, our political ideas and values place us in a larger and longer tradition in the evolution of political thought.

This is the first of three chapters that explore the important role that ideas play in animating politics and the political process. We begin with political philosophy, a subdiscipline within political science that involves a relatively small number of individuals. Political philosophers specialize in the elucidation of political values, the clarification of the proper ends of political life, and the elaboration of arguments about how political systems ought to operate if they are to successfully achieve their ends. In Chapter 4 we turn to a discussion of some of the major political ideologies. While often grounded in political philosophy, we will see that ideologies are coherent packages of ideas that are fundamentally aimed at mobilizing support and structuring political activity. As such, ideologies are action-oriented ideas that involve a greater number of people than political philosophy, which is essentially an activity confined to intellectuals. Finally, in Chapter 5 we discuss an analytic approach that aims to understand the role of ideas held by all members of a population. As we will see, political culture aims to describe and understand the varieties of political ideas and values held by everyone, whether they are aware of them or not.

It is perhaps unconventional to include a separate consideration of political philosophy in an introduction to political science, the judgment being that it is a subject for the specialist, something that requires more attention than an introduction to the discipline can afford. The passage from Aristotle indicates disagreement with this reasoning: in his view we are not capable of participating properly in politics unless we have directed at least part of our attention to the questions of political philosophy. If politics has the normative character that we ascribed to it in Part I, then it is difficult not to agree, at least in part, with Aristotle. Our own experience, though, also compels consent to the judgment that the proper study of political philosophy requires more attention than this text will permit. This chapter is not in-depth political philosophy but a short introduction designed for two purposes. One is to illuminate some of the philosophical background that underlies the long tradition of political discourse, especially given that until relatively recently most of that discourse took place within the context of political philosophy. The other purpose is to acquaint students with some of the principal thinkers of the Western political tradition and with the questions they addressed; those wishing to study politics in greater depth may gain an inkling of their interest or disinterest in the philosophical path. A qualification is necessary though. Reading about political philosophy (e.g., this chapter) is in no way a substitute for reading political philosophy itself. Students are urged to seek out the primary texts themselves (see list A at the end of this

**3.2
The Nature of Political
Philosophy**

chapter) or to collections of material selected from primary texts (see list B). In addition to primary texts, there are comprehensive treatments of the history of political philosophy in which each major contributor receives an insightful chapter (see list C).

Philosophy comes from two Greek words: *philos* meaning "loving," and *sophia* meaning "wisdom"; the philosopher is one who loves wisdom, and the political philosopher one who loves wisdom or seeks truth about the political world in particular (see Figure 3.1). Until the present century, most political philosophy was written by thinkers whose concerns were much broader than merely the political realm; what they said about politics was part of a larger whole, often part of a system that attempted to articulate the fundamentals of *all* knowledge. This is one reason why the study of political philosophy can be so specialized—a particular author's position on government or on political goods like justice or equality cannot be separated from his or her beliefs about the fundamental substance of the universe or about how we know the things we know. Nonetheless, thinkers as diverse as Aristotle and Marx have agreed that politics is ultimately (if not essentially) practical, and however abstract or esoteric the questions political philosophy addresses, they must ultimately connect with how humans live their lives within (or in contest with) the structures of authority and power of the communities and societies they inhabit.

Traditional questions of political philosophy include the following:

1. What is the good life for humans?
2. Who should rule?
3. What is the best form of government?
4. Is there a law higher than or prior to the civil law (that made by political officials) to which we are primarily obliged?
5. What is justice?
6. What is right?
7. What is liberty?

Take for example the first of these questions, "What is the good life for humans?" Note how this differs from asking "What do humans like to do?" or "What makes humans happy?" To say the good life consists in *being happy* is one way to answer the original query but so, too, is *being virtuous* or *being victorious in combat*. And the degree to which being happy seems more sensible or normal than the other responses reflects the philosophic tastes of our own place and time. We can disagree then, about the answers to our

FIGURE 3.1 Political Philosophy Is ...

"an effort devoted to gaining wisdom about the nature of human beings and politics." (Leo Strauss)

"a reflective discourse on the meaning of the political." (Sheldin Wolin)

"a critical and creative activity in which each generation participates in a continuous tradition." (Losco and Williams) question "What is the good life for humans?" On the other hand, we might agree that the human good is happiness but then disagree about the nature of happiness—is it pleasure or well-being?

On the other hand, why should we assume that there is just *one* human good (which, mind you, is not the same as claiming that there is only one human desire or pleasure)? Are we making certain assumptions or demonstrating particular beliefs about human nature? That there is, for example, one universal human nature that each of us exemplifies? It is quite common for philosophers to base their prescriptions for what humans ought to be, or do, or become, on claims about what humans *are*; it is just as common for philosophers to disagree on the fundamentals of human nature. For example, are humans fundamentally spiritual—that is, essentially souls with temporary residence in a body—or are they exclusively material beings? Are we by nature lazy or creative, consumers or participants, passive or active? A much stronger philosophical case for democracy can be made if we are by nature active, creative participants rather than lazy, passive consumers, but this way of arguing seems to suppose that our natures are fixed or given, rather than something constructed, and that our way of being is static and never dynamic. These and countless other questions are the stuff of political philosophy, which can be summarized as *critical systematic argument about the ends (purposes) of human life and about how our society or community should be ordered so that citizens can best attain those ends.*

If political philosophy addresses such questions, it does not do so in a vacuum but within a context that presents at least two relevant dimensions. One is the context of space and time provided by sociology and history. Each political philosopher cannot help but think and work within the context of the particular society in which they live; there are many different types of society, and each society has its own history. To illustrate, consider the suggestion made above that we could respond to the question "What is the good life for humans?" with the answer "to be victorious in combat." To contemporary North Americans, that might seem a strange answer, but it would not be so to Greeks of Homeric times, because theirs was a society in which the skills or virtues of the warrior were valued. In other warrior cultures or societies one might expect similar virtues or values (one warrior society many students understand is that of the fictitious Klingons of *Star Trek* fame, for whom the only honorable death is to fall in combat). To return to the Greeks, we find that by the time of Plato and Aristotle (fourth century BC) other virtues had displaced the warrior ethic, in part if not principally because the nature of Greek society had changed. At the time of the end of feudalism and the beginning of liberal modernity a significant social transformation occurred; we find correspondingly—and it would be odd if we didn't—that the political philosophy of early modernity is strikingly different from that of medieval society in the questions it considers, the mode of argument used, and the conclusions arrived at.

The other context we should note is one that in certain ways manages to transcend the particular historical and sociological contexts of the first dimension, allowing political philosophy to partake of a longer, deeper tradition. If this were not the case, none of us today could be Aristotelians, or Marxists, or Adam Smith liberals, but indeed, living breathing examples of the intellectual residues of each can still be found. In practice, the philosopher is not a solitary figure who thinks and writes but is someone engaged in critical, rational dialogue with the preceding body of thought. Almost any serious work of philosophy is a response to, or refutation of, or commentary on, or synthesis of, the work or works of other philosophers, many if not most of whom have been long dead (hence, the oft-quoted observation that all political philosophy is merely footnotes to Plato). In this way philosophy reaches across generations, types of society, and periods of local history to become a larger **TRADITION**, or more accurately, sets of (often competing) traditions within which individual philosophers are situated.

Of the two contexts we have identified—the socio-historical and what we might call the textual or intellectual—it is the latter which has most often been more evident to philosophers themselves as they work and which is often most explicit in their work. This is another reason why political philosophy is most fruitfully studied in some depth; to understand fully any one thinker requires familiarity with the intellectual tradition within which he or she is working and the thinkers he or she is addressing in his or her work (something that may at times be implicit rather than explicit). Although his brief overview cannot constitute a proper introduction to political philosophy, we hope it whets the appetite of students for studying political philosophy by providing just a little background to the work of three pairs of important thinkers.

3.3
Plato (427–347 BC) and
Aristotle (384–322 BC)

The stature that Plato and Aristotle continue to hold within philosophy says something not only about the remarkable quality of these two intellects but also about the society that could produce them. Both were active during fourth century BC Athens, the leading **POLIS** of the Greek city-states, and the particular problems and challenges of governing such political entities preoccupy both in their political writings. The *poleii* of this period were agrarian, pre-industrial societies, dependent for economic life on the continued exploitation of a large class of slaves, many of whom were foreigners captured in war.[1] These societies were primitive by our standards in terms of technology and practical science, but they were extremely advanced in terms of intellectual disciplines like philosophy and the cultivation of the arts. (Critics of modernity argue that we have simply reversed the equation and have become technologically proficient and culturally impoverished.) The relatively small size of these city-states made possible quite a diversity of political arrangements within Greek experience, many of which were extremely unstable. Hence, who should rule and how they should rule were very central questions of political philosophy in this period.

Athens was, during the time of Plato and Aristotle (and indeed from the sixth century BC until destruction by the Romans in the first century), a democracy in which the most important decisions were made by a body of all the citizens (the Assembly) or, rather, of all those who chose to attend the business of the Assembly. A Council of Five Hundred, chosen by lot from the body of citizens, set the agenda for the Assembly. While the tradition of democracy, including the word itself, dates from this period of classical Athens, neither Plato nor Aristotle were democrats, although Aristotle's objections to democracy were less categorical than Plato's. Remember, though, that democracy in Athens meant not the modern practice of electing representatives but actual government by the body of citizens (which, not including slaves, women, children, or foreigners, amounted to perhaps 20 per cent of the population).

One of the most striking features of Plato's philosophy is that it is presented in the form of dialogues (conversations) between young Athenian noblemen, at the center of whom (and representing Plato's own position) is the philosopher Socrates. In most of the dialogues (there are about 27) Socrates challenges the common sense beliefs or opinions of his companions concerning the nature of various virtues and other philosophic questions; he does this by rigorous questioning (the Socratic method), which leads the speakers into contradictions that reveal the flaws of their initial positions. In each case, Socrates tries to move the entire company from opinion, which is uncritical and conventional, to knowledge, which should be critical and disclose the true nature of things.[2]

Plato was an idealist: he believed that the true nature of the universe is ideal, or even intellectual, and that behind the constant

1 Slavery is slavery, but Greek slaves in classical antiquity could enjoy a considerable amount of freedom and authority *within* the households where they were kept and were probably better off than most medieval peasants or early nineteenth-century proletarians, all things considered. The fact of slavery was *not* an issue during the time of Plato or Aristotle; as an institution of civil society it was taken for granted.

2 This view of knowledge and philosophy is very much out of fashion in many circles of contemporary philosophy.

flux of empirical events and material appearances lies an enduring reality that can be approached only through thought. This is the world of the Forms, which, for Plato, are the fundamental nature of the universe, persisting behind or beyond the world as it appears. Just as our common sense can easily become preoccupied with the world of appearance or the material of the senses, so, conversely, knowledge requires the critical ability to achieve clarity with concepts and proceed to an intellectual apprehension of the Forms (or Ideas). All **IDEALISM**, one of the strongest currents in the philosophic tradition, has its roots in Plato's metaphysics.

In Plato's most famous political work, *The Republic*, the principal topic is the nature of justice or the matter of *how* the people are to be ruled. After demonstrating the weakness of current, conventional understandings of justice, Socrates presents his own (i.e., Plato's) understanding of justice by way of an analogy that is truly representative of the nature of Plato's politics and philosophy. Socrates convinces his listeners that the human soul has three parts: a rational part, a spirited or courageous part, and an appetitive ir-rational part. Justice in the soul consists of each part performing its own function, which means, among other things, that the rational part will dominate or rule the appetitive part (mind over body, intellect over senses) and will do this with the aid of the spirited part.

Justice in the *ideal* city will parallel justice in the soul, for the city will have three classes corresponding to the three parts of the soul. The rational part of the city will be the class of Guardians, whose business it is to deliberate about the city as a whole. Assisting them will be a class of Auxiliaries, courageous warriors who will preserve the city from external foes and internal dissension. The largest part of the city will be the body of citizens, the Artisans, who are concerned with the mundane business of acquiring wealth. Justice in the city will consist in each class performing the function for which its nature has fitted it: the Guardians ought to rule, the Artisans ought to make money, and not vice-versa. It is also Plato's belief that individuals are *by nature* determined for one class or another. Much of *The Republic* is concerned with the education and training that the small elite class of Guardians is to receive and with the nature of their living. Since they are to put the good of the city first, their own desires are least important, and for this reason *for this class* Plato recommends a primitive communism (no private property nor, for that matter, monogamous marriage). From the class of Guardians will come philosophers (or a philosopher) fit to rule, but, interestingly, since philosophers will love knowledge and wish to spend their time in contemplation of the Forms, philosopher-kings will have to be forced to rule.

Perhaps it is a little clearer now why Plato was not a democrat. In the first place, he did not have the belief in fundamental human equality that democracy, at least on one level, presupposes. Plato thought we have different natures, which means that most of us are suited by neither aptitude nor inclination for making intelligent political decisions. We are better fitted perhaps for combat or for acquiring wealth, and these are what we should do, leaving the business of governing to those whose natures are so gifted. Given the diversity of types of states present in classical Greece, most political thinkers offered a means of classifying different regimes, and Plato was no exception. In his five-fold schema, each state corresponding to the dominance of a particular type of individual, democracy was second from the bottom (see Figure 3.2). Whether or not we agree with Plato on this, we should acknowledge one fundamental sense in which he stands at the root of all Western political philosophy: his notion that ruling is something done for the benefit of those who are ruled not for the interest(s) of the rulers. Interestingly, the only way Plato saw to achieve this was to have the wise rule; in other words, the emphasis is on achieving rulers with the *best character*. Character is innate, that is, part of one's given nature, but it is also as such merely a potential or possibility that cannot be realized without the proper nurture or education. One of Plato's lasting achievements was his Academy, founded with a view to providing young Athenian nobles with the education that would develop the character that would fit them to rule. This school lasted for several centuries.

A student in Plato's academy, and later one of its teachers, Aristotle demonstrated a more empirical cast of mind than his mentor. Some interpreters stress the continuities between Aristotle and Plato, others the differences. We will look at some of the

Aristotle

FIGURE 3.2 Types of Regimes

PLATO

In *The Republic*, five types of REGIMES are presented, differentiated on the basis of the type of character which predominates in each. Starting with the ideal regime—aristocracy—each successive regime is presented as a degeneration from the one preceding, a series which ends in tyranny. There is a certain degree to which Plato implies that this descent from ideal to worst regime is inevitable.

	TYPE OF REGIME	CHARACTER OF DOMINANT INDIVIDUAL
BEST	**ARISTOCRACY** (rule of the noble)	the good and just man
	TIMOCRACY (rule of warriors)	the lover of victory and honor
	OLIGARCHY (rule of the wealthy)	the lover of money
	DEMOCRACY (rule of the poor)	the lover of liberty
WORST	**TYRANNY/DICTATORSHIP** (rule of the tyrant)	the lover of power

ARISTOTLE

In *The Politics*, Aristotle articulated the distinction that became most common through the centuries: between the Rule of One, the Rule of the Few, and the Rule of the Many. Each of these has a just form and a corrupt form, just being those directed to the common advantage and *corrupt* being those in which rule is for the advantage of those who rule. In later times, this six-fold typology was often shortened to simply monarchy, aristocracy (or oligarchy), and democracy.

JUST REGIMES	CORRUPT REGIMES
KINGSHIP (rule of one in the interest of all)	**TYRANNY** (rule of one for their self-interest)
ARISTOCRACY (rule of the few in the interest of all)	**OLIGARCHY** (rule of the few for their self-interests)
POLITY (rule of the many pursuing the interests of all)	**DEMOCRACY** (rule of the many for their self-interests)

differences that make a difference. Sinclair (1959: 210-11) contrasts Aristotle—"a middle-class professional man, a husband and a father, scientific observer and practical administrator"—with Plato—"the Athenian aristocrat, mystic, ascetic, [and] puritan"—and points out the following non-Platonic features of Aristotle's politics: "the value of family life, the pursuit of health and happiness, property, [and] respect for public opinion." Perhaps most important, for Aristotle, politics is in a very real sense the art of the possible.

Like Plato, Aristotle believed in Forms, but he believed that they are immanent, that is to say, inseparable from the matter that is common to particulars. This means that the forms are not something inaccessible to ordinary consciousness and that, for Aristotle, the realm of appearance (the phenomenal) *is* real. Hence, there is not the same dualism or radical dichotomy between idea and matter, mind and senses, that there is in Plato's metaphysics. A central notion in Aristotle's thought is the idea that everything has a **TELOS**, an end or purpose or goal to which it strives or is destined or develops. This marks the birth of **EPISTEMOLOGY**: the study of the nature of knowledge. The end or *telos* is contained in the essence of the object; to explain an object then requires identifying its kind or species, which allows us to understand its essence and hence the *telos* or end it serves. One implication of this teleology is a more universal or implicitly egalitarian view of humanity; whatever the differences in our nature, as human beings we share a common *telos*. Thus, Aristotle can state—something it is difficult to imagine Plato uttering—at the beginning of his *Metaphysics*: "All men by nature desire to know." Like Plato, Aristotle does not question slavery as natural and believes in a natural distinction between women and men; he thus accepts hierarchy and patriarchy, but he nonetheless presents us with only one human nature, of which there is an inferior or superior manifestation in particular individuals.

In both *Ethics* and *Politics*, Aristotle is concerned with how humans realize the *telos* that is uniquely theirs as humans. He draws here upon a distinction (missing in Plato) between theoretical and practical reason. Theoretical reason is appropriate for the study of nature; it uncovers necessary and universal laws that constitute knowledge or science. Practical reason is appropriate for human affairs, is situational or contextual, and produces wisdom or judgment. This view of the reasoning we bring to politics as fallible and something only gained through experience is one students may understand but not appreciate, since it implies that wisdom will be as much a product of age as of intelligence. Our *telos*, Aristotle argues, is to seek *eudaimonia*, which is often translated as happiness but is perhaps more accurately presented by the term "well-being." Well-being turns out to be living a life in accordance with virtue, which can mean the pursuit of intellectual excellence or acting on our desires in a rational way. In either case, realizing our *telos* does not simply happen but must be cultivated through education, and this in turn rests on the foundation of good laws. In this way, Aristotle's **ETHICS** leads to his politics; conversely, the purpose of political life is to present the opportunity for us to realize our *telos*—to live a virtuous life. We cannot be moral beings in a corrupt city or *polis*. Like Plato, Aristotle places little importance on the pursuit of

Plato

wealth and none on the pursuit of wealth for its own sake. Properly understood, money or wealth is simply the means that provides us with the leisure to take part in civic life, to cultivate our sense of virtue, and to develop and exercise wise judgment. The primary purpose of the state is educative, and we cannot benefit from this education unless we participate in the politics of the state.

The concept of citizenship is thus very central to Aristotle, as indicated by the quotation with which this chapter began. To be a citizen or, more exactly, to be a good citizen, it is necessary to fulfill the *telos* of being human, but here is the problem: not all can be citizens. To be a citizen is to have the right to share in judicial or deliberative office (*Politics*, III,iv,1) and Aristotle accepts, first, that certain classes of people (e.g., slaves, women, foreigners) will never possess citizenship and, second, that who does qualify as a citizen will vary from constitution to constitution (that is according to the type of government).[3] Whatever the type of constitution, the citizen will be one who is engaged in ruling *and* being ruled, and Aristotle defines the excellence of the good citizen as "consisting in a knowledge of rule over free men from both points of view" (*Politics*, III, iv,15).

3 One of Aristotle's preparations for his *Politics* was a study of 158 Greek constitutions.

Like Plato, Aristotle believes that political authority is properly exercised when it is directed to the common good. Hence, any regime that is directed to the common advantage is just, and any that pursues a partial interest is corrupt, regardless in either case of who rules (see Figure 3.2). It is interesting to note how Aristotle's discussion of types of rule differs from Plato's, and Aristotle is much less categorical about which is the best regime. On the one hand, being more pragmatic, Aristotle distinguishes between the best regime (i.e., the ideal), the best possible regime, and the most possible regime. He also seems prepared to accept that what kind of regime works best will depend on circumstances and social conditions, which will vary from *polis* to *polis*. Unlike Plato, though, Aristotle is inclined to the view that many heads are better than one (or a few); "Each individual may indeed, be a worse judge than the experts; but all, when they meet together, are either better than experts or at any rate no worse" (*Politics*, III, xi, 14).

Finally, regardless of the type of regime, an enduring issue in political philosophy to which Aristotle makes significant contribution is the issue of the sovereignty of law: should we be governed by the wisdom of wise rulers or by the impartial neutrality of laws? As we shall see below, the answer of modernity has been to institutionalize the principle of the rule of law, but as Aristotle notes, with the impartiality or neutrality of law comes inflexibility, an inability to account for differences in circumstance or application. Aristotle argues that ultimately the rule of law is to be preferred, and where there are matters that law cannot deal with adequately, these are best decided by many individuals rather than one (or a few). As to how we know which matters fall in the latter category, Aristotle is less clear.

Common to both these great thinkers, Plato and Aristotle, is the quest for a politics where rule is wise, virtuous, and directed to the advantage of all. For both, development of the character of those who rule is crucial and education is central. For Plato, this is a very special education for those with the nature that equips them for philosophy (which equals science). For Aristotle, the education of those who rule is more practical and gained more through experience than training or reflection, although these too are important. For each thinker, law is important, but whereas for Plato this is ultimately the eternal law of the Forms that transcends any particular *polis*, Aristotle is more concerned with the actual laws of constitutions, which may be just or corrupt. While there is much that is dead in the thought of each (especially their unquestioning acceptance of slavery and patriarchy), each also has much to say to us today, as indeed they have spoken to countless generations in the past two millennia.

3.4
Hobbes (1588–1679) and
Locke (1632–1704)

Thomas Hobbes has been described as the greatest of all English political thinkers, and there are very few ideas in liberal thought that do not stem from his work or from criticism of it. The first and perhaps the greatest of his critics was John Locke. Together, Hobbes and Locke first put into conceptual form the character of modern society and the liberal government that seems necessarily (to liberals) to go with it. Because of the degree to which liberalism has been the dominant ideology of the modern period and because we discuss ideology at greater length in the next chapter, the emphasis here will be less on the substance of Hobbes's and Locke's philosophies and more on the significance of each for liberalism.

The political event most crucial for Hobbes was the struggle between monarch and Parliament that shaped English politics in the 1600s and led to the Civil War, Cromwell's Commonwealth, the Restoration of the Stuart monarchy, and finally to the Glorious (or Whig) Revolution of 1688. This set of events marks England's adjustment from a feudal, traditional society to a modern, legal-rational polity—this is England's experience of the "liberal revolution" referred to earlier.

Not only was Hobbes aware of the social transformation his society was undergoing, he seems to have understood and welcomed it. Having decided for the new market-driven, Protestant, rational society, Hobbes intends to provide a political theory for the new age. His insight into the nature of post-feudal society makes him "modern" and "radical" for his own time and enduring for us today. At the same time he must argue in the language of his day, addressing those shaped by or attempting to defend feudal doctrines and practices; for this reason he can often seem archaic and "dated" to contemporary students. There is also a strongly conservative dimension to Hobbes, expressed in his fear of conflict, his concern for order and stability, and the paternalism of his theory of government.

Hobbes begins not with the community but with the individual. Individuals, for Hobbes, are logically prior to any group or collective formation, and this, in part, is what is meant by describing Hobbes's theory as atomistic. Hobbes believes that individuals are fundamentally bodies in motion, guided by their passions, the strongest of which is the fear of death. Two consequences follow from Hobbes's account of appetitive man.

First, human reason is instrumental: it exists and operates to serve the passions in obtaining their object (pleasure or the avoidance of pain). Reason thus has no "higher" status and provides no independent course of action for us to follow: all voluntary actions and inclinations we have are concerned with "securing a contented life" (*Leviathan*, Ch. XI).

Second, society is artificial: "All society therefore is either for gain, or for glory; that is, not so much for love of our fellows, as for the love of ourselves" (*De Cive*, Ch. I). Others are of value to us only instrumentally—that is, as means to our ends—and they have no intrinsic value in and of themselves. We value others for the power they have, and Hobbes defines power as a present means to some future end.

Because fear of death is our strongest passion, we desire satisfaction not only now but also in all future instances. Therefore, we desire power (a present means to a future end), and Hobbes proposes that "a general inclination of all mankind" is "a perpetual and restless desire of power after power, that ceases only in Death" (*Leviathan*, Ch. XI). A modest or moderate power is not enough, Hobbes notes, because we can never be certain it is enough. Men compete with each other for particular powers such as wealth, status, and authority. This competition in turn leads to war, because the most effective victory over one's opponent is that which causes their death.

Thus, Hobbes's basic and initial propositions about human nature place each individual in conflict with every other individual. You are my enemy because you want the same things I want, and presumably we both cannot have or enjoy them.

For Hobbes, the **STATE OF NATURE** is a hypothetical condition, a statement of what *would* be the case *if* we were to remove all social and political authority. Given the equality of our appetitive natures, he concludes that each person is the enemy of every other. The best defense in such conditions is a good offense: "there is no way for any man to secure himself, so reasonable as anticipation; that is, by force, or wiles, to master the persons of all men he can, so long, till he see no other power great enough to endanger him: And this is no more than his own conservation requires, and is generally avowed" (*Leviathan*, Ch. XIII). In other words, each individual, in order to preserve himself from defeat, must kill all others. Therefore, the state of nature turns out to be a state of war "and such a war, as is of every man against every man."

This Hobbesian conception of the state of nature as a state of war is one of the most powerful images of political thought: an

ANARCHY of the worst kind, a condition of violent stagnation that recommends itself to no-one. At the same time we should note that this condition is the product of a rational strategy undertaken in the absence of government, given the nature of human passions. The individuals in this state of nature are acting rationally on the basis of their appetites, and Hobbes tells us that their actions are not sinful or evil or unjust. Good and evil, justice and injustice, right and wrong—these can exist only when there is a commonly agreed-upon standard and a power to enforce it. Neither of these conditions exists in the state of nature.

Having established, then, that without authority men are in a horrible state of war *and* that their natures prevent them from escaping this condition, Hobbes then offers an apparent solution. This is an agreement of every man with every other man to be ruled by a common power (a Sovereign) who "shall act, or cause to be acted, in those things which concern the common peace and safety" (*Leviathan*, Ch. XVII). This is the great covenant (an agreement binding the parties to future compliance) by which **CIVIL SOCIETY** is created and by which individuals escape the state of war. Each individual surrenders the right to do whatever is necessary to defend him/herself from others and agrees to the protection provided by a Sovereign, who is thereby empowered to make laws and enforce them. We might note that Hobbes does not say that individuals in the state of nature actually could make such a covenant—his own description of their nature suggests they couldn't—but rather that if they were to escape the state of nature, this is what would be required of them.

The notion that political society is something to which individuals agree and which they collectively construct or implement in order to protect or further their self-interest as individuals signals clearly the way in which society is instrumental and artificial for thinkers like Hobbes. A central proposition of such theories is the notion that the purpose of government is the security and well-being of the individuals governed. Hobbes is justifying the state on the basis of its contribution to individual welfare. Note, he is not saying that the state provides individuals' welfare; rather, he claims that the state provides a framework of stability and security (through laws) in which individuals may pursue their own ends. Individuals are no less self-interested and driven by their passions or appetites in civil society than in the state of nature. What has changed is that the law enforced by the Sovereign protects individuals from the actions others might take on the basis of their self-interest.

For Hobbes it does not matter how governments come into being: their nature, their purpose, and their justification is the same. Because humans are the way they are, a Sovereign power is necessary to keep peace. Therefore, all Sovereigns are justified in exercising power. Without a Sovereign to keep the peace by enforcing law, men would return to the state of nature, which is a state of war. The surest sign of this, Hobbes suggests, is the destruction brought by civil wars, where authority is in dispute. For Hobbes, all government is legitimate. But, because government is justified on the basis of individual self-interest, the ends or purposes of government are public and not private. All governments will properly be concerned with providing for the welfare of their citizens.

Hobbes's hypothetical devices of a state of nature and of a covenant that establishes civil society are intended and designed to establish two points. One, for citizens, is the necessity of an absolute unlimited Sovereign to enforce the laws necessary for stability and security. The second, for rulers, is to stress that the justifications and purposes of government ultimately are the contribution that government makes to the individual pursuit of self-interest.

To make the Sovereign anything less than absolute is to invite conflict over power, and among other things, this would weaken the ability of the Sovereign to enforce the law. A Sovereign less effective in enforcing the law would be unable to adequately protect citizens from each other, and they would eventually revert to the state of nature. Hobbes's arguments for an absolute Sovereign are quite independent of his treatment of another question: what form shall the state take? To this Hobbes has two answers. The first is that it does not matter what kind of government there is as long as it has a monopoly of power and is unlimited in its authority. Second, Hobbes believes that democracy is not possible in practice and that monarchy is preferable to aristocracy. This means that while he considers it possible for the Sovereign to be one man, or an assembly of men, his preference is for the former. It is his belief that an assembly of men would suffer from internal conflict, largely because the members would be concerned as much or more with their own personal well-being than with that of the Commonwealth. It is worth remembering the contemporary context, though—all governments in Hobbes's day were absolute and unlimited in their exercise of power/authority. There was nothing "new" or "radical" in his suggestion that government must be absolute; he was merely affirming the status quo.

Liberty is defined as "the absence of external impediments" (*Leviathan*, Ch. XIV) in which light it appears that the state of nature is a condition of absolute (unhindered) liberty (since there is no authority). In the civil state accomplished by the Commonwealth, the impediments to liberty are provided by Civil Laws, that is, the laws made and enforced by the Sovereign. The establishment of government thus entails an agreement by the subjects that their liberty will be limited by the Sovereign, and these limits are established by the laws the Sovereign makes. It should be stressed that liberty is not confined by authority. If this were the case, then the establishment of an absolute Sovereign would also amount to the absence of citizens' liberty. It is *law* that limits liberty, and therefore how much or how little liberty citizens enjoy will depend on the nature of the law made by the Sovereign. Hence Hobbes's famous formulation: the liberty of citizens consists in "the silence of the Law." While Hobbes insists upon an absolute Sovereign, he also believes the Sovereign will permit subjects an extensive sphere of personal liberty, and this is done by the making of "good laws," which are defined as those that are "needful, for the good of the people, and withall perspicuous" (*Leviathan*, Ch. XXX).

There are two important points here. The first is that authority is not a personal possession of those who exercise it but something justified on the basis of the interests of those governed. The state exists and is justified solely for public and not private purposes. Second, the role of the state is to provide, through a framework of law, an environment of stability and security in which individuals continue to pursue the self-interest that lies at the core of their nature. The individuals Hobbes describes in the state of nature are the same ones who inhabit civil society: self-interested, appetitive, desiring power after power, competitive, and, however rational, subject to the strength of their passions. The institution of government does not seek to change men but rather to provide the conditions within which their natures can coexist peacefully and prosper. It does so through the framework of law, and the power that enforces this law, in Hobbes's view, must have no rivals, no limits, and no external authority to which it answers.

Any evaluation of Hobbes's political theory must give due consideration to the context within which he was writing. On the divide, as it were, between feudal society and modern market society, Hobbes gives us a vision of government for the new emerging society while still reflecting many of the assumptions and maintaining many of the formulations of the old. He is a radical conservative, a liberal monarchist, a modern thinker at work in an as yet pre-modern world. We should not evaluate Hobbes's work as the last word in modern liberal thought but as its initial systematic statement, and this means that there is much in Hobbes that survives in later philosophies, as well as much that is discarded.

Locke, curiously enough, is much more traditional than Hobbes when it comes to human nature, morality, and our relationship to society, but he is much more modern when it comes to his faith in institutions. In important ways, Locke has more confidence than Hobbes in our ability to use our reason and, recognizing the law of nature, regulate our passions and live together morally. For this reason Locke imagines that we could live peaceably and sociably in a state of nature without government but with property, money, and other features of social existence. Indeed, it is conflicts over property that in Locke's view form the greatest impediment to our peaceful existence in the state of nature, and it is for the protection of property (which, we should note, Locke defines as "life, liberty, and possessions") that we abandon the state of nature and create a political society.

Like Hobbes, then, Locke puts a **SOCIAL CONTRACT** at the beginning of civil society—a mutual agreement among those who wish security and stability. Unlike Hobbes, though, Locke writes as if the social contract is not hypothetical but a real historical event, and, unlike Hobbes he conceives this to be a contract *between* the Sovereign and the subjects. Therefore, the origin of government is the **CONSENT OF THE GOVERNED**, which constitutes a genuine notion of **POPULAR SOVEREIGNTY**. Locke even argues that the people have a right to revolution if the Sovereign becomes a tyrant or abuses the terms of the social contract. This also means that he is willing, unlike Hobbes, to place limits on the authority of the Sovereign. The unanimity of all participants in Hobbes's imaginary covenant is replaced by the more practical principle of **MAJORITY RULE** in Locke's version.

Perhaps the most important revision Locke makes is the notion that the Sovereign power can be divided; indeed, it *must* be divided with the executive and the legislative powers placed in different hands. This presents a clear expression of and argument for the doctrine of the **SEPARATION OF POWERS** that was to be so influential among designers of liberal constitutions. Contrary to Hobbes's preference for monarchy, Locke argues that the legislative power should be in the hands of an assembly, a body of men who together make the law but are also at the same time subject to it. Locke insists that the legislative power is the supreme power, in part because he also insists that the people have a right to alter the legislature when it acts contrary to the trust placed in it. By making a series of important modifications to the arguments that

Hobbes had advanced, Locke presents a picture of government much more familiar to us than Hobbes's absolute Sovereign. We should be clear that Locke was no more a democrat than Hobbes, but he did articulate the principles of popular sovereignty and of representative government. He simply assumed, as did most thinkers of his day, that the class of citizens who might vote and sit in the legislature would be limited to males who held a significant amount of property.

Hobbes had written within the context of the English Civil War, a struggle—complicated by religious issues—between the monarchy and those defending Parliament. In 1688 the Glorious Revolution installed William and Mary of Orange on the English throne and guaranteed a Protestant succession. More importantly, the new monarchs agreed to conditions that eventually resulted in the supremacy of Parliament and led to an increasing diminution of the active role of the monarch in political affairs. We now know that Locke's *Second Treatise on Government* was written in anticipation of the Glorious Revolution, and the outcome—a limited government of the propertied class represented in an assembly, subject to majority rule; executive power in the monarch, subordinate to the legislative power—corresponds rather well to the basic outlines of his theory.

3.5
Burke (1729–1797) and
Marx (1818–1883)

As Europe modernized through the Industrial Revolution in the eighteenth and nineteenth centuries, new ideas received expression and new political currents were unleashed. New forms of production created new economic actors who challenged traditional aristocratic privileges and pushed for a broadening of citizenship and access to political power. To a degree unseen in earlier epochs, political philosophy began to spill over into political ideology and increasingly strove not only to understand but also to change the world. Two pivotal historical events were borne of the liberal philosophy that arose in the early modern epoch, grounded as it was in notions of individual equality and liberty. We refer to the American (1776) and French (1789) revolutions. These political upheavals forever changed the political landscape and provoked widespread reaction in virtually all quarters of society. These ranged from a wholesale rejection of revolutionary change and a concomitant celebration of traditional practices and institutions (epitomized by Edmund Burke) to an enthusiastic embrace by others such as Karl Marx, who regarded these milestones as but another necessary step toward the ultimate revolution. According to Marx, the revolution that capitalism unleashed would eventually and inexorably end history by ushering in a communist utopia akin to John Lennon's utopia we imagined at the beginning of this chapter. Let us briefly consider these different philosophical reactions before turning to a general discussion of the ideological currents that arose from these philosophers (and others) of modernity.

The writings and speeches of Burke often seem to be the fount from which all modern conservatism flows, but it is not quite that simple. Although Burke sat in the English Parliament as a Whig for almost 30 years, he was both an aristocratic and a situational conservative. The key to Burke's apparent inconsistency (he could support the American Revolution while condemning the French Revolution) is the gradual way in which England became liberal, so that parliamentary, representative government coexisted with a traditional monarchy, landed aristocracy, and the absence of democracy. Burke supported *all* the fundamental institutions of his England. His most famous work is the *Reflections on the Revolution in France* (1790), written before but anticipating those darkest periods of that upheaval that became known as The Terror. Here he lamented that "the age of chivalry is gone. That of sophisters, economists, and calculators has succeeded, and the glory of Europe is extinguished forever."

In contrast to the revolutionary spirit, Burke preached a loyalty to traditional institutions:

> We know that we have made no discoveries, and we think that no discoveries are to be made, in morality, nor many in the great principles of government, nor in the ideas of liberty, which were understood long before we were born, altogether as well as they will be after the grave has heaped its mold upon our presumption and the silent tomb shall have imposed its law on our pert loquacity.... We fear God; we look up with awe to kings, with affection to parliaments, with duty to magistrates, with reverence to priests, and with respect to nobility.... instead of casting away all our old prejudices, we cherish them to a very considerable degree, and, ... the longer they have lasted and the more generally they have prevailed, the more we cherish them. (*Reflections*)

In addition to traditionalism, Burke's conservatism also celebrates the virtue of a natural aristocracy. He believed in the hierarchical ordering of society and that the privileged orders, namely the nobility and the clergy, were what gave society its civilization and refinement:

> Nothing is more certain than that our manners, our civilization, and all the good things which are connected with manners and with civilization have, in this European world of ours, depended for ages upon two principles ... I mean the spirit of a gentleman and the spirit of religion. The nobility and the clergy, the one by profession, the other by patronage, kept learning in existence, even in the midst of arms and confusions, and whilst governments were rather in their causes than formed. Learning paid back what it received to nobility and to priesthood, and paid it with usury, by enlarging their ideas and by furnishing their minds. (*Reflections*)

In stark contrast to Burke, Karl Marx saw revolution as the natural and inevitable consequence of the workings of the newly emergent capitalist economic system and of the class conflict that the cut-throat competition of the market had unleashed. Marx is undoubtedly the most influential figure in all of political ideology, and therefore a consideration of his thought provides a useful segue into a consideration of ideologies more generally. His theory drew upon and extended three currents in the history of ideas. The one most obvious is his transformation of the socialist and communist ideas of the early nineteenth century into something based less on utopian ethical theories and more on a social scientific appreciation of economic and political forces. Socialism has been dominated by Marxism (either directly or in opposition to it), and both liberalism and conservatism have been shaped by their struggles against Marxism.

Second, most of Marx's life was devoted to the study, analysis, and critique of capitalist economic theory and practice. In this effort he was part of the political economy tradition established by such liberal thinkers as Adam Smith, David Ricardo, and James Mill. One does not have to be a socialist to recognize the strength of Marx's critique of capitalism and the responses it has wholly or in part generated. The other major dimension of Marx's thought—and, in fact, his original occupation—was as one of a group of philosophers known as the Young Hegelians—left-wing disciples of Hegel, the Prussian idealist and conservative. Marx turned Hegel's idealism upside-down but retained certain features of its idiosyncratic logic, the result being what Marx called **HISTORICAL MATERIALISM**, which

Figure 3.3: Excerpts from The Manifesto of the Communist Party (1848), Karl Marx and Friedrich Engels

A spectre is haunting Europe—the spectre of communism. All the powers of old Europe have entered into a holy alliance to exorcise this spectre: Pope and Tsar, Metternich and Guizot, French Radicals and German police-spies....

The history of all hitherto existing society is the history of class struggles. Freeman and slave, patrician and plebian, lord and serf, guild-master and journeyman, in a word, oppressor and oppressed, stood in constant opposition to one another, carried on an uninterrupted, now hidden, now open fight, a fight that each time ended, either in a revolutionary reconstitution of society at large, or in the common ruin of the contending classes ...

The bourgeoisie, historically, has played a most revolutionary part....

The bourgeoisie, during its rule of scarce one hundred years, has created more massive and more colossal productive forces than have all preceding generations together. Subjection of nature's forces to man, machinery, application of chemistry to industry and agriculture, steam navigation, railways, electric telegraphs, clearing of whole continents for cultivation, canalization or rivers, whole populations conjured out of the ground—what earlier century had even a presentiment that such productive forces slumbered in the lap of social labor?

We see then: the means of production and of exchange, on whose foundation the bourgeoisie built itself up, were generated in feudal society. At a certain stage in the development of these means of production and of exchange, the conditions under which feudal society produced and exchanged, the feudal organization of agriculture and manufacturing industry, in one word, the feudal relations of property became no longer compatible with the already developed productive forces; they became so many fetters. They had to be burst asunder; they were burst asunder.

Into their place stepped free competition, accompanied by a social and political constitution adapted in it, and the economic and political sway of the bourgeois class.

A similar movement is going on before our own eyes. Modern bourgeois society, with its relations of production, of exchange and of property, a society that has conjured up such gigantic means of production and of exchange, is like the sorcerer who is no longer able to control the powers of the nether world whom he has called up by his spells. For many a decade past, the history of industry and commerce is but the history of the revolt of modern productive forces against modern conditions of production, against the property relations that are the conditions for the existence of the bourgeois and of its rule....

But not only has the bourgeoisie forged the weapons that bring death to itself; it has also called into existence the men who are to wield those weapons—the modern working class—the proletarians ...

The essential conditions for the existence and for the sway of the bourgeois class is the formation and augmentation of capital; the condition for capital is wage labor. Wage labor rests exclusively on competition between the laborers. The advance of industry, whose involuntary promoter is the bourgeoisie, replaces the isolation of the laborers, due to competition, by the revolutionary combination, due to association. The development of Modern Industry, therefore, cuts from under its feet the very foundation on which the bourgeoisie produces and appropriates products. What the bourgeoisie therefore produces, above all, are its own grave-diggers. Its fall and the victory of the proletariat are equally inevitable ...

The Communists disdain to conceal their views and aims. They openly declare that their ends can be attained only by the forcible overthrow of all existing social conditions. Let the ruling classes tremble at a Communistic revolution. The proletarians have nothing to lose but their chains. They have a world to win.

Working Men of All Countries, Unite!

Source: Freely available on the Internet. These excerpts are taken from:
<http://www.marxists.org/archive/marx/works/1848/communist-manifesto/>.

Engels and Lenin would later develop as dialectical materialism. More intriguing was Marx's exploration of some other themes in Hegel's thought, which led him to the notion of "alienation." Marx argued that it is our nature to be active, creative beings, expressing ourselves in and through the products of our labor—i.e., our activity with the materials of nature. We are alienated from our essence or nature when the conditions of our laboring activity are perverted. Marx early rejected capitalism because the wage-labor relation is alienating. That is, once we sell our labor power for a wage to an employer, our laboring activity is no longer freely creative. The products of our activity are no longer ours, the activity itself is now under the direction of another, and our relations to others are now mediated by impersonal things. In this way, Marx rejects capitalism less for its inequality and more for the assault on our freedom and dignity that this inequality entails. It is possible to extend Marx's critique from the division of labor and wage relations to the effects of technology and a culture of entertainment on our potential and actual development as freely creating agents. Just as much has been done in the world in the name of Marx that bears no relation to anything he ever wrote, so, too, his influence on any number of intellectual disciplines remains (and likely will remain) strong, quite irrespective of the future success or failure of the real-world movements that claim (or have claimed) to be motivated by his ideas.

Marx demonstrated key elements of nineteenth-century thinking in his work, in particular the recognition of human development, both individually and collectively as peoples or even as a "species." Human nature is not a static given but a potential to be developed or a possibility to be realized, and politics can be about providing the opportunities for the fullest flowering of human individuality or about removing the obstacles to this unfolding of human nature's richness.

3.6
Conclusion: From Philosophy to Ideology

There are two reasons for ending our sampling of political philosophers at this point. One is that political philosophy becomes increasingly less accessible to the educated lay person and more something that requires specialized training and background in philosophy to understand. While this is not universally so, it has become true of large areas of philosophy, especially those drawing upon thinkers from continental Europe, particularly in the second half of the last century. The second change is that political philosophy is very often less about the traditional objects of politics—institutions of government, political processes, etc.—and more about ontology, or theories of meaning, or linguistic analysis, etc. The second reason for turning from philosophy at this point in our examination is that political thought, up to and including much of the nineteenth century, was largely the work of a few thinkers who participated in a philosophic tradition. With the nineteenth century came the development of modern urban societies and of newspapers, the beginnings of mass culture, political parties, trade unions, public libraries, and lecture circuits. In short, political ideas began to be popularized and expressed in forms that, while grounded in the ideas of political philosophers, were no longer confined either to philosophers or a narrow circle of educated political actors. Beginning in earnest in the nineteenth century and continuing into the twenty-first century was the age of ideology.

Key Terms

anarchy
civil society
consent of the governed
epistemology
ethics
historical materialism
idealism
majority rule
polis
popular sovereignty
regimes
separation of powers
social contract
state of nature
telos
tradition

References and Suggested Readings

A. PRIMARY TEXTS IN POLITICAL PHILOSOPHY

Plato
>   Selected Dialogues (especially *The Apology*, Crito)
>   *The Republic*

Aristotle
>   *The Politics*
>   *The Nichomachean Ethics*

Hobbes
>   *De Cive*
>   *Leviathan*

Locke
>   *The Two Treatises on Government*

Marx
>   *Manifesto of the Communist Party*
>   *Critique of the Gotha Programme*

B. COLLECTIONS OF POLITICAL PHILOSOPHY

Ebenstein, William, and Alan O. Ebenstein, eds. 1992. *Introduction to Political Thinkers*. New York: Harcourt Brace Jovanovich.

Losco, Joseph, and Leonard Williams, eds. 1992. *Political Theory: Classical Writings, Contemporary Views*. New York: St. Martin's Press.

Porter, Jene M., ed. 1989. *Classical Political Philosophy*. Englewood Cliffs, NJ: Prentice Hall.

C. HISTORIES OF POLITICAL PHILOSOPHY

Plamanetz, John. 1963. *Man and Society*. London: Longmans.

Sabine, George. [1937] 1950. *A History of Political Theory*, rev. ed. New York: Henry Holt.

Strauss, Leo, and Joseph Cropsey. 1987. *History of Political Philosophy*, 3rd ed. Chicago: University of Chicago Press.

Wolin, Sheldon, [1960], 2004. *Politics and Vision: Continuity and Innovation in Western Political Thought*. Princeton, NJ: Princeton University Press

D. OTHER

Bowle, John. 1961. *Western Political Thought*. London: Methuen.

Halévy, Elie. 1972. *The Growth of Philosophical Radicalism*. London: Faber and Faber.

Held, David, ed. 1991. *Political Theory Today*. Oxford: Polity Press.

Horowitz, Asher, and Gad Horowitz. 1988. *"Everywhere They Are in Chains": Political Theory From Rousseau to Marx*. Scarborough, ON: Nelson.

Irwin, Terrence. 1989. *Classical Thought*. Oxford: Oxford University Press.

MacIntyre, Alasdair. 1984. *After Virtue*, 2nd ed. Notre Dame, IN: University of Notre Dame Press.

Sinclair, T.A. 1959. *History of Greek Political Thought*. London: Routledge and Kegan Paul.

Stace, William. 1955. *The Political Philosophy of Hegel*. New York: Dover.

FOUR | Ideology: Ideas for Political Action

"The whole history of civilization is strewn with creeds and institutions that were invaluable at first, and deadly afterward."
—Walter Bagehot, 1869

"I am an intellectual chap,
And think of things that would astonish you.
I often think it's comical
How Nature always does contrive
That every boy and every gal,
That's born into the world alive,
Is either a little Liberal,
Or else a little Conservative!"
—Sir William Schwenck Gilbert, "Iolanthe" (1882)

Few among us will become political philosophers, but many of us may come to adhere to an **IDEOLOGY** or at least hold beliefs of an ideological character. Terms like liberal, conservative, radical, progressive, feminist, or ecologist are commonly used to describe the positions staked out by political actors, their supporters, and their allies. Like many political science terms, ideology is employed in different ways. Here ideology will be defined as *a more or less consistent set of beliefs about the nature of the society in which individuals live and about the proper role of the state in establishing or maintaining that society.* It may be useful to compare ideology with political philosophy, which we discussed in the previous chapter.

Like philosophy, ideology is *systematic*: beliefs about one topic are related to beliefs about another, different subject. For example, beliefs about the nature (real or ideal) of society may be connected somehow to beliefs about the role(s) to be played by the state in society, which in turn informs beliefs about a particular policy such as gun control. It is sometimes useful to think of ideologies as sets of answers to questions that range from the very general and abstract to the concrete and particular. Also, like political philosophies, ideologies are *normative*. They are beliefs about how the world *ought* to be. A related dimension of ideology, but not necessarily of philosophy, is that it orients action or requires change in the

4.1
Ideology Defined

world, following up on the normative beliefs it contains. Ideologies typically offer or inform a program of action that seeks to transform the world from the way it is into what (for the ideology) is its ideal constitution. Conversely, the ideology may seek to protect a valued way of life from change. The capacity of ideologies to guide or even incite political activity is one principal feature that makes them interesting to social scientists.

In addition to promoting a specific view of how the world should be, an ideology very often presupposes definite notions about what the world *is* or employs unique concepts to explain or make sense of the world of experience. For example, both radical feminism and Marxism seek to eradicate inequality from the world, but each identifies inequality differently, and the equality each seeks to establish is distinct (although not necessarily incompatible). The primary concept Marxists have used to describe and explain the social relations of society is that of **CLASS**. For radical feminists, the structure of social reality is provided not (or not primarily) by class, but by **PATRIARCHY**, the historical subjugation of women by men through socially constituted gender relations. Feminists do not deny the existence of the economic or material relations indicated by the term *class*, but argue that these are not the *essential* relationships. The point of this example, then, is that ideologies can operate as different ways of seeing and understanding the social world(s) we inhabit, and this too is similar to the way philosophy can shape our perceptions.

Marx argued that the ruling ideology in any society will be that which protects and reflects the interests of the dominant economic class *even though* it may not be presented or understood by its adherents in such terms. Two of Marx's ideas here have been adapted by others who might agree with him on little else: one is the connection (often hidden) of ideas with interests; the other is the notion that ideologies are partial views of social and political reality and in this partiality or bias are incomplete or even untrue. And of course, it is not necessary for ideas to be true to be powerful or to regulate activity.

There are several ways in which ideologies differ from political philosophy. First, and perhaps most obvious, they are simpler, proceeding at a less sophisticated level of abstraction. Secondly, and related to the first, they are more popular and accessible to a broader public than philosophy. Finally, ideologies can be described as political philosophies geared for action; they are primarily about changing the world—or preserving it from change. The philosopher continues to ask about what the political world is and how it should be; the **IDEOLOGUE** has definite answers to these questions and seeks to put them into practice.

The implication here is that ideologies are fundamentally critical in their orientation; while this is often true, it is not universally so. Many ideologies are basically critical of the existing social and political arrangements (the **STATUS QUO**) and have presented programs for radical change. But ideologies may also justify a status quo and present a program that resists fundamental **REFORM**. When an ideological consensus emerges in a society, ideology may be much less about creating social change or transformation than about presenting competing solutions to problems or managing change brought about by other circumstances.

Our last general observation is that ideology, even more than philosophy, is determined by its general context. The socio-historical and intellectual contexts discussed in the treatment of political philosophy are equally as relevant to ideology and for the same reasons. At the same time, because ideology is oriented to political action, it is more sensitive than political philosophy to the actual politics of particular societies, and in this way it is more reactive to the specific contexts of place and time. There is much that does not make sense unless we pay particular attention to the way ideology reacts to specific circumstances. This allows us to explain why conservatives in countries like Britain and the United States want government to give greater freedom to market forces, while conservatives in Eastern Europe resist reforms that would do just that. Or why conservatives in the twentieth century are often difficult to distinguish from early nineteenth-century liberals. Comparative politics teaches us that, within any given society, an ideology or two will dominate, a couple of others may compete, and the rest are absent or so marginal as to elude the acquaintance of most citizens. Differences in the public support for gun control in the United States and Canada, or the contrast between the success of **SOCIALISM** in Europe and its absence in the United States, reflect the fact that the ideological landscape in each of these settings is distinct. The success in the United States of liberal conservatism with its distrust of the state is no doubt in part rooted in the birth of that country through **REVOLUTION** against a perceived tyrannical power. The viability of conservative and socialist parties in Europe in the past has probably owed something to the clarity with which class is perceived in formerly feudal societies. Each case deserves to be considered on its own merits.

Similarly, to be a liberal changed its meaning in the United States after the Depression and the Roosevelt New Deal, and seems

Communist
Monument

to mean something quite different today than it did even 25 years ago. How will ideologies that sustained themselves in the context of the Cold War redefine themselves in its absence? It is as much because of shifting temporal contexts as anything else that the meanings of liberalism, conservatism, and even socialism have been impermanent. For this reason it is useful to approach ideologies as having undergone changes that allow us to speak of different "generations." In turning to specific ideologies, we will examine the context in which the ideology arose and by which it was defined, as well as the ways in which successive changes in context have transformed its perspectives.

LIBERALISM is the first modern ideology and still remains the dominant ideology of the contemporary age. The context in which liberalism was born was that of reaction to the feudal structures of medieval society. From the mid-seventeenth to the early nineteenth centuries, liberalism received systematic articulation and refinement by a series of philosophers and political activists.

4.2
Classical Liberalism

The liberal reaction against the organic hierarchical structure of feudal society is seen clearly in a conceptual device that serves frequently as a starting point in early liberal thought: the "state of nature." This was a (usually) hypothetical construct of how humans would live, singly or together, in a condition without political authority or other ordering institutions. This type of speculation illustrates clearly three characteristics of liberalism:

1. a focus on and primary valuation of the individual;
2. the artificial nature of society in the liberal view; and
3. the rational, instrumental character of political institutions, which liberals justify on the basis of their contribution to the self-interest of individuals.

If medieval society embodied the dominance of social structure over individuals, then liberalism is the political philosophy of **INDIVIDUALISM**; political community, or what liberal thinkers call "civil society" is somewhat artificial, something we establish from our initial position as individuals in order to improve our personal well-being. Correspondingly, social structures or institutions are reasonable instruments (i.e., means we devise with our reason) that ought to maximize the well-being of individuals. Liberal thinkers have differed in identifying the character of well-being (security, pleasure, **SELF-DETERMINATION**), but they have agreed that it is this individual well-being that political society ought to secure. The verb "secure" is important here, for early liberals believed the state should provide a framework of laws and order within which individuals could safely pursue their own interests. They did not believe that the state should actually provide the tangible means of well-being to individuals. Early liberal thought, then, is not only about self-interest but also about self-reliance and self-regulation.

Liberalism is the ideology not only of individualism but also of freedom or liberty. The root of the term "liberal" is the Latin term "liber" which translates roughly as "freedom/liberty." Liberals believe that we are free by nature but that we surrender some of our liberty to live in society with others, a surrender made in exchange for some other good, like security. ("By nature," for liberals, we are also equal, but this receives less emphasis.) Government is seen by liberals to be a necessary evil, and so they seek to limit the extent of limitations on personal liberty imposed by law. Increasingly, this liberty has come to be expressed or defined through appeal to individual **RIGHTS**, which are claims sometimes made against other citizens but also and most importantly against the state. Instead of government being the property of *an* individual, it is—in theory—to serve the interests of *all* individuals; to ensure this, liberals argue for limits on the state. Such limits may be achieved by removing certain subjects from the compass of state authority (as in the device of rights) or by giving greater control over government to the individuals whom government is supposed to serve (as through **DEMOCRACY**). Either path embodies the notion of limited and rule-abiding government, or **CONSTITUTIONALISM**.

Constitutionalism means that there are established, understood rules concerning the exercise of power and authority, and that those who exercise power and authority respect these rules. In practice this means a set of limits or restraints on the scope of governmental authority or power, and the rules that provide this restraint embody a constitution, the most fundamental law of a polity. Clearly, constitutionalism is liberalism's response to the arbitrary, personal nature of absolute power as it developed at the end of the feudal period.

Popular sovereignty is the notion that the authority (or power) of the state is traced ultimately to the people who are governed within that state. Authority is entrusted to elites by the people and is to be exercised for their (the people's) interest. In those thinkers who employed the devices of a state of nature, popular sovereignty was indicated by the supposed "creation" of government through a collective agreement called a "social contract" or "covenant," and with this agreement individuals were supposed to pass from a natural state without government to a civil state with rational, accountable government.

Early liberals were somewhat uneasy about democracy and looked for other constitutional means of keeping rulers in check. In

Britain, liberals (called Whigs) pushed for **RESPONSIBLE GOVERNMENT**, and the so-called Glorious (or Whig) revolution of 1688 led to a system of responsible government that has been the model for most of the world's parliamentary constitutions. Responsible government means that the political executive is not able to act without the support of a majority in the legislature (the chamber of representatives). A different path to the same goal was the advocacy of **MIXED GOVERNMENT**, or a **SEPARATION OF POWERS**, as embodied in the American Constitution. Through history, mixed government had meant tempering government by one (monarchy) with government by the few (aristocracy) and by the many (democracy). This was the model for the American Constitution of a President, Supreme Court, and Congress, which are kept in balance by a system of checks and balances.

Whether they advocated responsible government or a separation of powers, liberals tended to agree on the necessity of **REPRESENTATIVE GOVERNMENT**. This means that an important part of the state (for some liberals the supreme part)—the legislature—should be composed of representatives of the people. We will find that many early liberals had a very narrow view of who should be entitled to sit in the legislature or vote for such representatives, but it was not a large step to move, as liberals eventually did, from supporting representative government to advocating representative democracy as the surest means of preserving citizens' liberty.

As important to the early liberals as *political* liberty was *economic* liberty, or **MARKET AUTONOMY**, meaning that the state leaves unregulated the private economic transactions of individuals. Again, this clearly contrasts with the feudal economy, which was heavily regulated by both church and state and which entailed a variety of authoritative transfers of resources from citizens to state and church. The classic liberal statement on economic matters has been considered the **LAISSEZ-FAIRE** doctrine of minimal government activity in the marketplace associated with the Scottish political economist Adam Smith, who in 1776 published his influential book *The Wealth of Nations*. The *laissez-faire* emphasis on the minimal state sometimes obscures the fact that market society did not "just happen" but required a variety of supportive policies and activities to be undertaken by the state—e.g., rules governing exchange, enforcement of contracts, stable currency, etc. In its early days, liberalism was as much about creating the conditions for a market society to flourish as it was about letting the market do its own thing.

In addition to political and economic liberty, liberalism came to argue for social or moral liberty (see Figure 4.1). The most famous statement of this strain of liberalism remains John Stuart Mill's essay *On Liberty*, which is about freedom of opinion, belief, and lifestyle. These concerns are consistent with an ideology of individualism; if individual well-being requires political and economic liberty, why not also social or moral liberty? In asking such questions, however, J.S. Mill went further than many previous liberals had been prepared to go. Liberal thinkers had often been quite conventional in their beliefs about public morality; while they had been unwilling to accept these beliefs merely because they were hallowed by convention or custom, liberals had instead sought rational justifications for existing moral conventions or legal restrictions based on morality. Since Mill's time liberals have been typically tolerant of moral and religious difference or plurality.

A final point to note is the importance of *reason* in liberalism, which espouses a *rational* individualism. Here the contrast is with the traditional character of feudal society, and we need simply recall liberalism's roots in that rationalist revolution known as the Enlightenment. The concern for representative, limited government is a belief that individuals can be protected from arbitrary, irrational authority through rational, predictable government. The market can be seen as a rational alternative to medieval rules and regulations. Liberal ethical theory looks to rational principle rather than traditional justification. In all these ways liberalism supposes that government, politics, and social life generally can be ordered by human reason in ways that will make individuals better off than they might otherwise be.

In short, the liberal perspective is that the world consists of rational, self-interested *individuals*, who are essentially prior to political society and by nature exist free and equal. The ideal for which liberalism strives is the preservation and enhancement of individual *liberty* within a system of enforceable rights under a government committed to the rule of law. Within such a framework, individuals will be able to cultivate their own particular good with security and at peace with others. The program of liberalism, at least initially, was to secure its ideal through *reform* of traditional institutions or

FIGURE 4.1 Libertarianism

A radical version of classical liberalism is alive and well in the United States today—**LIBERTARIANISM**. Advocating the radical extension of liberty to as many aspects of life as possible—provided that the free choices of individuals do not harm other individuals—modern Libertarians support such policies as the legalization of all drugs, the privatization of welfare programs, the elimination of laws barring pornography, prostitution, "victimless crimes," and the like. Organizing such an anti-political constituency for political power as libertarians has proven to be difficult. In the United States, the Libertarian Party was founded in 1972 and has campaigned in most presidential elections since then. In Europe, some "radical parties" embrace libertarian principles to greater or lesser degrees. For further information, see <http://www.libertarian.org>.

their actual replacement with rationally designed instruments of accountable *limited government*.

In the last century and a half, liberalism has been significantly transformed. The short explanation is that liberalism reacted to its own successes and shortcomings. It responded to the competition provided by socialism, to the demise of feudal society and with it (by and large) toryism, and to the pressures of a democratic political process that it (liberalism) helped to democratize. The vision of liberalism did not alter fundamentally: liberals continued (and continue) to seek a society in which individual well-being is maximized through the enlightened pursuit of self-interest within a progressively broadening and secure sphere of individual liberty. Over time, though, the breadth and scope of liberals' concerns have altered.

4.3
Reform Liberalism

On the one hand, with each success in securing individual liberty, liberalism has not halted but moved on to fresh matters. A modern liberal's concerns with racial and gender equality, rights for gays and lesbians, the continued absence of prayer in schools, and the public provision of goods such as education and health care—these would have struck early liberals as radical, perhaps outrageous, demands. Nonetheless, what the modern liberal wants is grounded on the same principles with which the classic liberal demanded representative government, the protection of property, or religious freedom.

At the same time, as liberals succeeded in implementing their political and economic agenda, they often came to the recognition that their liberal vision was as yet incompletely realized. Representative liberal government and a thriving private property market economy did not suffice to ensure liberty and well-being for all. This recognition led to two strategies: the reform of political and economic institutions and the reform of traditional social institutions as they touched upon issues such as education, the status of women and children, sexuality, and other areas of social and personal liberty. Like others we will call these modern (twentieth-century) liberals "reform liberals," in contrast to the "classic liberals" of the eighteenth and early nineteenth centuries.

When the status quo was the rigid, relatively authoritarian structures of feudal society, liberalism tended to emphasize the negative role of the state in restricting individual freedom. While liberals recognized that some restriction of the ability of individuals to act is necessary for social peace and security, they sought to minimize these restrictions, especially where they were fetters on economic and social progress. By the nineteenth century, in many nations, liberalism had become the new status quo, and yet many individuals were not appreciably better off or freer than they had been (or would have been) in medieval society. In the immediate aftermath of the Industrial Revolution, many of those in the lowest strata of society were clearly worse off. While the liberal revolution had brought political and economic liberty, it had not brought these freedoms—or their benefits—to all. This had two consequences for liberalism.

One was the recognition that the state (or government) is not the only institution (more correctly, set of institutions) that restricts the freedom of individuals. The institutions of civil society—the capitalist economy, the family, social norms and attitudes—can also restrict individual liberty. As J.S. Mill argued in *On Liberty*—and as we may often find true still today—personal liberty has as much or more to fear from public opinion and its pressures for conformity as from the activities of the state. Secondly, it is possible to see liberty not only in the negative sense of an absence of restrictions but in the positive sense of an ability to do this or that. For example, it may be legally possible for anyone to acquire property, but if the economic system does not provide real opportunity for those born in poverty to escape that condition, are they any freer than if they were legally barred from ownership?

In the nineteenth century some liberals came to see that individuals are denied freedom in the positive sense by the laws and institutions of a purportedly liberal society. At the same time, they increasingly accepted the notion of progressive humanity and with it the imperative to remove restrictions or impediments to that progress. The result of these developments was a shift in liberalism from emphasizing the need for greater freedom from the state to an emphasis on the need for greater equality in the enjoyment of liberty.

To enhance a positive enjoyment of liberty, to promote equality of opportunity, and to reform any number of institutions that diminish individual freedom, liberalism changed its posture toward the state. Liberals came to believe that the state in a liberal society can function to preserve and enhance liberty, to reform the institutions of civil society, and to provide opportunity for those disadvantaged by their ascribed social position. From the stance of *laissez-faire* and the minimal state, liberals moved to acceptance of an activist state, a government much larger than what liberalism originally envisaged. In short, then, a variety of problems associated with continued inequality and the lack of freedom provided the incentive for reform of liberalism—reform that took three main directions:

1. the incorporation of political democracy,
2. an expansion of rights claims by individuals, and
3. the abandonment of *laissez-faire* political economy.

One of the earliest and most significant revisions of liberalism was an incorporation of political democracy. Early liberal thinkers such as Locke had advocated representative government but had expected that the representatives would be drawn from and selected by the property-owning classes. The Industrial Revolution had created a large class of urban workers who, owning no property, had no political rights. It was this class (by and large) which socialism claimed to represent and to whom it appealed for support. Partly for reasons of principle and partly for the pragmatic purpose of heading off the socialists, liberals came to support extending the franchise (the right to vote) first to male members of the working class and, much later, to women of all social classes.

A second dimension of liberal reform was an expansion of rights claims on behalf of individuals. Rights may be understood as *entitlements individuals claim from the state or other individuals*. Entitlements may be moral or legal; in the latter case the state is legally obliged to respect or enforce entitlements. Although it is not always the case, rights are often about protections for something individuals value (like their lives, freedoms, properties, etc.). The extension of entitlements to individuals previously unprotected from the state or other individuals is a significant (and ongoing) development within liberalism. The extension of legal and political rights to women in the first decades of this century and the civil rights movement in the United States in the 1960s offer clear examples of reform liberalism in practice.

The third and perhaps most significant area of liberal reform was the abandonment of *laissez-faire* political economy and participation in the development of the twentieth-century **WELFARE STATE**. Advocates of the market economy, such as Adam Smith, firmly believed that if competition and market mechanisms were allowed to work unfettered by government regulation, the condition of the working class would be improved; over the long term wages would rise, prices would fall, and all would become wealthier. Similarly, liberal economists could argue that the tremendous economic growth created by capitalism more than compensated for any inequality by providing better than any other system might for those at the bottom of the economy. In practice, though, the liberal economy did not work as beneficially for the laboring classes or the unemployed as theory promised. Also, socialism claimed to offer a political economy which could improve the conditions of the least advantaged, employing the productive capacity of market society without reproducing its attendant inequality.

Abandoning the minimal state, reformist liberals looked to an activist state to overcome the weaknesses of *laissez-faire*, to moderate the inequalities and inequities of the market economy, and to act positively to enhance the actual liberty of all in society, particularly of those currently disadvantaged by the existing social arrangements. A wide variety of tools was developed and employed by liberals in power, including increasing regulation of economic life, actual intervention in the economy, and progressive application of levers of economic management, all culminating in the twentieth-century welfare state. Despite the scope and extent of these departures from *laissez-faire*, this reformed liberalism remained committed to the market and to private property. For this reason, despite what its critics have sometimes alleged, the activist state of reformed liberalism falls far short of the interventionist state of socialism. In this regard, too, it is notable that the liberal welfare state has usually been much less comprehensive and extensive than the welfare state constructed by social democrats or socialists (see below).

4.4
Classical Conservatism

CONSERVATISM seems the counterpart of liberalism—its natural opposite as day is to night or winter is to summer. But it is sometimes possible for liberals to be conservative or for conservatives really to be liberals. In the early 1990s in Russia, for example, "liberals" led by Boris Yeltsin pressed for the kind of economic system favored by North American "conservatives"—though Yeltsin's idea was similar to the economic vision of "liberals" in early nineteenth-century Britain. This sort of contradiction begins to dissolve if we realize that conservatism is even more bound to the contexts of place and time than other ideologies. Conservatism might be understood initially as a *disposition* to preserve what exists, to resist change, and/or to support the traditional ways of a community or society. The content of conservatism will thus depend on what already exists, what is traditional or prevalent in the community. (Those who would go further—i.e., bring back what is going or gone—may be termed *radical conservatives* or, more pejoratively, *reactionaries*). In a society where liberal values have become well-established or entrenched, conservatism may well seek to preserve liberalism from reform or radical change; in an authoritarian dictatorship, conservatism may support clearly illiberal ideas. The original conservatives who sought to preserve the traditional institutions and values of aristocratic society in the face of the liberal revolution need to be distinguished from those conservatives with whom we are familiar today. These initial conservatives can be identified by their British name, "tories" (a term also sometimes used by liberals to describe their opponents in the early days of the American republic).

If, generally speaking, liberalism is the ideology of the individual, conservatism is an ideology of the community, and **TORYISM** is the ideology of an idealized hierarchical community resembling late feudal society. In contrast to liberals, tories see the organic, hierarchical organization of society as natural; indeed, however organized, society or community is natural in the same way that family is. What is artificial is the distinction liberals make between the state of nature and civil society. Tories value whatever contributes to the coherence, cohesion, and continuance of this community: its traditions, conventions, time-honored institutions, structures, and practices. The conservative views these institutions (such as monarchy and the Church) or practices (traditional morality, deference to authority, performance of duty) as inseparable from a way of life handed down by history. The primary task of the state is to preserve the integrity of the community (which includes its institutions, practices, and values). In contrast to the abstract, often ahistorical character of liberalism, conservatism (especially the tory variety) venerates history and custom.

Toryism takes the position that individuals are necessarily (as history and experience demonstrate) unequal by nature. It is therefore not surprising if individuals are ordered and structured in society; on this view the hierarchical organization of society simply reflects the reality of different individual capacities and is essential to the community's survival. All individuals are not equal in talent or ability, though these inequalities need not be a source of conflict or social instability. Instead, individuals have the responsibility to recognize their natural abilities and, on that basis, to find and accept their "place" in the larger social order. Thus the aristocracy of feudal society is a natural governing class that has emerged through history on the basis of its superior endowments. Central to this vision is the recognition that such a natural inequality establishes mutual obligations between the superior and the inferior. The aristocracy holds a privileged position at the head of society, but it also has responsibility for the welfare of the less fortunate; it is privileged in its possession of political power, but it is also obliged to exercise that power responsibly in the general interest. It is essential that *each* individual, whatever their rank or station, perform the duties and responsibilities associated with that situation. This is because each individual—from monarch to slave—is but part of a larger whole *and* serves a larger or nobler purpose. Thus, in contrast to the liberal emphasis on freedom or liberty, toryism stresses order, stability, and adherence to duty. Privilege is necessary and right.

There is a certain ambivalence in the tory stance regarding power and authority. On the one hand, strong authority is necessary to sustain the organic structure of the community. On the other hand, inasmuch as the community is preserved through custom, convention, and tradition, the active scope or role for government is ideally quite small. Thus, tories favor a strong but relatively inactive state (besides, a state too busy will inevitably bring unnecessary change). Tory conservatism is comfortable with the absolute state if its authority is exercised by the right people: tories are fond of traditional institutions such as hereditary monarchy and of legislative assemblies so long as they are aristocratic or controlled by the privileged classes. It is when government becomes more democratic or representative of the non-privileged classes that tories become more supportive of the **LIMITED STATE**. These conservatives are fonder of constitutionalism than democracy. The ultimate source of authority for tories is often transcendent, such as God or the "natural order," in contrast to the popular authority grounding liberalism.

The foundation of the traditional aristocracy was the feudal relation between landlord and tenant. The secure identification of an individual with a place, a particular occupation, a clearly recognized set of duties and obligations, and a sound knowledge of one's inferiors and superiors—all this was challenged by market society. Small wonder that tories first resisted its triumph. In many cases, though, members of the landed aristocracy realized that there was no incompatibility between an aristocracy of birth and an aristocracy of wealth, and that wealth grounded in land could be supplemented with wealth gained in commerce and manufacture. Toryism eventually made its peace with the market economy, but in doing so, the conservatism it represented started down the road to liberalism. Tory antipathy to markets survives in the insistence sometimes found in conservatism that markets serve the good of the community, an insistence that is more in tune with economic nationalism than *laissez-faire*.

One of the strongest elements of toryism is its support of trad-itional values: religious, moral, and social. The religious and moral beliefs and practices of a society are regarded as part and parcel of its necessary structure; to challenge or reject them is to challenge the value or integrity of the community itself. Tories, then, will gener-ally be closely allied with the church (particularly if it is an officially sanctioned or established church) and, above all, are convinced of the importance of religion. Traditional moral values and practices will also be central to these conservatives, not simply as individual beliefs but rather as matters of public morality. Unlike the liberal, who may well share with the tory many beliefs about right and wrong but is willing to let individuals decide for themselves, the tory is not usually so tolerant but advocates an active enforcement of moral standards. If public opinion and censure are not enough to do this, then the state should be employed to uphold what is right. Tolerance is not generally a central feature of toryism.

Finally, just as liberalism stresses rationalism, toryism justi-fies itself on the basis of tradition. What has been handed down from generation to generation through history is regarded as right or worth preserving simply because it has withstood "the test of time." It is a temptation (to which liberals often succumb) to see this traditionalism as simply the irrational veneration of history, but it may with more insight be seen as symptomatic of a cautious at-titude towards the powers of reason. The liberal is confident that we can design institutions and programs to change the world in ways that will solve our problems; the conservative is not so sure. What passing "the test of time" may mean on this view is meth-ods or practices that have succeeded, have worked, whatever their limitations. The conservative is reluctant to throw these away for something new and untested, unproven.

The point has been made already that the content of conserva-tism is to a great degree dependent on the context: what is it that conservatives wish to "conserve"? If conservatism is a defense of the status quo against the efforts of those who would imple-ment serious reform or change, then there can be as many different conservatisms as there are status quos. If, then, at some time in the eighteenth and nineteenth century in most of Europe and many of her present or former colonies, liberalism became the status quo as represented by the dominant political and economic institutions, conservatism in such liberal societies should have a markedly liberal character.

**4.5
Liberal or Market
Conservatism**

At the same time, in describing tory conservatism, we encountered several ideas capable of surviving the demise of any fondness for feudalism. These were notions such as natural inequality, the importance of religion, the value of traditional morality, and a pessimism about human nature (what the conservative might claim is simply a "realism" about people). None of these is incompatible with the primary institutions of liberal society, in particular a constitutional, limited government and a private property market economy. Modern conservatism in liberal societies, then, has turned out to be, in almost every case, a mixture of toryism and liberalism. What makes this quite easily confusing is the variety of ways in which liberalism and conservatism may be combined. At the very least, all conservatives in modern liberal societies partake in the liberal consensus that accords legitimacy to a private property market economy, the basic institutions of constitutional representative government, and to the rule of law. This consensus is so complete in some societies (like the United States) that it is no longer recognized by many people as specifically "liberal." What distinguishes conservatives from each other is how much of this liberal consensus they have come to share and, on the other hand, what they reject in the liberal catalogue of values.

Consider in the first instance classic liberals who object to the changes brought about by reform liberalism. Wishing to preserve the status quo in the face of reform, these are "conservative liberals." They support a *laissez-faire* economy and the associated notion of the minimal state. They support representative government, are wary of extending popular democracy too far, and probably regard the American Bill of Rights (1789) as a code needing no expansion or supplementation. The moral values of the nineteenth century, stressing the virtues of the Christian family, sit comfortably with them. Over time, these conservative liberals have come to be called conservatives, just as reform liberals have become simply liberals. In fact, some of the most eloquent spokesmen of conservatism have been conservative liberals, such as Burke (who was a Whig and not a Tory) or Michael Oakshott.

A very similar position can be reached from a different angle. Imagine that as liberal political and economic institutions are entrenched, tories become reconciled to them but do not abandon their own beliefs about human nature, order and stability, change, and natural inequality. Since the liberal institutions they come to accept are the as yet unreformed institutions of classic liberalism—*laissez-faire* and limited representative government—there is very little to distinguish these liberal conservatives (conservatives who adopt liberal institutions) from the conservative liberals (liberals with a conservative disposition). The picture, though, is more complicated than this.

Two further variations on the conservative theme may seem odd or curious to many North Americans. Over time, most if not all tories made their peace with the economic side of liberalism, accepting and adapting to the modern industrial market economy. The critical issue here is which dimensions of their tory conservatism did they bring with their new allegiance to liberal economics? One of the features distinguishing tories from liberals is their belief in natural inequality. The inequality associated with a market economy thus poses no problem to tories adapting to liberal institutions. For a supposed "natural" aristocracy based on family and social class, the market economy substitutes an aristocracy based on wealth and economic class.

Classical conservatives, though, also possessed a belief in organic community that complemented their belief in natural inequality. If the least advantaged somehow have "inferior" natures, then this is the lot nature has given them and not something attributable to their own failures or lack of effort. So too, by this logic, the "superior" individuals of noble character are not self-made but naturally endowed with the abilities, temperament, intellect, or whatever it is that makes them "superior." In an organic conception of society, those naturally superior have an obligation towards their inferiors: to educate them, to present to them an example of proper conduct, and where possible to provide for those unable to provide for themselves. Tories who bring this sense of *noblesse oblige* to their adoption of liberal institutions will have a basis for agreeing to some of the measures brought in by reform liberalism, particularly those features of the welfare state that are designed to provide social relief to the least advantaged in society. It is important to understand the difference here: reform liberals reform the market economy in order to enhance equality of opportunity for individuals; market tories reform the market economy because they recognize the need to intervene to protect those least able to compete in an unfettered market.

Similar to market conservatism is European **CHRISTIAN DEMOCRACY**. Feudal society on that continent involved a close, albeit fractious, relationship between the state and the Roman Catholic Church. Liberalism, influenced by the rationalist Enlightenment and Protestantism, argued for a separation of church and state. Free-thinkers, dissenters, and non-believers were usually liberals. Particularly in those countries that remained predominantly

Roman Catholic, liberalism was seen to be the enemy of religion and the Church, and it was opposed to any official position for the Church in civic life. Moreover, many Church adherents identified liberalism and its modern ways with materialism, urbanization, and secularization—features believed to undermine the faith and the institutions in which it is most at home, the family and the local community. Christian Democratic parties were formed to oppose liberal parties and defend the Church and its values. Although they are Protestant in Scandinavia and the large German party appeals to both Protestants and Catholics, most Christian Democratic movements have succeeded in predominantly Roman Catholic nations. As Mény points out, in countries where *all* parties profess allegiance to the church, such as Ireland and Spain, Christian Democracy does not exist (1993: 66). Not surprisingly, Christian Democratic ideology has tended to support traditional Church positions on social and moral matters: opposition to abortion, civil divorce, and contraception; support for the traditional family; and deference to legitimate public authorities. The major difference between European Christian Democrats and secular conservatives has tended to concern the role of the state in the economy. Whereas Europe's secular conservatives (like American conservatives) are usually economic liberals advocating a minimal state, Christian Democracy has believed that economics should take second place to social concerns and, for this reason, has in the past supported state policies to protect or give relief to the poor or working classes, even when this has constituted what liberals would call "interference" in the marketplace. Interestingly, Pope Leo XIII wrote in his encyclical *Rerum Novarum* (1891) that "the public administration must duly and solicitously provide for the welfare and comfort of the working classes; otherwise that law of justice will be violated which ordains that each man shall have his due." The advanced welfare states of Western Europe have often been the product of a consensus (or compromise) between social democracy on the left and Christian Democracy on the right.

While Christian Democracy may be foreign to North American students, the association of religious adherence and conservatism is not. In almost any culture, in normal circumstances, adherence to the dominant religion will be somewhat conservative, preserving traditional values and ways of life. The degree to which a society or its politics have been secularized will have a bearing on the link between religion and politics. The religious right in the United States would alter a long-standing relationship of official religious neutrality. Like other conservatives, the religious right supports traditional moral values, grounded here in a fundamentalist reading of Christian scripture. These conservatives would like to see prayer in schools; believe in a strong law-and-order state (including capital punishment); and generally oppose abortion, feminism, rights for gays and lesbians, sex education in schools, and whatever else they identify with "secular humanism," a generic label for all the ills of modern society. What takes these conservatives further than others who might share part or all of the same concerns is their determination to use the state to further their religious agenda or to dismantle the laws that contradict it.

In the modern Western world, then, all conservatives are marked by a belief in the private property market economy and, by and large, agree on a *laissez-faire*, minimal state approach to this economy. As the end of the century approaches, they are concerned to reduce the size and scale of government operations and eliminate government deficits. In this sense, then, they are all fiscal conservatives. The one exception to this is the kind of conservatism—mainly European Christian Democracy—that continues to value social welfare just enough to justify government regulation of, or activity in, the market.

Clearly then, conservatism comes in any number of flavors today, although increasingly common to all versions is a belief in "fiscal responsibility," a general adherence to economic liberalism, and a strong commitment to moral principles, usually (but not always) of a traditional character and usually (but not always) linked to Christianity.

If toryism was a reaction against liberalism on behalf of a vanishing status quo, socialism was a reaction against the world created by successful liberalism. Some early socialists, it is true, were reacting with liberals against aristocratic society, but obviously they did so with a different vision and emphasis. The most significant socialist thinkers were motivated by a distaste for liberal society, particularly for the consequences of the market economy so central to the liberal vision. Socialism was *the* ideology of the nineteenth century, gaining significance after the effects of the Industrial Revolution had become obvious and after the liberal revolution had succeeded in dissolving feudal society in most of Europe.

Like liberals and contrary to tories, socialists begin with the proposition that humans are fundamentally equal; unlike liberals and in agreement with classical conservatives, socialists see humans as having an essentially social or communal nature. Socialists

4.6
Socialism, Communism, and Social Democracy

oppose the inegalitarian beliefs of tories and the individualism of liberals. In the latter case, socialists also disagree about the nature of equality or inequality that is present in society and that is acceptable or not. Liberals oppose the inherited or traditional inequalities of the hierarchical feudal condition; they are concerned to ensure that neither laws nor regulations deny individuals the same chances or opportunity to achieve their goals, protect their self-interests, or obtain well-being. Inequalities that result from differences in individual effort or from how individuals exploit the equal opportunity provided them are not problematic to most liberals and are quite acceptable or "natural" to many. Early liberals also accepted a wide range of existing structural inequalities; in asserting that all had "equal opportunity," these liberals were blind to those disadvantages of poverty, social class, and gender under which most of the population labored. To the socialist, the inequalities to which the liberal did not object were simply unacceptable. There can be no equality of opportunity in a class-ridden society, and individuals everywhere owe their outcomes as much to chance, inheritance, unequal opportunities, and structural factors as to individual effort.

The socialist might even agree with the liberal that in *abstract models* the market is impartial and rewards individuals, but in practice, the socialist argues, the market is partial to those with resources and rewards classes of individuals privileged in terms of assets like capital, or information, or education. The social science of the socialist is concerned with how individuals are privileged or disabled by their position within the social structure, a structure seen largely in economic or political-economic terms. What matters about individuals is their social relations, and, following Marx, the socialist sees these as class relations.

From the socialist perspective, the liberal revolution managed to replace an aristocracy of birth with an aristocracy of wealth. An elite founded on aristocratic tradition and birth-lines gave way to a privileged elite founded on economic power. Even worse, though, the reciprocal obligations that bound feudal lord to peasant and that were at least a meager compensation for the structural inequality of medieval society also vanished; the liberal allows such obligations to lapse in the belief that individuals are authors of their own fate.

While socialism is ultimately concerned with creating a society in which all individuals are genuinely equal, its concern in the present world is to eliminate what it sees as exploitation or subjugation of the least privileged classes in society; in seeking to do so, it gains little affection from those most advantageously positioned in society. Ideally, then, for the socialist the state is an instrument to be used on behalf of the exploited or underprivileged classes against the advantaged classes. Like the tory, but for different reasons, the socialist believes in a strong state, not the limited, minimal state of classic liberalism. The socialist tends to be wary of rights, then, because they are more effectively employed by those with resources than by those without, often to thwart the fundamental social change that socialists believe is necessary and because they privilege individuals against the collectivity. Unlike the tories, though, who are concerned that a strong state be in the right hands, socialists are (in theory at least) strong supporters of democracy; instead of rights that an elite minority can use to prevent the state from acting, socialists favor a strong state controlled by the majority. After all (the socialist reasons), those less advantaged are usually the majority rather than the minority. At the same time, successful social and political transformation should diminish the need for state activity. Socialists are in theory even more radically disposed towards democracy than liberals, then, with important exceptions that we will note below.

The most important task of the state, for socialists, is to regulate, to reform, even to replace the private property market economy of liberalism because of the inequality or alienation it creates. It is precisely the economic liberty or market autonomy which the liberal values that the socialist says is responsible for the inequality of capitalist society and for the consequent absence of genuine freedom for all those underprivileged in that society. In the place of private property, the socialist argues for collective or public ownership of the means of production, distribution, and exchange which capitalism employs (i.e., industry, transportation, financial institutions, etc.). In the place of market autonomy and the (mal) distribution it creates, the socialist calls for central planning and redistribution on rational egalitarian principles. These are of course the most contentious parts of the socialist position.

Within socialism, considerable difference arose about the degree of emphasis that should be put on **COLLECTIVE OWNERSHIP** and about those forms of democracy associated with liberal individualism. These and other differences lie behind the distinctions between **COMMUNISTS** or **MARXISTS**, after the nineteenth-century German philosopher Karl Marx, and socialists of a less radical variety, committed to at least some elements of liberal democracy, who called themselves **SOCIAL DEMOCRATS**. The fundamental distinction between socialism and communism was originally rooted in differences over democracy and about a revolutionary or reformist strategy of change. Both believed in the replacement of a private property market economy with a socialized (collective or public ownership) economy under the direction of the state. Since early in the twentieth century, then, it has been possible to distinguish clearly between socialism and communism. Socialism is democratic, reformist, and peaceful; communism is authoritarian or totalitarian, revolutionary, and if necessary committed to violent struggle. These differences are significant and underpin others. Communism is authoritarian in two important senses: it involves an anti-democratic concentration of power and a commitment to a total employment of the state on behalf of the revolution's ends. In the former case the Communist Party is not simply an elite acting on behalf of the **PROLETARIAT**, it is the *only* party permitted to exist, to organize, to solicit public support, and, most importantly, to gain office. The distinction between party and government is completely obscured, if it can be said to exist at all in any meaningful sense. No opposition to the Communist Party or its positions is tolerated or regarded as legitimate. By contrast, democratic socialism accepts the legitimacy of opposition, the inevitability of plurality within contemporary society, and the challenge of competing for public support within electoral democracy. The state and government are and remain separate from the party, even if it succeeds in winning elections.

Secondly, the Communist Party's monopoly on power goes hand in hand with a commitment to the total employment of the power of the state on behalf of the ends defined by communism. This complete exercise of the power of the state is often described as "totalitarian" as there is no recognized or protected area of privacy where collective oversight and control is prohibited. There is no sphere of society in which the state is not seen to have a legitimate interest. The distinction between private and public, so central to liberal thought, is erased on the basis that it is bogus and a barrier to the eradication of liberal capitalism.

In contrast with communism, over time socialism has also increasingly accepted the private ownership of property. In the past, elected socialist governments (for example, the postwar Labour governments in Britain) have nationalized private corporations in areas like coal-mining or steel production. While these efforts stopped short of attempting to replace the market as the primary means of allocation of resources and without having any designs on private property at large, today such partial nationalization has been the extreme edge of social democracy. Social democrats continue to worry about the influence and power of corporate property and, by the same token, are supportive of genuine collective ventures such as cooperatives or worker-owned businesses, but they are no longer committed to eliminating private corporations or to restructuring the entire economy on an alternative basis.

As socialism has in practice moved closer to the positions of social democracy, the contrasts we have made may seem like differences in emphasis rather than in kind. Indeed, as we move from communism to socialism to social democracy, we come to a point at which we approach the ideology of reform liberalism discussed earlier in this chapter. The telling distinction here comes down to the perception of the fundamental relationship of the individual to society and to other individuals. What marks the communist, socialist, and social democrat from liberals, however reformed or progressive these liberals may be, is a primary emphasis on the whole and on the collective basis of individual experience.

Stepping back and looking at the larger landscape reveals that in the past two centuries the ideological horizon has become narrower and less clearly defined. The common element eroding these distinctions is the pervasive success of liberalism, a success confirmed (not denied!) by the fact that few of those who are liberals call themselves such today. Liberalism's rivals on both the right and left have accommodated themselves to liberal society to a large, if still varying, degree. Within the ideologies of the Western world, then, there has been considerable convergence, which expresses itself as a consensus of values, *within which it is still possible for there to be quite polarized and passionate differences*, usually about the policies and programs that best reflect or realize those values.

So far our focus has been on the mainstream ideologies (or families of ideologies) conventionally arranged on the "left-right" spectrum and that seem at the end of the twentieth century to have fashioned a rough consensus about the central institutions of contemporary liberal democracy. Conservatism, liberalism, and socialism do not manage, though, to cover all the ideological bases. In the following, we will consider briefly (and sometimes too briefly) some other "isms," some of which challenge from within the consensus just noted and some of which stand outside (if not in direct opposition to) that consensus.

4.7
Beyond the Consensus

FIGURE 4.2 A Third Way?

In the past decade or so, an alternative has emerged that is distinct from the traditional left (socialism) or the parties of the traditional right (conservatives or liberals). Dubbed "**THE THIRD WAY**," this alternative, which represents something of a middle-ground between the two ideological extremes, accepts the market economy and capitalism as the only viable economic ideology. However, according to a prominent proponent, Anthony Giddens of the London School of Economics, the third way seeks to develop a new "mixed economy" in which public and private forces combine in new ways to help avoid market failures, constrain inequalities, and unlock new creative energies. Critical of the concentration of wealth under market capitalism, Third Way theorists emphasize education and a greater degree of genuine equality of opportunity as ways of spreading prosperity to a broader segment of society. These ideas became closely associated in the public mind with such recent political figures as former American President Bill Clinton, British Prime Minister Tony Blair, and German Chancellor Gerhard Schröder (see also the discussion of Blair's "New Labour" in Chapter 13).

4.7.1
Feminism

FEMINISM makes a strong claim to be considered a full-fledged ideology for it has a vision, a perspective, and a program. On the other hand, it can be misleading to speak of "feminism" when there are so many feminisms. No more than we would be willing to equate social democracy and communism should we be willing to treat the various schools of feminist thought as one and the same. In some cases, these varieties of feminism are the feminization of ideologies with which we are already familiar: hence liberal feminism, Marxist feminism, social democratic feminism, anarcha-feminism, etc. Other currents, particularly radical and postmodern feminism, appear to reject any accommodation with ideologies from the past. The approach here will be to outline what all these feminisms share to the degree they have a common vision and perspective.

Like socialism, feminism is in some senses easiest to approach through its perspective, its particular diagnosis of *the status quo*. Feminists see contemporary social relations as expressions of patriarchy, a structure of domination of women by men. The primary goal of feminism is to create gender equality and thus to dismantle patriarchy. Susan Moller Okin defines gender as "social institutionalizations of sexual difference," and notes that much of this sexual difference is not immutably biological, but is "socially constructed" (Held, 1991: 67). Feminists work to overturn these social institutionalizations and social constructions of sexual difference that have come at women's expense, seeking to create a

FIGURE 4.3 Excerpts from "The Declaration of Sentiments," Seneca Falls, NY (1848)

The history of mankind is a history of repeated injuries and usurpations on the part of man toward woman, having in direct object the establishment of an absolute tyranny over her. To prove this, let facts be submitted to a candid world.

He has never permitted her to exercise her inalienable right to the elective franchise.

He has compelled her to submit to laws, in the formation of which she had no voice.

He has withheld from her rights which are given to the most ignorant and degraded men—both natives and foreigners.

Having deprived her of this first right of a citizen, the elective franchise, thereby leaving her without representation in the halls of legislation, he has oppressed her on all sides.

He has made her, if married, in the eye of the law, civilly dead.

He has taken from her all right in property, even to the wages she earns ...

He has endeavored, in every way that he could, to destroy her confidence in her own powers, to lessen her self-respect, and to make her willing to lead a dependent and abject life.

Now, in view of this entire disfranchisement of one-half the people of this country, their social and religious degradation—in view of the unjust laws above mentioned, and because women do feel themselves aggrieved, oppressed, and fraudulently deprived of their most sacred rights, we insist that they have immediate admission to all the rights and privileges which belong to them as citizens of the United States ...

Source: <http://www.usconstitution.net/sentiments.html>.

world of structural equality in which women, as women, have full autonomy. Achieving these goals requires action on a variety of policy issues such as pay equity, reproductive choice, and childcare. One of the distinguishing marks of feminism has been its insistence on examining the dynamics of power within what is often regarded by "mainstream" political science as the private sphere, that is to say, the relations within families, within marriage, or the sexual relations of individuals. This focus is captured in the phrase "the personal is the political," which rejects the more orthodox dichotomy of private/public.

As with other ideologies, feminism's adherents differ in the intensity of their involvement, that is, the degree to which their perspective is wholly feminist. Just as there are radical and not-so-radical socialists or conservatives, there are radical feminists and not-so-radical feminists. "First wave" feminism sought to increase opportunities for women within the existing structures and processes of capitalist, liberal (patriarchal) society without challenging their legitimacy. Important strides were made in terms of gaining for women rights that were previously lacking or inadequately enforced, but many felt this was insufficient. Second wave feminists go further and challenge the very structures by which gender inequality has been reinforced and perpetuated. Second wave feminism, then, in many ways, and certainly for its more "radical" adherents, is a revolutionary perspective that calls for a fundamentally different kind of society and of social relations premised on the equality of the sexes. An early expression of this can be found in the "Declaration of Sentiments" that was signed by 68 women, including Elizabeth Cady Stanton, and 32 men, at a convention held in Seneca Falls, NY in 1848 (see Figure 4.3).

One effect of feminism upon the narrowly defined political realm has been a marked increase in the number of women in politics over the past generation. In some respects this has been even more noticeable in the number holding high political office. Nonetheless, women remain badly underrepresented in politics, even in the most "advanced" democracies. In addition, there have been few signs of a "feminization" of the political process. It was once predicted that the rise of women to positions of power would be accompanied by a shift to a politics less confrontational, adversarial, and partisan—that there would be a more constructive opposition of viewpoints. As yet such a change has not been evident.

Increasing numbers of women (and men) have embraced principles and goals of feminism, although it is fair to speculate about how many, outside the academic and intellectual communities, have progressed from the "first wave" to the "second wave." Moreover, feminism has, like nationalism or populism, found its home within many ideologies; only those who remain unabashedly traditionalist on moral and social questions are impervious to feminism.

4.7.2
Environmentalism

In 1962 Rachel Carson published *Silent Spring*, which documented in a powerful way the effect of pesticides, herbicides, and other man-made chemicals upon the environment. Many date the beginning of the environmental movement to the public awareness created by this book. **ECOLOGY** (the science) supplies the perspective, the way of seeing the world, that informs **ENVIRONMENTALISM** (the political movement, such as "Green" politics).

The ecological perspective is one of interdependence, looking at humanity and Nature through a systems approach that examines how species and their environment move in and out of balance with each other. Ecologists point out the ways that human activity in the world upsets the balance between creatures and their environment by destroying habitats, polluting the environment, using up non-renewable resources, transforming the climate, crowding out other species by over-populating the planet, etc. As humanity progressively makes the world a less hospitable place for life, which in its diversity is steadily diminishing, the quality of life lived by humans is also diminished. Ultimately, as the ecological perspective reminds us, there is a finite limit on the ability of the planet to sustain life. The human population and the resources it expends cannot grow *ad infinitum*.

The concern of environmentalism, informed by this ecological perspective, is to slow down and ultimately reverse the trend of an ever-increasing human consumption of resources and human domination and despoliation of "the environment." Certainly one obvious issue is the question of uneven economic development and the desire of much of the world's nations to "catch up" to the standard of living of advanced industrial societies, a process that would involve a tremendous acceleration in the consumption of resources and the production of associated wastes. Interestingly, though, its long-term effect might be to stabilize population, since there seems to be a strong inverse relationship between birth rate and standard of living. (For an environmentalist, the measure of "standard of living" in terms of output, consumption, or purchasing power is a symptom of the skewed perspectives of industrial societies.) Much attention in recent years has focused on the notion of "sustainable development," a term implying a modernization and enrichment of life that is neutral in its effects on the environment, or, as defined by the World Commission on Environment and Development (WCED, 1987), "development that meets the needs of the present without compromising the ability of future generations to meet their own needs."

As this indicates, environmentalism challenges the very economic and political-economic assumptions that have been central to the ideologies of the modern world; conservatism, liberalism, and socialism alike have accepted the desirability of economic growth and development without limits. According to dominant schools of economic thought, and to most economic policy-makers, the economy is "working" only when it is growing. Environmentalism is thus seen to be post-industrialist and post-materialist; a popular slogan among Greens has been "neither right nor left nor in the center," indicating their distinction from all established parties.

FIGURE 4.4 Eco-Terrorism—Extremism in the Name of Environmental Protection

While most environmentalists embrace non-violent means to advance their political ideas, a small but significant component of the environmental movement chooses to operate outside the institutions and processes of liberal democracy. So-called "eco-terrorists" deploy tactics that are typically designed to disrupt the public or destroy property associated with those believed to be enemies of the environment. For example, in 2003 a number of Hummer dealerships in Southern California were attacked by arsonists, causing millions of dollars of damage to these environmentally unfriendly vehicles. Similarly, some animal rights activists attempt to disrupt or destroy university research facilities where animals are being utilized in experiments. Most prominently, the Animal Liberation Front (ALF), active in almost three dozen countries around the world, has among its stated aims "to inflict economic damage on those who profit from the misery and exploitation of animals." Similarly the Earth Liberation Front (ELF), which describes itself as an "underground movement with no leadership, membership or official spokesperson" (see <http://www.earthliberationfront.com/elf_news.htm>), mounts attacks on property that it deems to be threatening life—human or animal. Founded in Britain in the 1990s, it spread to the United States; in March 2001 the FBI named the ELF as the most important domestic source of terror.

The program of environmentalism is diverse, comprehensive, and still very much contested. All agree on the need to reduce, if not somehow eliminate, the production and eventual release by humans into the environment of toxic substances. How this should be done is a question of competing strategies: while some look for non-toxic alternatives, some stress eliminating the need for such substances at all. Some will be concerned with the regulatory mechanisms already in place (or not), while others will urge using market mechanisms to provide incentives for polluters rather than legal sanctions as disincentives. An issue of some debate is whether it is more appropriate to develop new ecologically sound technologies, such as alternative energy sources (wind, solar panels, etc.), or to work to change the structure of societies and accordingly human consumption habits. All environmentalists wish to stop new development that is harmful to the environment, all wish to clean up or eliminate those activities that are currently harming the environment; the question for many is, is this enough? Or does sustaining the planet that sustains us require us to change our lives more drastically? Must humans eventually consider a process of de-industrialization?

A final area of considerable debate and disagreement within environmentalism and among Greens concerns the political strategy of the movement/party. Should Greens be active as a political party, thus giving legitimacy to the very system that sustains a material-ist and unsustainable development? Or should they concentrate on getting their message across to the general public? It can be argued that Green parties and environmental interest groups have had con-siderable success on the front of public education. The surest proof of this is the tendency of *all* political parties today to at least make the right noises about their concern for environmental issues, even if their policies don't always demonstrate this.

It may be useful to think of **NATIONALISM** in liberal democracies as a (usually) subordinate element within the broader ideologies of conservatism, liberalism, and socialism. By contrast, in authoritar-ian regimes, nationalism can become the dominant element in the ideology of the state.

4.7.3
Nationalism

By nationalism we may mean several things, but behind them all stands the idea of "the nation," a term indicating (as discussed in Chapter One) a common identity and purpose that unite people for political purposes. A nation exists where a people share a common language, culture, religion, customs, and a shared understanding of their collective history as a people. Nation-states as we understand them today only emerged in Western Europe at the end of the feudal period as the patchwork system of feudal kingdoms, duchies, and principalities was forged into larger territorial units under the developing authority of absolute monarchs. The work of creating among citizens an identity corresponding to these larger political units was something accomplished after the demise of feudal society and owes much both to the first- and second-generation ideologies we have discussed and to the institutions and practices they have established and sustained. The notion of a national identity depends to a large degree on the development of means of communica-tion and travel and on the standardization of laws and institutions. Each of these serves to break down the differences that define local communities and provide them with their own unique identity. Nationalism, then, is the political dispositions that promote and maintain the interests of "the nation," so understood. There are three general forms in which we might encounter nationalism.

The first sense of nationalism is *the goal of achieving political autonomy or independence for a people* (that is, for the "nation"). Typ-ically this nationalism is a movement by a specific people within a larger society for self-determination, which may be seen to require the separation of a territorial unit inhabited by the "nation"; the

departure of a ruling colonial power; or, less drastically, the granting of various measures of political autonomy. The nationalism of
self-determination seeks greater autonomy (e.g., state-building) for
a people whose common identity marks them as a "nation" (which
may itself be contested). This is the nationalism that inspired revolutions (or national liberation movements) within territories in the
developing world that were ruled as colonies by European powers.
It is also the nationalism that motivates action for self-determination
by a people not successfully integrated into the larger identity of a
nation-state, a people who usually constitute a cohesive minority
within that state. The desire of a significant portion of the Québécois in Canada or of the Basque and Catalan peoples in Spain for
political autonomy are contemporary examples. Finally, the desire
for self-determination is the nationalism that feeds the dreams of
peoples without a state to establish one, e.g., the creation of Israel or
the desire of Kurds for their own homeland.

A second sense of nationalism has the goal of creating, fos-
tering, or sustaining a common identity among the citizens of a
political state. In many cases this is an attempt to unite those who
otherwise do not see themselves as sharing a common identity (an
exercise often called **NATION-BUILDING**). This is the nationalism that
lay behind the creation of modern nation-states out of smaller communities and societies. That nations are often so constructed is more
obvious perhaps to citizens of newer nations like the United States,
Canada, and Australia, where peoples of various backgrounds and
experiences share a nation-state. In the case of Canada, at least, the
question of national identity (i.e., what it means to be a Canadian)
is very much still in debate. On the other hand, the disintegration
of what once was Yugoslavia, the divorce of the Czech Republic
and Slovakia, and the falling apart of the former Soviet Union indicate how the nationalism of nation-building can sometimes fail to
overcome and supplant the more particular identities of ethnic and
linguistic communities, which maintain their integrity within the
larger nation-state. In the absence of integration into a larger whole,
it is perhaps inevitable that such communities look for a degree
of self-determination. The failure to create a common Yugoslav-
ian identity is reflected in the desire of Croats, Serbs, Bosnians,
Slovenians, etc. to obtain and preserve their own geo-political
autonomy—and in their willingness to engage in brutal warfare
and widespread civilian destruction for that purpose.

The third sense we may attach to nationalism is an emphasis on the integrity or priority of the nation-state. This is a rather
vague description that covers a variety of stances that oppose

something we might with similar vagueness call internationalism. The tendency in foreign policy, for example, to act unilaterally, rather than in concert with other nations or through supra-national organizations such as the United Nations is one such expression; isolationism, in which a country withdraws from activity in the international arena, is another. (The United States has, at various times during the past century, exhibited both of these tendencies.) Free traders are economic internationalists; their counterparts are economic nationalists, who may advocate protectionism or national standards with respect to employment, environmental policies, or restrictions on foreign investment. In Canada the protection of cultural industries and the general concern to prevent cultural assimilation by the United States is a familiar example of nationalism in this last, and perhaps most politically benign, sense.

Each of these senses of nationalism—self-determination, nation-building, national preference—is compatible with the mainstream ideologies we have discussed. One could be a conservative nationalist, or a liberal nationalist, or a conservative internationalist, or a socialist who is nationalist on economic issues and internationalist on foreign policy, etc. At the same time, there are certain affinities or tendencies for specific ideologies to be nationalist or internationalist. Liberalism, because it celebrates the individual and not the group, very often favors internationalism and is suspicious of nationalism (which it rightly associates with conservatism). Communism or radical socialism is also internationalist, since it ultimately promotes solidarity with humanity as a whole or at least among the working classes worldwide. On this basis one might regard socialism and social democracy as more susceptible to nationalism than is communism. On the other hand, communist regimes have often been totalitarian authoritarian states, highly motivated to tap into nationalism whenever it has suited their purposes. Ultimately, all ideologies have demonstrated an ability to accommodate nationalism, depending on the circumstances and the context.

4.8 Beyond Ideology?

As indicated earlier, ideology is often viewed unfavorably; to be called an *ideologue*—someone who adheres closely to an ideology—is rarely a compliment. The supposedly negative features are that ideology is simplistic and one-sided, **DOGMATIC**, biased, and emotional. There is enough truth to each of these claims to merit a closer examination. We have noted that ideology is simpler than philosophy, and this is something that makes it accessible to the public. It is not far from simpler to simplistic, to the claim that the world is more complex than the picture ideology typically presents, a picture which for that reason is inadequate. This view of ideology as one-sided is related to the particular perspective that is often unique to an ideology. For example, Marxists may emphasize class struggle while feminists may focus on patriarchy. This suggests that there may often be validity to the characterization of ideology as one-sided. *Both* class and patriarchy may be features of contemporary social relations, but to take either by itself as the whole or dominant truth *is* one-sided. It may be then that part of the price ideology pays to be popular or accessible is to remain one-sided or at times simplistic. Is this too large a price to pay?

To call ideology dogmatic is to say that its adherents insist on the truth of their belief system come what may and will admit no exceptions, accept no challenges, or rethink no principles. This is of course an observation that speaks more about those who believe in an ideology and about the way they believe than about ideology itself. To adhere uncritically to an ideology may not be uncommon, but neither is it something necessarily entailed by ideology. To identify ideologies as biased is significant only if there is by comparison an "unbiased" way of thinking that is somehow more "objective" than ideology. With the demise of the myth of "value-free" inquiry years ago, it is not clear what that more objective way might be. Ideologies are no more or less biased than philosophies, theories, or any other systematic bodies of beliefs or ways of thinking. Ideologies *are* partial in the sense we identified above, given that they entail a specific way of seeing, but that is as much their strength as their weakness. Finally, the claim that ideologies are emotional is like the claim they are dogmatic: it is a claim about those who hold an ideology and about how it excites them. Ideologies often make emotional appeals on the strength of the symbols and slogans they employ, and one of the strengths of ideology may well be that as a simplified system it is capable of appealing to affect rather than intellect. Nevertheless, there is no reason to assert that this is the only appeal of ideology or even necessarily its strongest appeal.

Criticisms of ideology come down to one point which is well taken: ideology can become a substitute for independent thinking, for analysis, and for reflection. The individual attaches herself to a belief system and thereafter allows her judgment to be determined more or less automatically by the prescriptions of the ideology. Like all uncritical forms of thought, ideology employed in such a manner is deserving of disdain. However, there is nothing in the nature of ideology that requires it to be employed uncritically or dogmatically. And, in fact, there is ample evidence to suggest that most citizens are not tightly constrained by coherent ideological dispositions. Philip Converse (1964), for example, suggests that very few Americans—perhaps scarcely one in ten—make use of ideological concepts (such as "left" or "right") to structure their political thinking. Instead, most citizens seem to be ideological polyglots, capable of selecting from a number of (sometimes contradictory) ideologies in framing their political outlooks. As a result, the distribution of ideas among democratic citizens in the real world of political life is far more complicated than the world of ideologies might lead us to believe (Dalton, 2002: 13-31).

If we do not have ideology, then what? Moving in the direction of a *more* systematic, consistent, more nuanced way of thinking about politics brings us to political philosophy (although, as noted, where the line is crossed from ideology to philosophy, or vice-versa, is not clear). In some utopias, perhaps all citizens can be philosophers, but this is simply not a possibility in the society in which we now live, whatever might be the merits of such a state of affairs. In the opposite direction we move towards what might at its best be called an expedient approach to politics and what is at worst a wholly unprincipled, often inconsistent thinking about politics. Expedience can well avoid some of the pitfalls we have identified as possible companions of ideology, but it can also mean losing two of its central virtues. First, ideology is principled; fundamental propositions about what is right or wrong in the social and political realm run through an ideology and structure it. This means that its adherents are also guided by such propositions, and the consequence of this is that their political judgments and activity are not simply the product of the most narrowly defined or circumstantially constrained calculations of self-interest. Thus, political judgments gain some measure of objectivity, and in this way they become subjects for public debate, challenge, and re-thinking. These latter activities, of course, are at the heart of any meaningful democracy. Secondly, and not wholly unconnected with the last, ideology is goal-directed, animated by a vision of what is the best world, the best of all possible worlds, or the best we can make of this world. Political judgments informed by ideology, then, are oriented towards making the world in some way a better place (or preserving it from forces that would make it worse). Here, too, politics becomes more than simply reacting to circumstances or accepting the world as it is and surviving in it; instead of being the passive product of social and technological forces, ideology expresses our desire to shape our world, to engage in the kind of purposive action that is essentially human.

Key Terms

Christian Democracy
class
collective ownership
communists
conservatism
constitutionalism
democracy
dogmatic
ecology
environmentalism
feminism
ideologue
ideology
individualism
laissez-faire
liberalism
libertarian
limited state
market autonomy
Marxists
mixed government
nationalism
nation-building
patriarchy
proletariat
reform
representative government
responsible government
revolution
rights
self-determination
separation of powers
social democrats
socialism
status quo
"the third way"
toryism
welfare state

In our view, then, ideology—ideology that is employed and acquired critically in a manner that remains open to debate and challenge—has an important role to play in the real world of political citizenship. The catch, and there always is a catch, is to appropriate the good points about ideology—its systematic, principled, goal-directed approach to politics—while avoiding its pitfalls—its one-sidedness and the temptation it can bring with it to cease thinking for oneself.

References and Suggested Readings

Bell, Daniel. 1960. *The End of Ideology*. New York: Free Press of Glencoe.

Berlin, Isaiah. 1969. *Four Essays on Liberty*. Oxford: Oxford University Press.

Carson, Rachel. 1962, 1994. *Silent Spring* (with an Introduction by Al Gore). Boston: Houghton Mifflin.

Converse, Philip. 1964. "The Nature of Belief Systems in Mass Publics," in D. Apter, ed., *Ideology and Discontent*. New York: The Free Press.

Dalton, Russell J. 2002. *Citizen Politics: Public Opinion and Political Parties in Advanced Industrial Democracies*, 3rd ed. New York: Chatham House.

Dworkin, Andrea. 1976. *Our Blood: Prophecies and Discourses on Sexual Politics*. New York: Harper and Row.

Friedan, Betty. 1963. *The Feminine Mystique*. New York: W.W. Norton.

Giddens, Anthony. 1998. *The Third Way: The Renewal of Social Democracy*. Cambridge: Polity Press.

Huntington, Samuel P. 1957. "Conservatism as an Ideology." *American Political Science Review* 51 (June): 454-73.

Kolakowski, Leszek. 1978. *Main Currents of Marxism: The Founders*. Oxford: Oxford University Press.

Millet, Kate. 1970. *Sexual Politics*. Garden City, NY: Doubleday.

Nisbet, Robert. 1986. *Conservatism: Dream and Reality*. Minneapolis, MN: University of Minnesota Press.

Nozick, Robert. 1974. *Anarchy, State, and Utopia*. New York: Basic Books.

Oakeshott, Michael. 1962. *Rationalism in Politics*. London: Methuen.

Plamenatz, John. 1970. *Ideology*. London: Macmillan.

Sargent, Lyman Tower. 1987. *Contemporary Political Ideologies*, 7th ed. Chicago, IL: Dorsey Press.

World Commission on Environment and Development. 1987. *From One Earth to One World: An Overview*. Oxford: Oxford University Press.

Wolff, Robert Paul. 1970. *In Defense of Anarchism*. New York: Harper Torchbooks.

FIVE | Political Culture: The Collective Consciousness of a Polity

"Culture is a system of attitudes, values, and knowledge that is widely shared within a society and transmitted from generation to generation."

—Inglehart, 1990

"The study of public opinion has developed from a glorified kind of fortune telling into a practical way of learning what the nation thinks."

—Gallup and Rae, 1940

If political philosophy is the domain of philosophers and ideology the territory of political activists and partisans, then political culture is the world of all of us, regardless of our political education or our degree of political interest. By focusing on political culture in this chapter, we therefore extend our consideration of the role of ideas in political life to its natural maximum. Every society possesses a **POLITICAL CULTURE** (and, often, many political subcultures), and this broad term encompasses many elements concerning the intellectual dispositions (e.g., **BELIEFS, ATTITUDES, VALUES**) that people have about politics. A political culture is an aggregate like "the public" or "society"; it indicates a collection of the ideas of the individuals who comprise a community. For this reason it is something independent of the ideas of any *particular* individual. Each of us reflects, more or less, the political culture of the society we inhabit or have been raised in, and the "more or less," as well as the way in which we acquire political culture, can be particularly challenging to measure and demonstrate. Social scientists study political culture because they believe that what people think about the political world shapes their behavior, their consent, or their level of tolerance. It is often suggested that political culture defines the boundaries of political activity within a polity and in this way limits the realm of political possibility. Within any given society

5.1
Introduction: Defining Political Culture

certain policies are seen to be legitimate, others not; political debate, competition for authority, and the actual implementation of policy will generally occur within the boundaries of acceptability defined by the political culture. Many Americans view with suspicion the kind of government-funded and administered health care that their neighbors to the north in Canada take for granted or even venerate. Australians tend to espouse an egalitarianism that scorns the deference to authority for which the British, at least in the past, have been noted.

This chapter begins with a definition of political culture and a discussion of its main dimensions and sources. We then turn to a consideration of the primary means by which political cultures are created and shaped, looking at the processes of political socialization and of communication through the media. Like other topics in political behavior, analyses of political culture have come to rely heavily on public opinion surveys. Therefore, it is important for students to have at least a general understanding of what is involved in the measurement of attitudes, **OPINIONS**, and values through survey research. Finally in this chapter we consider how and why political cultures change. We will review some of the most influential work in the study of political culture by Harvard's Robert Putnam and the University of Michigan's Ronald Inglehart.

To begin historically, the academic study of political culture had its origins in precisely such observations about differences among countries in the political orientations of their citizens. American individualism, British reserve and deference, Italian passion and emotion, etc., all led scholars to reflect upon the notion of "national character" (Barker, 1927). These early works often were little more than exercises in cultural stereotyping by country, and the use of such generalizations in explanation was often problematic. For example, it was often held that the French experienced many political upheavals in their political history because they had a revolutionary culture. Can you see the difficulty with this kind of "explanation"? Does it not merely substitute "explanation" for a process of development that might be seen as a "description" of that same process? Still, national character studies usefully pointed up the fact that political understandings do seem to vary widely both across and within countries. The desire to understand these cross-national and intra-national differences led to the development of the concept of political culture and a variety of ways to observe it.

Let us begin by regarding a political culture as *the collective political consciousness of a polity* and then deconstruct this a little. First, consider the ways in which political culture is collective and not individual. As noted above, individuals reflect more or less a political culture, and this is for at least a couple of reasons. One is the size and complexity of modern societies, which are no longer homogenous communities. In a small, completely homogeneous community—that is, one where all have the same beliefs about politics, religion, ethics, etc.—it might be reasonable to expect each mature individual to reflect quite accurately the political culture of the community, because in such a society each individual is a miniature copy of the whole (this is akin to what French sociologist Emile Durkheim called "mechanical solidarity"). The pluralism of modern society, then, is one reason that the whole remains greater than the sum of its parts; the fluidity of modern society is another. That is, people do not spend their lives in one locale but often come and go many times in a life, great distances and small, and in doing so partake of many different cultures in different degrees.

There are also the effects of the increasing pace of social and technological change. In political terms, for example, the television age is less than 50 years old, which means that there are people whose beliefs about politics are still influenced, if not shaped, by their experience of a political world before the dominance of **MASS MEDIA**. For those under the age of 25, though, political knowledge and attitudes may be based principally if not entirely upon television news and political coverage. People's political dispositions and normative beliefs are often nostalgic, that is, influenced by how they remember circumstances at an earlier stage in their lives. Two or three centuries ago, an individual's way of life and experiences might not have been very different from those of her parent or grandparent; today no two decades are alike, and siblings born half a dozen years apart may seem to have grown up in different worlds. All of these considerations should clarify why we note that the beliefs, attitudes, or values of any particular individual tell us nothing about the political culture in general. We have to aggregate or collect the totality of beliefs present in the population to get a picture of the culture and hence of its effect on the world of political action. We should emphasize that it is only individuals who have beliefs, values, attitudes, etc. There is no sense to phrases like "society believes that ..." or "American values ..."; we are simply pointing out that the collective shape of our beliefs, attitudes, and values is very different from any particular individual's perspective.

Political culture refers to our orientations to political objects, and if this seems rather obvious, the point is to realize the diversity of objects that are political, a point we will clarify somewhat by talking about the kinds of attitudes involved—each kind of attitude corresponds to certain kinds of objects. More problematic is our description of political culture as "consciousness," for what do we make of the subconscious, or unconscious, or what is implicitly conscious but has yet to be stated? If a researcher enters the classroom and asks first-year university students to respond to questions about foreign policy issues, what is being measured? These students may have never considered the question: "which is the greatest threat to world peace: abject poverty or religious fundamentalism?" Is the response recorded actually measuring the student's attitude, or is the exercise actually *creating* attitudes that didn't previously exist? This is not a trivial point, because this *is* the way political culture is most often measured: through survey research. It is also the way that public opinion **POLLING** operates, and we will need to consider the possibility that public opinion is not measured but is rather *constructed* by those who purport to be measuring. The easiest way to avoid the question of consciousness would be to describe political culture instead as the way we as groups or as citizens of a country think about political objects; in this way we could see the answer to the question about which nation threatens world peace as shaped by the political culture, whether or not it was a newly minted opinion. As individuals, we are ultimately the bearers of political cultural properties, but like other forms of culture, political cultures are only identifiable in collective terms. The difficulty is that this formulation—the way we learn to think about politics—tends to focus again on individuals rather than on the collective product of individual consciousness.

5.2
Beliefs, Attitudes, Values

It is not accidental that we keep referring to beliefs, attitudes, and values, for while these terms may seem interchangeable, they can be used to refer to three distinct kinds of ideas that we have about politics. The initial distinction between cognitive, affective, and evaluative ideas in the political culture was made by Gabriel Almond and Sidney Verba in *The Civic Culture* (1963). And, as we noted above, each kind of idea refers to different categories of political object.

The distribution and content of our political knowledge represents the **COGNITIVE** foundations of our political ideas: these contain our knowledge about the political world and obviously will depend very much on our education about politics, whether formal or informal. Periodically we are informed that a low percentage of Americans can name their Member of Congress, or that large numbers remain unclear about just what Congress does, or about the division of powers between state and federal governments. Given the low importance attached to political education in the public school system, and the tendency of mass media to report events rather than explain them, low levels of political knowledge in the population should not surprise us. It can be seen, though, as an impediment to democracy or, alternatively, as the sign that not much is expected of citizens in our system; people inform themselves when they have pressing reasons to do so.

Of course, an absence of specific knowledge about politics does not always discourage individuals from developing and expressing rather strong political positions. Attitudes refer to those ideas that are laden with **AFFECT**: our dispositions for or against particular political objects. For example, one attitude social scientists measure is *support*, and David Easton (1965) has identified three foci of political support: (1) the community, (2) the regime (what we have called the state), and (3) the authorities (the government). These are useful and important distinctions. It is one of the strengths of democracy that it allows citizens to oppose the government while still supporting the state (the institutional system). In federal countries like the United States and Canada there may be important differences in levels of support for any of these three foci divided yet again between national and provincial or state level. Separatists in the Canadian province of Quebec who want the province to become an independent sovereign state, for example, attach support to a different kind of community than to others who live in that province.

Two other political orientations commonly measured are dispositions of **TRUST** and **EFFICACY**, which might, like support, be directed to the state (especially efficacy) and/or the government (especially trust). In the United States it has become customary to decry the rise of cynicism, alienation, and anger, and to bemoan the loss of trust in our political leaders and institutions. Polls taken since the early 1990s reveal that only about one-quarter of American adults express confidence that the federal government could be trusted to "do what is right" most of the time (down from 75 per cent in 1958).[1] Efficacy, on the other hand, measures the degree to which an individual feels that her participation or activity is worthwhile, meaningful, "makes a difference." Those who feel politicians never listen to the people, or that their vote makes no difference, are clearly low in efficacy. Many have noted an increase in the numbers of citizens expressing low levels of efficacy. Polling data (see Dalton, 2002) revealed that in 1994 two-thirds of Americans reported that "elected officials do not care what 'people like

1 See, for example, the Pew Research Center's "How Americans View Government: Deconstructing Distrust," 10 March 1998, <http://people-press.org/reports/display.php3?ReportID=95>.

me' think," for example (up from 49 per cent in 1987). Similar movements in public opinion have been identified in other liberal democratic polities.

It is striking that social scientists and public opinion pollsters alike have found very little good news in North America, particularly in the 1990s, insofar as support, trust, and efficacy are concerned. This is particularly true of public attitudes towards politicians, who now very often compete with lawyers for last place on the list of esteemed professions. In many cases, being a career politician or a political insider is now seen to be a liability for political candidates. In the 1994 national (congressional) election in the United States, only 38 per cent of eligible voters bothered to cast a ballot, and the 1996 presidential election recorded the support of less than half the registered electorate. All of this serves as evidence that something is not well with the political culture of North American democracies or with a political process with which citizens seem increasingly dissatisfied. Unfortunately, the list of possible causes or suspects—from the mass media to flaws in the institutional machinery, the professionalization of politics, the politicians themselves, the unreasonable demands of citizens, etc.—is too lengthy for us to pursue in this space.

We employ the term "values" to designate **EVALUATIVE** or normative ideas about the political world. Already we have considered such ideas at rather extended length in our discussions of political philosophy and ideology, both of which occupy a large place in the political culture of almost any polity. There are also (in most political cultures) certain evaluative ideas or norms that cut across the differences of ideology and yet which are too widespread to be the particular domain of philosophers. A commitment to democracy is one such idea, and one we expect to hold a central place in the political culture of democratic polities. The level of this commitment can vary considerably, though, as can the understanding of what is being supported or demanded by such a value. If democracy is based on the notion of *majority rule* as it is often held to be in North American societies, it is the case that in many European countries democracy means *consensus*, a more demanding standard. Nonetheless, in Western democracies we expect to find conservatives, liberals, and socialists all stressing their democratic credentials.

Central political values like democracy, or certain norms of justice, can be an interesting basis for comparison between political cultures; many political scientists have contrasted the political cultures of Canada and the United States by comparing key political values supposed to be dominant in each (Lipset, 1990). Canadians are said to demonstrate much greater *deference to authority* than Americans, meaning that they have more willingly accepted the necessity of hierarchy and authority and been willing to obey their "superiors." It is possible to imagine any number of axes we might construct with opposing value terms at either pole of each axis. The political culture of any polity could, in theory, be located at a point on the axis and compared with other cultures. One such axis might put egalitarianism at one end and elitism at the other. Most observers would probably put Australia, for example, towards the egalitarian end, meaning not that Australia is in fact a country more equal than others (although it may be), but rather that egalitarianism is highly valued in its political culture. The United States has traditionally been believed to value egalitarianism highly (although not as highly as liberty or enterprise), but the United States is also one of the developed world's most inegalitarian countries. Another axis might oppose "tolerance of diversity" to "pressure for conformity." Another might oppose "individualism" to "collectivism." There are numerous possibilities here.

Each of the ideas discussed in the previous section—beliefs, attitudes, and values—can be measured directly by asking individuals to respond to questions (and, of course, by aggregating the results) or indirectly by analyzing political speeches, party platforms, newspaper editorials, and the literature and songs of a people. What all this obscures is how modern the notion of such a measurable political culture is. Two hundred years ago in most modern polities *a* political culture that could be found among "the people" did not exist. The kind of political culture we have been describing in this chapter presupposes the development of a mass society, a society that overcomes differences of space, class, education, etc., to create a set of shared understandings or of contexts for dispute. This may be easier to see by thinking about some of the things that had to happen for a **MASS CULTURE** to emerge.

Let us begin with the creation of nation-states at the end of the feudal period, as discussed much earlier. This wasn't simply the consolidation of territory and people under one ruler but under one set of common rules, displacing local customs and traditions with the uniformity of law. Over time this also meant standardization of other aspects of social life, such as language, forging both a common pronunciation and spelling out of a variety of local variations or dialects. The invention and development of printing was of incalculable significance, especially once education ceased

5.3
Mass Culture and Socialization

to be the privilege of the wealthy and became in some small degree general and brought with it general literacy. General education was to a certain degree more practical, and perhaps necessary, once humans began to live in cities and towns rather than scattered through the countryside. Urbanization erodes a great deal of the distinctiveness of locality, especially insofar as cities, the sites of the development and application of technologies of every kind, become more and more alike over time. As railroads, then the automobile, and finally the airplane made travel a commonplace rather than an adventure, differences in lifestyle were further erased by the ease with which ideas and **INFORMATION** could also travel. No doubt the most significant contribution to the development of mass culture, though, and building on the rest of it, has been the emergence of electric and electronic means of communications. The telegraph, telephone, radio, television, cable and satellite communications, and now the personal computer not only give each of us windows on the wider world but make what each of us sees through the windows more and more alike. Finally, we may add the growth of the multinational corporation and the globalization of the marketplace to note the continued homogenization of mass culture to a degree that may soon (if it has not already begun) to erode the distinctiveness of national cultures.

Interestingly, the growth of a mass culture has paralleled the growth of a political public; at the end of the feudal period and during the first centuries of the modern era, the political class (those with political rights and political influence) comprised a small elite within the larger society. With the creation and development of mass society and of the mass culture that accompanies it, the pressure for representation of the broader public in the political system mounted. The creation of a political class that, in theory at least, includes adults of all classes and gender (in other words, *democracy*) was in most cases a belated response to changing social and economic realities unleashed by industrialization. On the other hand, we should also consider that many new nation-states, often artificially put together by colonial administrators, have yet to complete the transition to a mass society, a transition that is readily taken for granted in developed countries because most of the transformations took place in previous generations. These newer nations have yet to develop a national identity transcending region or tribe and have yet to forge a common political culture or strong institutions of civil society. Not surprisingly, political instability is not uncommon.

What we have been describing are the various means by which humans have shrunk the differences of space and time, which lead to differences in experience, ways of life, and ultimately of ideas and understandings—of culture. Some barriers between different cultures are less permeable than others—language, for example, which has always been closely linked to culture, or religious differences, or collective historical memories—but these too are probably less impenetrable than ever. As the forces that shape our culture have changed with modernization and the growth of technology, so too have the ways by which culture is transmitted from one generation to another in what is generally called **SOCIALIZATION**.

By socialization we indicate the processes by which individuals acquire the values and beliefs of their society or community. Our political dispositions are not innate but are learned or acquired at various stages of our experience of the world. Socialization is a means by which political culture is transmitted to new generations of citizens, and unless there is a conscious effort to do otherwise, the process is generally conservative—reinforcing the status quo, the values and norms currently popular or dominant in society—in part because socialization is usually a byproduct of other activities. Although not everyone would agree, it is possible to view socialization and education as different processes. Education is a deliberate attempt, on the part of others and/or ourselves, to impart or gain knowledge and skills or to refine talents and aptitudes. Taking or teaching a political science course is education, not socialization. Starting the school day with the national anthem or pledging allegiance to the flag are examples of experiences that socialize by generating attitudes or habits of mind.

Most discussions of socialization make two observations, one about *agents* which transmit cultural material and one about the *stages* or timing of socialization. For example, typical agents of socialization are parents, teachers, and peers, and this should not surprise us, since these are the people with whom we have primary contact

---

FIGURE 5.1 Documentary Films and Political Socialization

One of the most interesting developments in the last several decades has been the emergence of politically charged documentaries as spark plugs in enhancing the salience of particular issues or causes. For example, former Vice-President Al Gore's film *An Inconvenient Truth* (2005) has been credited with a significant increase in the public's concern over global warming. Widely viewed, the film has grossed over $24 million in the United States and over $49 million worldwide (as of June 3, 2007).

More controversially, Michigan native Michael Moore has directed a number of films that have been highly critical of the United States government and its policies. In *Bowling for Columbine* (2002), for example, Moore criticizes the permissive gun culture prevalent in the United States. In *Fahrenheit 9/11* (2004) Moore took aim at the Bush Administration's reaction to the terrorist tragedies in 2001 and the war in Iraq. Most recently, his film *Sicko* (released in 2007) points up the shortcomings of the American health care system in which there are 50 million citizens without insurance, 9 million of them children. Adding to his controversial stature, Moore often contrasts the American situation with a more preferred (i.e., more state interventionist) alternative found north of the border in Canada, where both gun control and universal public medical care are in place.

With audiences in the millions worldwide, it remains to be seen how viewing these highly charged "shockumentaries" will influence the socialization of American citizens (and those of other countries).

145

in our formative years when we are being inducted into our political culture. Pivotal or historic events, such as 9/11, may also play an important role in our socialization. Repeating the point made above, these agents do not (or do not *normally*) deliberately strive to socialize us, but they end up participating in our socialization by teaching us, playing with us, nurturing us, etc. The degree to which socialization is regarded as involving an unconscious accumulation of dispositions and habits on our part is also indicated by all the discussion of how we are socialized most in our early years and, like the proverbial old dog, become increasingly unwilling to learn new tricks as we grow older.

Discussion of the agents of socialization can tend to emphasize the personal dimension—how we are shaped by our interaction with other individuals. It is also the case that we are socialized by institutions or by individuals in their institutional capacity. The influence of our parents is profoundly personal, but at the same time it reflects the role of the institution we call the family. As the structure of the family changes and diversifies, we can expect increasing speculation and research into the effects on the socialization of children. Teachers are agents of socialization because of the institutionalization of education in our society. Once upon a time in most Western societies (and in parts of some of them still today) the Church was an important agent of socialization. In recent decades a new agency has risen to prominence: the television set—in part because the television set has taken over to some degree (and in some cases quite a large degree) the roles of parent, best friend, teacher, or even pastor. Again, television programs (generally) do not aim to socialize young viewers but to inform or, more usually, entertain them. It is in the process of informing or entertaining that they socialize by helping reinforce or transmit values, beliefs, or attitudes prevalent in our culture. If, for example, in all television programs, women are portrayed as stay-at-home Moms, then this may well transmit or reinforce the attitude that a woman's primary vocation is to find a husband and have children. This is one reason for the concern about stereotypes in the media: they tend to reinforce the attitudes responsible for such stereotypes. As increasing numbers of young citizens are linked through their computers and Internet sites like "Facebook" and "YouTube" we may see the emergence of yet another agency of socialization.

Socialization matters because it is the way a political culture is passed on from one generation to another, a transmission that is in all likelihood always somewhat imperfect or incomplete. Despite the disposition socialization has towards reproducing the status quo, each new generation will undoubtedly have its own perspective also. We will discuss the phenomenon of political cultural change later in this chapter, but suffice it to say here that cultures are not deterministic. Indeed, socialization is a life-long process, and no one is too old to change. However, to the extent that our formative orientations are formed early in our lives, when we are most impressionable, and that we become less susceptible to influence or unlikely to change our fundamental dispositions later, socialization warns us that there are limits to what is politically possible or what we can expect particular publics to support or accept.

To offer an extended example, we have noted the presence in political cultures of advanced industrial societies of the "value" that involves a belief in and commitment to democracy. This usually does not mean the kind of direct democracy practiced in ancient Athens, or the participatory legislature that Rousseau spoke of in *The Social Contract*, and with good reason—our societies are too large and the tasks of governing too specialized and continuous for much "government by the people." Not surprisingly, we are socialized not to demand or expect too much of a say in how we are governed. The institutional limitations to democracy are buttressed by cultural messages that are transmitted from generation to generation. The belief in democracy that is central to our political culture is at the same time a limited belief in democracy, just as the democracy of our institutions entails a limited public participation. Hand in hand with the belief in the legitimacy of democracy often goes the age-old suspicion of "the public" or of its competence to judge how authority and power should be exercised. The phrase "too much democracy is dangerous" seems to capture this ambivalence: democracy is good so long as it is kept within limits and not taken too far.

The socialization process in representative democracies often reflects and reinforces this ambivalence toward democracy. Consider the amount of democratic decision-making that citizens are likely to encounter in non-governmental organizations or institutions. Most areas of individual life—the family, the school, the Church, the workplace—are dominated by authority structures of a non-democratic (if not authoritarian) nature. When we consider that it is primarily within such settings that citizens are socialized, it should not surprise us that many citizens are ambivalent about democracy nor that non-democratic or authoritarian attitudes are not infrequently encountered within a nominally democratic political culture (Eckstein, 1966).

For many of us living today, the history of the world beyond us has footage, a set of remembered television images on file somewhere in our minds—the film of Jack Ruby shooting Lee Harvey Oswald, astronauts golfing on the moon, crowds milling back and forth at the Brandenburg Gate as the Berlin Wall came down, the twin towers of the World Trade Center collapsing, and so on. So, too, for most of us, our perceptions and attitudes (if not our knowledge and understanding also) of political figures and institutions are mediated by images relayed by television or headlines in newspapers (although more likely the former than the latter). One of the most important contributions to the mass culture described in the last section, and certainly what shapes it most today, is the mass communications technologies or media developed in this century. We are living today in "the television age" of politics, and it is noteworthy that we are just beginning to grasp the significance of this, just as it is easy to overlook that the television age in the United States is less than 50 years old (if dated from the Kennedy-Nixon debate of 1960). In this debate, it has been widely argued that Kennedy's youthful appearance in contrast with Nixon's haggard look (complete with a "five o'clock shadow") contributed to the former's subsequent victory in the presidential context. It is easy to overlook because of the extent to which television today dominates not just the coverage of politics (to the degree that many newspapers like *USA Today* are clearly modeled on television-style presentation of news) but the way politics is practiced—from the domination of election campaigns to the centrality of the scheduled or unscheduled news conference to the presentation of congressional business on a specialty cable channel. Does this matter?

Representative democracy rests in part on an ongoing relationship between the people and the political elites they elect. Crucial to this relationship is the information available to the public about their representatives through media such as newspapers, radio, and television. When accountability is provided for by the granting or withholding of support at election time, an informed vote requires information about the performance (past, present, and promised in the future) of candidates. Citizens can only evaluate their government on the basis of the information that is accessible to them. The interest of citizens is obviously in having the most thorough and penetrating information brought to their attention.

The reason it *does* matter how media such as television deliver the news, then, is that in a mass political culture, especially a democratic mass political culture, citizens require information about what the state, government, and politicians are or are not

Mediated reality

doing. The only means of delivering this information regularly and reliably to the general public is the resources of the mass media. Most citizens cannot inform themselves directly, and other possible sources—academic studies, government documents, private consultants—have too many limitations, ranging from bias to lack of timeliness to being prepared for a specialist public. The media, in short, plays a public role, and it is a key institution of civil society in any liberal democracy. To play this public role the media must be free from government censorship or other influence—what is normally meant by a "free press." Media firms are clearly aware of their public role, for they draw attention whenever they feel their liberty or privileges threatened.

From the beginning (newspapers) to the present (the Internet), the preponderance of news delivery has been through private companies, and the situation of private organizations performing a public function presents several interesting situations. One underlying issue here is the matter of accountability. Public institutions (or those who run them) must ultimately answer to the people either directly or through their elected representatives; private organizations must answer only to those who own them—the shareholders, who may be few or many. It is possible to regulate private corporations to force their compliance with certain public objectives, but the difficulty with regulating the press beyond a certain point is the possibility that governments might use the excuse of "public objectives" to exert political influence or even censorship of unfavorable publicity. Ultimately, the public requires not regulated but "responsible" journalism, which means the onus is on a self-regulated media. Insofar as the media are concerned to fulfill the public role of providing citizens with the best available information in an accessible and timely fashion, this is not problematic, but there are pressures inherent in the private ownership of media firms, and in the nature of the medium itself, which get in the way of this public responsibility.

By definition almost, private companies exist for the purpose of making a profit; those that do not generate a surplus for their owners will not be around long—unless their owners have very deep pockets and some reason for wanting to lose money. It is true that there have been media firms, particularly in the newspaper age, which were run not primarily for profit but to get a particular point of view before the public, to advance the interests of a particular party, or to provide some philanthropic patronage. These kinds of operations are increasingly rare and occupy a most minuscule share of the media market. Like almost everything else today, presenting the news is a business, and as a business it is expected to pay dividends to its shareholders. This raises the possibility that where there is a conflict between performing the public role (practicing responsible journalism that presents the public with critical, quality information) and realizing the private end (maximizing profits), shareholders will expect or want the latter to predominate. We are not saying that presenting quality information through responsible journalism cannot be profitable, just that there is no guarantee that it will be, and perhaps in today's mass society, there is less likelihood it will be.

This is because modern media companies are primarily concerned with two activities other than presenting the "news" that citizens need—selling advertising and providing **ENTERTAINMENT**—and the two are obviously linked. Media firms—newspapers, radio, and television alike—depend for the largest share of their revenue on the sale of advertising. Naturally, this creates pressures to provide whatever is most attractive to advertisers. Advertisers in turn will turn to those newspapers or TV stations that attract the most readers/viewers (or those most likely to buy the advertiser's service/product). If entertainment attracts more readers/viewers than does quality political journalism, or if sensational, superficial political journalism attracts more attention than serious, nuanced analysis, it is not hard to see how the need to stay profitable influences media products. Thus, most modern metropolitan newspapers are no longer only (or even primarily) about the presentation of news but are multi-dimensional publications that entertain readers in any number of ways. Television, of course, is a medium that is primarily about entertainment. Among others, Neil Postman (1985) has written about how the entertainment imperative also extends to the way that newspapers and television gather and present the news.

At least three kinds of exceptions exist to this hijacking of the serious public role of the mass media by the more profitable imperatives of entertainment, but like many exceptions they only prove the rule. One is the rare private media firm that caters to a market of serious information-seekers, people willing to pay for quality, responsible journalism presented as the only (or main) fare. This is particularly true of journals and magazines that can survive on grants, endowments, and subscriptions and hence eschew advertising revenue. Or, such publications can offer to advertisers a particular type of reader who suits the demographic profile that marketing research has identified as a potential buyer or client. Some newspapers, such as the *New York Times* or the *Washington Post*, cater to a more serious readership. These papers are able to do so by selling advertising space to sponsors who wish in turn to sell their product to this presumably higher income clientele. Such a paper, however influential and respected, remains outside the mainstream of popular culture; it is not read by many in the middle or working class. A second potential source of uncompromised journalism is public broadcasting, where radio and television are owned by the state, usually through an arm's-length arrangement like a Crown corporation (the Canadian Broadcasting Corporation [CBC], the British Broadcasting Corporation [BBC], etc.). Because funding comes from the state, such broadcasters are also released from the imperatives of pleasing advertisers and appealing to the markets that advertisers want. Here too, though, there are problems. If these networks succeed in attracting an audience of significant proportions, they do so often by offering a different or superior entertainment to the commercial networks. The serious documentaries and news affairs programming they present are usually among their least-watched shows, meaning that, again, serious journalism remains on the margins of popular culture. In recent decades, governments have been less willing to fund state enterprises like public broadcasting, which forces the networks to rely on popular subscriptions or fund-raising or turn to advertising as a principal revenue source. Once this happens, the same imperatives that determine the content of commercial television become the norm here too. A third possibility arises as a result of technological developments that have increasingly meant that "narrowcast" media with closely defined clienteles are replacing the traditional broadcast media aimed at a more general audience. A part of this involves the great expansion of "specialty" channels, but here also there seems to be a trade-off between ratings and seriousness of content. The more entertaining and visually focused—like CNN or Headline News or even NewsWorld—the larger the ratings; the more political and serious—C-Span—the smaller and more specialized the audience.

We have been discussing how the need for profitability of privately owned media firms leads them to present all manner of content, most or much of which has little to do with the public function of informing citizens for democratic judgment and participation. There are really two sets of issues here: one is the role of private ownership and profitability, which affects all types of media; the second is the nature of the particular medium itself and how this shapes the messages it delivers, and here the principal concern of most critics is with the limitations of television as a medium (privately *or* publicly owned).

The way in which concern with profitability shapes the way media firms operate is accentuated by the increasing concentration of ownership within the media world and the integration of media firms into larger corporate entities. In the second half of this century, the independent newspaper and the non-affiliated television station have become increasingly rare; newspaper chains and media companies that own strings of stations are now the norm. The next stage of concentration is when different branches of the media world are integrated in one corporate entity. Thus, the same company may own a television network, a movie studio, publishing interests, and recording companies. Cable distribution companies own specialty channels and operate cellular phone networks. The final stage is when these media conglomerates are themselves part of larger corporations that include non-media concerns like brewing, manufacturing, or financial services.

The increasing degree of corporate ownership and concentration raises several issues. First of all, it ensures that profitability will be a fundamental concern, if not *the* consideration before which all else must give way. It also means that the individuals who run media firms may themselves have no media background or experience but impressive credentials in achieving management objectives. Secondly, chain ownership and **CORPORATE CONCENTRATION** has tended to reduce the diversity of views put before the public in two ways. One, particularly in the newspaper world, has been the elimination of competition; few communities have more than one paper, and in many parts of the country all papers are owned by the same corporation. Secondly, even where there is competition, as may be more likely in television or radio, it can work to make companies more alike rather than different, as they copy each others' successes and learn from each others' failures. Lots of studios make Hollywood movies, but that's the point: they all make Hollywood movies. Unfortunately, opinion and information are areas where diversity rather than uniformity is what best suits the interests of the consumer. Finally, the degree of corporate ownership of media outlets raises questions of conflict of interest. One of the reasons a free press is central to liberal democracies is its ability to keep governments honest by shining the light of publicity on their misdeeds. But what if the government's actions are in the interests of the corporate sector that owns media firms, *or* if they are contrary to those interests? In either case, can the public expect a full, objective, critical discussion of the issues in the media outlets controlled by these interests? The state is not the only source of power in contemporary society; in capitalist economies there can be considerable power based on private wealth. Traditionally, the independent press has had as impressive a record in exposing abuses of private power as it has in blowing the whistle on public figures. The concentration of media power in the hands of a few large corporations endangers the ability of the press to be an effective public watchdog (Herman and Chomsky, 1988).

A wholly separate source of issues surrounds not the ownership of media but the nature of the media itself or, more exactly, of the medium by which information is transmitted. The concern of culture critics ever since Marshall McLuhan coined the phrase "the medium is the message" is that television, which has become the dominant medium, is unable (or unlikely) to present the kind of information that citizens need to evaluate properly their governments and representatives. One of the most compelling examinations of the limitations (or dangers) of the medium that is television is Neil Postman's *Amusing Ourselves to Death: Public Discourse in an Age of Show Business* (1985). The point at the heart of Postman's analysis, and indeed of all criticisms of television, is that it is image based. Images entertain, amuse, perhaps shock or amaze, but they do not easily permit (or encourage) debate, analysis, or thoughtful reflection. Postman argues that "embedded in the surrealistic frame of a television news show is a theory of anticommunication, featuring a type of discourse that abandons logic, reason, sequence, and rules of contradiction." He concludes that Americans are "the best entertained and quite likely the least well-informed people in the Western world" (1985: 105-06). The medium Postman opposes to television is, of course, the printed page of books, magazines, and perhaps newspapers. One of his arguments, though, is that the incoherence, triviality, and irrationality of television is leaking into other forms of communication, like newspapers and magazines, and that a public which is dependent on television for its information and culture will begin to think about the world in ways which mirror this medium: "How delighted would be all the kings, czars, and führers of the past (and commissars of the present) to know that censorship is not a necessity when all political discourse takes the form of a jest" (1985: 141).

Interestingly, an increasing body of evidence suggests that the public is finding the jest less and less amusing. The shallowness and anti-intellectual biases of television cannot, perhaps, always manage to amuse and entertain, particularly when coverage of what is supposed to be serious—elections, policy struggles, political crises—cannot be avoided. We have noted above the increasing disillusion with and distaste of the public for politicians and public officials. This would not seem consistent with the thesis that all television does is entertain—and where else can we look to explain public attitudes towards political actors *but* television? The last media topic we will explore, albeit briefly, is the peculiar relationship of journalists and politicians in "the television age"—briefly, because like many other aspects of the television age, the relationship of journalists and politicians is still evolving.

As Lance Bennett (1980, 1992), among others, has pointed out, journalists and politicians exist in an uneasy symbiosis: each is dependent on the other for what they need. Political actors need (preferably favorable) publicity; journalists need (preferably topical) information. This creates the potential for mutual accommodation and cooperation in many ways. A journalist who asks embarrassing questions risks getting shut out of future stories or not recognized at the next press conference. The journalist who presents the politician in a favorable or sympathetic light may well receive some inside information or background somewhere down the road. A politician who has the qualities the particular medium is looking for—snappy quotes (print), photogenic features (television), a sexy voice (radio)—is more likely to receive publicity than someone boringly verbose, physically "unattractive," or plagued with a squeaky or whiny voice. Most meetings between press and politicians are not spontaneous events but routine encounters both plan for: the scheduled press conference, the so-called scrum in the corridors of Congress, the office interview, the campaign bus or plane, etc. It is, of course, in the interest of both parties to make these encounters appear more spontaneous than they in fact are, so that much of the cooperation between the two sets of actors is hidden from the innocent public. In the last couple of decades, though, much has changed in the relationship between politicians and journalists, and it has changed largely because of the realization of the importance of television.

From journalists, we witness increasingly the phenomena associated with what has been called **JUDGMENTAL JOURNALISM**. This represents their response to the increasingly manipulative behavior of politicians in the attempt to control the outcome of their encounters with the media. The political **MANIPULATION** of the media in the television age is itself a product of the realization that politicians no longer control the content of the news. Each of these points needs a little further explanation.

Consider the fundamental character of political news in the age of print compared with political news in the age of television. In the former, the primary news takes the form of words. Politicians appear in the news through their statements (something that remains true or becomes even truer in the radio age). This means that politicians control the content of the news; whether delivering speeches, speaking from prepared texts, or responding to questions, they determine what will or will not be available for report. Journalists may choose to ignore these words, but on the printed page or the airwaves of radio without the words of politicians news is empty or just journalists' opinions. Moreover—and this is easily overlooked—in these pre-television times, the words politicians were speaking (and journalists recording) were being spoken *not* to journalists but to other politicians (in Congress, say) or to sections of the general public. This placed journalists in the role of supposedly neutral or objective observers or "reporters" to those sections of the public not present at these speeches. The ability of journalists to put their own "spin" on events was also limited by the fact that the spoken word is, or can be made to be, a matter of public record.

When the medium changes to television, which is image based, all kinds of material *other* than the speaker's words and their meaning become capable of transmission. The tone of voice, the delivery of a speech, nervous habits, a perspiring brow, yawning or amused faces in the audience, the dress and physical appearance of the candidate, whether the speaker is using notes, etc.—these and countless other aspects can now be shared with the wider public through television, and which of these is shared is no longer in the control of the politician but rather of the television cameraman, director, or producer. Television newscasts can edit footage to select the images to present, images that may or may not be flattering to political actors. And images *because* they are images "do not lie." They may be irrelevant to almost anything, but they can and do create impressions that may become relevant to everything. With the advent of television, control over the content of the news shifts, at least temporarily, to the journalists.

Over time, discerning politicians and their advisors realize what works and doesn't work on television. Political parties learn to judge what kinds of candidate attributes will or will not play well on the small screen. In any number of ways, political actors seek in the television age (in a way they never needed to in the print age) to manage the encounter with journalists. This means trying to control the timing, the setting, and the nature of the meetings between politicians and reporters. Attention is paid to the personal appearance of candidates in a way that was never quite done before; venues where politicians speak are scouted for how they will look on television and for the possible camera angles that will be used to portray the candidate; staged media events become the staple of election campaigns and sometimes of the "normal" non-election political day; "spin doctors" attempt to influence media interpretations and reactions. Political actors are no longer addressing words and through them ideas to (portions of) the public, but rather they pitch their message to the media in the hope that the images the media presents to the public will be favorable. In other words, politicians and their support staff try to manipulate the medium.

It is in part this attempt by political actors to use television in their favor that has turned reporters (by experience a cynical lot) into "judgmental journalists." No longer content to be simply the conduit through which politicians send their message to the public, journalists have become self-conscious about their own role—and the role of their medium—in the process. An attendant irony is that while television has become the dominant medium, there are still large numbers of print journalists covering politics and trying to find something to say about a presentation that is geared for the medium of image—television. Bennett (1992) reports that in the 1988 American election campaign the average television "sound bite" was 9.2 seconds, down from 14 seconds in 1984. As he notes, "It is hard to discuss the meaning of any 9.2 second slice of a text, particularly when such slices are constructed to stand alone, rendering the rest of the text something like a serving utensil" (1992: 23). Not surprisingly, journalists have less and less to report on the issues, or what candidates are saying, because the issues are increasingly irrelevant, because the candidates have less and less of substance to say. The attention of journalists turns to the campaign itself, to reporting how the parties and candidates are trying to manipulate journalists and the public in the attempt to gain support. Bennett reports on a study of the 1988 American election by Marjorie Harris, which found that coverage in the print media from September to election day was devoted two-thirds of the time to discussing the parties' campaign strategy: "In short, the campaign became its own news. The media reflected on their own role as never before, resulting in redundancy, self-referential logic, and loss of context, which are the hallmarks of postmodern symbolics. The media couldn't get out of their own loop" (1992: 26). As journalists become increasingly disillusioned with the political efforts to manipulate their media, it is small wonder that political figures are increasingly despised by a public less and less interested in politics. The technology that seems to offer the greatest potential ever for getting information to the public has in fact spawned a medium that leaves citizens less well informed than ever and by and large not a bit concerned about it. Worst of all, there seems to be very few practical ideas about how to make things any different.

W e have described how, in the course of their business, politicians seek to manage their encounters with journalists or, in less polite terms, seek to manipulate or "spin" the media. The ultimate aim of this activity, though, is not journalists but the

**5.5
The Politics of
Public Opinion**

wider public, the consumers of media. In an age where popular sovereignty has become a fundamental political value and political legitimacy rests (in the long if not the short term) on support from the public, political figures seek not merely to win elections but if possible to remain high in public opinion in the times between such contests. While political elites thus have an interest in an informed public, it is an interest in a public that is favorably informed, and political actors use their resources to enhance their public image whenever and wherever possible. In part, this emphasis on continued popularity rather than simply the ability to win an election campaign is the product of the development and increasing presence of public opinion polls. What we often overlook is that these polls are as much about the *construction* of public opinion as they are about its measurement.

Modern polling is a social science using refined techniques based on probability theory to enable investigators to obtain data from a relatively small sample of individuals and yet have a reasonable confidence that their findings are an accurate representation of the larger population. No-one (to our knowledge, at least) challenges the mathematical foundations in probability theory on which scientific polling rests, nor do we need to dwell on the practical difficulties encountered in actually taking a poll. What makes poll results somewhat artificial—what we might call "constructs" of public opinion—are several other characteristics.

First of all, the questions asked in an opinion survey are typically hypothetical, "what if ...?" kinds of statements that involve no actual commitment or activity on the part of the respondent. A pollster might ask "If there were an election today, which party would you vote for?" Is there any reason to believe that your answer today, when you know there is no election, would be the same as your actual vote today, if there were in fact an election? In other words, because you know the question is purely hypothetical, you know there is nothing at stake for you in your answer, and you are in fact free to answer however you like because there are no real-world consequences for you.

A second element, somewhat related to the first, is the very nature of *opinion*. A survey researcher simply wants your responses to her questions; very rarely will you be asked *why* you responded as you did and never will you be asked for evidence or logic to support your answer. Polling, in this way, does not seek judgments or expertise, in part because it is not equipped to make such distinctions, in part because those who do polls don't care. Polls are very egalitarian: everyone's opinion is equally valid. We are not arguing here that some people's opinions are more valid but rather that everyone's *considered judgment* is worth considerably more than their opinion. Indeed, a fool's judgment, based on thoughtful consideration of evidence or reasons, may be worth more than the ill-considered, hasty response of the genius. Again, the hypothetical or artificial character of the polling situation comes into play. When we make real decisions with consequences in the real world, we are more likely to consider evidence, possible outcomes, ethical considerations—in short, all the things that go into a judgment but do not necessarily inform an opinion. Similarly, while it is one thing, in the abstract, to say that all people's opinions are equally valid, in practice we are likely to consult the individuals who, our experience teaches us, have the knowledge and experience to give us sound advice. Thirdly, public opinion polls can only claim to represent opinion at a given moment in time (or what amounts usually in practice to the period of a few days during which the poll was conducted). A poll taken the first week of June 2007 can only speak about what was believed or known by respondents during the first week of June 2007, for who can say that public opinion wasn't changed significantly by subsequent events, perhaps even moments after the poll was taken? For this reason, polls are often described as giving us "snapshots" of public opinion, and it is only the eagerness of news firms to report poll results that obscures to us that they are inevitably "old news."

Finally, perhaps the most important aspect of modern polling that makes it a "construction" of public opinion, is a complex of issues dealing with the way that questions are worded and presented to respondents. Consider, for example, possible differences in the answers respondents are permitted. A *categorical* format permits only two (or perhaps three—"agree," "disagree," "don't know") responses; an *ordinal* format allows one to rank several choices, or assign a number to indicate the degree of response; an *open-ended* format allows the respondent to reply in words of their own choosing (see Figure 5.2). Clearly the open-ended format is the most informative in terms of the range and accuracy of responses that it permits; ordinal and categorical formats force respondents into choosing between respectively fewer options and hence to select a response that may be a less than completely accurate statement of their position. On the other hand, pollsters want answers that are quantifiable and do not leave a great deal of room open to interpretation, and here categorical and ordinal formats are much superior to the open-ended question, which may in fact produce no two responses alike.

FIGURE 5.2 Questions and Answers

OPEN-ENDED QUESTIONS	ORDINAL QUESTIONS	CATEGORICAL QUESTIONS
What do you think of the performance of the Bush Administration?	On a scale where 1 is poor and 10 is excellent, rate the performance of the Bush Administration.	The performance of the administration of George W. Bush is (a) good (b) bad (c) don't know.
What are the important issues you feel government should address?	Rank the following issues in terms of their immediate importance: the environment, the deficit, unemployment, the war in Iraq.	Winning the war against terror is more important than economic growth: (a) agree (b) disagree.
What qualities are most important for a successful political leader?	In terms of their campaign performance, rank these Democratic presidential candidates from best to worst: Hillary Clinton, Barak Obama, John Edwards.	

As important as the range of responses permitted (or not), is the wording of poll questions. Consider the two questions in Figure 5.3; are they identical, or does the wording used in each tend to invite one response rather than the other? Indeed, every student (and particularly any who have taken a multiple-choice examination, for opinion surveys are often just simplified multiple-choice questionnaires) knows how important the wording of a question can be and that there may be no such thing a neutral question. Complicating this further is the circumstance that a poll is a set of questions, in which one question, seemingly innocuous on its own, takes on greater significance when viewed in light of what precedes and/or follows. Questionnaires may be designed so as to "set-up" particular questions. Consider the two scenarios in Figure 5.4; neither of these is neutral, each could be seen as an attempt to influence the final question, in the first case in a manner unfavorable to the president, in the second case in a fashion favorable to her approval rating. Admittedly, our examples are a little crude; if nothing else, pollsters would likely not put these questions quite so proximate but intersperse them with others less obviously pointed than these.

The final point to consider is that most public opinion polls are conducted by private companies who sell their social scientific/ survey research expertise to various clients. Chief among these are

FIGURE 5.3 Poll Questions

Do you agree with the following statement?

Taxes are an unwelcome intrusion of the state upon the property of the individual.

    (a) agree   (b) disagree   (c) don't know

Taxes are necessary to pay for public goods like education and health care.

    (a) agree   (b) disagree   (c) don't know

political parties, governments, interest groups, and media companies. With the possible exception of the latter, each of these clients commissions opinion surveys not so much because they want to know what public opinion is but because they hope to use the results of public opinion surveys as ammunition in their efforts to secure (or block) specific public policies. To be more precise, they will commission polls with one eye on ascertaining the state of public opinion. If the results are (or can be interpreted in a way) favorable to their cause, they will publish or publicize the results in

FIGURE 5.4 Examples of Polling Questions

SCENARIO A
1. Comparing your financial position today with what it was before the last election, do you find yourself (a) better off, (b) worse off, (c) about the same?
2. What was your opinion of the tax increases introduced by President Smith: (a) in favor (b) opposed (c) no opinion?
3. Taxes are an unwelcome intrusion of the state upon the property of the individual: (a) agree (b) disagree (c) don't know.
4. President Lois Smith is doing a good job: (a) agree (b) disagree (c) don't know.

SCENARIO B
1. Rank the following issues in order of their importance to you:
   (a) unemployment (b) an aging population (c) the environment
   (d) health care costs.
2. Taxes are necessary to pay for public goods like education and health care: (a) agree (b) disagree (c) don't know.
3. What is your opinion of President Smith's increases in the taxes on gasoline and tobacco products: (a) agree (b) disagree (c) don't know.
4. President Lois Smith is doing a good job: (a) agree (b) disagree (c) don't know.

an effort to influence policy-makers or convert the unconverted, in either case with the argument that "public opinion" is on their side. If the poll results are less than favorable, they are unlikely to see the light of day, particularly when commissioned by private organizations. Governments use polls to get an idea what public reaction is likely to be to particular policies under consideration; it can be embarrassing when polls are made public showing opinion opposed to the policy direction of the government. On the other hand, governments that simply follow the path of least resistance are criticized for "governing by polls" and, given what we have been discussing, rightly so. For not only is the measurement of public opinion a hypothetical, undiscriminating "snapshot," it is also constructed at least in part through the ingenuity of survey designers. Since there are myriad ways one can ask questions, limit the possibilities of answers, choose not to ask other questions, create moods or influence attitudes by careful wording of questions and intelligent sequencing and juxtaposition of questions, the business of the pollster is not about finding "the truth"; there are any number of "truths" to be uncovered by the pollster's art or, more accurately, science. Given that polling companies serve a paying clientele, it would seem desirable that, wherever possible, the "truth" the poll reveals be the "truth" the client was looking for.

These observations about polling are not meant cynically or pejoratively but simply reflect the observation that the principle *raison d'être* of polling is not investigative (to uncover previously obscure truths) but *rhetorical*: to convince, persuade, or otherwise motivate someone or something. The notion that polls are somehow objective, disinterested, neutral measures of public opinion is a myth born out of a failure to understand how polls are constructed and the purposes for which they are designed, and this myth is maintained by pollsters who wish to capitalize on the added influence that this supposed objectivity gives to their results. This point notwithstanding, pollsters are increasingly aware of the need to behave responsibly and professionally, since ultimately their livelihood depends on the willingness of representative samples of individuals to give up their time to answer survey questions. They have, therefore, a vested interest in safeguarding the legitimacy and reputability of public opinion surveying. For this reason, pollsters have developed an elaborate code of conduct (see Figure 5.5) governing responsible polling, disclosing sufficient information for the informed reader to evaluate the scientific merit and representativeness of published poll results.

FIGURE 5.5 Standard for Minimal Disclosure of Poll Results

As polling data assumes greater importance in contemporary political systems, the American Association of Public Opinion Research (AAPOR) has articulated a "Code of Professional Ethics and Practices" to which its members must adhere. Part 3 of this code outlines the organization's "standards for minimal disclosure." According to these guidelines, all polls should include the release of:

1. Who sponsored the survey, and who conducted it.
2. The exact wording of questions asked, including the text of any preceding instruction or explanation to the interviewer or respondents that might reasonably be expected to affect the response.
3. A definition of the population under study, and a description of the sampling frame used to identify this population.
4. A description of the sample selection procedure, giving a clear indication of the method by which the respondents were selected by the researcher, or whether the respondents were entirely self-selected.
5. Size of samples and, if applicable, completion rates and information on eligibility criteria and screening procedures.
6. A discussion of the precision of the findings, including, if appropriate, estimates of sampling error, and a description of any weighting or estimating procedures used.
7. Which results are based on parts of the sample, rather than on the total sample.
8. Method, location, and dates of data collection.

The entire code can be found at <http://www.aapor.org/ethics/code.html>.

It has become a cliché to note that we live in an era of rapid change. It has been over three decades since Alvin Toffler documented the effects of this as individuals experienced "future shock" (1970). At the level of societies, however, the concept of culture invokes expectations of continuity rather than change. Individuals are thought to acquire political culture cumulatively through processes of political socialization that begin in early childhood and continue through the life cycle. The structures that provide for these socialization experiences—families, schools, churches, communities, and governments—should manifest considerable continuity over time. As a result, a perspective based on political culture expects change normally to be a slow process (Eckstein, 1992: 270-71). A review of two influential arguments advanced recently to describe and explain political cultural change will illustrate the ways in which a perspective based on expectations of cultural continuity can also accommodate development and change.

5.6
The Problem of Political Cultural Change

Robert Putnam's research illustrates nicely both the political culturalist orientation towards cultural continuity and also its adaptation to explain cultural change. First, Putnam's influential study of the performance of regional governments in Italy since 1970 (*Making Democracy Work: Civic Traditions in Modern Italy*) turns up a particularly striking example of political cultural continuity. Civic communities rich in **SOCIAL CAPITAL** (trust, norms of reciprocity, civic mindedness, and sociability) for the past 900 years in Italy's north have nurtured strong, capable regional governments since they were introduced in 1970. However, in the south, a similarly long-lived more autocratic, less civic-minded culture meant that contemporary Italy lacked the political cultural requisites for effective democratic institutions. In this way, "... social patterns plainly traceable from early medieval Italy to today turn out to be decisive in explaining why, on the verge of the twenty-first century, some communities are better able than others to manage collective life and sustain effective institutions" (Putnam, 1994: 121).

In a subsequent article on American political culture, Putnam (1995) touched off a heated controversy by identifying a critical decline in the vitality of America's civil society (social capital) in recent decades. As a result, he advances a pessimistic interpretation of cultural change in the United States, one that holds negative implications for the continued health and vitality of American democracy. He musters a variety of evidence to support his contention. Opinion polls suggest, for example, that between 1973 and 1993 the number of Americans who reported attending a public meeting on town or school affairs in the past year declined from 22 per cent to 13 per cent. Similar declines are reported on many measures of American engagement in politics and government, regular church attendance, labor union membership, and other civic organizations (such as the Red Cross, Boy Scouts, etc.). More evocatively, however, Putnam points to the paradox that while more Americans are bowling than ever before, between 1980 and 1993 league bowling decreased by 40 per cent. Americans, it would appear, are increasingly "**BOWLING ALONE**" (Putnam, 2000). As a result, they are less apt to encounter their fellow citizens in a social setting and less likely to develop the kinds of interpersonal relationships that are conducive to social capital formation and vital democracy.

How is this change in American political culture to be explained? Putnam identifies four possible explanations: the movement of women into the labor force (with attendant declines in the participation of women in such organizations as PTAs, Federation of Women's Clubs, League of Women Voters, and the Red Cross);

FIGURE 5.6 Bowling Alone?

Robert Putnam's provocative thesis—symbolized by the image of
Americans "bowling alone" and not in leagues—that Americans are
joining fewer groups and socializing less with one another has provoked
a lively debate among sociologists and political scientists. Some argue
that Putnam's diagnosis is too pessimistic, and that he mistakes a *change*
in the nature of the social engagement of Americans for a decline in
their social relationships. Women, for example, are arguably more likely
to be socially connected through the workplace than they were several
decades ago, when they may have been prime supporters of parent/teacher
associations and church groups. The growth of "virtual communities"
on the Internet connect individuals in novel ways that Putnam's analysis
discounts. Information collected by the National Opinion Research
Center's "General Social Survey" (GSS), an annual survey of opinions and
social trends, points to some counter-evidence, for example. A comparison
of GSS data from 1974 and 1994, for example, shows that membership in
some groups (church-related groups, hobby clubs, etc.) did decline over the
period. However, membership in some kinds of groups actually went up
over that period. An *Atlantic Monthly* article replying to Putnam's "Bowling
Alone," was titled "Kicking in Groups." Along these lines, the proportion of
Americans reporting memberships in "sports clubs" went up from 17.9 per
cent in 1974 to 21.8 per cent in 1994; membership in fraternities went up
from 4.7 per cent to 5.7 per cent, while membership in professional groups
went up from 13.2 per cent to 18.7 per cent over the two decades. See
Nicholas Lemann, "Kicking in Groups," *The Atlantic Monthly*, April 1996.

residential mobility and suburbanization; marital instability and the
decline of the "nuclear family"; and the privatization of leisure by
television, the Internet, and other electronic technologies. Each
of these complex factors has the effect of eroding the connection
between Americans and their communities. If the vitality of American democracy is to be assured, according to Putnam, it is imperative to restore civic engagement and civic trust.

Another prominent interpretation of cultural change in the
United States (and elsewhere throughout the world) has been advanced by Ronald Inglehart (1990, 1997). Inglehart was impressed
by the tumultuous and turbulent politics of the "radical 1960s"
in America. He sought to explain the rebelliousness of the young
generation at that time to their distinctive socialization experiences associated with the unprecedented affluence that would shift
the political cultures of generations and, in so doing, advanced a
general explanation for the cultural consequences of material affluence. His basic argument is that generations will adopt cultural
dispositions consistent with the level of material (economic and
physical) security or insecurity they experience, especially during

the formative years early in their lives. Drawing on the insights of Abraham Maslow, Inglehart hypothesized that the postwar "baby boom" generation was the first to experience widespread economic affluence and conditions of (relative) material security. By contrast, their parents' generation would have experienced two world wars and a worldwide economic depression. The result, according to Inglehart, would be a generational difference in political values and political cultures.

Inglehart's research is based on analyses of large numbers of public opinion surveys in which (among other things) he contrasts the political values and priorities of different age cohorts (groups born within the same time period and who, as a result, share common socialization experiences). Older generations in Western publics were expected to be preoccupied with what Maslow termed "physiological" and "safety" needs. Inglehart labels these "materialist" values and associates these needs with individuals assigning highest priority to government actions that provide for economic growth, fight inflation, and provide a strong armed force to defend the country and maintain order in the nation. The success with which these lower order needs were met in the 1950s and 1960s meant that the baby boom generation was able largely to take these values for granted. As such, they were free to cultivate higher order needs on Maslow's hierarchy: belongingness, esteem, and ultimately self-actualization. As indicators of these, Inglehart included the value priorities of "having more say in government," "freedom of speech," and the importance of preserving nature and beautifying cities.

The political tumult of the 1960s, then, sprang from generational differences in political socialization experiences that represented a profound gap between young and old. The older generation bemoaned the cultural dissoluteness associated with their liberal-minded ("sex, drugs, and rock 'n roll") offspring; and the young, for their part, were being admonished "not to trust anyone over 35." Inglehart's analyses suggest that, in a variety of countries, post-material values are more prevalent in the youngest age cohorts and least frequently encountered in older ones. As younger generations replace older ones in the population, then, Inglehart expects the politics of **POST-MATERIALISM** to become increasingly prominent. Recent evidence suggests that such a culture shift may well be under way. Between 1973 and 1990, the proportion of citizens with post-materialist values was steady in Britain and the United States (at about 20 per cent), but nearly tripled in West Germany to 36 per cent of the population (Dalton, 2002: 96, Table 5.2). This politics,

Inglehart argues, will be less organized by traditional political parties and organizations and instead be more protest-oriented and more focused on social movements (such as the feminist movement or the ecological movement).

Cultures normally serve as relatively stable orientations, but as we have seen cultural change can and does occur. Both the continuities and the discontinuities in culture over time are accounted for by changes in the processes and content of political socialization. The causes of these changes are many and varied. However, in a world characterized by rapid change, political cultures serve as a kind of ballast, ensuring that societies are not buffeted randomly by these changes. Rather, as Inglehart explains, "Old worldviews are remarkably persistent, shaping human behavior long after the conditions that gave rise to them have faded away (Inglehart, 1990: 426).

The twentieth century has witnessed the further creation and sophistication of a mass culture in developed societies and, consistent with the expansion of the political class to include all adults, the development of a mass political culture. These transformations have relied upon the successive emergence of media of communication, which have served to shrink the worlds of place and time, and media that have come to be less and less about merely the transmission of information and increasingly about entertainment and diversion. Just as citizens have come increasingly to rely on mass media (and, among these, to rely predominantly on television) to inform them about the political world, politicians have become increasingly dependent on the media to put them in touch with an ever-increasing electorate. This, in turn, is symptomatic of a more general dependence of contemporary politicians upon social scientific expertise to manage their encounter with the public. The use of public opinion polling, sophisticated marketing techniques, advertising expertise, controlled access to the media, professional image consultants, and public relations experts is standard practice now in attempting to maintain a favorable public image. It is not cynicism to regard these attempts at managing the public perception of the political world as manipulative. To the extent that these attempts at manipulation succeed, they make a sham of whatever democratic process exists. To the extent that they fail (and it is remarkable, given the expertise and effort which is behind them, how often they fail) they undermine democracy by alienating the public from the political realm.

**5.7
Conclusion**

Key Terms

affect

attitudes

beliefs

"bowling alone"

cognitive

corporate concentration

efficacy

entertainment

evaluative

information

judgmental journalism

manipulation

mass culture

mass media

opinion

political culture

polling

post-materialism

socialization

social capital

trust

values

References and Suggested Readings

Almond, Gabriel, and Sidney Verba. 1963. *The Civic Culture: Political Attitudes and Democracy in Five Nations*. Princeton, NJ: Princeton University Press.

Barker, Sir Ernest. 1927. *National Character and the Factors in its Formation*. London: Methuen.

Bennett, W. Lance. 1980. *Public Opinion in American Politics*. New York: Harcourt Brace Jovanovich.

———. 1992. *The Governing Crisis: Media, Manipulation, and Marketing in American Elections*. New York: St. Martin's Press.

Dalton, Russell J. 2002. *Citizen Politics in Western Democracies*, 3rd ed. Chatham, NJ: Chatham House.

Eckstein, Harry. 1966. "A Theory of Stable Democracy." Appendix to *Division and Cohesion in Democracy: A Study of Norway*. Princeton, NJ: Princeton University Press.

———. 1992. *Regarding Politics: Essays on Political Theory, Stability, and Change*. Berkeley, CA: University of California Press.

Gallup, George, and Saul Rae. 1940. *The Pulse of Democracy*. New York: Simon and Schuster.

Herman, Edward, and Noam Chomsky. 1988. *Manufacturing Consent: The Political Economy of the Mass Media*. New York: Pantheon Books.

Inglehart, Ronald. 1990. *Culture Shift in Advanced Industrial Society*. Princeton, NJ: Princeton University Press.

———. 1997. *Modernization and Postmodernization: Cultural, Economic, and Political Change in 43 Nations*. Princeton, NJ: Princeton University Press.

Inglehart, Ronald, and Christian Welzel. 2005. *Modernization, Cultural Change, and Democracy*. New York: Cambridge University Press.

Lipset, Seymour Martin. 1990. *Continental Divide: The Values and Institutions of the United States and Canada*. New York: Routledge.

Postman, Neil. 1985. *Amusing Ourselves to Death: Public Discourse in the Age of Show Business*. New York: Penguin.

Putnam, Robert D. 1995. "Bowling Alone: America's Declining Social Capital." *Journal of Democracy* 6,1 (January): 65-78.
<http://muse.jhu.edu/demo/journal_of_democracy/v006/6.1putnam.html>

———. 2000. *Bowling Alone: The Collapse and Revival of American Community*. New York: Simon and Schuster.

———. 1994. *Making Democracy Work: Civic Traditions in Modern Italy*. Princeton: Princeton University Press.

Toffler, Alvin. 1970. *Future Shock*. New York: Random House.

THREE | the evolution of liberal democracy

SIX | Liberal Democracy: Emergence and Dimensions

"Man's capacity for justice makes democracy possible, but man's inclination to injustice makes democracy necessary."
—Reinhold Niebuhr, *The Children of Light and the Children of Darkness*, 1944

"... for the first time in all history, more people on this planet live under democracy than dictatorship."
—President William Jefferson Clinton, Inaugural Address, 1997

As former President Clinton's comment above suggests, more than ever before we live in an age of **DEMOCRACY**. The events of the past several decades, including the collapse of communist authoritarianism in large sections of the world and the replacement of many military juntas and dictatorships in others, suggest the imminent achievement of the democratic idea worldwide. For a variety of reasons we will summarize below, such democratic triumphalism may be premature. A longer historical perspective is necessary both to appreciate the larger context of political development within which the current advance of democracy has taken place and to appreciate the uncertainties that have risen to confront the latest "wave" of democratization. In this chapter we turn our attention to an explanation of the emergence and development of the liberal democratic state in the Western industrial world. We then discuss the syndrome of processes and institutions that constitutes **LIBERAL DEMOCRACY**. This establishes the intellectual foundation for the chapters that follow in the text in which the main variations in liberal democracy as it is practiced in the modern world are outlined.

6.1
Introduction

6.2
Historical Foundations of
Modern Democracy

It is customary to trace the Western roots of democracy to ancient Greece, particularly to the city-state (polis) of Athens. In the relatively intimate setting of Athenian democracy, it was possible for politics to be highly participatory, engaging the energies and attention (at least at times) of a considerable portion of the population. However, once the community became too large, either in territory or population, this kind of politics was no longer practical. In the Roman **EMPIRE** that emerged to replace Greek civilization as the dominant political organization in Europe, on the other hand, politics was not participatory (except in a limited sense, for limited periods, in the capital) but military in tone and spirit. It was the organization, extent, and skill of Rome's armies that kept Rome together, just as ultimately it was military defeat at the hands of the Goths and Vandals that brought the empire to an end. Interestingly, what was missing in either case, city-state or empire, was an adequate professional bureaucracy (which, of course, is an advantage Chinese dynasties had over their European counterparts). Without it, the city-state could not expand beyond a certain size, except militarily. Empires could grow so enormous because they were primarily about military security not about providing public or political goods to their enormous populations. Nation-states would not emerge in Western Europe until the end of the feudal period.

The end of the Roman Empire (and the beginning of the medieval period) was brought about by the migration of several peoples from Eastern Europe and Central Asia. Nomadic warrior societies pushed westward by other peoples behind them, these tribes eventually defeated the armies of an aging, decaying empire. Much of the politics and society of the medieval period reflects an uneasy marriage of tribal customs and traditional ways with imperial remnants such as Roman law and the **CATHOLIC CHURCH**. Pagan tribes were eventually converted to Christianity, while tribal customs and rules were incorporated into codified laws, and vice-versa. The political product was something identified as feudal society or **FEUDALISM**.

We can describe feudal society as a product of the encounter of tribal chiefdoms with the remnants of the highly developed Roman state. In feudal society, authority was fragmented—a characteristic that marked the medieval period until late in its development. Tribes, united for military purposes under a powerful chieftain or king, would become dispersed upon settlement after victory. Authority would then be exercised by local nobles, whose position, initially at least, reflected military rank or prowess. Although there were attempts to reunite Western Europe by reconstituting the

FIGURE 6.1 Western European Political History

	CLASSICAL ANTIQUITY 400 BC–400 AD	MEDIEVAL AGE 400–1400	MODERNITY 1400–?
FORM OF GOVERNMENT	Polis to Empire	Feudal fiefdom to Nation–state (absolute monarchy)	Constitutional monarchy to Representative government to Liberal democracy
CENTRAL MORAL–POLITICAL CONCEPTS	virtue citizenship	natural law divine right	popular sovereignty individual rights
ECONOMIC MODES	slavery military agricultural	agrarian military commercial	commercial industrial market activity
RELIGION	pagan	Catholic Christianity	from Christian pluralism to secularism
INTELLECTUAL APPROACH	philosophical	scholastic	scientific

Roman Empire—most successfully under Charlemagne—it would be accurate to say that a medieval emperor was at most a "chief of chiefs" rather than someone who personally governed the "empire." This last point is important; medieval authority, reflecting its tribal roots, was largely personal.

The personal nature of authority in the medieval period is indicated by the dominance of traditional justifications. Hereditary monarchy, a product of this period, is a classic example of the selection of leaders based on **CUSTOM**, tradition, and adherence to "accepted ways." At the same time, there was considerable effort on the part of leaders to secure claims to charismatic authority: the "**DIVINE RIGHT** of kings" is a theory that claims leaders are anointed and justified by God in their exercise of power. The religious unification of Europe under Catholic Christianity meant that rulers were not only claiming justification under the same God but that medieval politics often focused upon the relationship between the state and the Church or between secular and ecclesiastical authority. Feudal society was subject to a dual authority—that of the secular state and that of the Church. A central question at any time and often a primary source of conflict was thus the issue of the relationship between Church and state. For the most part, weak, fragmented political power was complemented by a universal Church exercising considerable authority in a variety of contexts. This contrast reflects another: governments were weak and fragmented because they ultimately rested more upon power than authority, but the physical ability of rulers to exercise power was limited by various factors (most principally the absence of resources and the difficulty of transporting them quickly). The influence of the Church on the other hand reflected a universal authority grounded in a common religious creed but often hampered by an absence of power. In this way, rulers sought favor from the Church in order to enhance their legitimacy, while the Church often required the power of the local state in order to enforce authoritative decisions or policies. The desire of either Church or state to have the upper hand or final word set the stage for many of the conflicts of medieval politics.

The feudal economy was essentially a subsistence economy in which producers were primarily concerned to provide for their own consumption plus a share for the feudal overlord. Over the centuries the subsistence economy was transformed by the gradual emergence of markets. These institutions, where goods could be bartered and sold, complicated the economic foundations of feudalism by orienting an increasing amount of production not for subsistence but for commerce. Commercial activities in turn stimulated, and in turn were stimulated by, the growth of towns and cities. Cities in turn became attractive settings for the increasing numbers of artisans and crafts workers. All of these movements contributed to breaking down the relatively rigid feudal hierarchy and encourage a more complex division of labor in economy and society. Also undermining the foundations of the feudal order were the rise of absolute monarchies, especially in England, France, and Spain. These political systems concentrated power in the monarch's hands, greatly reducing the independence and power of the aristocracy. Improvements in communication and transportation also had a corrosive effect on feudalism by breaking down the isolation of feudal communities and bringing them into contact with a larger and increasingly market-dominated world. As a result of these forces, by the fifteenth and sixteenth centuries, feudalism was in decline in most parts of Western Europe, though vestiges would remain for at least another two centuries

The **LIBERAL REVOLUTION** that marks the passage from **MEDIEVAL SOCIETY** to what we recognize as modernity was a great transformation in Western Europe, an event or process to which most Western nations owe their political institutions and the central concepts of their political culture. More specifically, we have seen that feudal society was eroded by tremendous social transformations, chief among them **THE REFORMATION, THE ENLIGHTENMENT** (the "age of reason"), and the **MARKET ECONOMY**. In place of an organic, hierarchical, traditional society, these phenomena created an increasingly individualistic, fluid, pluralistic society in which reason and science replaced custom and divine intention as central standards by which policy and institutions could be evaluated. In contrast to a rigid order of entrenched social positions, the new society was premised on the liberation of individuals from arbitrary, traditional, involuntary bonds and on the replacement of these with relationships of rational self-interest. This new society was not one to which feudal political institutions could be accommodated. Material pressures demanded new institutions, and the cultural changes we have examined undermined the traditional justifications of medieval authority. The liberal revolution is the political counterpart of these social transformations. In addition to new ways of organizing religious life, new approaches to understanding the human and natural world, and new ways of organizing economic production, Western Europe undertook to reorganize its political life, to establish new institutions and structures of authority, and to justify them in ways consistent with the social changes that had taken place and that were continuing to be at work. This new political order, in brief, is the product of what we are calling the liberal revolution.

We may use the term **REVOLUTION** in at least two senses. One indicates a radical (i.e., comprehensive) change or set of changes. Another is to describe a sudden event that brings about radical change. The liberal revolution should be understood in the former sense, because the radical change Europe underwent did not necessarily occur suddenly or violently and sometimes took place gradually and (relatively) peacefully. Revolution in the second sense (a sudden series of events bringing radical change) is often the result of the failure to accommodate political institutions to a changing society or set of social values. The **FRENCH REVOLUTION** of 1789, perhaps the most striking example of a revolution in this dramatic sense, can be seen as such an eruption created by an intolerable tension between the old political order and the new social forces created by economic and cultural change. These most drastic revolutions are often the least surprising, because the need for change, or the desire for change, is so clearly evident to so many. What the English call the Glorious or Whig Revolution of 1688 was simply one of several significant changes in English life over the course of a century or more. In fact, the Whig Revolution was only dramatic in that it replaced the ruling Stuart dynasty with a monarchic family (William and Mary of Orange) willing to acknowledge parliamentary supremacy. This relatively bloodless transformation had very little immediate effect on the ordinary citizen because in many if not most respects Britain had already been transformed from feudal society into something else. In fact, we might go further and suggest that revolutions that are accomplished gradually, without violent disruption to a society and its citizens, are more likely to succeed in the long run.

Students might observe that the United States has not undergone a liberal revolution. The original British North American colonies were largely populated with immigrants from Europe who espoused modern values, concepts, and liberal institutions. The War of Independence arose from a conflict between relatively liberal colonies and an imperial administration under George III, exercising an absolute authority towards the colonies. In fact, many Whig politicians in Britain supported the colonial cause. The **AMERICAN REVOLUTION** was the revolt of a society more modern and liberal against the remnants of medieval authority exercised by the monarch. As future monarchs left colonial policy to Parliament, liberal self-government came to colonies such as Canada and Australia peacefully and gradually.

In short, the liberal revolution is the political restructuring that accompanies a transformation from a traditional, agrarian, organic society to a rational, market-oriented, pluralist society. It is a stage through which various societies have passed at different times, depending upon their history, culture, and prevailing conditions. It is by no means obvious that every society *must* undergo such a transformation, but it is common to all so-called "Western" nations. Such a transformation is behind the development of modern notions of legal-rational authority and such central normative concepts as justice and democracy. It also has informed the understanding of state and government indicated above. The liberal revolution stands in the background of the constitutional systems or governmental institutions we examine in Part Four and, indeed, is presupposed by our discussion of the modern state throughout this book.

**6.3
From Representative
Government to
Representative
Democracy**

We have already said something above about the logical relationship between liberalism and democracy. In the aftermath of the liberal revolution though, this relationship was not obvious to liberal thinkers; it was overshadowed by their acceptance of the traditional criticisms of democracy. Instead of democracy, liberal thinkers were concerned to establish **REPRESENTATIVE GOVERNMENT** and to replace absolute monarchy with parliamentary sovereignty. This is obvious in the political writings of the foundational liberal thinkers, Thomas Hobbes and John Locke.

Hobbes was certainly no advocate of democracy, but it should be noted that he understood the term literally as the rule by (all) the people, which he considered an impossibility. Nonetheless, his justification of government was that in a state of nature, individuals acting out of self-interest would create the Sovereign (the authority of the state) to protect them and would create this authority through a covenant (agreement) of each individual with every other. This is very much like an argument for popular sovereignty in that the authority of the state is traced back to the interests of the subjects themselves. By virtue of the device of the covenant, Hobbes says more than once that the subjects are the "authors" of the Sovereign's actions. On the other hand this covenant is an entirely hypothetical event; the popular sovereignty Hobbes describes is only apparent.

Like Hobbes, Locke begins with a social contract, a mutual agreement among those who wish security and stability, but unlike Hobbes, Locke writes as if such a contract is a real historical event. The social contract is an agreement between the Sovereign and the subjects, so that for Locke government has its origin in **THE CONSENT OF THE GOVERNED**. The unanimity of all participants in Hobbes's imaginary covenant is replaced by the more practical principle of **MAJORITY RULE** in Locke's version. Locke argues that the legislative power should be in the hands of an assembly, a body of men who together make the law but are also at the same time subject to it. It is important to note that Locke's theory does not (nor was it intended to) describe the workings of a democracy. But it does describe a liberal parliamentary government and articulates several of the ideas and conventions that have become integral to liberal **REPRESENTATIVE DEMOCRACY**. Like many philosophers, Locke believed that government requires rationality, and he would have restricted the political community to those who are rational; like many of his time, Locke believed that most people are not (or do not demonstrate) sufficient rationality to merit rights of political participation. Those who did demonstrate such sufficient rationality were thought to be those with productive property. In this respect Locke did not challenge the existing arrangements, which limited the right to vote for Parliament (and to sit in Parliament) to a small wealthy class, but rather the relationship between the legislature and the monarchy.

A British
Suffragette

When representative government became democratic, this involved extending the **FRANCHISE** (the right to vote for representatives) from a small propertied class to virtually all adult citizens. This happened in stages, often in the face of much opposition and resistance, and was only completed in the twentieth century in most contemporary democracies. Among other things, these extensions of the democratic franchise involved (1) eliminating property qualifications as a condition of the franchise; (2) the recognition of women as persons equally entitled to political rights; (3) the removal of restrictions based on racial, ethnic, or religious grounds; and (4) a lowering of age limits to present levels.

On the other hand, extending the right to vote did not alter the basic functioning of representative government; the same institutions, conventions, and practices continued to operate as before, with representatives perhaps even gaining more autonomy from the immediate demands of constituents as their constituencies became more pluralistic. Moreover, the significance of extending the franchise depends on the importance of the vote within the institutions of liberal representative government. Certainly, to gain the right to vote is important for citizens previously denied that right, but it is significant as much for the symbolic importance attached to full citizenship as for any power gained. Undeniably, each expansion of the franchise has required elected officials—singly or in parties—to be more responsive to the section of the electorate thus enfranchised than they might otherwise have been. Nonetheless, one reason this act of voting fails to carry more weight is the nature of the ongoing relationship between the voters and their representatives.

The first legislatures emerged gradually from the medieval period in Britain. Elected representatives served as members of a legislature; in its original configuration—as an assembly of feudal lords—Parliament consisted of members with no legal obligations to their retainers (constituents) but were bound only by a moral obligation to consider the well-being of their constituents. So too, today, apart from the necessity of facing constituents in periodic elections, legislators typically have no legal responsibilities to their constituents. This absence of accountability for the period between elections can be called **REPRESENTATIVE AUTONOMY**, and it is a feature of most contemporary democracies. The most eloquent defense of the autonomy of the elected representative is that provided by **EDMUND BURKE** in a 1776 speech to his constituents in Bristol following his election to the House of Commons (Figure 6.2). The autonomy Burke was advocating is not mere freedom or license: the representative is "free" to follow his own judgment rather than that of his constituents, and in this sense he or she acts as their "trustee." In this **TRUSTEE MODEL OF REPRESENTATION** (as it has come to be known), the elected representative is not free to do whatever he or she likes but rather enjoys a freedom to use his or her reason to *judge* what is in the constituents' best interest. This view of the representative's role is consistent with Burke's underlying conservatism. He believed that voters should elect the most able and qualified candidates and then defer to their (presumably better) judgment. What Burke did not admit is that this creates a problem for constituents whose representative does not follow their opinions, judgments, etc. How does the constituent know whether or not the representative is making a thoughtful, informed decision about what is in their interest, or pursuing some other agenda— perhaps one of personal interest?

In defense of Burke, we might note that in an age before universal state-funded schooling, the level of education attained was more or less proportionate to wealth. The vast majority had little or no formal education and, one could argue, did not possess the tools to make rational informed judgments. This social reality provided ammunition not only for the autonomy of representatives but against any notion of making the political system more democratic: how could one, in an increasingly complex and technical world, consider giving the vote to people who could neither read nor write? This also indicates that prior to universal compulsory education, the class rule by the propertied interests could be defended on the basis of factors—such as expertise or education—other than class, which were nonetheless very much associated with class.

Since the United States was founded on classical liberal as opposed to classical conservative positions such as Burke's, the "trustee" conceptualization of representational roles has never resonated well with American political culture. Instead, most Americans feel that their elected representatives should subordinate their own views and act on the basis of their constituents' wishes—something referred to as the **DELEGATE MODEL OF REPRESENTATION** (Bernstein, 1989). As we will see in subsequent chapters, within the world of parliamentary democracy, representative autonomy describes the relationship between legislator and constituents, but it does not account for the actions of representatives. Instead, modern members of Parliament (MPs) elected in parliamentary regimes are governed almost exclusively by the dictates of party discipline, which remains central to government stability. Individual autonomy only comes into full play on those rare issues on which a "free" vote is held— so-called "matters of conscience," such as capital punishment or

FIGURE 6.2 Edmund Burke on the Representative (excerpts)

Certainly, Gentlemen, it ought to be the happiness and glory of a representative to live in the strictest union, the closest correspondence, and the most unreserved communication with his constituents. Their wishes ought to have great weight with him; their opinions high respect; their business unremitted attention. It is his duty to sacrifice his repose, his pleasure, his satisfactions, to theirs—and above all, ever, and in all cases, to prefer their interest to his own.

But his unbiased opinions, his mature judgment, his enlightened conscience, he ought not to sacrifice to you, to any man, or to any set of men living. These he does not derive from your pleasure—no, nor from the law and the constitution. They are a trust from Providence, for the abuse of which he is deeply answerable. Your representative owes you, not his industry only, but his judgment; and he betrays, instead of serving you, if he sacrifices it to your opinion.

... government and legislation are matters of reason and judgment, and not of inclination; and what sort of reason is that in which the deliberation precedes the discussion, in which one set of men deliberate and another decide, and where those who form the conclusion are perhaps three hundred miles distant from those who hear the arguments?

To deliver an opinion is the right of all men; that of constituents is a weighty and respectable opinion, which a representative ought always to rejoice to hear, and which he ought always most seriously to consider. But *authoritative* instructions, *mandates* issued, which a member is bound blindly and implicitly to obey, to vote, and to argue for, though contrary to the clearest conviction of his judgment and conscience; these are things utterly unknown to the laws of this land, and which arise from a fundamental mistake of the whole order and tenor of our constitution.

Parliament is not a *congress* of ambassadors from different and hostile interests, which interests each must maintain, as an agent and advocate, against other agents and advocates; but Parliament is a *deliberative* assembly of *one* nation, with *one* interest, that of the whole—where not local purposes, not local prejudices, ought to guide, but the general good, resulting from the general reason of the whole. You choose a member, indeed; but when you have chosen him, he is not a member of Bristol, but he is a member of *Parliament*. If the local constituent should have an interest or should form a hasty opinion evidently opposite to the real good of the rest of the community, the member for that place ought to be as far as any other from any endeavor to give it effect....Your faithful friend, your devoted servant, I shall be to the end of my life: a flatterer you do not wish for.

Source: *Speech to the Bristol Electors*, November 3, 1774; ‹http://press-pubs.uchicago.edu/founders/documents/v1ch13s7.html›.

abortion. In the United States, party discipline is much less rigid, and members are not at all bound to vote along party lines, although there are more alliances within parties than outside them. In theory, this should provide elected representatives more freedom to follow their constituents' wishes. However, critics argue that the freedom from party discipline makes American legislators more susceptible to the influence of lobbyists and not necessarily to the wishes of their constituents.

The liberal revolution created a new form or style of government, in some cases dramatically redesigning the institutions of state (as in France), in other cases changing the rules and conventions that determine how existing institutions function (as in Britain). In the former instance, government by a monarch and noble-born aristocracy was rejected for a **REPUBLICAN** form of government, a republic being a nation of citizens equal in political rank and status (at least in theory if not practice). In the latter case, the monarchy was retained, but its power diminished (as it would continue to be reduced). In either instance, the common theme is the **DEPERSONALIZATION** of authority and power. No longer was the power of the state to be seen (as it was in feudal times) as a possession or right of the individuals (or families) wielding it but rather as something exercised on behalf of "the people." The essentially "liberal" idea at the core of the liberal revolution was that *the power and authority of government exist for the sake of the interests of the individuals governed.* The "rule of men" was to be replaced with the "rule of law." Reflecting its connection with the Enlightenment, the liberal revolution was about replacing arbitrary, unpredictable, personal power with rational, predictable, impersonal authority. One device for realizing these possibilities is a constitution and, as important or more so, is the commitment to **CONSTITUTIONALISM**— an acceptance that the constitution places limits on the way power or authority can be exercised within the state. This distinction is not academic; there have been many examples of states with constitutions that the political authorities have simply suspended or set aside whenever it became expedient to do so. Liberal constitutions are designed to protect individual citizens from the possibility of an arbitrary absolute authority by placing roadblocks in the way of the emergence of such a power. The nature of these roadblocks, and other constitutional provisions designed to make government predictable, law-abiding, and not arbitrary or capricious—including those embedded in **RESPONSIBLE GOVERNMENT** (parliamentary systems), or **CHECKS AND BALANCES** (the American Constitution), or **JUDICIAL INDEPENDENCE**, or entrenched individual **RIGHTS**—will be examined in greater detail in subsequent chapters.

It is worth stressing, though, that the liberal revolution was not initially democratic. The modern state of Western Europe and its colonies was liberal first and only later democratic, and when it became democratic, this was usually through a series of gradual, cautious expansions of the class of those with political standing. With the exception of the United States, a typical pattern for Western democracies was an evolution from responsible government to representative government to liberal democracy. The significance we underline here is that liberal democracy has been the product of considerable development within the liberal nation-states that resulted from the demise of feudal society. This is one point of considerable difference between the beginning of **LIBERAL MODERNITY** in the late seventeenth century and where we stand at the beginning of the twenty-first century; today the liberal states are (more or less) democratic. There have been several other developments, equally or more important.

One has been the continued growth and development of market society, which began in trade, grew exponentially with the development of manufacturing as a result of the Industrial Revolution, and has been periodically renewed by the emergence of new technologies. In the twentieth century, and particularly in the postwar period, market society in the industrialized West has become a mass consumer society, by which we mean that an increasing proportion of production and consumption involves items that cannot be considered basic necessities of life. It is still possible at this time to note that only 80 years ago the mass entertainment industry as we know it today did not exist. In part a consumer society has been accomplished through the continuous exploitation of the possibilities afforded by science and technology, in part it has been a fruit of the historical exploitation of peoples both domestically but especially abroad in the age of **IMPERIALISM** that has continued in one form or another since the nineteenth century.[1] It has also meant the creation of a large **MIDDLE CLASS** of professionals and skilled workers that did not exist at the beginning of the modern period.

The development of the post-industrial societies of the West also reflects and has reinforced changes in the nature of **CIVIL SOCIETY.** By civil society we mean the areas of social life that are organized or governed by institutions or authorities other than the state or government. Three primary institutions of civil society in Western society have been the family, the Church, and the market economy. It is clear that in the past century or so the role of the first two has been radically changed or has declined significantly, while the third may no longer qualify (if it ever did) as standing sufficiently outside the scope of governmental activity. All voluntary activity falls within the scope of civil society and, in the view of many, the healthier the institutions of civil society, the healthier the political community will be. Certainly, a decline in the ability of civil society to take responsibility for large areas of social life will put pressure on the state to take up the slack, impelling it to take on tasks for which it may or may not be suited. This is the last theme that we will be exploring at length in this text, namely, the phenomenal growth of the state during the twentieth century and the contradictory pressures on it today to both contract its expenditures and revenues and yet continue to provide the public goods

1 In fact imperialism is much older than the nineteenth century; one need only think about the Spanish, Portuguese, French, and British conquest of the "New World" from the sixteenth century onwards or the development of the slave trade. In the nineteenth century, European countries divided up Africa among themselves and exploited its lands and peoples as cheap sources of labor and materials. Today, multinational corporations continue to shift production to developing nations' cheap labor markets, and the movement of components of a finished product within a vertically integrated company but across state borders accounts for a good deal of world trade. In the United States, for example, one recent estimate suggests that 50 per cent of all imports and 30 per cent of all exports occur as a result of transfers within multinational firms. Similarly, Western financial institutions like the World Bank and the International Monetary Fund project and approve loans on the basis of criteria that often seem more consistent with the interests of the developed world creditors than those of the developing world clients.

2 It should be noted that the definition of democracy employed by Huntington hinges on essentially two criteria that are relatively easily met. First, a state is classed as democratic if at least half the adult males are permitted to vote and, second, if there is a responsible executive who must maintain majority support in an elected parliament or is chosen by periodic popular support. Some scholars have been critical of this minimalist conceptualization of democracy. Larry Diamond, for example, estimates that while 117 of the world's 191 states (61.3 per cent) in 1995 could be classified as "formal democracies" in Huntington's sense, only 76 (39.8 per cent) could be classed as "free states" or "liberal democracies" when additional criteria are added. These criteria include substantial freedom of belief, opinion, discussion, assembly, publication, etc.; a free and independent press; political equality of citizens; the rule of law; the existence of multiple and ongoing channels and means of expressing and representing interests; real power lying with elected officials; constitutional checks on executive power; open access to political institutions to all groups; and others (Diamond, 1996: 27).

FIGURE 6.3 "Three Waves of Democracy"

First Wave (1828–1926): 29 democracies established
    First Reverse Wave (1922–1942)
Second Wave (1943–1964): 32 democracies established
    Second Reverse Wave (1961–1974)
Third Wave (1974–?): about 60 democracies established

---

that citizens have come to expect from it. There is an argument to be made that the state has grown as a result of the changes we have been discussing; the rise of democracy, the growth of an affluent middle class, and the decline in the significance of civil society have all created pressures for the state to expand and provide new programs, initiatives, and regulation.

With the liberal revolution of the eighteenth and nineteenth centuries, then, came a constellation of factors that we have come to regard as constituting "modernity." The unleashing of a series of social, cultural, and economic forces during this transformation began a process that would culminate in the widespread adoption of democracy by a majority of states in all parts of the world. This process of democratization during the modern phase has not been smooth and cumulative, however. Instead, Samuel Huntington (1991) has argued that democracy has spread—and retreated—through a succession of waves (see Figure 6.3). With each successive wave, however, the number of democracies increased, and now, as the quotations opening this chapter suggest, for the first time in history a majority of people in the world live in states that can be described as "democratic."[2]

According to Huntington's provocative analysis, the first wave of democratization was initiated by developments in the United States, unfolded slowly over almost a century, and was responsible for the creation of about 29 democracies. The rise of authoritarianism and fascism in the period between the two world wars of the twentieth century reversed some of the advance of democracy in the first wave and reduced the number of democracies to about a dozen by 1942. A second wave of democratization followed the defeat of Germany, Italy, and Japan in World War II, and approximately 32 new democracies were formed. Some of these were created in haste by European colonial powers as they withdrew from parts of their former empire in the postwar period. Many of these newly independent former colonies faced tremendous developmental challenges, and their democratic institutions did not fare well. As a result, by the beginning of the current period of expansion in

1974, the number of democracies in the world stood at about 39. According to Huntington, the current wave has produced the most rapid and far-reaching expansion with almost 70 new democracies being added.

Accounting for the diffusion and retrenchment of democracy over time is a difficult and complex enterprise. The spread of democracy seems to embody a diffusion process whereby leaders and citizens in some countries are led to push for the kind of democracy at home that others enjoy elsewhere. In this respect, the communications revolution of this century has made it much easier for citizens in previously isolated or "closed" societies to learn of the progress of democracy in other countries. However, the pattern of expansion followed by consolidation in some cases and collapse in others invites us to speculate about the potentially destabilizing effects of democratic transition. Clearly, in some cases the open competition associated with the electoral process unleashes forces that some new democratic institutions may not be able to control. In other cases, unrealistic expectations about improvements in living standards and quality of life may have been raised by the achievement of the kinds of procedural reforms associated with democratization. Disillusionment may well set in if the positive improvements in quality of life expected to accompany democratization are not forthcoming.

In this respect, Huntington and a number of scholars of democratic consolidation have contemplated whether or not there will be a third "reverse wave" of collapses in some of the democracies established after 1974. While there is some evidence to suggest that the period of dramatic expansion has ended, the prospects for consolidating democracy in many of the recently democratized states is far from clear. Certainly, General Pervez Musharraf's October 12, 1999 **COUP D'ÉTAT** in Pakistan and the two-day coup d'état against constitutional Venezuelan President Hugo Chavez in April 2002 signal the continuing fragility of some democratic states, even ones once thought to be relatively successful in their consolidation efforts. Similarly, Freedom House, a respected non-governmental organization monitoring the state of political liberties around the world, is increasingly concerned by the erosion of democracy and political freedom in Vladimir Putin's Russia.[3] Huntington's own view is that the answer to this question is tightly bound up with two factors: continued economic development in the new democracies and the receptivity to democracy of non-Western cultures (1997: 4). With respect to the former, the recent economic setbacks experienced by the previously buoyant Southeast Asian countries

3 See the news release from Freedom House, "The Erosion of Democracy in Russia Continues" (March 3, 2007), <http://www. freedomhouse.org/template. cfm?page=70&release=480>.

(Thailand, South Korea, and Indonesia in particular) may well threaten the nascent progress that democratizing forces have made there. Other scholars also stress the need to deepen the roots of democracy beyond the electoral process alone, arguing that a reliance on the process (elections) rather than the substantive democratic principles that make elections meaningful (popular control, constitutional government, individual liberty, and political equality) potentially dooms us to a third "reverse wave" (Diamond, 1996).

The transformation of all of the new democracies into full "liberal democracies" is far from certain, and conclusions must therefore be tentative. In fact, the terrorist attacks of 9/11 have led some to question this optimistic view of the inevitable spread of democracy. Within the framework of liberal democratic institutions and values, the twentieth-century state has expanded so much in its scope, its organization, and its complexity that our political vocabulary, rooted in eighteenth- and nineteenth-century models, sometimes fails to capture adequately the nature of modern government. At the same time, questions that were debated during the expansion of government earlier in this century continue to challenge citizens and policy-makers alike. Specifically, reform in Eastern Europe and the former Soviet Union, ideological change in the West, economic globalization, levels of governmental indebtedness, and emerging social and environmental issues have breathed new life into an old and enduring debate: what is the proper role of the state?

The assumption by the state of new responsibilities (or, what is sometimes more relevant today, its retreat from certain activities) does not occur without considerable debate or opposition. Very different conceptions exist about the proper role or functions of the state, and often quite distinct interests are represented by positions taken on these issues. In part, then, the nature of the state is a product of ideology, and the level of state activity at any point in time may reflect an ideological consensus, a balance of ideological forces, or the temporary dominance of one viewpoint over others. As we saw in Chapter Four, underlying ideological positions are often perceptions of interest, people's conception of their own needs and wants as experienced from a particular social position. It is generally on the basis of such perceptions of interest that people turn to the state for action or, conversely, object to governmental policy. It is particularly important to ask who the state serves or represents given that modern societies are typically fragmented in terms of classes, or interests, or ethno-linguistic identities (in short, in terms of all the particular communities or groups that may exist within the larger polity and that complicate the relationship between state and society).

While it may be fine in theory to say that the state should represent everyone or all groups, this may in practice be neither possible nor desirable. Who is represented by the state? This will depend in large measure on the nature of the political process (the means by which individuals and policy preferences are transmitted from the public to the government). In any polity there are crucial questions about the adequacy of the political process to respond to the interests of the citizens generally or for particular groups or interests within the polity. To assume that the actions of government reflect a consensus concerning the role of the state in society is to assume (unwisely) that the political process gives all interests and parties a political voice equal to their social strength. For any number of reasons this is not likely to be the case, as we will see below.

While the remainder of our discussion will focus on liberal democracy as the system that characterizes the political systems of Western Europe, North America, and most of the rest of the world's economically developed nation-states, it is worth noting that no two liberal democracies are exactly alike. Each reflects the way certain ideas and principles have been refracted by the history of the given society, and each is rooted in the political culture of the historical community involved. Liberal democracies are products of a process of development, one by no means finished or exhausted. The liberal notions of justice and democracy prominent today are far from identical to those that first emerged some 300 years ago. When examining the changes that liberal democracies have undergone, it is possible to ask if there is a point at which they cease to be liberal democracies and are better described otherwise. It is also possible in our contemporary state to ask about the directions in which liberal democracy could or should evolve. At this point, however, it is appropriate to set aside our discussion of the historical emergence of democracy and consider the conceptual and definitional challenges that the concept of democracy entails.

In essence, democracy literally means "rule of the many." Its origins are in two Greek words, *demos*, meaning "people," and *kratos*, meaning "power" or "rule." Observing democracy in practice, however, reveals a bewildering array of variations. According to one recent survey, there are more than 550 "subtypes" of democracy discussed in the empirical and theoretical literature

6.4
Democracy Defined

(Collier and Levitsky, 1996). Democracy was contrasted in classical literature with the "rule of the few" (aristocracy) and the "rule of one" (monarchy). Today, "democracy" is more often understood as the "rule of the *people*," as implied in Lincoln's famous phrase in the Gettysburg Address about a government "of the people, by the people, and for the people." As we noted in Chapter One, democracy is a form of **POPULAR SOVEREIGNTY**—the idea that the authority of the state derives from the people who are governed. What distinguishes democracy is its insistence that the authority of the state not only *derives* from the public but ultimately *rests with* the public in one fashion or another. In some way, the people must actually be involved in the exercise of the authority of the state, or those who exercise the authority of the state must be accountable to the people. Democracy is subversive of authority by insisting that power ultimately belongs to the ruled, not the rulers.

How do the people rule in a democracy? When societies were smaller and the scope of government was much less than it has become today, it was conceivable that "the people" might exercise authority themselves. In such a **DIRECT DEMOCRACY**, citizens themselves would determine policy. As communities became larger, more fragmented, and the tasks of the state became more complex, the direct participation of the people in government became increasingly impractical, and democracy came to mean the popular choice of delegates or representatives who govern *on behalf of* the people. In classical times, people understood by democracy the direct participation of all citizens (i.e., male property-owners) in the task of government; since the liberal revolution, democracy has been generally understood as a form of representative government in which people choose their rulers. Moreover, as Rousseau (the first major Western thinker to embrace democracy fully) recognized, if people choose representatives to rule them, there should be some means by which the people keep their representatives accountable. As we have seen earlier in this chapter, however, there are disagreements among democratic theorists about how a representative should act (as a trustee or as a delegate of their constituents), but in either case it is agreed that electors should periodically be given an opportunity to reward (re-elect) or punish (throw out) the politician who fails to fulfill their expectations. In short, then, in direct democracy, citizens exercise authority and power personally; in representative democracy, citizens choose delegates to exercise authority and power on their behalf—an exercise for which these delegates must answer to the people at some subsequent point in time.

In contemporary democracies, then, much comes down to the quality of the "choice" that citizens have between rival rulers. This "minimalist" or "elitist" conceptualization of modern democracy was clearly articulated by an economist, Joseph Schumpeter, in the late 1940s. As an economic theorist, Schumpeter was convinced that political consumers, like consumers of other goods and services, retained supremacy as long as they were presented with sufficient choice and so long as "political producers" were subject to unfettered competition in the same way that economic producers were allowed in economic theory. Accordingly, Schumpeterian democracy is defined as "... that institutional arrangement for arriving at political decisions in which individuals acquire the power to decide by means of a competitive struggle for the people's vote" (Schumpeter [1942] 1950: 269). Obviously, modern liberal democracies are examples of representative democracy, but there are also moments of direct democracy within these states, primarily through referendums and initiatives. Here the decision-making undertaken by elected representatives is supplemented by occasional direct participation by the citizenry, direct participation which may be more or less binding on the government.

The executive and judicial functions of the state have rarely been exercised directly by the body of citizens and certainly not in modern times. Even a thorough democrat might concede that under contemporary circumstances these tasks should be carried out by delegates of the people. In the modern era it has not been unusual for members of the executive to be elected, but commonly this applies only to the chief executive (especially in presidential systems) or heads of state. As we will see shortly, most democracies are of the parliamentary variety. In these systems, members of the executive are indirectly elected to their executive offices; as a result of the fusion of powers, they are available to participate in the executive only if they have been elected as legislators. Moreover, in the modern state, executive and judicial responsibilities are carried out by large bureaucracies staffed by (unelected) professional public servants.

While the most immediate and involved participation of citizens in government is the direct democracy of referendums, even this is a limited activity. Unlike many cases where decision-making is the final act in a whole process that involves debate, deliberation, and amendment, voting in a referendum occurs quite apart from the process by which the question is formulated and brought forward for decision. Both electing representatives and the direct democracy of the referendum and initiative are examples of non-participatory

FIGURE 6.4 Majority Rule

Sometimes, democracy is erroneously defined as "majority rule"—erroneously so defined because democracy may require consent of more than the majority and often gets by with the consent of something less than the majority. It is quite possible to require unanimity, although this would diminish greatly the chances of accomplishing anything and is quite impractical in any but the smallest decision-making bodies. In such small assemblies, though, a demand for consensus may well require that all—not simply a bare majority—agree. (By convention, within the Westminster model of parliamentary government, cabinet decisions are supposed to be matters of consensus.) There are any number of degrees of consent between unanimity and a numerical majority (50 per cent + 1); the consent of two-thirds of the eligible voters is a common requirement for constitutional decisions.

Even more common than levels of consent greater than a simple majority are levels that represent less than a majority. Sometimes a plurality (having more support than any other option or candidate or alternative) is sufficient. Many electoral systems will award victory on the basis of much less than a majority of the votes cast, and even an electoral majority may mean much less than a majority of the citizens (because all do not or cannot vote). Commonly a majority is required in the legislature to pass a motion, but this is simply a majority of those present, who may be but a handful of the legislators and thus who in turn represent only a very small portion of the citizen body. More important than the actual presence or absence of a numerical majority is adherence to three other notions intrinsic to democracy. One is the principle that the level of consent (whether a majority, plurality, two-thirds of the citizen body, etc.) be determined, agreed to, and a matter of public knowledge prior to the consent being polled. The second principle is that those who take part agree to abide by the outcome, regardless of which side of the issue they end up on. In other words, the process legitimizes all decisions, not simply those with which we agree. Thirdly, we would argue, this puts the onus on the winning side, and especially governments that gain control of the policy process, to implement policies that all can at least live with, even if they don't approve of them.

democracy. **PARTICIPATORY DEMOCRACY**, which requires that citizens be involved in the discussion and informed debate that precedes decision-making, is the democracy of small societies, of town hall meetings, and sometimes of the workplace, but it is something few see as a viable option in today's plural societies. Recognizing these challenges, conceptualizations of participatory democracy often emphasize the extent to which citizens can *learn* to be participatory democrats in the political sphere by sharing in the exercise of decision-making power in other spheres of their social life such as families, schools, churches, interest groups, and workplaces (Pateman, 1970).

Clearly, then, democracy is something that may be present in a political system in a variety of ways and with various degrees of intensity. At the very least, to qualify as democratic a system must present its citizens with the opportunity of selecting political elites in competitive, periodic elections. This is the very least, and it is possible for democracy to entail much more. We could construct a continuum beginning with an absence of public input and ending with a maximum of public involvement. Actual political systems or states fall somewhere on that continuum to the degree that they reflect these democratic elements. It should also be noted that most of the systems we recognize as democratic do not go very far beyond the minimum of periodic elections.

If we continue to regard democracy as "rule by the people," then critical examination suggests that liberal representative government, even with a universal franchise, presents a bare minimum requirement of democracy. Following Schumpeter, it does so only to the degree that citizens participate in the selection of rulers. We should acknowledge that this is often the extent of the participation that our liberal representative democracy grants to its citizens. This also means that the justification of such a democracy comes down to the significance of a popular selection of political officials.

In classical liberal democratic theory, the selection of representatives through popular periodic elections is justified as an important and rational activity by which citizens transmit their preferences for policies or their position on issues by matching their self-interest to the stated positions or platforms of candidates and/or parties. In other words, in liberal democracies, informed and interested citizens employ their vote in a rational fashion in response to the issues of the day and the policy options articulated by competing electoral candidates. In this way, democracy ensures popular sovereignty by implementing the common will—or at least the will of the majority—once voters rationally select responsible individuals who govern on the basis of the mandate supplied by their supporters. A comparison is sometimes drawn by liberal theorists between the functioning of the free market in the economy and the free exercise of the suffrage in democratic politics. In the market, demand by consumers is held to represent their rational choice of the objects corresponding to their self-interest, and the level of consumer demand will determine the supply of corresponding goods by producers. By analogy, political candidates fit the role of producers, competing to offer the best package of goods—i.e.,

6.5
Representative Democracy Considered

policies or programs—that will respond to the demands or desires of voters (the consumers). It is the responsiveness and accountability of governments, driven by the vitality of electoral competition that produces them, then, that determines the health of a democracy.

Several problems attend this depiction of **ELECTORAL ACTIVITY**, not the least of which is the large body of empirical evidence that reveals that it is not an accurate representation of actual citizen behavior. Studies of political behavior, for example, have indicated several characteristics of voters that run contrary to the portrait drawn by classical democratic theory. One is a lack of interest and involvement in the political process. The majority of citizens participate in the political system only by voting, choosing not to engage in any number of other voluntary activities such as running for office, campaigning on behalf of a candidate, writing a representative, etc. Even more troubling to some is the low turnout in national elections where such participation is entirely voluntary. As the data in Figure 6.5 illustrate, in the United States, where the onus is on citizens to register if they wish to vote, barely half the electorate participates. In many Western democracies (e.g., Australia and Italy), voting is no longer a privilege or a right but a legal requirement enforced by penalties.

A further concern for classic liberal theorists is the finding that voting is often a very non-rational activity. In other words, voting behavior is not primarily the result of an evaluation of the fit between self-interest and the policy options articulated by candidates, but rather it is often the byproduct of other, non-rational factors such as socialization, habit, affect (emotion), misinformation, and/or manipulation. In addition, early social scientific voter studies identified unexpected anti-democratic or non-democratic attitudes. Many individuals seemed to display attitudes identified as authoritarian; in particular some seemed prepared to defer to authority while others manifested a (perhaps unhealthy) desire to exercise authority over others. Typically, such attitudes were identified among the "apathetic," the non-participators.

What are we to conclude from these empirical findings? Do they speak to us about the character of ordinary individuals and confirm the anti-democratic prejudices that have prevailed through so much of human history? Or do they tell us something about a society that permits little in the way of democracy and demands even less from its citizens? For example, given the autonomy of government from its citizens—that is, the actual lack of direct input by citizens into decision-making—is there any reason for citizens to take an active, rational interest in politics? Should they bother

FIGURE 6.5 Cross-National Differences in Voter Turnout

AVERAGE TURNOUT OF ELIGIBLE VOTERS %; NUMBER OF ELECTIONS FROM 1960-1995

Australia	95%	14	Belgium	91%	12
Italy	90%	9	Luxembourg	90%	7
Iceland	89%	10	New Zealand	88%	12
Denmark	87%	14	Germany	86%	9
Czech Republic	85%	2	Netherlands	83%	7
Norway	81%	9	Canada	76%	11
France	76%	9	United Kingdom	75%	9
Ireland	74%	11	Japan	71%	12
India	58%	6	USA	54%	9
Switzerland	54%	8	Poland	51%	2

It is worth noting that some of these figures, particularly the American ones, would change if the turnout of *registered* voters were considered.

The International Institute for Democracy and Electoral Assistance (IDEA) in Stockholm has recently made available a wealth of voter turnout data from all over the world. See ‹http://www.idea.int/vt/index.cfm›.

Source: Adapted from Mark Franklin, "Electoral Participation," in LeDuc, Neimi, and Norris, 1996: 218.

to take the time and effort to become informed about issues when there is little if any opportunity to employ that information? Is it possible to argue that the behavior of citizens very much reflects the opportunities given them (or not)? It would seem that there are two sets of impediments to citizen participation—one institutional and the other cultural.

In the first place, the electoral machinery of many, if not most, democracies does not in any way register, let alone reward, a "rational" vote (where rational indicates a vote cast on the basis of a judicious consideration of policies, issues, and programs). The representative who is elected, or the leader of the party to which she belongs, has no real knowledge about why she received more votes than any other candidate. There is no way for you as a voter to indicate on your ballot that you support this party for its economic and foreign policies, but you oppose its stand on social programs and legalized gambling. Nor is there any way to distinguish your ballot so informed from mine, which supports the same party because of its promises on social programs and despite its economic policies. This lack of specificity in the way the ballot records one's support makes all talk by winning parties about having received a mandate to carry out specific policies most dubious.

Ultimately, the democratic vote amounts to a transmission of trust or statement of faith rather than a set of instructions or directives, and in this case, affect, or habit, or socialization may be just as "rational" a basis for decision as any calculation of enlightened "self-interest." We should not expect voters to act "rationally" when the political process in which they are active does not encourage rationality, take notice of it, nor in some cases even permit it. But if, in both theory and practice, we recognize that governing requires rational decision-making, then it seems odd not to ask whether the participation of the people in the political system should not also entail rationality and, therefore, a set of institutions and practices that permit and indeed require such rationality.

In the second place, the institutional limitations to democracy are buttressed by cultural messages transmitted from generation to generation. We have spoken above about political culture as an aggregate of the beliefs within a society or community about the political world, and we identified a belief in democracy as a central feature of our contemporary political culture. At the same time, this is a limited belief in democracy, just as the democracy of our institutions is a very limited public participation. Hand in hand with the belief in the rightness of democracy goes the age-old suspicion of "the public" or of its competence to judge how authority and power should be exercised. The phrase "too much democracy is dangerous" seems to capture this ambivalence: democracy is good so long as it is kept within limits and not taken too far. This equivocal stance toward democracy is very often transmitted, if not reinforced, by the socialization process.

When empirical studies undermine the portrait of democratic voting as rational decision-making, they also undermine liberal democracy's traditional claims to legitimacy.[4] If modern democracy claims to be *the* good form of government because it realizes popular sovereignty, and that sovereignty turns out on close examination to be largely symbolic or merely formal, then the claim to legitimacy is seriously undermined. If liberal democracy fails to give citizens an actual role in governing, and if it fails to encourage rational activity in the selection of rulers, what does it do?

If liberal democracy is distinguished from other political arrangements by the popular selection of elites, then much depends upon the nature and significance of this selection process. Commonly, the modern definition of democracy makes reference to "periodic, competitive" elections. But how competitive is it? For decades incumbent members of the House of Representatives who seek re-election have success rates of greater than 90 per cent (re-

4 Some defenders claim that individuals may not choose to be active in politics if the system is effectively addressing their concerns. In this case, non-participation does not mean disengagement, or non-attentiveness, but merely satisfaction. Individuals who are inactive may still be monitoring the political system and its outputs, and they may be ready to act if and when they become concerned. In this respect, they may resemble a group of parents with young children at a swimming pool. The parents might appear to be simply idling away a day at the poolside, but in reality they are closely monitoring the scene, ready to intervene the moment something goes awry (see Zaller, 1999).

election success rates for incumbent senators are more variable, but still they are quite high). In addition, the significance of competition is that it is supposed to make our choices more meaningful by increasing the range of options presented to us. There is a variety of ways in which the choices we confront may be more or less meaningful. We might be concerned about the number of choices, the ideological diversity or range of choices offered, the clarity of competing positions advanced, the responsibility of candidates for positions advanced or to be implemented (i.e., is there any point evaluating the relative promises and commitments of candidates A and B if there is no guarantee that the party leadership will listen to A or B, or allow them to follow through on promises made?), or the accuracy of the available information about the candidates or policy options at stake. As we will see, there are very real differences in the electoral and party systems of liberal democracies, differences that make a difference to the quality of choice the voters can make and to the quality of representation they receive. If the quality of choice with which citizens are presented is diminished for any reason, then so, too, is much of the value that can be claimed for liberal democracy.

Increasingly, the modern state must be democratic to be legitimate; yet, at the same time, the impression persists that often our institutions present a democratic façade behind which a largely undemocratic politics persists. Our political culture is effectively democratic; ideologies that are elitist and anti-democratic remain at the margins. The 1997 trial and conviction of Timothy McVeigh (who was subsequently executed in May 2001) and Terry Nichols (who is currently serving a life sentence) for the bombing of a federal office building in Oklahoma City draws attention to the vitality of anti-system sentiment among some minorities. Similarly, the "unabomber" (Ted Kaczynski) trial in 1998 drove home a similar message concerning the persistence of counter-cultural sentiments and the potential for these marginalized critics to disrupt the system through domestic terrorism. Fortunately, however, Americans by and large remain strong supporters of democracy. Of course, this commitment to democracy and freedom has only strengthened in the aftermath of 9/11, though some might question the potentially adverse impact on civil liberties of some of the anti-terrorism measures adopted in recent years.

It is easy for citizens who have grown up within a democratic political system to take it for granted. Historically, though,

6.6
Distrust of Democracy

the allegiance to democracy is rather recent, something perhaps obscured by our knowledge that a democracy existed in ancient Athens, one that was in some senses more direct and participatory than that of today. On the other hand, Athenian democracy was limited to a small body of citizens (who were property-owning males), and the democratic period in Athens was denounced by many of its leading citizens. Recall that neither Aristotle nor Plato were democrats, and it seems that few among the educated classes mourned the passing of democracy in ancient Greece. Early critics of democracy had at least two concerns. First of all, democracy was seen to be inherently unstable, to degenerate easily into demagoguery and tyranny. The term "demagogue" indicates someone who incites the crowd by playing upon its fears, vanity, or prejudice and who becomes its leader by such flattery or deceit. In ancient experience, these leaders, originally acclaimed by the people, came to exercise power absolutely and without restraint, thus becoming *tyrants*. For the ancients, tyranny was the worst form of government, being roughly equivalent to (and receiving the same scorn that we today would reserve for) personal dictatorship. A second fear was that democracy involves a rule by the larger part of the people *against* the lesser part in what has been called in more recent times a **TYRANNY OF THE MAJORITY**. Instead of being ruled by all the people for the general welfare, democracy may become a rule by one class or group (albeit the largest) for its own interest, an interest that may involve exploiting or persecuting a minority.

Underlying these criticisms of democracy has very often been a relatively low opinion of "the people," that is to say, of ordinary citizens, who were assumed to be ignorant and irrational (an assumption that has informed elitist attitudes throughout the centuries). Such fears of "mob rule" or "the crowd" became more prevalent in the latter decades of the nineteenth century during the first wave of democratization when the industrial revolution had created a large and impoverished working class that was pressuring for inclusion in the political process (LeBon, [1893] 1960). Accordingly, the argument runs, a certain amount of power must be kept in the hands of an enlightened elite to keep government from being usurped by a tyrant, or to shelter minority interests, or simply to protect the benefits and achievements of culture and civilization. We might point out that the fear of a "tyranny of the majority" has often been raised by a minority occupying economically, politically, or socially privileged positions. Nonetheless, in large plural societies, the possibility of a majority (particularly of a religious, linguistic, or ethnic nature) oppressing a minority *is* a

The Statue of
Liberty, New
York City

potential problem for fully participatory models of democracy. In those societies where the unequal exercise of power also ensures that the mass of the population remains poor and uneducated, fears about democracy may not be ungrounded. Rather, it is the possibility or the reality of authoritarian dictatorship that is to be feared in these settings where majorities lack basic skills necessary to challenge authority. Not surprisingly, then, democracy remained a suspect form of government from the time of Aristotle until the late eighteenth century when thinkers like Jean-Jacques Rousseau began to make a strong case for its legitimacy. It was a few generations later that reforms began to make representative liberal governments into representative liberal democratic governments. The dangers of democracy were less apparent once the general population began to be neither poor nor ignorant. Certainly the success of democracy in the United States in the nineteenth century did much to recommend it to other liberal nations.

6.7
The Costs and Benefits of Democracy

Our examination of political history and practice reveals an ambiguous commitment to democracy; the democracy we have is quite limited and within the limited scope of electing representatives is often incomplete or compromised. At the same time our ideologies, our constitutions, and even our foreign policy rest on a formal commitment to democracy, however vaguely defined. What we have not done yet in this chapter is examine why it matters whether or not our politics is democratic or whose interests are best served by having a democratic polity. If we can clarify these questions, then we may also illuminate why it matters (or doesn't) that our present experience of democratic politics is limited in the ways we have identified.

In Chapter One we suggested that one hallmark of the modern era in politics has been the replacement of traditional and charismatic forms of legitimacy with legal-rational grounds and that these latter have come down to basically two: justice and popular sovereignty. These are alternate means of procuring legitimacy; a government will be seen as legitimate if it exercises authority correctly (justice) or because it implements a popular will or mandate. Consequently, it should not surprise us that virtually every government claims to provide justice and to carry out the public will. This should alert us to the possibility that governments that are not democratic might claim to be so—and the likelihood that governments will often be less democratic than they claim. The concept of legitimacy helps to explain what interest governments or rulers may have in democracy. Democracy, from the perspective of those in power, may be *a means of securing support for the exercise of power.* Those who enjoy the exercise of power and authority may wish for just enough democracy to grant them legitimacy but not enough to put serious constraints on their exercise of authority and power. We have acknowledged that democracy is not the only means of realizing popular sovereignty, but we have also suggested that anything less than the actual participation of the people in some way is only an "apparent" popular sovereignty. It may well be that it is in the interest of elites to have a popular sovereignty that is only apparent rather than one that is effective. But it is harder to see that this is in the long-term interest of citizens.

The whole point of the liberal revolution against medieval authority was to secure individuals from the arbitrary exercise of power, and the kind of power justified by traditional or charismatic grounds could offer no such guarantee. As we have indicated, there are two fundamental ways to be secure from arbitrary power. One is to constrain the use of power so that it cannot harm us, and the second is to exercise that power ourselves. The latter is the end of democracy, the former is the aim of justice. Further, our commitment to democracy may be weak or take second place if justice appears to be doing the job of protecting our interests. This will be particularly true if justice seems more convenient or efficient than democracy. The critic of (more) democracy will point out, and often quite rightly, that democracy is expensive, that it slows down the work of government, that it is economically inefficient and tends to burden the marketplace, that it involves a commitment by citizens to activity that may not be attractive (or as attractive as other leisure pursuits), that it is simply too time-consuming, or that it presupposes a level of political knowledge and experience that citizens do not presently have (and that it would be too expensive to provide them with). It is best, on these grounds, to keep government small, manageable, economic, and in the hands of experts. Such an argument gains strength when it can be demonstrated that justice secures us from the arbitrary or injurious use of that power by governmental elites. Given the establishment of constitutionalism, of the rule of law, and in particular of the entrenchment of individual rights in normal and constitutional law, it is tempting to conclude that democracy has become something of a luxury, perhaps something superfluous. According to this argument, governments may best be kept honest by an appeal to the courts when our rights have been infringed—a method that is more efficient and convenient for the community at large (although it may not be for the individuals who must make such appeals) than wholesale political participation.

On the other hand, this last view overlooks the relationship between democracy and justice. Who protects, interprets, and defines our rights—politicians or judges? Can rights be secure if those who protect, interpret, and define them are not accountable to the public? Democracy is a possible means of keeping those who safeguard the citizens' rights accountable to the citizens. Similarly, social justice involves a variety of difficult decisions about the distribution of social values, the criteria by which distribution should take place, and about what kinds of inequalities should be tolerated. Who should make these decisions? If social justice is an entitlement of the people, rather than a gift from rulers, then perhaps there is a function for democracy here that is not optional. With political economy, we encounter various options concerning the degree to which the state should engage in regulating the market or intervene in the economy generally. Who should determine the character of the state's management of economic life? Here some argue that democracy is a potential means by which the state can be made responsive to the needs of all classes, not merely those of the economic elite or of the dominant economic class. Are they right? At the very least, justice issues point out the interest that citizens might have in democracy, regardless of whether it is convenient, or easy, or efficient.

**6.8
Conclusion:
The Prospects for
Democracy**

Finally, at the beginning of the twenty-first century, we can ask what are the prospects for democracy? In the 1980s and 1990s a great number of countries in Eastern Europe, Asia, Africa, and Latin America embraced some form of democracy after generations of authoritarian or totalitarian rule. As we saw earlier in this chapter, the initial two waves of democratization were followed by reverse waves in which some of the newly emergent democracies fell back into authoritarianism. Will this pattern be repeated in the aftermath of the third wave? What are the constraints working against the growth of democracy and perhaps even towards its contraction? What is the likelihood that popular participation will be further extended or strengthened?

In the past, democracy often came into being or was extended as the result of revolution or as political leaders responded to public pressure or unrest. It is probably a safe generalization to say that those in power do not voluntarily relinquish any unless it is in their own interest to do so. Perhaps political parties committed to greater democratization will be elected in the future, and perhaps circumstances will arise to make greater democracy an attractive option to those in power. Revolution for a *more* democratic polity does not seem likely so long as Western economies are relatively healthy; people seem more likely to take radical political action when they have less to lose (or, conversely, when they have more at stake). It is much easier, unfortunately, to be definite about the impediments or constraints on democracy in contemporary society.

One challenge is the plural character of modern societies. The apparent inability of the United States to replace the dictatorship of Saddam Hussein in Iraq with a viable democratic regime shows clearly that erecting representative institutions alone is insufficient to ensure that a divided society will come together in successful democratic governance. More broadly, it is increasingly impossible to speak with any accuracy of "the people" or about a public will; there are typically several or many peoples and a variety of wills within the public. At least three different problems are presented by such plurality. One is the possibility that any democratic majority might systematically exclude a people or peoples, a result that can only be destabilizing over the long term. At the very least, the legitimacy of the state will be quickly eroded in the view of those excluded consistently. Secondly, it may not be possible, given the institutions in place, to manufacture a majority. In that case, the decisive voice is that of a plurality. Here then, a minority ends up deciding for all, which may well be unjust and may also be destabilizing. Finally, democracy has traditionally provided a means of collective decision-making. This implies that people have a common interest or are able to make the compromises necessary to reach a solution satisfactory to their competing interests. As the plural character of modern society grows and is more sharply defined, compromises between competing interests may well become more difficult to reach; instead of a collective decision-making process, democracy becomes the arena for irreconcilable, competing voices seeking outright victory rather than compromise.

The increasingly complex world in which our politics is situated presents another set of challenges for democracy. One is that it has helped fuel the tremendous growth of government in the last century. While there is much action and more rhetoric about making government smaller and simpler, success has been limited, and the utility of many cutbacks remains uncertain. Apart from the sheer size of government and the challenges that its "volume of business" present for democracy, the business of government has become, like society at large, increasingly technical. Informed

Key Terms

American Revolution
Edmund Burke
Catholic Church
checks and balances
civil society
consent of the governed
constitutionalism
coup d'état
custom
delegate model of
representation
democracy
depersonalization
direct democracy
divine right
electoral activity
the Enlightenment
empire
feudalism
franchise
French Revolution
imperialism
judicial independence
liberal democracy
liberal modernity
liberal revolution
majority rule
market economy
medieval society
middle class
participatory democracy
popular sovereignty
the Reformation
representative autonomy
representative democracy
representative government
republican
responsible government
revolution
rights
"three waves of democracy"
trustee model of
representation
tyranny of the majority
voter turnout

decision-making requires informed decision-makers, and democratic decision-making requires an informed citizenry. We are told that citizens are more informed and better educated than ever before, but they are not always informed or educated about government, or politics, or about the substance of political decisions. Where the bulk of that information is received through a medium like contemporary commercial television, there is reason to doubt that they are adequately informed for democratic decision-making. There is no reason why they could not be so informed, but it is not obvious that all (or even how many) citizens are sufficiently interested to become so informed or are willing to invest the time to do so.

Democracy carries an implicit endorsement of the political sphere; by inviting or even requiring citizens to participate in the exercise of authority and power, we indicate that this is an important, worthwhile activity. Such an approach and attitude can be traced back to Aristotle's view of humans as essentially political animals. For Aristotle, politics was a noble, worthy human activity (unlike making money, which was activity fit for slaves). It is not much of an exaggeration to say that in our contemporary democracies the situation is reversed; making and spending money is celebrated, while politicians and political activity are despised and distrusted. Again there is an irony here: much of the public disenchantment with the political realm stems from its failure to be more democratic or to be as democratic in practice as it is in theory. The public hears political promises made in order to gain its support; the public grows cynical as politicians in power backtrack or renege on their commitments. Political actors seek to manage public opinion in order to co-opt the minimal accountability they must submit to and manage to alienate a wary public. In the process, the whole political process is discredited, and instead of agitating for more democracy, citizens turn away from the limited democracy they have.

While a healthy democracy may be difficult to achieve and maintain, we need not conclude on such a pessimistic note. The spread of democracy worldwide is something to be applauded, and the alternatives to democracy are unpleasant to say the least. We should bear in mind that democracy is *both* an ideal *as well as* a description of a certain type of political system. The two are not necessarily the same. We need not have perfection to have something worthwhile, and we should not let shortcomings associated with the realization of democracy in the political world blind us to its virtues (Mueller, 1999). Democracies are works in progress, and political science can help by identifying best practices and institutional improvements. In the remainder of this book, we chart the basic variations in the practice of liberal democracy around the world, and invite you to judge how well these institutional configurations embody and express the ideals of democracy.

References and Suggested Readings

Publishing information is not provided for texts in political thought which are either out of print or widely available in contemporary editions.

Barber, Benjamin R. 1984. *Strong Democracy: Participatory Politics for a New Age*. Berkeley, CA: University of California Press.

Barraclough, Geoffrey. 1967. *An Introduction to Contemporary History*. New York: Pelican.

Bernstein, Robert A. 1989. *Elections, Representation, and Congressional Voting Behavior: The Myth of Constituency Control*. Englewood Cliffs, NJ: Prentice-Hall.

Collier, David, and Steven Levitsky. 1996. "Democracy 'With Adjectives': Conceptual Innovation in Comparative Research." Unpublished. Berkeley, CA: University of California, Berkeley, Department of Political Science.

Dahl, Robert. 1956. *A Preface to Democratic Theory*. Chicago, IL: University of Chicago Press.

Diamond, Larry. 1996. "Is the Third Wave Over?" *Journal of Democracy* 7, 3 (July): 20-37.

Held, David. 1987. *Models of Democracy*. Cambridge: Polity Press.

Hill, Christopher. 1969. *Reformation to Industrial Revolution*. Harmondsworth, UK: Penguin.

Huntington, Samuel P. 1991. *The Third Wave: Democratization in the Late Twentieth Century*. Norman, OK: University of Oklahoma Press.

——. 1997. "After Twenty Years: The Future of the Third Wave." *Journal of Democracy* 8, 4 (October): 3-12.

Jones, A.H.M. 1986. *Athenian Democracy*. Baltimore, MD: Johns Hopkins University Press.

LeBon, Gustave. [1893] 1960. *The Crowd: A Study of the Popular Mind*. New York: Vintage.

LeDuc, Lawrence, Richard Neimi, and Pippa Norris, eds. 1996. *Comparing Democracies*. Thousand Oaks, CA: Sage.

Macpherson, C.B. 1977. *The Life and Times of Liberal Democracy*. New York: Oxford University Press.

Mansfield, Jane. 1980. *Beyond Adversarial Democracy*. New York: Basic Books.

Mueller, John. 1999. *Capitalism, Democracy, and Ralph's Pretty Good Grocery*. Princeton, NJ: Princeton University Press.

Pateman, Carol. 1970. *Participation and Democratic Theory*. Cambridge: Cambridge University Press.

Rousseau, Jean-Jacques. 1762. *The Social Contract*.

Rudé, George. 1964. *Revolutionary Europe: 1783-1815*. Glasgow: Fontana.

Schmitter, Philippe C., and Terry Lynn Karl. 1991. "What Democracy Is ... and Is Not." *Journal of Democracy* 2, 3 (Summer): 75-88.

Schumpeter, Joseph. [1942] 1950. *Capitalism, Socialism and Democracy*. New York: Harper.

Watkins, Frederick. 1957. *The Political Tradition of the West*. Cambridge, MA: Harvard University Press.

Zaller, John. 1999. "Perversities in the Ideal of the Informed Citizenry." Paper presented at "The Transformation of Civic Life" Conference. Middle Tennessee State University, Murfreesboro and Nashville, Tennessee (November 12-13); <http://www.mtsu.edu/-seig/paper_j_zaller.html>.

FOUR

the institutions of liberal democratic states

SEVEN | Democratic Governance: Presidential and Parliamentary Variants

"The principles of a free constitution are irrevocably lost, when the legislative power is nominated by the executive."

—Edward Gibbon, *Decline and Fall of the Roman Empire*

Having traced the philosophical and historical origins of democracy, we are now in a position to assess the institutions and processes characteristic of contemporary liberal democracies. Looking at what these polities do will occupy us for the rest of this text. This chapter briefly introduces the main functions all states perform and identifies the key institutional arrangements that liberal democracies have adopted to perform these functions. We will then turn to a discussion of two models of democratic governance that differ in terms of the relationship of the political executive to the political legislature. Presidential systems, as we shall see, separate these branches of government, while **PARLIAMENTARY SYSTEMS** merge or fuse them. There are far-reaching consequences that follow from this fundamental difference, which we will also explore briefly in this chapter.

7.1 Introduction

7.2
Constitutions and Constitutionalism

Perhaps the most basic and important distinction to be drawn in comparative politics is between constitutional and non-constitutional governments. We might define a **CONSTITUTION** as *a body of fundamental or basic rules* (indeed, the German Constitution is called the Basic Law) *outlining the structures of power and authority and the relations between these and the people.* In short, constitutions are a set of basic rules that make the exercise of political power law-abiding and non-arbitrary. Laws that politicians make that stand in opposition to the legal provisions of a constitution can be struck down by the legal system and declared illegal in a process called **JUDICIAL REVIEW**.

Normally, but not necessarily, these rules are codified in a written text. However, not all constitutions take this form. For example, when Walter Bagehot published a book entitled *The English Constitution* in 1867, he analyzed not a written document but rather the actual structure of the power and authority of the British state. In not having a written text, the British Constitution is unusual among modern democracies. There are, however, written parts of the British Constitution, including such documents as the *Magna Carta* and the *Act of Habeus Corpus*, successive electoral reform acts, the *Statute of Westminster*, etc. These bits and pieces of acts of Parliament, judicial rulings, and even unwritten rules define political relationships between institutions of state and between the British state and the people; they function as constitutional rules in the absence of a body to enforce them *because the relevant political actors accept them as constitutional.* While no one doubts that Britain is a constitutional monarchy, this unusual feature of British politics introduces some ambiguity into the political system, and some critics claim that it is time to codify constitutional **STATUTES** and practices in that country.

By contrast, when Americans talk about their Constitution, they are referring to a written document, a body of law that serves like a legal blueprint for the edifice of the state. This is more typical of countries, and in the American Constitution we can see the basic features of most constitutions. Not all constitutions will address all of these topics, nor give equal stress to each of them, but they do the following:

1. Define who exercises authority and/or the institutions and processes by which authority is exercised and, in either case, what kind of authority (or function of the state) is involved. Examples of this would include indicating that the chief executive is an elected **PRESIDENT**, or stipulating

Super Forum
enlightening
British don't have a written constitution their politicians accept the rules instead of finding loopholes to circumvent the written document. only works if people agree on what those rules are. So far so good But there is no written Bill of Rights to protect people

that **LEGISLATION** must receive the support of a majority in both houses of the legislature, or specifying the maximum time permissible between elections or rules concerning the qualifications for holding office, etc.

2. Outline the relationships between and the priority of the various primary institutions and offices (or branches) of the state. The various checks and balances of the American system of separated powers would fall in this category, as would the fusion of powers of the parliamentary model, if constitutionalized (as it has been in Canada, Australia, and New Zealand, for example). The relationship of the head of state to other fundamental institutions may be addressed here.

Both (1) and (2) cover the basic elements of political systems or types of governmental regimes. In addition, constitutions may (but do not necessarily) address the following:

3. If applicable, divide jurisdictions between levels of government and define other fundamental relationships between them. This is a necessary task in federal states, and we will discuss what this means at greater length in Chapter Eight.

4. Establish the rights of citizens with respect to the state, and indicate how they may seek redress for violation of these rights. The first ten amendments to the American Constitution comprise what is known as the Bill of Rights. Criticism of the British Constitution for its lack of enshrining such "positive rights" for its citizens has been growing. Since 1988 there has been a vigorous campaign in that country pressing for the adoption of a constitutionally entrenched (and hence legally protected) "Bill of Rights" (see Chapter 12). Canada is one state with a "constitution similar in principle to that of the United Kingdom" (Preamble to the Canada Act, 1867), and for many years this included the absence of a written bill of rights. However, as part of a series of constitutional changes in 1982, the country adopted a "Charter of Rights and Freedoms." The experience of Canada before and after the adoption of the Charter underscores the point that the extent of judicial review—and therefore the reach of judicial power—is greatly enhanced by the presence of an entrenched rights code. This has enormous significance for the operation of the political system.

5. Indicate the conditions that must be satisfied to amend the constitution. In general, because constitutional rules are considered more basic and fundamental than other types of legal and political directives, constitutional changes are more difficult to achieve than other forms. Amending formulas may be simple or complex, rigid or flexible, and there is no necessary link between these two dimensions.

The American amendment process appears to be fairly simple, but it turns out in practice to be rigid; over 10,000 amendments have been proposed since 1787, but only 26 have passed (ten of which constituted the Bill of Rights and were passed in 1789). As might be expected, a constitutional amendment in the United States can be proposed at the federal level or at the state level. In the former case, a proposal must receive a two-thirds vote in both houses of Congress. In the latter instance, a proposal may be made by a national convention called for that purpose if requested by two-thirds (34) of the 50 states. In fact, this latter method of proposal has never been used. Once proposed, an amendment must be *ratified*, which requires approval by three-quarters of the states, either through approval by the state legislatures or by constitutional conventions held in the states. It is up to Congress to choose the method of ratification, and ratification by conventions was used only once (to end Prohibition). It should perhaps also be noted that at each stage, by either means, the margin of approval is much greater than a simple majority (50 per cent + 1); this is common to constitutional votes and reflects the belief that the basic rules should not be constantly changing.

By contrast, the Basic Law of Germany has a simple and flexible **AMENDING PROCEDURE**: a vote of two-thirds of the members of both houses of the federal legislature. In this case, the provision that the members of the *Bundesrat* are delegates of the *Länder* governments makes such a simple procedure capable of securing the consent of both levels of state. As a result it has been possible for the German Constitution, although less than 60 years old, to be amended with great frequency. Interestingly, though, there are parts of the German Constitution that cannot be amended, including the existence of a federal system and some fundamental individual rights.

A more important distinction relating to constitutions exists, however. For example, the written constitution adopted by the then-totalitarian state of the Soviet Union would lead an uncritical reader to believe that citizens of that country were as well or better

The American Constitution

protected than their counterparts in any genuine liberal democracy. Of course, we know that in practice political authorities in that state completely ignored the provisions laid down in that document. The existence of constitutional documents, then, does not guarantee the existence of constitutional rule. This may be thought of as a distinction between the formal (written) constitution and the **MATERIAL CONSTITUTION** (the actual structure). Ideally, the formal describes the material. Just as a map becomes out of date when high seas wash away a coastline or a dam floods a valley, so too parts of the written constitution can cease to describe the reality of the state; just as maps are redrawn to reflect a changing world, constitutions sometimes must change to match new political realities.

To describe the idea that the state will be limited by a written constitution, we will use the term **CONSTITUTIONALISM** (a term we briefly introduced in Chapter One). Constitutionalism has several requirements. In addition to the rules that define what governments may or may not do (or how they may or may not do it), there must be a forum where disputes about the meaning of the constitution and whether or not it has been adhered to can be heard and decided. This, we have seen, is the function of a high or "supreme" or special constitutional court. It follows then that there should also be a means of enforcing constitutional rules and rulings. In theory this would mean some other institution of the state, such as the police or military, willing to employ force on behalf of the authority of the supreme or constitutional court. In normal practice, if ever, constitutions don't work this way. Perhaps the most important facet of constitutionalism is its requirement that all political actors abide by the constitutional rules of the polity, and where these are in dispute, all recognize the legitimacy of the body designated for deciding these disputes and abide by its rulings. We might call this disposition on the part of political actors a constitutional ethic or norm; without it, constitutions will be merely symbolic documents. By analogy, when one agrees to play a game, one has also agreed to abide by the rules of that game and accept the word of the duly constituted umpire if there are disputes about what is acceptable or not. You cannot, because a rule is contrary to your purposes, simply set it aside in the middle of the game. And yet, when a political leader "suspends" a constitution because of supposed "instability" when all that is threatened is her own electoral chances, that is all that she has done. In such a case, there is a constitution but no constitutionalism. Ultimately, constitutionalism cannot be forced, or enforced, but must become such an integral part of the political culture that political actors cannot conceive of doing other than as the constitution permits. This is one reason why it is important that the body of constitutional rules remain in touch with the central values, beliefs, and aspirations of the population of the polity.

<table>
<tr><td>

7.3
Basic Functions
of the State

</td><td>

Within the wide diversity of states and the multiplicity of constitutions that define them, a few basic functions are common, and indeed it is arguable that such functions must be performed in some way in any political society. It is important to keep distinct the **FUNCTIONS** that governments perform from the **INSTITUTIONS** that perform these functions and to keep both of these distinct from the **TYPE OF SYSTEM** or constitution that arranges the institutions and their relationships.

</td></tr>
</table>

We will begin with the classic threefold distinction, which revolves around three different aspects of one inescapable fact: governments *decide*—this is what it means to have power, to be authoritative. In all collective enterprises, short of achieving unanimity, someone or some group must decide for the rest *and* do so in such a way that the rest acknowledge their right to do so. The most basic function of the state, then, is one of **DECISION-MAKING**. Because authority is now generally exercised through the impersonal instrument of law, the decision-making function is often called the **LEGISLATIVE** function, "legislating" being the business of making laws. We should recognize, though, that the decisions made by government may be quite different from law. On the one hand, whereas laws are rules that apply more or less universally and continually, some decisions (e.g., to appoint an ambassador, to declare a national disaster, to recognize a citizen's outstanding bravery) may be one-time and quite particular. On the other hand, while laws are generally statements about what may or may not be done, or about what must or must not be done (i.e., they "permit" or "prohibit," "prescribe" or "proscribe"), many authoritative decisions are about conferring benefits (like pensions), or providing public goods (like education or health care), or encouraging economic activity (through subsidies, loans, or setting interest rates, etc.). Most of us meet government more often through these kinds of programs than by encountering "the law." In this sense, the decision-making function is broader than law and is better captured by the term **POLICY-MAKING**. **POLICY** in turn can be defined broadly as *any course of action or inaction that government deliberately chooses to take.*

In any organized society, decisions—whether particular, rules, or programmatic—must be made in an authoritative way. Institutions, processes, and the systems that organize both will determine at least three things:

1. *who* will make these decisions,
2. *how* these decisions will be made, and
3. *which* decisions can or cannot in fact be made.

These three variables—the "who," "how," and "what" of decision-making—will vary considerably from polity to polity or, even more so, from one type of political system to another. As might be equally obvious, the variables of "who," "how," and "what" will also apply to other functions of the state.

To make a decision is one thing; to implement it or carry it out is another matter altogether. It is probably safe to say that most of us are better at making decisions than at realizing them, and most of us would rather make decisions than implement them, given the choice. Nonetheless, if decisions are not somehow put into effect, they become meaningless. Just as the kinds of decisions governments make can vary, so too will **IMPLEMENTATION** of decisions. In the case of a law, it may mean enforcing sanctions or penalties against those who do not obey; with a policy or broad program it may involve the delivery of services, or the payment of funds, or the maintenance of physical plant, etc. In either case, a complex organization of resources, human and otherwise, is required to carry out what was intended in the authoritative decision. This function is typically called the **EXECUTIVE** or administrative function of the state. By and large, this is entrusted to the permanent **BUREAUCRACY** that characterizes the state as a form of social organization. Modern government consists (to a large degree) of many bureaucracies, organized to deliver programs, enforce laws, or administer regulations. Collectively, these various government departments that implement decisions are sometimes called "the bureaucracy."

Finally, wherever authoritative decisions are made and implemented, there will be disputes, and the kinds of disagreement will be as various as the decisions and their implementation. Consider the "who," "how," and "what" of decision-making again—each of these is a possible source of dispute. Was the decision made by the person or body authorized to make such decisions? Was the decision made according to the procedural rules set out for decision-makers? Was the decision one that can in fact be made by decision-makers? Someone or some body must have the responsibility for answering these questions or settling these disputes; if not, the legitimacy of the state could be undermined. This function of **ADJUDICATION**, or dispute settlement, has commonly been called the **JUDICIAL** function.

Judgment of disputes concerning the authoritative decisions of the state usually falls into one of two very broad categories: disputes about the decision itself or about the implementation of the decision. Roughly speaking, this corresponds to a distinction between matters of law and matters of fact. Most criminal and many civil cases, for example, are of the latter kind: what must be judged is the guilt, innocence, or liability of the accused party; the law itself is not at issue. In most constitutional cases, by contrast, what is in dispute is the law itself, its validity, or, in many cases, its meaning. Here judgment is primarily about *interpretation*. As with decision-making, so too for decision-adjudicating: there are variations with respect to who adjudicates, how they adjudicate, and what they may adjudicate. If all societies require authoritative decisions, and thus making them is a primary function of *all* governments (or states), then necessarily these societies will also require decisions to be implemented and disputes about decisions to be settled—the executive and judicial functions will be as basic to government as the legislative function.

FIGURE 7.1 Functions of the State

FOUND IN ALL STATES	MAY ALL BE FOUND IN A SINGLE STATE, BUT NOT NECESSARILY, AND NOT IN SAME PRIORITY	FOUR MOST PERSISTENT TYPES OF STATE ACTIVITIES
1. Population control: fixing of boundaries, establishment of citizenship categories, census taking.	1. Pattern maintenance: to keep in power those who have power, wealth.	1. The maintenance of internal order.
2. Judiciary: laws, legal procedure, and judges.	2. Organizing for conquest.	2. Military defense/aggression, directed against foreign foes.
3. Enforcement: permanent military and police forces.	3. Pursuit of wealth.	3. The maintenance of communications infrastructures.
4. Fiscal: taxation.	4. The welfare state.	4. Economic redistribution.
— Kottak (1991: 129)	5. The mobilization state.	— Mann (1990: 69)
	— Deutsch (1990: 24–25)	

Various political thinkers have ascribed other functions to the state, and in most cases what these indicate are more specific ends or goals that governments provide or seek to accomplish. These purposes or goods are, in fact, what governments use their decision-making and implementing power to accomplish. These particular goals or functions that constitute the business of the state will vary considerably according to the type of society, the level of technology, period in history, etc. For example, we might say that it is a function of governments to ensure that citizens achieve an adequate level of education; 200 years ago few, if any, governments would have recognized such a task as their responsibility. On the other hand, defense of citizens and their possessions from aggression, internal or external, has been recognized as a purpose of the state probably as long as there have been states (see Figure 7.1).

7.4 Institutions

Regardless of their form, constitutions have a common function: to provide a fundamental definition of the structures and processes of authority. Decision-making, implementation, and adjudication are common to all political communities that have a state, and the alternative designation of these functions as the legislative, executive, and judicial functions indicates a relationship with the primary institutions responsible for performing these functions in the modern state. Whether functions are named for institutions or vice-versa is a moot point. It is important to appreciate that this division is relatively modern and that the correspondence of functions and institutions is not always as direct as may first appear. At most, an institution has primary responsibility for the function but often requires the approval or consent of one or several other

Virginia Assembly

institutions of the state. To indicate this more clearly we need to discuss the actual organization of institutions within a system or type of government. First, though, some general comments about each institution are in order.

7.4.1
Legislatures

A legislature may be described as a body of individuals organized for the purpose of legislating, or making the laws that will be binding on the community. The history of legislatures is interesting and significant. In medieval times, monarchs who wished to mobilize the public to some great purpose (going to war, mounting a Crusade, etc.) would periodically summon representatives of the various classes (or "estates") to an assembly, where they would be expected to give their approval to the business the monarch set before them. The usual classes or estates summoned were members of the Church, the aristocracy, and representatives of the townsfolk and free peasantry. Two points are worth noting. One is that the original purpose of such assemblies was to give approval (and thus legitimacy) to decisions that had already been made by the monarch but that required public compliance in order to be implemented

FIGURE 7.2 Legislatures

BICAMERAL			UNICAMERAL
BRITAIN [Parliament] House of Lords House of Commons	**CANADA** [Parliament] Senate House of Commons	**AUSTRALIA** [Parliament] Senate House of Representatives	**SWEDEN** Riksdag
UNITED STATES [Congress] Senate House of Representatives	**JAPAN** [Diet] House of Councillors House of Representatives	**GERMANY** Bundesrat Bundestag	**NORWAY** Storting **NEW ZEALAND** House of Representatives
FRANCE Senate National Assembly	**ITALY** Senate Chamber of Deputies	**SWITZERLAND** Council of States National Council	**ISRAEL** Knesset
NETHERLANDS First Chamber Second Chamber			**DENMARK** Folketing

successfully. One of the changes that accompanied the end of feudalism and the beginning of liberal government was the insistence by legislatures upon taking a more direct hand (if not primary responsibility) for making decisions. The second point of significance is that from their earliest beginnings, legislatures were representative, although not democratic. In practice then, a legislature is an assembly of representatives entrusted with the authority to legislate, and it is organized for that purpose.

It is also for historical reasons, generally, that many legislatures actually consist of two chambers, or "houses" of representatives. As noted, the summoning of the estates meant assembling the representatives of different classes, who could hardly be expected to sit and deliberate together. Hence the distinction in the British legislature between the (House of) Lords, for bishops and nobles, and the (House of) Commons, for commoners (townsfolk and free peasants), a distinction that persists today. In most cases though, the reason for continuing to have two chambers, or a **BICAMERAL** legislature, is to embody different principles of representation, particularly in federal countries (see Chapter Eight below). Thus in the United States, the House of Representatives is based on the principle of **REPRESENTATION BY POPULATION**, while the senate is based on the principle of equal representation of the states. Names of some legislatures, bicameral (two houses) and unicameral (one chamber), are listed in Figure 7.2.

Executives are the highest ranking individuals in organizations; this is true of businesses, universities, or charities as it is of nation-states. Modern executive offices within the state are a result of the successive limitation, formalization, or replacement with a civilian counterpart of the traditional office of monarch. Historically, European absolute monarchs were both makers and administrators of the law; a key accomplishment of the liberal revolution was giving real legislative power to legislatures or parliaments. This has meant that political executives in the modern period have been primarily concerned with what we have identified as the executive (or administrative) function, that is, overseeing the administration or execution of authoritative decisions. This is the day-to-day functioning of government, or what might be called the ongoing activity of governing, and as the size and level of government activity has expanded so enormously in the past two centuries, so too the scope of the administrative side of the state has grown in significance, especially given that this includes all of the vast bureaucracies involved in delivering government programs and other public goods.

Before examining the different forms that the modern executive takes, it is necessary to explain a simple but crucial distinction between **FORMAL** and **DISCRETIONARY POWER** or authority. Formal authority is governed by rules, is procedural, and is often exercised in the name of the organization or body by an individual who is its representative. One should not conclude that because formal authority excludes individual discretion or decision that it is unimportant; formality attaches a legitimacy to decisions, and this allows others to recognize their validity. For example, when students graduate from university, their diploma is signed by the university president (or equivalent official), and without this signature it would not be a valid diploma. The signature is a formality, though, in that the university president does not personally decide whether or not to sign each student's diploma. Instead, as long as certain rules and procedures have been satisfied (the student has a passing grade in a sufficient number and mix of courses, all outstanding fees have been paid, etc.), the signature of the university president is automatic *and* informs one and all that this student *has* satisfied the requirements of the university degree. At the level of the nation-state, the **HEAD OF STATE** is the executive whose task it is to perform formal functions on behalf of the state, as well as ceremonial duties, which likewise do not involve great matters of decision but satisfy certain international and domestic requirements of etiquette. Whether the head of state carries out *only* formal and ceremonial functions will depend on the constitution of the state concerned, but where this is so, the head of state may be referred to as a **FORMAL EXECUTIVE**.

Obviously, not all power, and not all executive acts, are formal. There is a considerable range of executive decisions that involve actual discretion or judgment on the part of those who make them. The fact that there are no rules or procedures that executives must follow in these cases is the reason we call this kind of decision-making *discretionary* power or authority, although it is probably just what we normally think of as what power and authority involve—making decisions. To give just one example that anticipates our discussion of constitutional systems below, consider the difference between lawmaking in Canada and the United States. In both these countries, as in many democracies, a bill that passes the legislature goes to the executive for approval. In Canada, this is a mere formality: the governor general, as a head of state whose role is largely (although not completely) formal, has no choice but to "give assent" to the bill and thus make it law. In the United States, by contrast, the president (who is head of state, but who is not a merely formal executive) has several choices, including the option of vetoing (canceling or negating) the legislation; this is the discretionary power a formal executive lacks.

As noted above, modern executives can be explained as various transformations of traditional monarchy. In **CONSTITUTIONAL MONARCHIES** (which are all parliamentary systems, like Canada, Britain, Belgium, Sweden, and others), the role of the monarch has been limited and formalized; what discretionary executive power remains is transferred to a **POLITICAL EXECUTIVE**. This means, first, that unlike the monarch, who usually achieves office by birth and rules of hereditary succession, the political executive is designated by the operations of the political process, which in liberal states is representative and democratic. It also means that these countries have a **DUAL EXECUTIVE**, consisting of a formal executive (the monarch) and a political executive (usually a **PRIME MINISTER** and **CABINET**).

The historical assumption underlying traditional monarchy (and aristocracy) was that of a natural hierarchy of superior and inferior natures, natures that are at least in part inherited. The Enlightenment liberal view, by contrast, is that all humans are in essence of one common nature, equally deserving of rights and respect. The political community corresponding to this view cannot accept any "natural hierarchy," but is an association of free and equal citizens; a government of free citizens is called a **REPUBLIC**.

FIGURE 7.3 Executives

UNLIMITED STATES	CONSTITUTIONAL STATES	
AUTHORITARIAN RULER	**SINGLE (UNIFIED) EXECUTIVE**	
Absolute Monarch	Strong President	United States
	DUAL EXECUTIVE	

	CONSTITUTIONAL MONARCHY
	    Head of State: Monarch (formal)
	    Head of Government: Prime Minister
	    (political)
		Australia, Belgium, Canada,
		Denmark, Japan, Luxembourg,
		Netherlands, New Zealand,
		Norway, Spain, Sweden,
		United Kingdom

	REPUBLIC (1)
	    Head of State: Weak President (formal)
	    Head of Government: Strong Prime
	    Minister (political)
		Austria, Germany, Greece,
		Iceland, Ireland, Israel, Italy,
		Portugal

	REPUBLIC (2)
	    Head of State: Strong President (political)
	    Head of Government: Prime Minister
	    (political)
		France, Finland, Poland, Russia

Logistically, the simplest path to a republic would be to replace the monarchy with a civilian office whose occupant was chosen by the citizen body, that is, a president. Traditional institutions like monarchy, though, are often deeply imbedded in the political culture and life of a country, so that not only does the monarch resist being deposed, but the monarchy commands fierce loyalty from considerable portions of the public. In practice, then, to replace a monarch with a presidency has often been difficult, requiring revolution, or conquest and reorganization by a foreign power, or a military coup. Normally, a president will embody the role of head of state and carry out the formal and ceremonial executive functions. In systems with a single executive (like the United States), the president will also have responsibilities of a discretionary or political nature. The extent of these will depend, though, on the relationship of the presidency to other institutions like the legislature, and thus it depends on the nature of the constitutional system. For the moment, we can consider the president to be the civilian equivalent of a monarch, the extent of his/her power dependent on the place of the presidency within the constitution (see Figure 7.3).

In systems of separated executive and legislative power, a president will be accountable to the people, directly or indirectly. Not all republics are democratic though, and when authoritarian rulers take the title of president, the civilian equivalence of absolute monarchy is achieved. In either case, democratic or authoritarian, we have so far been talking of a strong president, that is, a unified or single executive. In countries where the monarch's role was diminished and formalized, there emerged a political executive exercising the bulk of discretionary power. This was the experience of parliamentary systems (to be discussed in greater detail below), where the executive, strictly speaking, is a collective body—the cabinet. At the head of the cabinet, and thus the **HEAD OF GOVERNMENT** in these countries, is a prime minister. The dual executive in parliamentary systems was initially in most cases a pairing of monarch and prime minister. In some parliamentary countries, the monarchy has been replaced with a civilian head of state, normally designated as president. Here, then, is a dual executive of a president who is head of state (a mainly formal office) and a prime minister who is head of government (wielding discretionary power as chair or head of cabinet). As a generalization, the presidency as sole executive is strong, but a presidency as head of state within a dual executive (such as in parliamentary systems) is weak. For reasons that will be clearer when we have examined the differences between systems with fused powers (parliamentary) and separated powers (presidential), the most "powerful" executive office in democratic or constitutional regimes is that of prime minister in a parliamentary system.

The third institution of the state—the **JUDICIARY**—is in normal cases part of the state but not part of politics. By judiciary we indicate magistrates or judges and the courts over which they preside. The task of the courts and their officers is the administration of justice, or what we have described as adjudicating disputes about authoritative decisions. A central principle of modern liberal justice (perhaps *the* principle) is the **RULE OF LAW** (see also Chapter Twelve), which can be summarized as *the requirement that all citizens, rulers and ruled alike, obey known, impartial rules*. In short, no-one is above the law, including the highest political officials. For this to be true, and for the law to be impartial, the ideal of **JUDICIAL INDEPENDENCE** must be met. This means that officers of the court, and judges particularly, must be free from political interference, that is, remain free from being influenced by those in positions of authority or

7.4.3
Judiciaries

FIGURE 7.4 Judicial Independence

Theodore Becker has defined judicial independence as

a. the degree to which judges believe they can decide and do decide
   consistent with their own personal attitudes, values, and conceptions of
   judicial role (in their interpretation of the law),
b. in opposition to what others, who have or are believed to have political
   or judicial power, think about or desire in like matters, and
c. particularly when a decision adverse to the beliefs or desires of those
   with political or judicial power may bring some retribution on the
   judges personally or on the power of the courts. (1970:144)

In practical terms, this means that judges must have an adequate salary that
is secure from interference by political actors; that their term of office must
also be secure, with removal prior to the end of term occurring only for
"just cause"; and that the appointment process is free of political pressure or
influence.

power (see Figure 7.4). To the degree that judicial independence is
realized in modern democracies, the ordinary business of the courts
is a legal, not political, matter.

Two activities of the courts do have unquestionably political
significance. One is the interpretation of law, the other is hearing constitutional cases. In applying laws to particular cases, judges
are always engaged in interpretation of the law, that is, clarifying
the meaning of the words in the statute and their relevance to the
case at hand. This has political significance when the interpretation
judges give a law has unexpected consequences, especially when
these are contrary to the intention(s) of lawmakers. Law is an instrument politicians use to make policy; if the courts interpret law
in a way different than legislators intended, then judges are making
policy—whether they intend to or not. Whether political actors
can restore the original policy by making a new, differently worded
law depends on a number of legal and political factors.

The most intentionally political role of the courts is to uphold
the constitution, the framework of basic law that defines relationships between rulers, institutions, and citizens. If governments are
to be limited in their activities by a set of rules such as a constitution
provides, then there must be a forum where challenges to actions of
the state or government can be heard and authoritative judgments
delivered. While many question the need for the courts to make
policy, few challenge the legitimacy of the constitutional role of
this institution. The scope of this role depends on the nature of the
constitution and on the organization of the courts.

FIGURE 7.5 Judicial Review

Democracies with judicial review:
   Australia, Austria, Canada, Denmark, France, Germany, Iceland,
   Ireland, Italy, Japan, Norway, Sweden, United States

Democracies without judicial review:
   Belgium, Finland, Israel, Luxembourg, Netherlands, New Zealand,
   Switzerland, United Kingdom

Source: Lijphart, 1984: 193.

In most countries, courts are organized hierarchically in a pyramid that culminates in a high court from which there is no further legal appeal. The rulings of this court are binding on all lower courts, and this ensures some uniformity to the application and interpretation of the law and, to the degree that uniformity imparts fairness, delivers justice. The high or **SUPREME COURT** is often the final court of appeal for all criminal and civil cases heard at lower levels of the court system. In many countries it also hears constitutional challenges, but in some cases (for example, Austria, Germany, Italy, Portugal, Spain, France, and most countries of Eastern Europe) there is a special constitutional court that only deals with this type of case.

As noted, the actual role of the courts in respect to constitutional matters will depend on several variables. In most cases, the courts will be able to rule on whether government bodies or office-holders have exceeded the authority the constitution allots them. An important, but more specialized function is disputes between levels of government, a central question in countries with a federal constitution. Perhaps the most important variable is whether the courts are empowered to perform judicial review, that is, whether the courts are able to rule on the validity of laws passed by the legislature. The possibility of judicial review is enhanced by the inclusion in the constitution of a code or charter of citizens' rights, because this provides a set of standards that the courts can use to evaluate legislation, but there are several other variables involved in judicial review. "Concrete" review, for example, refers to consideration of a law resulting from an actual case tried under that law. Usually this means that the defendant charged under the law chooses to challenge the constitutional validity of the law. In the United States, appeal of an actual case to the Supreme Court is the only way judicial review by this body can happen. In Canada, the device of **REFERENCE** makes it possible for governments to use the courts to rule on the constitutionality of a bill or law in the absence of an actual case.

Reference is an example of what is called "abstract" review, that is, review in the absence of a case. In some countries, only abstract review is possible; in others there is a time limit to the possibility of abstract review after the passage of a bill; and in some countries review *must* take place before a bill actually becomes law. In France, for example, the Constitutional Council may not overturn a bill once the president has signed it into law, so bills are referred to this special court after passage by the legislature and before presidential assent. Where abstract review is possible, there are usually rules about who can make such a reference to the courts. In some countries, like Sweden, judicial review is constitutionally possible, but rarely happens; in the Netherlands by contrast, judicial review is constitutionally prohibited.

7.4.4
Institutional Configurations

As the discussion of institutions makes clear, it is difficult to separate legislatures and executives from the types of political systems in which they are found. By a political (or constitutional) system (or type) we mean to indicate two things:

1. the relationship between the institutions just discussed—legislatures, executives, and judiciaries—and
2. how responsibility for the functions of the state is allocated' among these institutions.

Fortunately, there is less variety than one might think among the world's democracies. We will outline some of the principles that distinguish the principal varieties and then in the subsequent two chapters explore these types in greater detail.

Perhaps the most obvious basis of distinction has been the relationship of the institutions of state. The parliamentary system of Britain epitomizes a concentration of powers in the hands of the political executive, whereas the presidential system of the United States exemplifies the separation of powers over three branches of government. The fundamental distinction separating these kinds of democratic regimes is the fusion of executive and legislative power in parliamentary systems and the separation of executive and legislative powers in presidential systems.

Lijphart (1984) identifies **PRESIDENTIALISM** with a political (and not merely formal) executive that is not drawn from the legislature and is not responsible to the legislature. This is in clear contrast to the parliamentary executive, which is normally both drawn from, and remains responsible to, the legislature. Sartori identifies a system as presidential "if, and only if, the head of state (president) i) results from popular election, ii) during his or her pre-established tenure cannot be discharged by a parliamentary vote, and iii) heads or otherwise directs the governments that he or she directs" (1994: 84). In democracies, a presidential executive is elected by the people directly, as in France or Finland, or indirectly, as in the United States where the device of an electoral college is employed. The "classic" presidential model is the American system of separated powers, where the entire executive has no standing in or responsibility to the legislature.

While the British system of parliamentary government was the product of a revolution against absolutist monarchy, the American system of separated powers was in part the result of revolution against the **CONCENTRATED POWERS** of the British Crown. We say "in part," though, because revolution in and of itself cannot explain the distrust of government that has been so imbedded in American political culture and the Constitution (France, after all, has had several revolutions and yet has one of the most activist states and political cultures in the democratic world). The framers of the American Constitution were also intrigued by the causes of the collapse of the ancient republic of Rome and worried about the possible rise and dominance of factions within the body politic. They drew heavily on Locke's notion of a clear separation of the executive and legislative powers of the state and on Montesquieu's ideas about the separation of powers. To some degree, the revolution and the pre-revolutionary experience of the colonials only reinforced the antipathy to government that had brought many of them to the New World in the first place.

While, as we will see, the parliamentary system has evolved from very non-democratic origins (sovereignty embodied in the person of the monarch) to increasingly representative and democratic formations, the American system begins with the liberal notion of popular sovereignty. The people entrust sovereignty to the institutions of the state by means of a constitution, which is their safeguard against abuses of power by those who exercise it. Although it is commonly observed that the constitution framers were wary of government, it is clear that they were pretty hardheaded about the people too. As James Madison wrote in *Federalist Paper No. 51*:

7.5
Exploring Presidentialism

If men were angels, no government would be necessary. If angels were to govern men, neither external nor internal controls on government would be necessary. In framing a government which is to be administered by men over men, the great difficulty lies in this: you must first enable the government to control the governed; and in the next place oblige it to control itself. A dependence on the people is, no doubt, the primary control on the government; but experience has taught mankind the necessity of auxiliary precautions.

In fact, Madison displayed a particularly modern confidence in institutions, in the ability to secure justice through the clever design of institutions and procedures. In several respects, it is the *Constitution* that is sovereign in the American system of government.

The most fundamental principle of this Constitution is a radical **SEPARATION OF POWERS**. This is accomplished by the creation of distinct "branches" of government and the restriction that no individual may serve or hold office in more than one of these branches at the same time. The president is not and cannot be a member of the legislature. The same is true of members of the cabinet, who are appointed by the president. American cabinet secretaries are not responsible to the legislature, collectively or individually, but rather are individually responsible to the president. As a result, there is no body that can be identified (as in parliamentary systems) as the current government or the government of the day. In the United States reference is often made to "**THE ADMINISTRATION**" (more commonly, the "Clinton Administration" or the "Bush Administration," etc.), which encompasses the president, cabinet, and White House officials. The task of each secretary is to oversee the administration of his/her government department and advise the president concerning needs and problems concerning the ability of the public service to deliver policy consistent with the Administration's purposes. This means a role primarily of implementation of policy determined elsewhere, either in the legislature or by presidential aides and advisors. This cabinet is not a collective executive, and for this reason it rarely meets as a whole. In comparative terms, the American cabinet is small: 13 secretaries, the president, vice-president, and a few cabinet-level executives—such as the head of the Central Intelligence Agency (CIA) and the Ambassador to the United Nations—bring the total to around 20 members. White House officials number around 1,500 individuals, freshly appointed with each change in president and hired to provide a range of support

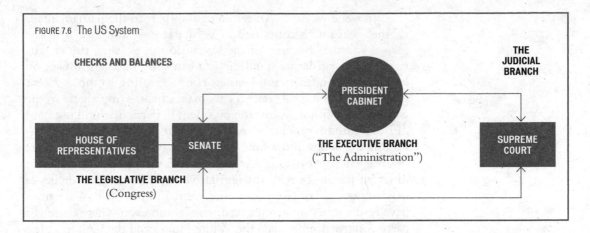

FIGURE 7.6 The US System

CHECKS AND BALANCES

THE JUDICIAL BRANCH

PRESIDENT CABINET

HOUSE OF REPRESENTATIVES

SENATE

THE EXECUTIVE BRANCH ("The Administration")

SUPREME COURT

THE LEGISLATIVE BRANCH (Congress)

and advisory services to the chief executive. The organization and functioning of this bureaucracy is very much at the discretion of the president and will reflect his leadership philosophy and style. In this structure will be found the president's closest policy advisors, and these aides may often wield more influence on public policy than does the cabinet secretary of the relevant department.

The flip-side of the separation of powers in the American Constitution is a set of checks and balances designed to keep any one branch of government from gaining power at the expense of the others. This is one of the "auxiliary precautions" to which Madison referred and is based on the premise that "Ambition must be made to counteract ambition" (Federalist Paper No. 51). The actual checks and balances are numerous, but their effect is that no branch of government can fully perform its function without at least the acquiescence of the other two. Thus, while each branch of government has primary responsibility for carrying out the function for which it is named, the other two branches also have a role with respect to that function. The legislature legislates (makes law), but, as noted above, the president has the ability to **VETO** legislation, and the Supreme Court by exercising judicial review can declare laws to be unconstitutional. By the same token, with a two-thirds vote in both houses, Congress can overturn a presidential veto, and through a complex procedure involving the state legislatures, the Constitution can be amended. The president makes high-level appointments, from ambassadors and cabinet secretaries to Supreme Court justices, but the Senate of the legislature has the ability to hold hearings on these appointments and in some cases (e.g., Supreme Court appointments) to deny them. And so on.

In some ways the American counterpart to the parliamentary cabinet is as much contained in White House staff as it is in the formal cabinet. Because of the separation of powers, the executive has no legislative standing and can only have an impact on legislation by influencing legislators or appealing to those whose partisan or ideological attachments makes them sympathetic to the executive's position. While the president in particular will not have difficulty finding members of Congress to sponsor legislation reflecting the policy aims of the Administration, there is no guarantee of sufficient support to ensure passage. It is frequently the case that different parties control the legislative and executive branches (a majority of the last two dozen mid-term and presidential elections have resulted in "divided government"), and even where there is a party congruence between the White House and the Congress, the weakness of **PARTY DISCIPLINE** means there are no safe bets. While observers have noted a strengthening of party voting (a situation in which a majority of Democrats oppose a majority of Republicans, or *vice versa*, on legislation), which, although becoming more common in recent years, is still a far cry from the virtual unanimity of party control over legislative voting that exists in many parliamentary regimes. On the other hand, the defeat of any bill or measure in the legislature is simply that; there is no question of confidence or of the consequences we associated with the lack of confidence in parliamentary regimes. Parties are weak in part because there is no requirement of responsible government, which works in parliamentary systems as a powerful incentive to create mechanisms of discipline. The weakness of parties means that party labels provide no infallible guide to the voting behavior of legislators: Democrats may vote against legislation sponsored by a Democratic president or supported by the party leadership. Republicans in one chamber might fall overwhelmingly behind a bill but block its passage in the other house of Congress.

Another means by which political power is fragmented, and at the same time a means of balancing the executive and legislative branches of government, is the device of fixed, staggered elections. This balances the branches in that neither has the power to dismiss the other and call an election (in most parliamentary systems the executive can dissolve the legislature and seek early elections, and in Austria the legislature can dissolve itself). Members of the first chamber of Congress (the House of Representatives) serve a two-year term, and senators (members of the second chamber) serve a six-year term, with one-third of the seats contested every two years. The presidential term of office is four years, and no president may

FIGURE 7.7 Parties

Political parties are organizations that serve several functions in the political system, and we discuss them in greater detail in Chapter Twelve. America's parties are the oldest in the world, but are less cohesive than many of their counterparts in other countries. A distinction is sometimes made between the **PARLIAMENTARY** (or legislative) **PARTY**, which consists of all elected members of a party and the **PARTY-AT-LARGE**, which also includes constituency officers and citizens who are members of the party. It is often said that after an election the party-at-large often loses control of the parliamentary party, and this is particularly true if the parliamentary party is in government. Another distinction is between **ELECTORAL PARTIES**, which are parties that contest elections by fielding candidates, and **LEGISLATIVE PARTIES**, which are those parties that actually win seats in the legislature. When we talk about a country's party system, we are talking about the number and strength of the legislative parties. Obviously the number of legislative parties cannot be greater than the number of electoral parties, but the reverse is often true.

serve more than two terms. Thus, a Congress elected at the same time as the president may change radically halfway through his term, and a president re-elected may find that many of his congressional allies have gone down to defeat. In fact, it is normal for the president's party to lose seats in the "mid-term" congressional elections. This was dramatically the case, for example, in 1994, when the Democrats not only lost 52 House and 8 Senate seats, but they also lost majority status in both houses for the first time in four decades. As a result of this, whereas the 103rd Congress, elected along with President Clinton in 1992, was dominated by the president's agenda on deficit reduction, economic stimulation, gays in the military, and health care reform, the 104th Congress was dominated by the resurgent Republican Party's "Contract With America." Similarly, since the Democrats regained control of the House and Senate in the elections of November 2006, Republican President Bush has had greater difficulty in securing legislative support for his initiatives.

The presence of fixed terms of office removes some potential uncertainty that turns up in parliamentary systems, however. There is, on the other hand, no **GOVERNMENT FORMATION** process, nor are there any of the difficult procedural or constitutional questions about **DISSOLUTION** or defeat of government that arise in parliamentary situations. The business of government tends to be conducted within the constraints provided by the fixed electoral terms and the corresponding congressional calendar, providing considerable predictability to the conduct of public affairs over an Administration's term of office.

Another institutional means of fragmenting power in the American system is found in the division of legislative power across two co-equal chambers of houses. Because all legislation must secure majorities in both houses if it is to be forwarded to the president, this system is referred to as one of "**STRONG**" or "**SYMMETRICAL**" **BICAMERALISM**. The House of Representatives, the lower house in this system, is comprised of 435 members, each elected from single-member districts according to the principle of representation by population (with at least one member for each state). Senators, however, are elected to represent the states in the federal policy process. Each state returns two senators, regardless of the size of the state (in the 104th Congress, 54 senators, a sufficient number to pass legislation, came from states comprising only 20 per cent of the population of the country). While co-equals in the legislative process, the two houses are not identical. All revenue bills, for example, must originate in the House of Representatives. While the House can bring impeachment charges against a president, only the Senate can try the case. The Senate can scrutinize high level executive and judicial appointments, and therefore presidents worry about instances when the Senate is not controlled by the president's party (the June 2001 defection of Senator Jim Jeffords of Vermont from the Republicans to sit as an independent tipped the balance in the Senate in the Democrats' favor).

To the outside observer, one of the most striking characteristics of the fragmentation of powers in the American system is the elusiveness of public policy, elusive in three ways. First of all, it may simply not be possible to effect public policy, because political actors with conflicting policy preferences are able to thwart each other using the checks and vetoes built into the system. Policy proposed by the president may not be able to marshal enough support in one or both houses of Congress. Legislation passed by Congress may fall to a presidential veto; presidents can veto legislation by sending it back to Congress with an explanation of the reasons for rejecting it. In this case, the veto can only be overridden by Congress if the bill is passed again by two-thirds majorities of both the Senate and the House. Only about 4 per cent of all vetoed legislation is able to clear this hurdle. In addition, a president can exercise a "**POCKET VETO**" whenever Congress adjourns within 10 days of passing a bill. In this event, the president can simply refuse to sign the bill into law and by doing nothing simply let the bill die.

Passing legislation in such a system is elusive because in order to secure passage through so many possible veto points, a series of compromises and trade-offs is often necessary, diluting the effect or changing the outcomes of policy along the way. In recent Congresses, 9,000 to 11,000 bills have been submitted by members every two years (up from 144 bills introduced in the 1st Congress). Only a small percentage survive to become laws, however, and those that make it through this process often bear little resemblance to their initial drafts. To do so, the bills must pass both in the House and the Senate, after which any differences that result from amendments in either chamber are worked out by a conference committee (and subsequently approved by each house) before they can go for presidential approval. At any point along this path, a failure to act is sufficient to kill a piece of legislation. The need to compromise and build coalitions along this tortuous road inevitably blunts the edge of legislation and dilutes its ideological content. Astute legislators can often attach "riders" to bills in return for their support. These amendments often have nothing to do with the topic of the bill itself.

Legislation creating public policy is elusive in the sense that it is often difficult for citizens to know who properly to credit for policy successes or determine who should shoulder the blame for policy failures. There will be no shortage of actors claiming to have played the crucial role in a popular policy and no shortage of finger pointing among political actors when there is dissatisfaction with government's performance. This elusiveness of public policy, in all three senses, may well contribute to the large-scale public dissatisfaction with government and with politicians, and it may account in part for the low turnouts of voters in American elections. Ironically, in a testament to the strength of the American political culture and the effectiveness of the socialization process, Americans appear to revere their Constitution when it may be exactly this constitutional system that leads them to distrust their government and their political classes.

When the American executive and legislative branches are able to work together, they must still satisfy the review of their actions performed by the courts. The United States has one of the world's longest and busiest traditions of judicial review, dating back to the celebrated *Marbury vs. Madison* case of 1804. One reason for this is the inclusion in the American Constitution of a Bill of Rights, which provides a set of criteria the courts can apply to their review of legislation. Because the American Constitution reserves rights to citizens on the one hand, and to the states on the other, the ability of the federal government to act is constrained from the outset. In the 1930s, a conservative Supreme Court overturned legislation that was central to President Roosevelt's "New Deal" package of measures designed to combat the social and economic effects of the Depression. Roosevelt threatened to try to amend the Constitution in ways that would allow him to change the composition of the court. On the other hand, in the 1950s and 1960s, a liberal Supreme Court made landmark civil rights rulings that signaled the end of racial segregation and led directly to significant civil rights legislation in the Kennedy and Johnson years. Both examples illustrate the importance of the judiciary as a third branch of government in the United States.

7.6
Exploring Parliamentary Systems

The British Parliament at Westminster has been called the mother of all parliaments, and indeed most parliamentary constitutions offer variations on the basic arrangements put in place by the Whig Revolution of 1688, itself the product of struggles predating the English Civil War of 1642. The word "revolution" implies a turning upside down, and just such a reversal occurred in the respective roles of the monarch and of the legislature. Prior to 1688, the monarch made decisions (acted) and expected the legislature (particularly the House of Commons) to give formal approval (ratification) to these executive acts. Since 1688, the reverse has been true: the legislature acts and the monarch gives the formal approval (assent) which legitimizes these actions.

This diagram is misleading in two respects. In the first place, the shift presented should be understood as one of relative influence in government; the British system is one of parliamentary supremacy, not legislative supremacy. In the British Constitution neither the monarch nor the legislature can act alone (legislative supremacy implies the latter) but must act together:

$$\text{Parliament} \; = \; \begin{array}{l} \text{The Monarch} \\ + \text{ House Of Lords} \\ + \text{ House Of Commons} \end{array}$$

Within this whole that is Parliament, the Revolution of 1688 reversed the priorities of the players; the play goes on with the same actors, but they have been required to exchange roles.

The second respect in which the characterization is inaccurate is that it leaves out the cabinet (and prime minister) and thus implies more power for the legislative chamber called the House of Commons than is actually the case. As we will see, it is actually the cabinet that exercises discretionary power within parliamentary systems, the cabinet that is the government of the day. This cabinet, though, is linked to the legislature in two important ways, which require explanation. First, though, we should explain the origin of cabinet government.

While absolute monarchs were ultimately responsible for all activities of the state—as Louis XIV said, "L'État c'est moi" ("I am the state")—they normally delegated much of the actual labor to trusted advisors. Over time, assistance to the monarch was recognized in a set of offices, each with its own title and particular set of functions (looking after the treasury, or the King's cavalry, or granting licenses to trade, etc.). Individually, those holding such offices had a title like Minister or Secretary, and collectively they met as advisors to the monarch (in Britain this body was known as the Privy Council). Originally, the monarch appointed his/her ministers from the ranks of the aristocracy, choosing favorites and dismissing them once they fell out of favor. This is the origin of the cabinet: a body of officials individually responsible for administering a portion of the state bureaucracy and collectively forming the "government" of the day. As a body performing the executive function of the state, the cabinet is a **COLLECTIVE EXECUTIVE**.

The cabinet arose, then, as a body of advisors serving the monarch, with a limited relationship to the legislature. In Britain, after 1688, this changed in two ways. It was necessary for the monarch to choose his/her ministers from the more powerful chamber of the legislature; this, a result of social, economic, and political changes, was no longer the House of Lords (representing the aristocracy), but the House of Commons (representing the propertied interests of an emerging market society). In other words, those who were actually carrying out the executive function (and functioning as a collective executive) were also to be legislators drawn from the lower chamber of the legislature. This dual membership of cabinet members in both the executive and the legislature is called a **FUSION OF POWERS**, and it is common to almost all parliamentary systems.

The second change brought about by 1688 was the requirement that the cabinet (or Ministry, or Privy Council) have the continued support of the most powerful chamber of the legislature—the House of Commons. This is known as "maintaining the **CONFIDENCE**" of the legislature, and in bicameral parliaments, the lower or popularly representative chamber is the one that matters—it is the confidence chamber. Maintaining the confidence means being able to sustain the support of a majority of legislators present in the chamber on all important votes concerning government policy or expenditure. This requirement that the executive

FIGURE 7.8

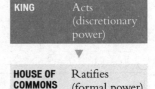

(the cabinet) have the support or confidence of the legislature (the lower chamber) is the principle of **RESPONSIBLE GOVERNMENT**, and it is *the* most important feature that distinguishes parliamentary government from all others. It is a principle intended to keep the executive accountable to the legislature, and in British politics it meant that instead of pleasing the monarch, the cabinet must be ultimately pleasing to the House of Commons. Any cabinet that fails to maintain the confidence of the legislature is expected to resign and be replaced by another that is able to command such a majority.

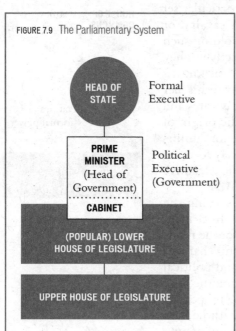

FIGURE 7.9 The Parliamentary System

Both the fusion of powers and responsible government in Britain (and many other countries) are **CONVENTIONS**. A convention is an unwritten rule that is nonetheless binding because all parties agree to it (and the reason they agree to it is usually because it works, or works best, to do so). In the case of responsible government, the convention that a government failing to win majority support in the legislature must resign has a clearly practical basis. If the cabinet cannot gain the support of a majority, it cannot get its policies or its expenditures passed, and if it cannot make policy or spend money, it cannot govern.

Linking the political executive—the cabinet—to the legislature by means of responsible government and the fusion of powers has had (at least) two other consequences of note. One is the emergence of the prime minister at the top of the political executive, so much so that as head of government the prime minister is the most powerful individual in a parliamentary democracy. One popular account has it that the office of prime minister emerged to prominence in Britain in the eighteenth century when German-speaking British kings stopped attending cabinet meetings because of their lack of facility with the English language. Historian Christopher Hill notes, though, that George I "stopped attending the cabinet not because of any lack of linguistic ability but because he had so little authority there" (1969: 216). Since it was now necessary for the cabinet to maintain the support of the House of Commons, monarchs had to choose ministers who could command that support, individuals with great following and influence among the members of Parliament. Once installed in cabinet, it was these individuals who would determine government policy. Should the King, for example, insist on policy contrary to

234

the wishes of the cabinet, he would risk its resignation, the loss of the government, and setting himself at odds with the entire House of Commons. After the Civil War and the Revolution of 1688, British monarchs were reluctant to antagonize Parliament so far. Since the eighteenth century in Britain, and now the norm in most parliamentary systems, the prime minister (as chair of cabinet and thus head of government) controls most of the discretionary executive authority of the state, and, given the fusion of powers which links the cabinet and prime minister to the House of Commons, usually dominates (if not controls) the legislature's business.

The second development, and one which clinched the dominance of the prime minister and cabinet within the parliamentary system, was the emergence of strong (disciplined) parties. Students are no doubt fully aware of the central role of political parties within contemporary politics, and we will discuss the nature and functions of political parties in greater depth below; what may be less familiar is the fact that in the early days of representative parliamentary government, there were no political parties. Individuals stood for parliamentary election on their own merits or reputations, neither representing nor sponsored by some larger organization or association. Within the legislature, it is true, individuals did not act as complete "independents" but associated in factions or groups, which might be organized around an ideological disposition, a religious affiliation, personal influence and obligations, naked ambition, or resentment of another group currently in power. Selecting individuals to the cabinet was in part a calculation of which factions' support they might bring or control and thus contribute to putting together a legislative majority (which responsible government requires).

Because the convention of responsible government requires the cabinet to maintain the support of a majority, this provides a great incentive for political leaders to organize their supporters and provide some greater measure of predictability and discipline to their legislative behavior. In parliamentary systems the stakes are high, because failure to maintain a majority means losing office. Consequently, in British parliamentary experience strong parties (now the norm in parliamentary regimes) replaced loose factions. What makes parties strong is their ability to discipline members through rewards for loyal behavior and sanctions for failure to support the party leadership. As parties have developed, they have come to dominate the political process of democratic states, so much so that being elected to Parliament as an "independent" is now a rather exceptional accomplishment. In many cases, the rules

FIGURE 7.10 Responsible Government and Parties

The division of Parliament (in Britain, Canada, and some other former British colonies) into a government side and an opposition side and the designation of the leader of the largest party not in government as the Leader of Her (His) Majesty's Loyal Opposition are carry overs from the time before disciplined parties. Members of the House would simply declare themselves for or against the government of the day, and take their seats on the appropriate side of the chamber.

of parliamentary procedure have been revised or rewritten to reflect (or ensure) the reality that the primary actors within the system are parties, not individual members.

Strong parties provide structure and predictability to activity within a parliament. As organizations that provide means for leaders to discipline members, parliamentary parties are hierarchical and (largely) run from the top down. To some degree, then, although party discipline is a product of the conditions created by responsible government, it also tends to undermine responsible government as a means by which the legislature keeps the executive accountable. This is so because party discipline means that party leaders in the cabinet have firm control over the votes of their members in the legislature. The executive dominance described above is thus confirmed and strengthened with the development of strong, disciplined parties. Ultimately, the executive answers not to the legislature, but to the electorate.

At its most basic, the essence of parliamentary government is the relationship between the executive and the legislature, something expressed most succinctly as *responsible cabinet government achieved through a fusion of powers*. This means several things. First, the government in power consists of a cabinet, which is a committee of individuals exercising executive power. Exercising executive power means in turn that each of these cabinet members (usually called ministers) is the executive or head of a government department or set of related departments. The area of responsibility of a cabinet minister is known as a **PORTFOLIO**. Second, the cabinet ministers are drawn from the ranks of the legislature, to which, as a body, they remain collectively responsible. While ministers answer individually to the legislature for their portfolio, collectively the cabinet must retain the support (confidence) of a majority in the legislature. Failure to do so means the end of this particular cabinet and thus the defeat of the government. Although each minister has a particular portfolio, government policy for any and all portfolios is approved by the cabinet and must have the public support of all members of cabinet. This is known as the principle of **CABINET SOLIDARITY** or of **COLLECTIVE RESPONSIBILITY** and indicates most clearly that this is a collective executive.

The head or chair of the cabinet is the prime minister, sometimes misleadingly described as a "first among equals," misleadingly because the prime minister is usually pre-eminent among ministers and in many parliamentary systems determines everything that matters about the cabinet, from its size to its membership to its structure to its style of decision-making. As head of cabinet, the prime minister is thus head of government and the chief political executive in most parliamentary systems (examples where this is not true will be discussed in the next chapter). Parliamentary systems thus have a dual executive, for someone *other* than the prime minister will occupy the position of head of state, a formal executive with largely formal and ceremonial functions. Whatever the title of the head of state—king, queen, president, grand duke—it is the prime minister as head of government who exercises most of the authority of the state in a parliamentary system.

Because parties are so central to parliamentary systems, it makes a real difference to these systems how many parties there are in the legislature, what their relative strength is, and how accurately their representation in the legislature mirrors their support in the electorate. In other words, a fundamental difference between parliamentary systems is the nature of their **PARTY SYSTEM**, and the party system is largely a function of (or associated with) the **ELECTORAL SYSTEM**.[1] (Both of these systems will be explained and discussed in greater detail in Chapter Nine below, and students may wish to skip ahead and skim portions of that chapter before continuing here.) Differences related to parties and electoral systems are absolutely crucial for determining how strong or weak, in the sense of being able to pass its preferred legislation, the government of a parliamentary system will be. For this reason, a brief overview of these factors, as they affect government formation and survival in parliamentary systems, is in order.

In terms of electoral systems, we want to distinguish between **PLURALITY** systems, where the candidate with the most votes is declared the winner (as in Canada, the United States, and Britain), and proportionate representation systems, where candidates from parties are awarded seats on the basis of the vote for the party. The plurality system is sometimes called a "winner-take-all" system, because the margin of victory makes no difference to the outcome; if I finish with 9,999 votes and you have 10,000, you win the seat

1 In some cases, it is clear that it was the party system that led to a proportionate electoral system being adopted, but it is this type of system that reinforces a multi-party system and ensures a high degree of proportionality among parties.

and I have nothing to show for second place. The same result happens if I finish with 1 vote and you have 19,999. The plurality system is not good at reflecting the amount of support that winners receive, and this is not only true on a constituency by constituency basis but also as a whole when the results are aggregated for all electoral districts. As a general rule, and this becomes more likely the more parties there are contesting the election, plurality systems *overcompensate winners* and *penalize losers* (see Figure 7.11).

For a variety of reasons (to be discussed in more detail in Chapter 9) the plurality system has two tendencies with which we are concerned here. One is to deliver a parliamentary majority to the winner of the election, i.e. to ensure that one party wins more seats in the legislature than all other parties combined. Given the tendency of plurality electoral systems to be associated with two party systems this observation may seem trivial, but it is true also of countries like Canada with many electoral parties. The second tendency is that there is no necessary correspondence between a party's parliamentary strength and its electoral strength; as a general rule winning parties will receive a higher share of seats in the legislature than their share of vote would warrant, and other parties will be correspondingly penalized by the system. In this way, the parliamentary majority of the winning party is often *manufactured*, meaning that the party won a majority of seats but received less than a majority of the vote. Figure 7.11 illustrates these tendencies at work in Canada in 1867 and 2000, though similar examples may be taken from Britain or other countries with plurality systems. The tendencies we have associated with plurality systems here are even more likely when the number of parties increases.

Proportionate representation electoral systems do not produce these electoral system consequences. The close correspondence between share of parliamentary seats and share of electoral vote has two consequences of note for us here. One is the tendency to sustain a multi-party system, and the significance of this will be more apparent as we proceed. The other is the virtual impossibility of manufacturing a majority. Since the system does not over-reward or penalize parties, the only legislative majorities that result will be fully "earned," that is, reflective of a majority of the votes cast by the electorate. The greater the number of electoral parties, the less the likelihood that one will command an absolute majority of support, and since proportionate systems sustain multi-party environments, legislative majorities for a single party are rare in these systems.

FIGURE 7.11 Disproportionality and Canada's Electoral System

1867			2000		
PARTY	**% SEATS**	**% VOTE**	**PARTY**	**% SEATS**	**% VOTE**
Conservatives	**60**	**50.1**	**Liberals**	**57.1**	**40.8**
Liberals	40	49.9	Canadian Alliance (Reform)	21.9	25.5
			Bloc Québécois	12.6	10.7
			Progressive Conservatives	4.0	12.2
			New Democratic Party	4.3	8.5

Hence, the distinction we are making between majoritarian and proportionate parliamentary systems may be explained:

ELECTORAL SYSTEM		PARTY SYSTEM		TYPE OF PARLIAMENTARY SYSTEM
plurality	+	two-party	=	majoritarian
proportionate	+	multi-party	=	proportionate

By a **MAJORITARIAN SYSTEM** we mean one where the electoral and party system create a general tendency or normal expectation that following an election, one party will have control of a majority of seats in the legislature. By a **PROPORTIONATE SYSTEM** we mean one where the electoral and party system create the conditions where following an election each party will have a share of seats corresponding to its share of vote, and for one party to control a majority of seats in the legislature will be the exception rather than the rule. A couple of clarifications are in order.

It should perhaps be emphasized that we are speaking of general tendencies here, not absolute relations; for every generalization we make there are (or could conceivably be) exceptions. Not all plurality electoral systems produce two-party systems (as the Canadian illustration in Figure 7.11 has clearly demonstrated), but on the other hand the persistence of a multi-party system in a plurality electoral system creates pressures for electoral reform. It is safe to say that plurality systems tend to reflect and sustain two-party environments and that proportionate systems tend to reflect and sustain multi-party environments, but there are counter examples to each generalization. Similarly, while it is not impossible for a party to win an absolute majority in a proportionate system with a multi-party environment, so too there is no guarantee that a plurality system will always produce a legislative majority for the winning party. What we are concerned with here is the usual or "normal" outcome of the system, because this will govern the expectations and calculations of the political actors and create the conventions and norms of institutional behavior within these systems.

If the majority of the world's democracies are parliamentary, then we should also note that of the 22 parliamentary systems that have been continuously democratic since 1945, 15 (Germany, Italy, Sweden, Norway, Denmark, Finland, Iceland, the Netherlands, Belgium, Luxembourg, Ireland, Austria, Switzerland, Malta, and Israel) fit our classification as proportionate; three (Britain, Canada, and India) are majoritarian; and two (France and Australia) represent special cases in part because they have neither (single-member) plurality nor proportionate representation electoral systems (see Lijphart, 1994: 2). Of these latter two, France has been more like proportionate systems and Australia more like majoritarian systems. Three European countries that became democratic in the mid-1970s—Greece, Portugal, and Spain—are also proportionate, as are most (if not all) of the newly created democracies of Eastern Europe and the former Soviet Union.

The first set of differences we can note concerns the nature of government in these two types of parliamentary system. If majoritarian systems tend to produce control of the legislature by one party, through a majority that is often manufactured by the electoral system, then obviously the government (cabinet) in such systems will *normally* be drawn from the caucus of the winning (majority) party. This is what is known as a **MAJORITY GOVERNMENT**, although it should more precisely be called single-party majority government. In other words, the cabinet is drawn from one party, which happens also to have a majority of the seats in the legislature (or in the house of the legislature that serves as the confidence chamber). Given strong party discipline, the requirements of responsible government (i.e., that the cabinet retain the support of a legislative majority) are more or less automatically fulfilled, and one expects single-party majority governments to be very stable. This circumstance also provides for the strongest possible form of government, since a majority of legislators necessary to pass legislation are subject to the discipline of the governing caucus (and a prime minister). It is this situation that leads critics of parliamentary systems to describe the prime minister as an "elected dictator." Although majority government is possible under any legislative system currently in use, it is much more likely in countries with plurality electoral systems and less likely where there is proportionate representation.

Suppose, though, that no one party wins a majority of seats in the legislature; who will govern? If the cabinet continues to be drawn from the members of one party in the legislature, this will constitute a **MINORITY GOVERNMENT**, so called because the government controls (through party discipline) the votes of only a minority of members of the legislature. One might expect that the party that forms the government in this situation will be the largest of the parliamentary parties, but this is not necessarily the case. Meeting the requirements of responsible government will clearly be more of a challenge for minority governments; a legislative majority for the government will require the cooperation, active or passive, of at least one other party in the legislature. The general expectation might be, then, that minority governments will be less stable and less strong than single-party majority governments because the possibility at least exists for defeat of the government in the legislature. The stability of minority governments depends on some other factors, though, foremost being the type of parliamentary system, a point we will explain below.

The other possibility, if no one party controls a legislative majority, is to draw the cabinet from two or more parties that *between them* do control a majority of legislators. This is what is known as **COALITION GOVERNMENT**, which typically means a formal agreement between political parties indicating three things:

1. an agreement jointly to form a government;
2. a division of the cabinet seats between the parties and the allocation of specific portfolios, including that of prime minister; and
3. an agreement about policies that the government will implement, or positions it will take on key issues.

In many countries, coalition governments are the norm, and in others they arise occasionally. For example, a recent study of 13 Western European governments that experienced coalition governments between 1945 and 1999 (Belgium, Denmark, Finland, France, Germany, Ireland, Italy, Luxembourg, the Netherlands, Norway, Portugal, Sweden, and Britain) found that coalitions comprised fully 69 per cent of all cabinets formed over that period (Müller and Strøm, 2000).

In countries where the norm is for the electoral system to produce no clear winner, where no one party controls the legislature, the expectation will be that some sort of coalition will be formed. In some countries, the size and/or the strategic position of the largest party may make a minority government resting on **LEGISLATIVE COALITIONS** as attractive or feasible as forming an executive coalition. In countries

FIGURE 7.12 Coalitions

EXECUTIVE COALITION
Where two or more parties formally agree to govern, dividing the cabinet posts between them, and (usually) agreeing on a joint policy platform.

LEGISLATIVE COALITION
Where two or more parties agree to vote together in the legislature, but do not share the executive between them.

ELECTORAL COALITION
Where two (or more) parties agree to work together in an election, usually agreeing not to run candidates in the same constituencies, provide mutual support, etc. Implicit in such electoral alliances is the possibility of working together in legislative or executive coalitions.

FIGURE 7.13 Majority, Minority, and Coalition Governments

SYSTEM OF GOVERNMENT	MAJORITARIAN	PROPORTIONATE
(Single-party) Majority	the norm	abnormal
(Single-party) Minority	abnormal	the norm
(Executive) Coalition	exceptional	the norm

with proportionate representation electoral systems, with what we have called proportionate parliaments, minority government will be more likely and will more likely be regarded not as a temporary expedient but a case of "normal politics." Our observations about majority, minority, and coalition government in the two types of parliamentary systems are summarized in Figure 7.13. As we noted above, while it is possible for any of these types of government to be formed in either of the types of parliamentary system, there is in either system a "normal" type of government and an "abnormal" type, abnormal because it works contrary to the tendencies of the electoral and party systems. In addition, we note that minority government may not be the norm, but it is extremely common in proportionate systems. Coalition government in majoritarian systems is not simply abnormal but usually happens under extraordinary circumstances like the state of national emergency associated with war.

The distinctions we have been discussing have a bearing on two very fundamental aspects of parliamentary government: how it comes into being and how it is dissolved. In the constitution of every parliamentary country, a government formation process is outlined, explicitly or implicitly. Contrary to popular perception, and to the way politics is reported in the media, parliamentary governments are not selected by the people but by the legislature. Elections in parliamentary countries return a set of representatives to the legislature; then the government formation process begins, and it can be simple or complex. Simple, complex, or in between, government formation in the parliamentary system involves variations on the following basic procedure:

1. the head of state invites someone from the legislature to form and head (as prime minister) a government;

2. the prime minister designate presents a cabinet to the head of state, and they are sworn in as ministers of the state, or of the Crown, or whatever is appropriate; and
3. the new cabinet government meets the legislature and receives its confidence (or does not).

In majoritarian systems, in the normal course of things, the government formation process is extremely simple, and it resembles the British model discussed earlier. When no party commands a majority, there are two logical choices of whom to invite to form the government: (1) the leader of the largest party in the legislature and (2) the leader of the party that formed or led the previous government.[2] This may be a matter of judgment for the head of state, it may be that there are established conventions about how this decision ought to be taken, or there may be explicit rules in the constitution that instruct the head of state on how to proceed. In European proportionate systems, the individual invited to form a government is often called a **FORMATEUR**. Once a *formateur* has been designated, he/she must decide whether the condition exists to govern as a single-party minority or whether it is more prudent to share power with another party or parties. There are advantages either way. A minority means not having to surrender portfolios or commit to a formal policy agreement, but it also means risking defeat in the legislature at any time and making policy compromises on issues to avoid this fate. Coalition government brings stability and predictability at the cost of sharing power and making policy compromises. The decision whether or not to seek partners will depend in the final analysis on the balance of circumstances and on the expectations generated by the parliamentary system. In majoritarian systems, because the absence of a majority is seen to be a (temporary) aberration, and because coalition is not common, leaders will likely prefer to govern as a minority, expecting to improve their fortunes through an election at the earliest convenient opportunity. In proportionate systems, where coalition is the norm, *formateurs* are likely to seek partners unless conditions for a long-term viable minority government are clearly present.

Regarding the **TERMINATION** of governments in parliamentary systems, majority governments (almost always found in majoritarian systems) usually end at the time of their own choosing, either serving the maximum time constitutionally permitted or choosing to face the electorate sooner because they believe they are currently well placed to win the election. In some parliamentary systems, for example, majority governments have to seek a fresh mandate

2 Consider the situation where there is a "pariah" party—one that no other party will cooperate with, like the situation of the Communists in postwar Italy. Even if this party finishes first, to invite it to form the government is futile because no other party will vote with it. Suppose also that the party that led the previous government has finished fourth in a five-party parliament. In this case it may be the second-place party that is best placed to lead a government.

FIGURE 7.14 Termination of Parliamentary Governments

1.   Change in the party composition of the cabinet:
     (a)   following internal dissension between coalition partners
     (b)   following defeat in the legislature
     (c)   following constitutional intervention (executive dismissal—see
           discussion of France in Chapter Eight).

2.   A formal government resignation, which may come about for any
     of the reasons listed in 1, leading to a new government, but not
     necessarily involving a change in the party composition of the cabinet.

3.   A change in the prime minister:
     (a)   forced retirement (through cabinet or party revolt)
     (b)   voluntary retirement
     (c)   for health reasons.

4.   An election, which may be "forced" by any of the preceding events,
     but which may also
     (a)   be anticipated by a governing party choosing to maximize its
           electoral chances at a particular moment, or
     (b)   be required because of constitutional limitations on the life of
           parliament or because of fixed election dates.

after four years; the closer governments get to their constitutional
deadline before calling an election the more likely it is that they
are unpopular with the public and are simply delaying an inevitable defeat. Paradoxically then, while serving the longest term is a
measure of government stability or durability, it can in fact mask
political weakness. The point to note is that if a majority government resigns there is little choice but to call an election, since no
other party or combination of parties in the legislature can govern
successfully.

The other (fairly) common reason for government changes in
majority situations is because of a change in prime minister. This
is typically a voluntary retirement, usually coming near the end of
a term of office, as appears to be the case in the recent replacement
of British Prime Minister Tony Blair by Gordon Brown. However,
prime ministerial change can come about as a result of a caucus
revolt such as that which replaced Prime Minister Thatcher with
John Major, or by an assassination, as in the case of Swedish Prime
Minister Olaf Palme. In majoritarian systems with flexible terms,
it is often expected that a prime minister sworn in without having
faced the electorate as party leader will do so at the earliest possible
opportunity and so "earn" his or her mandate.

Minority governments can end for the same reasons as majority governments, but they are much more likely to be finished by a defeat in the legislature, by a loss of confidence. With few exceptions, loss of a confidence motion means the end of the government in parliamentary regimes. One exception is Switzerland, where the executive, having passed the investiture vote, is not subject to legislative votes of confidence. A partial exception is Germany, where the legislature can terminate the government only with a vote of **CONSTRUCTIVE NON-CONFIDENCE**, which means that in addition to rejecting the current executive, the legislators must agree on a successor in whom they have confidence. Budge and Keman's (1990) study of 20 democracies between 1950 and 1983 found that defeat in the legislature was the most frequent cause of termination for minority governments.

In coalition government situations, a cause of government termination arises that is not so likely in single-party governments (majority or minority), namely, internal cabinet dissension. As we have observed, cabinet government is a collective executive, and the failure of cabinet members to work together and support a common policy platform signals an inability to govern. While this is possible in single-party governments, but not likely given the mechanisms of party discipline, it is very possible once we have coalition (multi-party) governments. Although coalitions involve a formal agreement about portfolios and a policy platform, disagreements about either (let alone other factors such as personality clashes between party leaders) may arise during the life of a government. Failure to resolve these conflicts may lead to the collapse of the coalition, or its defeat in the legislature, and hence its resignation. The greater probability of internal collapse in coalition governments is the primary reason for their reputation for "instability," especially as compared with single-party majority governments, and this is accordingly a key basis on which majoritarian and proportionate systems have been compared.

As we have seen earlier in the chapter, in a parliamentary system the head of state is a largely formal office, performing "a number of significant symbolic, procedural and diplomatic functions" (Gallagher et al., 1992: 14). In many cases like the British, the office of the head of state is a remnant of the traditional monarchy or has evolved from modifications of the same. Of the 19 parliamentary democracies of Western Europe, the head of state in seven is a monarch and in Luxembourg a grand duke; in the remainder the head of state is a president. Of the 11 Western European presidents, six are elected directly by the people, and five are elected by

FIGURE 7.15 Degrees of Confidence

In addition to the cases of Switzerland and Germany, some other variations on the issue of legislative confidence (or non-confidence) are worth noting. First of all, in most of the majoritarian systems modeled on the British Parliament, the idea that a vote of non-confidence should be followed by the government's resignation is merely conventional, not a legally binding constitutional rule. In theory, governments could continue to try to govern following one or several such votes of non-confidence. In practice, though, if the legislature has truly lost confidence in the executive, continuing to govern will not be feasible, since it will not be possible for the government to gain approval for its legislation or its financial resolutions. In most other parliamentary systems, the requirement of resignation after defeat on a confidence vote has been constitutionalized. Here, too, there are variations. In Finland, the president is not required to accept the resignation of the government but "may" do so (and, in practice, is unlikely not to do so). In France and Sweden, defeat of the government requires the vote of an absolute majority in the legislature (that is, a majority of all legislators, not just a majority of those present at the time of voting). In Spain, a motion of non-confidence in the prime minister must specify his or her successor.

Source: Laver and Schofield, 1990.

the people's representatives in the legislature. In four countries, the office of the head of state departs from the parliamentary norm in significant ways. In three countries (France, Finland, and Portugal, arranged in descending order of applicability) the president exercises discretionary power in ways more like the strong president of the American Constitution. In the remainder of the European parliamentary systems, heads of state perform functions as described in the quote with which this paragraph began.

Beyond the symbolic and ceremonial roles of the head of state, there are two other political purposes this office serves. One has to do with the requirement that there always be a legal government in office; in most cases the most important political duty of the head of state is to see that this is so, whether this means an active role for the head of state in the government formation process or in implementing constitutionally prescribed procedures.[3] In either case the head of state is supposed to serve as the representative of the whole people, "above" partisan politics and serving no particular interest or interests. Where heads of state manage to maintain the public respect for their office by observing these conventions of political neutrality, they are also in a position to act or intervene in times of constitutional crisis or deadlock, and they can use their influence to ensure stability. A good example of this was the decisive role

3 One exception is Sweden, which has transferred this role to the speaker of the legislature.

of King Juan Carlos of Spain in that country's transition from a dictatorship to a liberal democracy. As with other dimensions of parliamentary politics, so too the role of the head of state may be somewhat different in majoritarian and proportionate systems.

The size of cabinets in parliamentary systems is determined by the prime minister, but it reflects a number of concerns. First, prime ministers have to reward their political supporters with a place in the executive. They may have to assign some posts to representatives of particular groups or regions. Or they may choose to invite their strongest rivals in the party to have a seat at the cabinet table to keep them from being too critical of the government. Thus, representational and political considerations are important. The second factor that has had a large bearing on the size of cabinets has been the growth of the state, particularly in this century. An increase in the scope of government leads to new programs, new departments to implement and administer them, and thus to new ministries and portfolios. One could argue that this is not an inevitable development, that ministers could double up, taking responsibility for more than one portfolio, or that (as in Britain) not all department heads or administrators (i.e., ministers) need be considered in the cabinet. This is true, but it ignores the prestige that comes with cabinet status and the importance of this means of reward to prime ministers seeking to consolidate their hold on a parliamentary caucus. All things being equal, then, as the size of the state increases, we would expect the size of cabinet to grow also.

The point this chronicle should emphasize is the pre-eminence of the prime minister. Not only are ministers appointed by the prime minister and continue to serve at his or her pleasure, but it is the prime minister who may determine the size and structure of cabinet, decisions which will depend very much on his or her philosophy and leadership style. The complete dominance of the cabinet by the prime minister is something we would expect more of single-party governments, majority or minority, than of coalition cabinets, where questions of size, structure, and functioning will be part of the negotiated agreement among coalition partners. As Laver and Shepsle point out, cabinet decision-making is also very much a question of how "individual cabinet ministers are constrained by key political institutions" (1994: 5). Figure 7.18 presents the various models of cabinet decision-making they discuss.

Although we will have much more to say about policy-making in Chapter Eleven, at this point a few remarks are in order concerning the role of the cabinet and prime minister in policy-making. To put it baldly, in parliamentary systems the cabinet

FIGURE 7.16   Parliamentary Heads of State

A. MONARCHS
Belgium, Britain, Denmark, Luxembourg (Grand Duke), Netherlands, Norway, Spain, Sweden; exercised through a governor general: Australia, Canada, New Zealand.

B. (WEAK) PRESIDENTS
1. directly elected: Austria, Iceland, Ireland.
2. elected by legislature: Germany, Greece, Italy, Malta, Switzerland.

C. (STRONG) PRESIDENTS
all directly elected: France, Finland, Portugal.

monopolizes policy-making. We have described responsible government as perhaps the distinguishing feature of parliamentary government, meaning specifically the requirement that the cabinet maintain the confidence of the legislature. Given the strength of party discipline in most countries, this confidence is virtually guaranteed for any party (or combination of parties) that controls a majority of the legislators in parliament. The result is that responsible government takes on a new meaning, namely, that the cabinet is "responsible" for everything! Deciding what government will do, or not do, when it will be done, and how; drafting regulations or legislation and presenting the latter to parliament; overseeing the implementation and ongoing administration of policy—all of these are in the control of the cabinet, and that leaves very little. This is why parliamentary systems are usually described as having strong executive and weak legislatures or, to put it another way, as being systems characterized by **EXECUTIVE DOMINANCE**. Executives may be more or less stable, depending on the status of their majority or the nature of the coalition that comprises it, but whatever the composition of the government, the relative centrality of the cabinet within the system remains. This dominance is emphasized if we consider the principal challenges to it that exist.

Clearly the solid foundation upon which modern cabinet government rests is strong party discipline, and those parliaments with unstable coalitions are often those in which, for one reason or another, this coherence is lacking. This is the exception rather than the rule, because there is every incentive for parties to develop mechanisms to enforce discipline and thereby enhance the odds of their own political survival (an undisciplined party risks alienating an electorate uncertain of what it stands for). The sanctions that party leaders employ will be a mixture of inducements and punishments. The

FIGURE 7.17 Size of Parliamentary Cabinets (1945–90)

COUNTRY	AVERAGE SIZE	RANGE OF SIZE
Italy	24	15–32
France (5th Republic)	22	15–36
Britain	21	16–33
Belgium	20	15–27
France (4th Republic)	19	13–26
Germany	18	13–22
Sweden	18	14–21
Denmark	17	12–22
Norway	16	13–19
Ireland	15	12–17
Netherlands	14	10–18
Austria	13	11–16
Finland	13	7–18
Luxembourg	8	6–10

Source: adapted from Steiner, 1995: 99.

control that the cabinet and, more usually, the prime minister have over appointments (to judicial office, commissions, boards, even second chambers of the legislature) means an abundance of rewards for loyal behavior—quite apart from the hope of landing someday in cabinet or even in the prime minister's office. The penalties for disloyalty can be as varied, from exclusion from scarce positions of influence or additional remuneration, to exclusion from the party caucus (which, in those legislatures where the rules give privileges to parties, amounts to being silenced), to being dropped down or off the party's list of candidates for the next election. The effect of these mechanisms of party discipline is to internalize any dissent and thus remove it from public view. This is one purpose of meetings of the party caucus (the parliamentary party); held behind closed doors, these meetings allow backbenchers to challenge the decisions of leaders, and in some cases they have led to reversals on policy. More often than not though, it appears that caucus functions to allow leaders to instruct backbenchers on what is expected of them: how they are to vote on issues, what the party's public position is on matters, etc. Successful internal challenge of cabinet dominance is rare in parliamentary systems.

A second possible challenge to the dominance of the cabinet is the presence of a strong second chamber in those systems with bicameral (literally, "two house") legislatures, especially when the

---

FIGURE 7.18 Models of Cabinet Decision-Making

EFFECTIVE POWER RESTS OUTSIDE THE EXECUTIVE
1. **BUREAUCRATIC GOVERNMENT:** The power to make public policy rests in this instance with the bureaucracy. In this case who is in cabinet or control of the legislature makes little or no difference to policy.
2. **LEGISLATIVE GOVERNMENT:** The legislature makes policy and the cabinet's role is simply that of implementation.

EFFECTIVE POWER RESTS WITH THE EXECUTIVE
3. **PRIME-MINISTERIAL GOVERNMENT:** Policy-making takes place within a collective executive that is dominated by the prime minister.
4. **PARTY GOVERNMENT:** The cabinet is subject to the parliamentary caucus, which can force policy options. Clearly this is most feasible in a single-party government.
5. **CABINET GOVERNMENT:** This is the classical counterpart of collective responsibility—a decision-making process that is also collective and is usually protected by conventions of confidentiality.
6. **MINISTERIAL GOVERNMENT:** In this model, one of autonomy within a collective executive, each minister has significant if not primary influence for policies that fall under his or her portfolio.

---

powers of the two houses are equal or symmetrical. As we have seen, responsible government directs the attention of the cabinet to the popularly elected or "first" chamber of the legislature. It is also with respect to the behavior of members in this chamber that party discipline will be most effective. In bicameral legislatures it is possible that the party (or coalition) that controls the first chamber (and the cabinet) does not have a majority in the second chamber or is less able to control party members in this chamber. Where this is so, the constitutional powers of the second chamber will make a clear difference to the dominance of the cabinet. If the second chamber has weak powers, the cabinet will not be seriously challenged by its dissent; if its powers are strong, the cabinet may well find here an effective opposition. Where the second chamber has the ability to veto or block legislation coming from the first chamber, it will be in a position of potential challenger to the government. As Lijphart notes, this is enhanced by having the second chamber represent a different constituency, or be (s)elected on a different basis than the first chamber. Of the world's democracies, he judges four to satisfy these twin conditions of strong or symmetrical bicameralism: Australia, Germany, Switzerland, and (as we have seen) the United States. The latter, of course, is not parliamentary, and, as we have noted, Switzerland represents a rather exceptional case in several respects. In short, in most parliamentary democracies, the second chamber does not present an effective opposition to cabinet government.

A third possibility is the addition of a strong presidency to what is otherwise a system of responsible parliamentary government. This has been the experience in Western Europe of France (Fifth Republic) and to a lesser extent Finland (and even lesser, Portugal) and in Eastern Europe of several fledgling democracies, most notably Poland and Russia. These are exceptions to the parliamentary norm, and we will explore in the next chapter the reasons for creating a strong head of state in parliamentary systems. In most cases, though, this has not been to oppose an over-strong cabinet government but to provide stability to weak multi-party systems.

In normal circumstances, then, parliamentary government means a relatively unhampered executive dominance over the legislature and a relatively coherent control by the cabinet of policy-making and implementation. This means that parliamentary government is, all else being equal, *strong* government, able—if it is willing—to put the power of the state behind the problem-solving it undertakes (not that this guarantees a solution). The ability of parliamentary government to act decisively and quickly is one of its advantages among democratic systems. This does *not* mean that parliamentary government is absolute; there are at least two other possible checks on the policy-making of cabinet government. One (albeit absent in many parliamentary constitutions) is the judicial review of legislation or other constitutional judgments issued by the high courts concerning government actions. Where judicial review is possible, merely the possibility of it taking place may constrain governments from certain policies. Ultimately, though, the judgment that no cabinet government in a parliamentary democracy can escape is that of the people. Periodic, competitive elections offer citizens the opportunity to register their approval and disapproval of government policies and to replace one government with another. One could argue, in fact, that it is only on the premise that the political process delivers effective popular control over government that the powerful centralization of power in the hands of cabinet government can be justified. Where this premise is false, there is little that parliamentary government cannot do, and, as in earlier days, citizens must rely on the wisdom and moral restraint of their rulers.

As we have indicated earlier, strong presidents also exist in parliamentary systems in several of the new democracies to emerge out of Eastern Europe and the former Soviet Union. As these are all less than two decades old, it is premature to pass judgment on their effectiveness, and in many cases the exact nature of the relationship between presidency and the parliamentary executive is still not clear or is clearly still evolving. The rationale for having a strong presidency in these countries is once again to counteract potential or perceived instability in the political system. In most of these countries, authoritarian regimes were in place for a considerable period, which means that the political culture has not developed or sustained the attitudes and practices that are associated with democratic politics. Similarly, political pluralism is also new to these regimes; once officially one-party systems, free elections have now produced extremely fragmented multi-party systems. In Poland, for example, the first truly free parliamentary elections returned 29 parties to the Sejm (Poland's legislature), the largest winning only 13.5 per cent of the seats. Over time, in such regimes, one expects parties with similar ideological leanings to merge and consolidate their support, while other parties (such as Poland's Beer Lovers Party) may eventually disappear. Clearly though, forming a government in such fragmented parliaments is a challenge, and sustaining a coalition is always more difficult the more fragmented the party system. Not surprisingly, Polish President Lech Walesa and Russia's Boris Yeltsin both tried to emulate the French presidency in the early stages of their newly emerging democracies. Whether a strong presidency is merely a temporary expedient for these parliamentary systems until they establish institutional stability and loyalty to democratic traditions, or something that will persist as in the French Fifth Republic to date, is something too early to judge.

**7.7
Conclusion**

The weakness of a presidential system with separated powers was one of its attractions for those who designed it, insofar as they wished to avoid absolutism and tyranny. Such systems are likely to be preferred by anyone who wishes to minimize the role for government and maximize the scope for private (individual) freedom. It also means that policy-making can be difficult and is often stymied by stalemate. As we noted earlier, the successful export of the American system to other countries has been rare. Sartori (1994) lists 18 countries outside the United States with presidential democracies; apart from the Philippines, all are in Latin America, and only three— Costa Rica (1949), Venezuela (1958), and Colombia (1974)—have been uninterruptedly democratic for more than 20 years (and even here, Venezuela experienced a short-lived coup d'état in early 2002, and Columbia is struggling to maintain internal order against a variety of guerrilla forces). Sartori concludes as follows:

Ironically, then, the belief that presidential systems are strong systems draws on the worst possible structural arrangements—a divided power defenseless against divided government—and fails to realize that the American system works, or has worked, *in spite* of its constitution—hardly *thanks to* its constitution. (1994: 89)

One reason for mistaking the presidential system as strong may be the misperceptions of the *American* president (i.e., as world leader, military commander, etc.) alluded to above. Another may be the misidentification of those systems where a strong president adds stability to (or is intended to stabilize) a parliamentary regime.

What we have glimpsed in this chapter is the great variety of constitutional arrangements that can exist, structuring relationships between executives and legislatures within systems that otherwise have a great deal in common. Common to presidential systems is the feature that political executives are not drawn from and/or not responsible to legislatures. It remains the case that apart from the United States and the few stable Latin American examples of American-style separation of powers systems, the world's democratic nations have followed the parliamentary route. In a distinct minority of cases, this has been a presidentialism without a separation of powers, and for that reason this weak form of presidentialism might evolve into something resembling the more passive head of state we typically associate with "normal" parliamentary regimes. Portugal, for example, has abandoned its flirtation with strong presidentialism, and it may be that other systems with strong presidents might do so also as they stabilize. We are left with a great variety of parliamentary systems, so much so that for almost every generalization we can offer, there is at least one exception to the rule. The strongest distinction remains that between systems that put power in the hands of one party (majoritarian) and those that tend to produce coalitions (proportionate). In the next chapter we will turn to a wholly different basis for distinguishing among democratic polities, namely, the extent to which political powers are concentrated in the national governments or decentralized through subnational levels of government.

Key Terms

adjudication
amending procedure
bicameral
bureaucracy
cabinet
cabinet solidarity
checks and balances
coalition government
collective executive
collective responsibility
concentrated powers
confidence
constitution
constitutional monarchy
constitutionalism
constructive non-
   confidence
conventions
decision-making
discretionary power
dissolution
dual executive
electoral coalition
electoral parties
electoral system
executive
executive coalition
executive dominance
formal executive
formal power
formateur
functions
fusion of powers
government formation
head of government
head of state
implementation
institutions
judicial
judicial independence
judicial review
judiciary
legislation
legislative
legislative coalition
legislative parties
majoritarian system
majority government
material constitution

References and Suggested Readings

Bagehot, Walter. [1867] 1870. *The English Constitution*. Oxford: Oxford University Press.

Becker, Theodore L. 1970. *Comparative Judicial Politics: The Political Functionings of Courts*. Chicago, IL: Rand McNally.

Bogdanor, Vernon. 1988. *Constitutions in Democratic Politics*. Aldershot, UK: Gower.

Budge, Ian, and Hans Keman. 1990. *Parties and Democracy: Coalition Formation and Government Functioning in Twenty States*. Oxford: Oxford University Press.

Gallagher, Michael, *et al*. 1992. *Representative Government in Modern Europe*, 2nd ed. New York: McGraw-Hill.

Hill, Christopher, 1969. *The Good Old Cause: The English Revolution of 1640–1660*. London: F. Cass.

Lane, Jan-Erik, and Svante O. Errson. 1999. *Politics and Society in Western Europe*, 4th ed. Newbury Park, CA: Sage.

Laver, Michael, and Kenneth A. Shepsle. 1994. *Multiparty Government: The Politics of Coalition in Europe*. Oxford: Oxford University Press.

———. 1996. *Making and Breaking Governments*. Cambridge: Cambridge University Press.

Lijphart, Arend. 1984. *Democracies: Patterns of Majoritarian and Consensus Government in Twenty-One Countries*. New Haven, CT: Yale University Press.

———, ed. 1992. *Parliamentary versus Presidential Government*. Oxford: Oxford University Press.

Mény, Yves. 1998. *Government and Politics in Western Europe*. Oxford: Oxford University Press.

Müller, Wolfgang C., and Kaare Strøm, eds. 2000. *Coalition Governments in Western Europe*. Oxford: Oxford University Press.

Neustadt, Richard. 1986. *Presidential Power*. New York: Wiley.

Parenti, Michael. 2007. *Democracy for the Few*, 8th ed. New York: St. Martin's Press.

Redman, Eric. 1973. *The Dance of Legislation*. New York: Simon and Shuster.

Riggs, Fred W. 1994. "Conceptual Homogenization in a Heterogeneous Field: Presidentialism in Comparative Perspective," in Mattei Dogan and Ali Kazancigil, eds., *Comparing Nations: Concepts, Strategies, Substance*. Oxford: Blackwell. 72-152.

Rossiter, Clinton, ed. 1961. *The Federalist Papers*. New York: Mentor.

Sartori, Giovanni. 1994. *Comparative Constitutional Engineering*. New York: New York University Press.

Strong, C.F. 1963. *A History of Modern Political Constitutions*. New York: Capricorn Books.

Zeigler, Harmon. 1990. *The Political Community*. New York: Longman.

EIGHT | Governing Territory: Unitary and Federal Systems

"In a single republic, all the power surrendered by the people is submitted to the administration of a single government; and the usurpations are guarded against by a division of the government into distinct and separate departments. In the compound republic of America, the power surrendered by the people is first divided between two distinct governments, and then the portion allotted to each subdivided among distinct and separate departments. Hence a double security arises to the rights of the people. The different governments will control each other, at the same time that each will be controlled by itself."
— James Madison, "The Structure of the Government Must Furnish the Proper Checks and Balances Between the Different Departments," *Federalist Papers # 51*, February 6, 1788

Thus far we have tended to speak about *the* state or *the* government. However, where you and I live, we elect representatives to at least four and often more "nested" levels of government (local, county, state, and national or federal governments). Clearly, in this country governments are numerous; in addition to the federal and state levels, a recent census of governments shows that in addition to the federal government and those of the 50 states, there are 87,525 governments in the United States (US Census Bureau, <http://ftp2.census.gov/govs/cog/2002broch.pdf>). The division of responsibilities and **JURISDICTIONS** across these various levels of government constitutes an important feature of our political life that must be understood. As we shall see, the United States is not exceptional in this regard. This chapter deals with the feature that in almost every country, the state exists at different levels, and rarely are people subject to only one government. Countries vary, however, according to the amounts of power they distribute to each of these levels of government and in the institutional and legal mechanisms by which they distribute it. Some countries centralize most power in the hands of national (i.e., country-wide) political actors and processes. Others decentralize large amounts of power to subnational units of government. This territorial distribution of power is independent of the type of democratic system (parliamentary or presidential) that

8.1 Introduction: Decentralization and Centralization

we have been discussing and therefore merits a separate treatment in this text.

We will review a number of options that countries face concerning the territorial distribution of power. Extreme centralization and extreme **DECENTRALIZATION** represent only the end-points on a continuum representing the territorial concentration or fragmentation of political power. A virtually infinite array of choices between these extremes are available to states. Choices with respect to the territorial distribution of power reflect a balancing of several important considerations. First, since virtually all countries are large enough to contain significant geographic variations, there is a natural desire to provide citizens with outlets beneath the country-wide institutions of government through which they can attend to their particular needs and desires. By the same token, however, too much decentralization may threaten the very survival of the country by encouraging citizens to identify first and foremost as members of their local or subnational community rather than with the country as a whole. All states must strike a balance between centripetal and centrifugal tendencies and thereby achieve something approaching an optimal territorial distribution of powers given what is shared and what is geographically differentiated among their citizens. This is a complex and dynamic undertaking, for what is acceptable or optimal at one period in time may not remain so for long.

8.2
Definitions: Federal, Confederal, and Unitary Systems

A number of institutional arrangements that consolidate particular patterns of centralization and decentralization have been adopted by groups of states in the world today. This section establishes the core definitions of three general forms of territorial governance: confederal, federal, and unitary systems. In this respect, it is important to distinguish between a constitutional division of sovereignty across various levels of government and a simple decision on the part of one level to voluntarily share power with (or "delegate authority" to) other levels of government. Whereas the former divisions are more difficult to change, the latter can be arbitrarily modified by the level that retains sovereignty. The three terms defined in this section represent the primary choices in the constitutional **DIVISION OF POWERS**. In general, the forms of government they represent can be ordered from the most decentralized types of loosely integrated and largely autonomous states (confederal systems) to the highly centralized states that leave most power to be exercised by country-wide political institutions that produce decisions for all citizens. While distinguishing among these three terms is important, however, it is worth remembering that they represent only three choices from the continuum of centralization/decentralization, and within these concepts there is considerable scope for variation.

Where there is only one sovereign level of government—that is, where all subordinate levels exercise delegated authority—a **UNITARY STATE** exists, as in Britain, where all sovereignty ultimately rests with Parliament. At the other extreme is a situation where the regional or subnational governments are supreme, and the national authority is entirely their creation and servant. Such is a **CONFEDERATION**, and although the first constitution of the United States embodied confederal principles, none exist in the world today. Between these two poles—a unitary state at one end, and a confederal state at the other—are all federal states, where each of the two levels of government is sovereign in some respect(s). Within this condition, though, there is an enormous range of possibilities, from systems where the weight of the central government is so dominant that it might as well be unitary (hence very *centralized*), to such a weak central government that it might as well be confederal (hence very *decentralized*). Thus, we might present the possibilities as follows:

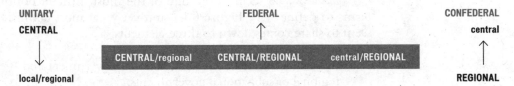

On the other hand, what this obscures is the real possibility within what are constitutionally unitary states for a considerable decentralization of authority through delegation to regional and/or municipal governments. In this way a formally unitary constitution might in fact allow a division of power much more decentralized than a federal constitution where the central government has clear dominance. The distinction we made earlier between material and formal constitutions is useful here too. While the authority of subordinate governments may in fact be delegated, and this means it may legally be revoked or altered by the central government, the limitations imposed by the political traditions, expectations, fiscal realities, etc. may impose limits on the practical ability of the central government to "re-occupy" areas of jurisdiction once delegated.

FIGURE 8.1 Definitions of Federalism

Federalism is a political organization in which the activities of government are divided between regional government and a central government in such a way that each kind of government has some activities on which it makes final decisions. (William H. Riker, in Greenstein and Polsby, 1975: 101)

A federal system of government consists of autonomous units that are tied together within one country. (Steiner, 1995: 123)

In a federal system there are two levels of government above the local level, each enjoying sovereignty in certain specific areas. (Mahler, 1995: 31)

It is a political system in which most or all of the structural elements of the state ... are duplicated at two levels, with both sets of structures exercising effective control over the same territory and population. Furthermore, neither set of structures should be able to abolish the other's jurisdiction over this territory or population. (Stevenson, 1989:8)

The method of dividing powers so that the general and regional governments are each, within a sphere, co-ordinate and independent. (K.C. Wheare, *Federal Government*, London, 1953; 11)

FEDERALISM seems to be one of the most difficult political terms to define—see Figure 8.1—and yet what most definitions seem to share comes down to three elements:

1. the state is divided between a national government and regional or subnational governments;
2. the powers of government are constitutionally allocated between these two levels of government; and
3. each level of government possesses some **AUTONOMY** from the other, meaning either that neither can destroy the other, that each has the final say in some area(s) of jurisdiction, or both.

As noted, authority exists at more than one level in virtually every country (excepting perhaps micro-states or city-states); what makes for federalism—in our view—is the constitutional independence of two levels of government. The government of the United States cannot abolish the states, nor can the states dissolve the federal government. Municipal or local governments, by contrast, are entirely creatures of state governments. The authority to make or abolish municipal governments is one of the powers of the state level of government in the American Constitution. One way to understand this distinction is the notion of **DELEGATION**. Authority is delegated when it is transferred from one body to another, but the original body retains the right to take the authority back at any point in the future. Most of the authority that is exercised by public servants working in government bureaucracies is power delegated by the legislature that, in theory, it could revoke at any time. Delegated authority or power is "on loan," however permanent this may seem. Municipal government is typically, as in the United States, delegated from a higher level of government. Federalism, by contrast, means two levels of government, each of which exercises authority not delegated by the other.

It is also noteworthy that the federal dimension of a constitution is one that can be subject to considerable evolution or development over time. The United States began as a confederation, re-constitutionalized as a relatively decentralized federation, and became by the mid-twentieth century much more centralized than the Founding Fathers would ever have dreamed possible (or wise). By contrast, Canada began as a very centralized system, so much so that it was characterized by observers as (and formally, still is) "**QUASI-FEDERAL**"; it is now one of the world's most decentralized federations. Why federal systems are so flexible is something we will discuss after looking at the component features of federal constitutions. After discussing the features of systems that satisfy the definition of federalism, we will look at quasi-federal elements (including home rule), and then at decentralization within unitary states. What we must do first, though, is establish the rationale for structuring the state at more than one level.

Writing in 1995, Gregory Mahler noted that of 178 nation-states in the world, only 21 claimed to be federal, but included in these were five of the world's six largest countries (Russia, Canada, the United States, Brazil, and Australia); he also noted that China, which is not federal, nonetheless has some federal characteristics (1995: 31). Intuitively, it makes sense that *larger countries* would have more than one level of government; to govern from one center is simply not efficient or prudent. While administrative decentralization can achieve efficiency without creating an autonomous second level of government, in many cases the latter was often preferable, especially in days before modern communication and transportation. Territorially based *cultural or linguistic minorities* often provided a rationale for decentralization and/or federalism, as these groups often demanded autonomy from centralizing and homogenizing policies. This was the case in Canada, where English

---

FIGURE 8.2
Units of Federalism

The national level of government in federal systems is sometimes called the central government, or the national government, or, as in Canada, the federal government. The subnational or regional governments go by a variety of names:

CANADA Provinces
GERMANY Länder
SWITZERLAND Cantons
UNITED STATES States
BRAZIL States
INDIA States
AUSTRALIA States

8.3
Why Federalism?

and French communities had to be brought together in the process of state-formation. Switzerland, with its four linguistic communities, is an even more striking example than Canada of a country that has employed federalism to safeguard cultural entities. Political and social tensions based on linguistic and cultural difference have also transformed Belgium from a unitary state to an extremely decentralized federal-like structure. *Historical factors* also contribute to the rationale for federalism. A very simple reason that large countries are likely to be federal is that they are often the product of a union of smaller territories, colonies, or even countries that have wished to retain some measure of autonomy in the new polity and have achieved this through regional or subnational governments. Two other powerful incentives for such separate entities to unite are *economic reasons* (to create a viable or competitive market or to secure access to necessary resources) and fear of a *common foreign enemy* (or potential enemy).

8.4 The Division of Powers

It should be obvious by this point that federalism, if it entails the autonomy of both levels of government, will require a written constitution where this autonomy is articulated and entrenched. One of the devices we will expect in a federal constitution is a division of powers between the two levels of government. Among the powers so divided will be the ability to make laws in certain fields (i.e., jurisdictions), the power of administering laws, and the capacity to raise and spend money. This division is what is sometimes called the "federal bargain" between the two levels of government, and in a truly federal system, neither level of government can alter the federal bargain without the consent of the other level.

8.4.1 Legislative Powers

Let us begin with the division of legislative powers, the core of any federal constitution. Here a comparison of the American and Canadian experiences (among others) is particularly instructive, since despite the obvious similarities between these countries, the two federal systems formed under quite different circumstances and followed different developmental paths over time. The term "division of powers" suggests that there is a fixed set of jurisdictions that we can simply apportion in some way (like a deck of cards or Grandma's china dishes) between two parties. In fact, it turns out that dividing powers between levels of government is more difficult than this, and it is problematic with respect to both the principle(s) on which the division is based and the means used to accomplish it.

Consider the principle first; one might assume it is simply a matter of assigning matters with a "national" dimension to the central government and matters of a "regional" nature to the subnational governments. But what constitutes a "national" matter (and remember we are dealing with subjects of legislation, not particular cases)? Some matters, such as matters connected to defense, foreign trade, treaties with foreign powers, minting currency, the postal service, etc., seem obviously national in character, and we would be surprised at finding them not assigned to the central government. Other subjects are not so clear cut: the regulation of labor relations, the environment, building and maintaining highways, education— in each of these cases an argument could be made either way, and in the real world these are sometimes "national" and sometimes "regional" responsibilities.

Matters are also complicated by the fact that the division of powers is a prime means of establishing which level of government will predominate, that is, how centralized or decentralized the system will be. When constitution framers want a centralized constitution, as the Fathers of Confederation did in Canada, they will try to give as many of the powers, or certainly what they believe to be the most important powers, to the national government. By contrast, in Switzerland, which was originally (and is nominally still) a confederation, the cantons are in theory "sovereign" and legislate in most areas according to their internal constitutions. It often turns out that whether you see something as a "national" or "regional" matter depends on which level of government you happen to favor! As we have already noted, federal systems also have a remarkable capacity to evolve (within a constitutional division of powers) from decentralized to centralized systems, and vice-versa.

Assuming that one can establish a principle of dividing the powers between the two levels of government, the means of indicating this in the constitution are various. Put most simply, the headings of power (the subjects concerning which a government may make law, that is, jurisdictions) must be enumerated in the constitution for one, or the other, or both levels of government. The simplest approach is to enumerate the powers of one level of government and indicate that everything else belongs to its counterpart. By and large this is the approach of the American Constitution, which enumerates the powers of the national government; places certain prohibitions on the national and state governments, respectively; and indicates that all other powers "are reserved to the States, respectively, or to the people" (Tenth Amendment). The Tenth Amendment is an example of a **RESIDUAL CLAUSE** (or "reservation clause"), which indicates which level of government will receive powers not expressly allocated in the constitution. This is an important device, since constitution-makers will not list every possible area of government activity, especially those yet to be invented! For example, the American Constitution pre-dated the invention of air travel, telecommunications, and nuclear power, each of which require regulation by the state at some level. In the American case, then, the powers of the states are not enumerated, but residual, which on some interpretations at least, implies state supremacy. On the other hand, in addition to its enumerated powers, the government of the United States is given the power "to make all laws which shall be necessary and proper" for carrying out its enumerated powers (the so-called "elastic clause" of Section 8, Article I), something open to a possibly very wide interpretation. In Canada, the federal constitution adopted in 1867 gave the federal government the right to legislate for "the Peace, Order, and Good Government" of the country.

In Germany, the regional governments, the *Länder*, hold the residual power under Article 70 of the Basic Law, which means the power to legislate in areas not expressly granted to the federal government. In addition, and an element with no Canadian or American parallel, the *Länder* can also legislate in the expressly federal areas when and to the degree that the federal government has declined to do so (Article 72). On the other hand, three separate reasons that justify the federal government taking over a legislative field from the *Länder* mean that the jurisdictions of the latter, while "exclusive," are hardly secure (see Mény, 1993: 201). The net result is a very large area of concurrent jurisdiction, over which ultimately the federal government has final say. As we will see below, the balance between the German federal state and the *Länder* is more a function of the bicameral legislature than of the division of legislative powers.

The German example illustrates the possibility of **CONCURRENT** legislation, where both levels of government may occupy a field of jurisdiction. In the United States, Article 6, Clause 2 (the "supremacy clause"), which states that "This Constitution, and the Laws of the United States ... shall be the supreme Law of the Land," is regarded as implying federal paramountcy. Section 109 of the Australian Constitution explicitly states federal paramountcy, and the courts have adopted the same principle in Canada, although whether Peace, Order, and Good Government clause provides justification of this is not fully clear. If provincial and federal laws should conflict, the constitution specifies that the federal law will prevail. This is a statement of **PARAMOUNTCY**, which addresses a matter *not* restricted to cases of concurrent jurisdiction. It might be that the levels of government, each legislating within its constitutionally defined jurisdictions, come into conflict—which law will prevail?

One point that deserves some attention is the tendency of federal constitutions to deviate from their original form or from the balance originally intended. Canada, originally conceived as a very centralized federation, has become one of the world's most decentralized federal systems, while it is generally agreed that the United States has evolved in the opposite direction: from decentralized to centralized (or at least potentially so). In the course of this evolution, Americans put down a secessionist attempt from the South in 1865. Canada, by contrast, confronts a serious political problem stemming from the nationalist aspirations of a significant proportion of French-speakers living in the province of Quebec. Having risen sharply over the past several decades, the tide of support for an independent state of Quebec appears to have subsided somewhat since the 1995 referendum on independence. At that time, the prospect of independence was rejected by the narrowest of margins (50.4 per cent to 49.5 per cent, a difference of only several thousand votes). Despite the recent downturn in support, separatist forces are unlikely to disappear, and movement leaders promise to hold more referendums until they are successful in obtaining independence for the province. How could these neighbors evolve so differently in their pattern of territorial governance?

There are several factors at work here. Obviously the character of a federal bargain can be altered deliberately through constitutional amendment, although this is made less likely by the requirement that such an amendment obtain the consent of both levels of government. In the United States, the Fourteenth, Sixteenth, and Seventeenth Amendments to the Constitution are seen to have limited states' rights.

Judicial interpretation of the constitution in response to challenges based on the division of powers is another powerful force in differentiating the Canadian and American experiences with federalism. By declaring a subject to be within (*intra vires*) or beyond (*ultra vires*) the jurisdiction of one or the other level of government, supreme courts can transform the federal bargain or, indeed, halt its evolution. During the Depression of the 1930s in both Canada and the United States, the Supreme Court of each country ruled unconstitutional extensive social and economic legislation of the federal government on grounds that it encroached on the powers of the provinces and states, respectively. In fact, in both countries there have been broad periods in which rulings from the courts have tended to favor the expansion of the relative power of one level of government or the other. It should also be noted that these cases were often the result of individuals challenging the jurisdictional constitutionality of a law and not because one level of government was objecting to actions by the other.

Another important factor in the evolution of federalism has been social and economic change. As a result of new technologies or a changing economic structure or demographic transformation, powers that once seemed central or important to constitution-framers become less important, and matters once regarded as minor (or not yet foreseen) become of great importance. In Canada, for example, many areas were originally assigned to the provinces in the belief they were not areas of national importance nor required much government expenditure. Because of technological and social change, two such areas—health care and education—have become among the largest areas of government program spending. Similarly, roads and highways, which have ended up under provincial jurisdiction, had a much different significance in the days before the invention of the automobile.

Finally, we should note that the relative weights of the levels of state within a federation will depend to a considerable degree also on the use that governments make of the powers the constitution gives them or of opportunities to expand or extend the boundaries of these powers. In the United States, President Roosevelt continued to push for expanded governmental powers despite rejection by the Supreme Court of his New Deal legislation, and after 1937 he met with success. In Canada, decentralization occurred in part at least because strong provincial leaders were unwilling to have their governments play the "merely local" role that centralists such as Canada's first prime minister, John A. Macdonald, had envisaged in 1867. As we have noted, the extent of the power of the German *Länder* is very much a function of the decision by the federal government to act in a field. Much of the twentieth century witnessed the tremendous expansion of government, and in most federal countries this occurred at both levels of the state, that is, national and subnational. The last decade or so has been marked by a retreat of government in the face of massive accumulated debts. In most cases this has meant a downsizing of government activity and spending but not necessarily a change in *constitutional* powers. Nonetheless, in some cases, levels of government may look to off-load responsibilities to their counterpart. This may be particularly

Texas Capitol

relevant in cases, as we will see below, where the government's capacity to raise revenue does not match its spending responsibilities.

In short, a variety of factors combine to shape the ongoing evolution of the "federal bargain" within federal systems. The fact that this may lead to a deviation from the original settlement of powers upon the governments by the constitution does not make it wrong or right. It just happens, and what matters more than its fidelity to the intentions of "founding fathers" is its effect on the ability of the two levels of government to be responsive to the problems of their common citizenry.

The American and Canadian constitutions appear to assume that it is normal for the level of government that makes laws in a particular field also to administer legislation in that jurisdiction. Such is not the case in Germany, where Article 84 of the Basic Law establishes that the *Länder* will implement and administer laws passed by the federal government. Not only is the executive responsibility for most (if not all) laws passed to the *Länder*, but according to Article

8.4.2
Administrative Powers

83 of the Basic Law the *Länder* are empowered to execute federal laws "as matters of their own concern" (Mény, 1993: 209). This allows for considerable policy variance among the *Länder*, for *how* a program is delivered is very often as significant as any variable in determining its success. In this way, then, the legislative dominance of the German federal government is balanced by the administrative monopoly of the *Länder*. In 1989 *Länder* public servants outnumbered federal public servants in (then) West Germany by a ratio of 5:1; in Canada, by comparison, the ratio is almost 1:1. At the beginning of the new millennium in the United States, there are approximately 2.9 million civilian employees of the federal government and approximately 16 million state and local civil servants.

8.4.3 Fiscal Powers

As each of us is aware from time to time, governments do more than make and enforce laws; they also (or as a result of legislation) spend money through programs and collect taxes to fund their expenditures. The term "fiscal" directs our attention to the revenues and spending of governments. Just as the autonomy we associate with genuine federalism requires that each level of government be able to make laws in some areas without the consent of the other level of government, so, too, we might argue, federalism requires that each government have the authority to raise the revenues necessary to finance its expenditures. In the best of all possible worlds each government's revenue capacity (which is not the same as its revenue authority) will match its expenditure needs, but in the real world, for many reasons, this is often not the case. In some cases the constitution may allocate revenue sources (e.g., types of taxation) unequally between the levels of state, perhaps reflecting a judgment of unequal need. In 1980 the United States government funded 23 per cent of the expenditures of local and state governments (Janda, et al., 1989: 121); by the 1990s, this figure had risen slightly to more than 25 per cent. The amount of money being transferred was substantial. Despite the attempts of the Reagan Administration to cut back on federal subsidies to other government levels in the 1980s, these payments still amount to about $250 billion a year (1997 figures). Other countries' experience with intergovernmental transfer payments varies. Hague et al. report that 60 per cent of the Australian states' revenue comes from the federal government (1993: 273). In Canada in 1996, about 16 per cent of provincial revenues ($26.5 billion) came in the form of grants from the government of Canada (Finances of the Nation, 1997: 8:3 and B:5). Obviously, the more financially autonomous the various levels of government are, the more opportunity they have to behave independently.

The means by which fiscal **TRANSFERS** are made from one level to another are various. One useful distinction is between **GENERAL PURPOSE** and **SPECIFIC PURPOSE TRANSFERS**, the former being transfers to the general revenue of the recipient government, the latter (called "grants-in-aid" in the United States) being monies targeted for specific programs or program areas. The bulk of transfers from the federal government come in the form of specific purpose transfers, which normally (but not always) go to the individual states and municipalities on an equal per capita basis. Here, too, it is useful to distinguish between **CATEGORICAL GRANTS** and **BLOCK GRANTS**, the former being funds to be spent in a particular area meeting a more or less stringent set of federally set conditions, the latter being monies intended for expenditure in particular policy areas, but over which the recipient governments exercise complete control. About 10 per cent of all federal aid to state and local governments has been in the form of block grants. This practice had been declining through the 1980s, but beginning in 1995 and extending into the new millennium the flow of federal aid funds from the federal to state and local governments through these grants began to increase as a result of the new Republican majority in Congress wishing to transfer welfare spending (in particular) to locally administered programs.

Approximately 90 per cent of all federal transfer payments to subnational levels of government come in the form of categorical grants. As noted, these grants are a means by which the federal government gains policy leverage in a field in which it has no constitutional legislative competence. For example, the availability of national aid for elementary and secondary education beginning in 1965 was a powerful incentive for communities to desegregate their educational system. And during the energy crisis of the 1970s federal highway assistance to states was made conditional on the adoption of a 55-mile-per-hour speed limit. All states did so (though this requirement was finally repealed in 1995).

Discussion of the division of powers directs our attention to federalism as a relationship between governments, federal and regional. Yet, as we have seen, an underlying rationale for having two levels of government may well be to represent different populations or cultures traditionally identified with the territorial subunits. Representing the people in two different dimensions,

8.5
Bicameralism in
Federal States

national and subnational, can be accomplished, then, through having two levels of government, one corresponding to each dimension of society. It is also possible to represent the two dimensions of society *within the national government*, and this is the function of a bicameral legislature and more specifically of the second chamber of a bicameral legislature in federal systems. In other words, in a federal polity, the second (or "upper") chamber of the legislature represents in some way the people or governments of the subnational or regional states.

In most bicameral democracies, the lower chamber, the one to which the government is responsible, is elected on the principle of **REPRESENTATION BY POPULATION**, sometimes articulated as "one person, one vote." If consistently adhered to, this principle will give the people *of the country* equal representation in the legislative chamber: each citizen's vote will carry the same weight. This also means that more populous regions or federal units will have a greater number of representatives than less populous areas. In the United States, after the 1990 census California had 52 representatives in the House of Representatives, while seven states had just one. In federal countries, then, the second chamber will serve to represent the regional or subnational units in some way. This is what Lijphart (1984) calls "**INCONGRUENCE**": the two chambers of the legislature are constituted on distinct bases, that is, they represent wholly different constituencies.

The simplest way to do this is give an equal number of seats to each unit. Thus, in the United States, each state elects two senators to the Senate, regardless of state population. In Germany, by contrast, each *Land* is represented in the *Bundesrat* by three, four, or five votes, depending on its population, and the members of the *Bundesrat* are appointed by the *Land* governments, which means that this chamber is in fact a federal council representing the governments of the *Länder*, rather than a legislative chamber representing constituencies. Within federal democracies, the Canadian Senate is something of an anomaly. First of all, the Canadian Senate is a patronage chamber: the senators are chosen by the prime minister and tend to be party members rewarded for loyal service. Senators serve until age 75, regardless of whether they are active in their service (see Figure 8.3) This non-democratic appointment system deprives the Canadian Senate of legitimacy and ensures its subordination to the democratically elected House of Commons. Secondly, the Canadian Senate represents regions rather than provinces; prior to the incorporation of Newfoundland as the tenth province (with six Senate seats) in 1949, there were four regions with 24 senators each

---

FIGURE 8.3
Canadian Senatorial Privilege?

The Canadian Senate drew critical attention in the late 1990s when it suspended one of its members, Senator Andrew Thompson, for failing to attend its sessions. Appointed to the Senate in 1967, but a resident of La Paz, Mexico for many years while a senator, Thompson attended only 14 daily sittings since 1990. He had been able to collect his full pay (a salary of CDN $64,400 plus a $10,000 tax-free allowance) by claiming sick leave and by showing up to re-qualify for membership whenever necessary. The Senate eventually found him in contempt of the body for not responding to the chamber's request that he return to answer questions on his attendance record. He resigned his position in March 1998, 20 months before his scheduled retirement.

(Atlantic Canada, Quebec, Ontario, and the West), plus one for each of the territories. This creates a very unequal representation in provincial terms, one which satisfies almost no-one.

As important as the basis of representation in second chambers, and often related to it, is the power of the second chamber relative to the first or "lower" house. In parliamentary systems, normally the second chamber cannot bring down the government; the first chamber is the *confidence chamber*. For this reason, there is often a requirement that bills (i.e., legislative proposals) involving the expenditure of money be introduced in the first chamber, although this is also required in the American Congress, which has no rules of confidence. The key issue here is whether or not the second chamber has the ability to veto or block legislation coming from the lower house. There is a strong argument to be made that second chambers that represent the regional states must have some such ability if they are to represent their constituencies effectively in the national government. This is what Lijphart calls "**SYMMETRY**" between the chambers of the legislature, and the combination of incongruence and symmetry creates what he calls "strong **BICAMERALISM**." In other words, under such conditions, the two houses of the legislature have a relatively equal weight in the legislative process, or conversely, the upper house does not simply give formal approval to what emerges from the lower chamber. Of the five federal systems included in his study of 21 democracies, Lijphart concludes that four (Australia, Germany, Switzerland, and the United States) qualify as strongly bicameral; the one that does not is Canada (1984: 99).

It is important to remember, though, that the ability of the upper chamber to defeat or block legislation from the lower chamber must be matched by a willingness to do so. If party discipline is weak, then such a possibility is more or less continuous. The American Congress provides perhaps the clearest example of two legislative chambers with more or less equal weight in the legislative process, so much so that most bills move through the two houses simultaneously rather than sequentially, as is the parliamentary norm. A bill may survive either or neither chamber, but then again, bills in this system are not "government" bills and their fate has no bearing on the term of the political executive. In parliamentary systems, where the requirements of responsible government have produced strong parties, the conditions of strong bicameralism will tend to come into play only if the party or parties that control the government are in a minority in the upper chamber. In such a case, "the opposition" controls the second chamber.

In contrast to American bicameralism, in parliamentary Australia most legislation is government legislation, and any defeat presents implications (if not indications) of non-confidence. In 1975, the "opposition" controlled the Australian Senate and refused passage to the Labour government's appropriations bills (which authorize government expenditures) when they were received from the lower chamber. In the view of the opposition, this constituted a vote of non-confidence in the government, whose resignation it demanded. The prime minister and his party argued that parliamentary government requires the confidence of the lower chamber only, a position that is true by convention in some democracies and constitutionally established in others. On the other hand, a government that cannot get parliamentary authorization for its expenditures is a government that cannot govern. In a move that remains controversial, the governor general dismissed the Labour government and ordered new elections for both houses of the Australian Parliament, elections won by the opposition Liberal-Country coalition. Significantly, it is the "incongruence" of the two chambers in a federal system that leads to the possibility that the majority in either chamber could be controlled by a different party or group of parties, something made more likely when elections for the chambers take place at different times.

Part of the difficulty in the Australian case was the lack of clarity concerning the significance of a defeat in the second chamber for the survival of the government. Such a problem does not exist in Germany. Constitutionally, only the lower or first chamber (the *Bundestag*) can defeat the government, so any defeat of legislation by the second chamber (the *Bundesrat*) is simply that. In addition, the veto exercised by the *Bundesrat* is qualified: it is an absolute veto only on matters that touch upon the interests of the *Länder*. On all other matters, the lower house may override the veto of the upper chamber with a second vote of its own. This means that on non-*Länder* issues, the veto of the second house is a very limited **SUSPENSIVE VETO**. Such a device gives second chambers power but not the ultimate ability to thwart the government.

This inability of a second chamber to stymie a government is particularly attractive in systems where the second chamber lacks the democratic legitimacy of the first or popularly elected chamber. In (non-federal) Britain, for example, the House of Lords is a remnant of the days of feudal aristocracy, being composed of a mixture of hereditary and life (appointed) peers. Such a representation of class and privilege is difficult to reconcile with the norms of democracy and egalitarianism, which have been proclaimed (if not fully

FIGURE 8.4 Reforming the British House of Lords

	COMPOSITION IN 1999 (PRE-REFORM)	COMPOSITION IN 2007
Archbishops and bishops	26	26
Life peers (appointed)	485	629
Hereditary peers	759	0
Hereditary peers under the *House of Lords Act 1999*	0	92
Total	1,270	747

realized) in the twentieth century and, not surprisingly, is unique to Britain. At any rate, since 1911, the House of Lords has had only a suspensive veto over legislation, and in 1949 the length of that "suspensive" period was reduced from two years to one. The idea of reforming the Lords has been around for a long time. Traditionally in favor of the abolition of the second chamber, the currently governing Labour Party moderated its stance in the early 1990s to advocate instead a two-stage reform process. In 1999, Tony Blair's Labour government introduced the House of Lords Bill, which would have removed all seats for hereditary peers. In order to speed passage of the bill in the face of opposition from the Conservative-dominated life peers, the government agreed to a compromise in which 92 seats would be retained for hereditary peers, at least until a second round of reforms is undertaken (to come after a Royal Commission has reported on ways to modernize the structure) (see Figure 8.4 for a comparison of the composition of the Lords before and after the Blair government reforms). As it stands now, however, the reformed Lords has eliminated some of the most egregious vestiges of aristocratic privilege in the British system.

Canada's upper chamber represents an unsatisfactory compromise between the British second chamber and the American Senate, which represents the regional units of state (the federal function). It has been pointed out that Canada's Senate was designed as a chamber of "sober second thought" in order to protect the interests of property against possible incursions by the policies of a popularly elected (and therefore intemperate) lower house. For that reason, Canadian senators were, and remain, appointed by the governor general on the advice of the prime minister. Such an appointed body offends the principles of democracy (see Figure 8.3), but it also fails to perform the federal function of a second chamber adequately, because the prime minister's appointees can hardly be said to represent either the provincial populations or the provincial governments.

One consequence of the lack of perceived legitimacy of the Senate is that Canada has not faced a crisis such as the Australian situation of 1975. The rare instances when the Senate defeats legislation coming from the House of Commons are not seen to have implications of confidence, and the Senate seems to have avoided defeating any legislation that might be seen to have such an import. A more subtle tactic is to amend legislation and send it back to the House of Commons. If such legislation comes back a second time in its original form, the senators are likely to give it reluctant passage. Not surprisingly, there have been no shortage of calls to reform the Canadian Senate, and most focus on improving its capability of representing the provinces (their peoples or their governments). It is difficult to argue with the proposition that if the Senate cannot perform the function of representing the provinces adequately, it has no reason for existing.

8.6 Home Rule and Decentralization in Unitary States

In the preceding sections we have employed a fairly orthodox definition of federalism that insists that the two levels of government—national and regional—must be autonomous of each other, and we have indicated several ways in which this can be true. In this section we want to consider several situations that do not satisfy the strict definition of federalism but that have a similar effect or may accomplish the same purposes as federalism.

HOME RULE is another concept closely related to federalism; it exists when a territory or region within a unitary state achieves autonomy or **SPECIAL STATUS**. In other words, a particular government exists in this region but not others. The obvious basis for such an asymmetry is clearly cultural, focusing on a minority language, ethnicity, and/or religion. Britain is a unitary state, but there have been initiatives that establish some measure of home rule for the country's predominantly Celtic peripheries. For example, Northern Ireland had a devolved bicameral parliamentary assembly that operated between 1921 and 1972. At that time it was suspended and ultimately eliminated as a result of the often violent communal conflict between Protestants and Catholics in the province. A Northern Irish Assembly was reinstated in 1998 as part of the "Good Friday Agreement," but has been suspended several times since then. Most recently, it was reinstated in May of 2007.

Elsewhere in the British Isles, both Wales and Scotland have more recently established regional assemblies. Although the Welsh

FIGURE 8.5 Devolution Referendums in Scotland and Wales

	SCOTLAND		WALES	
	1979	1997	1979	1997
% of those voting in favor of a separate assembly	52	74	20	50
% turnout	33	60	59	50

overwhelmingly rejected the question in a 1979 referendum, a majority of those voting in Scotland were in favor, but the turnout was too low for the result to count. The Labour Party that came to power in the summer of 1997 did so after campaigning in favor of **DEVOLUTION** for Scotland and Wales. Devolution in this context involves transferring powers and a measure of self-government to Scottish and Welsh parliaments. As a result of this campaign promise, Prime Minister Tony Blair's government held referendums in both regions. Scotland voted strongly in favor of a separate Scottish parliament, and as a result one was created following elections in 1999. One week after the Scottish referendum, a narrow majority of Welsh residents voted in favor of a Welsh assembly also, and one was established in Cardiff Bay the following year. The assemblies that were put in place as the result of these referendums are quite different, however. The Scottish Parliament is able to overturn British legislation, raise its own finances through taxation, and introduce bills in areas not retained by the national parliament in Westminster. The Welsh Assembly, on the other hand, was initially empowered only to amend Westminster legislation in areas specifically devolved to it, and it relies solely on money transferred from London. However, the *Government of Wales Act 2006* has established the ability of the National Assembly for Wales to make its own legislation on devolved matters such as health, education, social services, and local government. As such, while the Scottish Assembly remains more powerful than the Welsh, the difference in capability is less than it has been in the past.

As extensive as the home rule provisions anticipated in Britain are, however, it is worth remembering that these two assemblies exist "at the pleasure" of the central government in Westminster; it is not inconceivable that they might be disbanded at some future point, if the central government so desires. Other European unitary states have also devolved some autonomy to distinctive regions. The Finnish island of Åland, which has a large Swedish-speaking population, has extensive autonomy or home rule, including a parliament with powers over health policy, education, and environmental policy (Lane and Ersson, 1991: 219). In Denmark, the Faroe Islands and Greenland each have their own legislature and executive.

Finally, we should note the trend within even centralized unitary states for a wholesale decentralization of power. This normally results when a whole new level of regional government is created. In some cases this is the result of ideology, but there is a strongly pragmatic basis to decentralization: as the size and extent of the state have grown, it has become more difficult or inefficient to try to govern from one center. Decentralization often entails establishing administrative districts and corresponding offices for the purposes of administering the programs and enforcing the laws made by the national government. In this sense the state is decentralized but not the government, as there are no regional legislatures or separate structures of representation. Decentralization of the administrative or bureaucratic apparatus can also provide a basis, though, for the development of autonomy in other ways. Spain, constitutionally a unitary state, has for many years endured nationalist or separatist pressures from various ethnic divisions, and in some regions (most notably the Basque) there has been terrorism and violence. The response of the Spanish government has been to create a system of regional governments and, in areas where unrest has been greatest, to negotiate considerable autonomy for the regional governments. Spain now has a system of 17 autonomous regional governments, each with its own executive and legislature, but the powers enjoyed by each depends on agreements negotiated with the Spanish state. Four of the most nationalist regions—Catalonia, the Basque Country, Galicia, and Andalusia— have achieved a considerable degree of autonomy. Thus, although Spain is not strictly speaking a federal system, it contains considerable degrees of asymmetrical regional autonomy, attaining in some cases what might be considered home rule.

In the 1970s and 1980s two other highly centralized ("Napoleonic") states, Italy and France, each established new tiers of regional governments. In Italy, five of the 20 Italian regions created were given "special autonomy" to reflect the cultural and ethnic distinctiveness of particular border regions where there had been some separatist sentiment at the end of World War II. These regional governments are democratically elected and exercise a wide range of powers. Still other mechanisms may be found to decentralize power in unitary states. In the Scandinavian countries, for example, decentralization has been achieved not by creating regional governments, but by delegating to and increasing the autonomy of local governments.

In the second half of the twentieth century, the emergence and development of the European Community—now called the **EUROPEAN UNION** (EU)—has presented the possibility that federalism cannot only arise within a nation state (e.g., Belgium), or through the union of what had been colonies into a state (e.g., the United States or Canada), but also serve as a system for governing associated sovereign nation-states. What began as a limited trade association among six nations (the European Coal and Steel Community, created in 1951) became a commitment to the creation of a common market and united policies on matters such as transportation and agriculture (the European Economic Community, created in 1957). Most recently, the scope of the EU's authority has extended with the introduction of a common currency, the euro (adopted by most of its member states), customs union, and even defense and foreign policy. Along with this expansion of functions has come a broadening of membership, from the original six countries (France, Germany, Italy, Belgium, the Netherlands, and Luxembourg) to nine countries in 1973 (adding Britain, Denmark, and Ireland), to 12 in the mid-1980s (with the addition of Greece, Spain, and Portugal), to 15 member states (when Austria, Finland, and Sweden joined in 1995), to 25 members in May 2004 (with the accession of Cyprus, the Czech Republic, Estonia, Hungary, Latvia, Lithuania, Malta, Poland, Slovakia, and Slovenia), to its current complement of 27 members (when Bulgaria and Romania joined in 2007). The dramatic expansion of the EU does not seem to have ended: entry negotiations began with Turkey and Croatia in October 2005. As of January 2005, there are more than 459 million inhabitants of the EU, making this a formidable force in the contemporary world. This is an extraordinary set of developments on a continent that was twice the focal point of world wars in the last century.

As the scope of the EU has enlarged and as expansion of membership has accelerated, questions have been raised about its present and future governance. Currently, the governing structure of the EU looks like that of no other political system we have discussed. There are four main political institutions, as well as a Court of Justice. The complexity of the relationship among these units is clear from Figure 8.6.

Taken together, they define a complete and increasingly autonomous political system at the European level. As time passes, the EU operates more and more like a state, giving rise in some quarters to fears of an emergent European "superstate." Citizens in many countries carry EU currency in their pockets and travel abroad using burgundy EU passports, and citizens in 13 countries

8.7
Supranational Federalism?

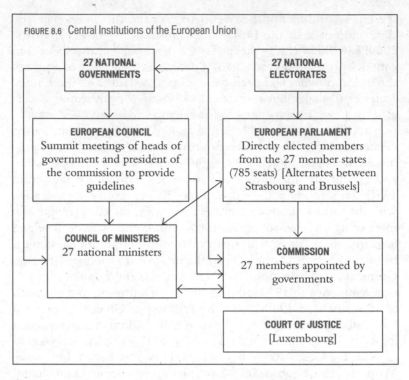

FIGURE 8.6 Central Institutions of the European Union

(the EU signatories to the *Schengen Agreement* of 1985) enjoy freedom of movement across member state borders with no border inspections.

The legislative branch—the European Parliament—is directly elected by citizens in member states across Europe in elections held every five years. The 785 seats in the European Parliament are apportioned among the member states according to population, but smaller states are over-represented in relation to larger ones. The powers of the Parliament depend on the subject being considered. Much of its work is advisory to other EU bodies, but they have expanded in recent years, particularly in terms of budgetary and executive oversight and concerning the accession of new member states.

The European Commission, which is both similar to and different from a "cabinet," consists of 27 members appointed by the member states, normally after they have completed a distinguished career in domestic politics. Each individual member assumes a portfolio consisting of a field of policy. These individuals swear an oath promising to pursue European and not narrow national interests in the discharge of their duties. The Commission must be

Some Flags of the
European Union

approved by Parliament before it takes office. Although the Commission is responsible for initiating legislation, its proposals may be overruled by the Council (see below), and it may be requested by the Council to draft proposals on a particular subject. Similarly, while the Commission is the body that monitors compliance by member states with EU policies, its ability to enforce implementation is weak. The authority of the Commission suffered greatly in 1999; as a result of widespread financial scandals and allegations of corruption, it was forced to resign by the European Parliament.

The most powerful body with respect to policy making in the EU is the Council of Ministers, which represents the governments of the member states. Each country's seat is filled by a minister from its government. Which minister attends a Council meeting depends on the topic under discussion. One meeting might bring together all transportation ministers of member states to discuss trucking regulations; another might involve all health ministers considering home-care standards. On all issues except the EU's budget, the Council is the final step in the decision-making process. Whereas the early decades saw each member of the Council wield a veto, more recent years have seen the emergence and spread of "qualified majority voting." The most important topics are reserved for meetings of the heads of state/government (prime ministers and presidents), and these are known as "European Council" meetings. They are carefully prepared and closely watched as leaders plot the future of this extraordinary emergent political system.

Initially, the EU institutions created a regime that was closer to a confederation than a federation in that member states have surrendered very little of their national sovereignty to the larger body. To be sure, even today, when EU laws take precedence over legislation passed by national governments, each state is free to withdraw at any time. Many of the issues critical to the future of the EU—from further economic and political integration to the establishment of a European defense force—will hinge on whether or not the member states will surrender more authority to its institutions. As the failure of all members to agree to the adoption of common borders and the euro shows, getting all 27 to move at the same speed toward closer integration is a tall order. However, one must be impressed with the remarkable progress that has been made towards the establishment of a common political association in a part of the world better known for its conflictual past than its record of cooperation.

What all of the examples in this section demonstrate is that while the number of countries that qualify as federal may be few when the definitions are strictly applied, there are any number of ways in which political systems may incorporate elements of federalism or apply federal solutions to their problems without actually adopting federalism. It is our hunch that, formally or informally, federalism is something the world's citizens are going to see more rather than less of in the coming decades.

References and Suggested Readings

Burgess, Michael, and Alain-G. Gagnon. 1993. *Comparative Federalism and Federation.* Toronto: University of Toronto Press.

Canadian Tax Foundation. 1997. *Finances of the Nation, 1997.* Toronto: Canadian Tax Foundation.

Elazar, Daniel. 1987. *Exploring Federalism.* Tuscaloosa, AL: University of Alabama Press.

Hague, Rod, et al., 1992. *Comparative Government: An Introduction*, 3rd ed. London: Macmillan.

Janda, Kenneth, Jeffrey Berry, and Jerry Goldman, 1989. *The Challenge of Democracy*, 2nd ed. Boston: Houghton-Mifflin.

Lane, Jan-Erik, and Svante O. Ersson. 1991. *Politics and Society in Western Europe.* Beverly Hills, CA: Sage Publications.

Lijphart, Arend. 1984. *Democracies: Patterns of Majoritarian and Consensus Government in Twenty-One Countries.* New Haven, CT: Yale University Press.

Mahler, Gregory. 1995. *Comparative Politics: An Institutional and Cross-National Approach.* Englewood Cliffs, NJ: Prentice-Hall.

Mény, Yves. 1993. *Government and Politics in Western Europe*, 2nd ed. Oxford: Oxford University Press.

Nugent, Neill. 2006. *Government and Politics of the European Union*, 6th ed. Durham, NC: Duke University Press.

Stanley, Harold, and Richard Niemi. 1994. *Vital Statistics on American Politics*, 4th ed. Washington, DC: CQ Press.

Stevenson, Garth. 1989. *Unfulfilled Union: Canadian Federalism and National Unity*, 3rd ed. Toronto: Gage.

Wheare, K.C. 1963. *Federal Government.* London: Oxford University Press.

Key Terms

autonomy
bicameralism
block grants
categorical grants
confederation
concurrent
decentralization
delegation
devolution
division of powers
European Union
federalism
general purpose transfers
home rule
incongruence
jurisdictions
paramountcy
quasi-federal
residual clause
representation by population
special status
specific purpose transfers
supranational federalism
suspensive veto
symmetry
transfers
unitary state

FIVE | the political process in liberal democracies

NINE | Cleavage Structures and Electoral Systems

> "How can you govern a country in which there are
> 246 kinds of cheese?"
> —Charles de Gaulle, 1958 (*The Columbia Dictionary of
> Quotations*, Columbia University Press, 1993)

Part Four described the main institutions through which liberal democracies are governed. In the next two chapters, we attempt to breathe life into these structures by looking at the social divisions that give rise to the conflict and competition so necessary to the vitality of liberal democracy. With an understanding of the ways in which social divisions can be seen to structure political competition, we then turn to the rules governing the conduct of elections. As we shall see, the nature of social divisions and the formal rules governing the electoral process combine to influence the number and character of political parties in liberal democracies. We have already seen that the number of parties, and the nature of party competition, has significant implications for the operation of democratic governance in political systems. Chapter Ten will explore in more detail the kinds of organizations that form to give political expression to demands of groups defined by different cleavages.

One of the recurring themes in definitions of politics is the resolution of conflict and, we might well ask, conflict between whom and over what? Part of the answer is contained in our observation about the character of most modern societies: they are pluralistic aggregations of several or many communities—their identity is multiple. The conflict states must resolve is sometimes a dispute between individuals, but it is as often, and perhaps more importantly, about competition between different segments of society, and it is competition for influence, if not control, over the policy outputs that government delivers. In turning to cleavages in this chapter, we are looking at the bases of division within a society, that is, the societal sources of the peaceful competition and conflict that is resolved through the political process.

The fundamental nature of these divisions is recognized by Lane and Ersson (1991: 11) when they describe cleavages as "the so-called raw materials of politics which political parties mold by aligning themselves in a party system facing the electorate in competitive elections. Public institutions offer decision-making mechanisms for handling issues that somehow relate to the cleavages in the social structure." Similarly, Gallagher *et al.* (2006: 264) describe cleavages as "the actual substance of the social divisions that underpin contemporary ... politics."

Building on the work of Lipset and Rokkan (1967), Gallagher *et al.* (2006: 264-65) suggest that a cleavage involves three dimensions:

1. a "social division" between people in terms of some central characteristic,
2. a collective identification in terms of this social division, and
3. some organization that gives "institutional expression" to this collective identification.

Each of these points deserves expansion. The first suggests that not only do people identify themselves in terms of a common characteristic but also that this is a basis for distinguishing themselves from others who do not share in this defining criterion. There are, in fact, many different bases on which such divisions may rest, but the most compelling are those that turn out to be, at least in some degree, *ascriptive*. By this adjective we would designate characteristics that are somehow innate (**RACE**), or inherited (mother tongue), or (for at least one's formative years) involuntarily assigned (**RELIGION, CLASS**). This allows us to distinguish the **IDENTITIES** on which cleavages rest from those identities or identifications that are more consciously selected or manufactured, such as an ideology, or a political party, or an interest group. Each of these latter may, in fact, be linked very closely to a cleavage (e.g., socialism and class; Christian Democratic parties and religion) but need not necessarily be so connected.

The second element of cleavages also indicates how the distinction we have just made is not entirely artificial. You could hardly belong to a political party or an interest group without being aware of or identifying yourself as a member of these organizations. It is entirely possible, if not in fact often the case, that we do *not* identify ourselves in terms of our race, or mother tongue, or class. We each have racial or ethnic, linguistic, and class characteristics, but we may not see these as the things that determine who we are and what we want. Very often these characteristics become "visible" to us only in the presence of others, whose characteristics are different. In this sense, a cleavage does not rest on the fact of difference but on the *perception* of difference.

Thirdly, though, the perception of difference is by itself not enough to make a cleavage politically relevant. The collective identification of people in terms of their common characteristic must lead to some political action, and this will in all likelihood express itself in some form of organization. This is where cleavages may link up with ideology, or political parties or interest groups. Hence members of the working class, conscious of their collective identity and **INTEREST**, may adopt a socialist ideology, establish trade unions, support the Social Democratic Party, etc. The careful reader will have noticed that something extra slipped into that last sentence, namely, the addition "and interest." We need this, or something like this, to explain how we get from consciousness of our identity in terms of a social characteristic to organization for political action on the basis of this identity. To be conscious of my religious or ethnic or class identity has no political significance unless it also means that I have an interest that is connected to that identity and that this interest is not being met, or is threatened, or requires protection, by the government. The division at the basis of a cleavage must be not simply a difference in identities but a *difference in interests*, where interest directs us to what a group (or individual for that matter) wants or believes it needs. Its political interests will be receiving the public policies that it wants or needs and enduring none that are contrary to its wants or needs. In our view it is a difference in interest (real or perceived) that is critical to the movement from collective identity to organization for political action. This is the difference between cleavages that remain latent and those that become manifest in the body politic. This may become clearer if we look at some of the more common cleavages within modern societies.

9.2
Some Cleavages Examined

At the risk of oversimplification, cleavages are the product of history: either significant changes in the nature of a society (a religious schism, the emergence of a new economic system, the impact of technology, etc.) have conspired to differentiate its people on a fresh basis, or wars, conquests, or political union have put together different peoples into one society. By and large either or both of these are true of the cleavages considered below.

9.2.1
Religion

One of the oldest cleavages in most Western democracies, and one that had much to do with the emergence of modern society in Western Europe and its dependencies, is that presented by religious difference. This is also a cleavage that can most seriously threaten the peace and stability of a society. The Reformation in Europe led to, or served as an excuse for, any number of civil wars and wars between nation-states. Interestingly, even today most European countries remain overwhelmingly Catholic *or* Protestant, and it is not an exaggeration to say that in most of the world still religious pluralism is either unknown or a source of tension. One need only think of the world's persistent trouble spots to identify clashes that are based, in whole or in part, on religious difference: Bosnia, Northern Ireland, Cyprus, Kashmir, Lebanon, etc. In countries where religious differences have remained matters of civil conflict, the political questions have focused on the role of the state in protecting a religion's values or traditional practices. For a variety of historical reasons, countries where there is a strict constitutional separation of church and state, as in the United States, have been rare. If not constitutionally, then in practice, or perhaps traditionally in past practice, the state has tended to favor one religion or another in some of its policies, and this creates resentment or demand for equity from other religious denominations. In some European countries (and among some of the Christian right in the United States) the religious cleavage is not so much interdenominational but between those who continue to defend a wholly secular state and those who would make religious values once again part of official decision-making or who seek to make pubic policy consistent with church teachings. We should perhaps also note that in talking about the religious cleavage we are talking as much (if not more) about a social identification than about any commitment to a particular spirituality. In many cases the conflict between adherents of rival creeds has little to do with theology or devotion and everything to do with a way of life and identification within the community. In plural, secular North American society, religious belief and practice is often seen to be simply a matter of personal choice; in many other societies, religious affiliation has a much more collective and social character; religion cannot be so simply or neatly extricated from other aspects of life.

A variety of different but similar variables can be treated here. Despite the increasing doubts that scientists have with the concept of "race," we can easily note the existence of many societies in which race has been (Uganda) and/or remains a significant cleavage (the United States, South Africa, Malaysia). Most of these cleavages are the unhappy legacy of colonialism and imperialism. In many other cases, though, political union or conquests or dynastic marriages have joined different ethnic and linguistic communities (which are not so distinct "racially") in one society. English and French in Canada; Flemish and Walloon in Belgium; or French, German, and Italian in Switzerland are more striking examples of advanced democracies with a significant **ETHNO-LINGUISTIC CLEAVAGE**, but countries like Spain, France, and Britain also score high on indices of ethnic diversity (see Lane and Ersson, 1991: 75). It is important to understand that these cleavages are never just about language but also about cultural differences rooted in or sustained through linguistic difference. In some cases, like the Scottish or Welsh in Britain, the cultural differences may in fact have survived the demise or decline of the native tongue. As we will discuss shortly, such ethno-linguistic cleavage seems rarely to exist in isolation but is rather often linked to another such as religion or class. In and of itself, the ethno-linguistic cleavage mobilizes its supporters around issues relevant to the survival of the culture, such as measures protecting and preserving use of language, education, and other cultural supports. In some cases freedom from discrimination or redress for historic injustices will also be high on the agenda. Most important is some kind of political power with which to guarantee favorable policies. For political majorities this is not a problem; ethno-linguistic minorities, though, will seek some manner of constitutional protection, special representation, and/or autonomy within the system.

9.2.2
Ethno-linguistic

This cleavage is a function of size (i.e., population) and distance (i.e., geography), in that without a significant separation of population there can, by definition, be no center and **PERIPHERY**, but there is more to it than this. As in all other cleavages, the difference *has to matter* in some way. Virtually all societies—city-states or micro-states excepted—will have a geopolitical center, and what makes it the center is not its geographic location but its *centrality* or importance within the society. The political center could be the largest city or most populous region; it may be the political capital and/or the most economically developed and productive region. In most cases, then, this centrality will be a source of resentment to regions or areas that feel disadvantaged or excluded by not being at the center. **METROPOLE** and **HINTERLAND** is another way of characterizing the halves of this cleavage, which is apt in that hinterland has the connotation of a region exploited or used for the benefit of the metropole, something that is very likely to cause resentment among those who inhabit the hinterland. In the case of Italy, recent growth in support in northern provinces for political movements with separatist agendas points in a more disruptive direction. Italy is governed from Rome, which is situated in the more populous, but also poorer, southern half of the country. As in most modern countries, the Italian state performs a redistributive function, which in this case means that the industrialized urban north subsidizes the more rural, poor south. Northern support for separatist parties means a wealthy hinterland seeking to be free from a needy metropole.

In some cases, the center-periphery cleavage accounts for what is commonly called "political **REGIONALISM**," which exists whenever the identification with a particular territory within a larger geographic whole becomes a factor in political activity. By itself, though, identification with a particular territorial region will not normally constitute the basis for political action and something else must unite and motivate the people within this region. For example, Canada exhibits a complicated amalgam of regional politics that illustrates the significance of more than one cleavage. There are many cases, as in Western or Atlantic Canada, where the observed regionalism reflects primarily a center-periphery cleavage, but there are other cases, such as in the Province of Quebec, where regionalism is based on another cleavage or cleavages (in this case primarily religious and/or ethno-linguistic divisions). Similarly in the British case, regionalist sentiment in Wales and Scotland incorporates and reflects a center-periphery dimension along with historical and cultural factors.

The urban-rural cleavage illustrates an important point, namely, that for a cleavage to play a significant role in a country's politics, there must be some measure of balance between the two sides of the division. To speak of an urban-rural cleavage in the Middle Ages, when there were few cities, would be rather silly, but the same is just as true in many parts of the industrialized world today where more than 80 per cent of the population lives in cities. This doesn't mean that there isn't a contrast and often a conflict of interest between those who live in the cities and those who still live in the country. Indeed, rural Americans tend to be more socially conservative than their urban counterparts, and thus appeals by politicians and parties to "family values" tend to resonate more strongly in rural areas. Equally, opposition to gun control is strongest in rural America. Access to quality health care, Internet communications infrastructure, and some government programs are other concerns disproportionately felt by residents of rural areas. Some have argued that these issues are driving a resurgence of rural-urban conflict in the United States (and in other countries), but the balance of power is so clearly held by urban dwellers that the cleavage is probably less significant than it once was. It may well be that in many places the urban-suburban cleavage is as relevant as the urban-rural once was.

9.2.4
Urban-Rural

There are several compelling reasons for arguing that class has become the most significant of the cleavages in contemporary politics, and most observers would agree that the politicization of class has been important in many Western European countries (Gallagher *et al.* 2006: 268-69). It is even possible to see the rural-urban cleavage, in many cases, as rooted in class differences. Certainly all countries are not characterized by ethno-linguistic difference, or religious distinctions, or center-periphery conflicts, but all have economic classes. Two factors must be kept in mind here, though: *how* we define and identify class, and that class, like other bases of identity, may remain a **LATENT CLEAVAGE** in some systems.

9.2.5
Class

Class, in any society, represents social stratifications that give differential access to resources and other societal goods. How these classes are to be defined and identified depends, in part, on perspective. Marx, for example, defined classes *structurally*, in terms of the organization of the means of economic production in any society, and believed that the capitalist mode of production created essentially two classes: owners and workers. For Marx, modern politics would be the class struggle between these two classes (and eventually the victory of the working class). In fact, in modern industrial (or now post-industrial) economies, the structure of capitalism is much more complex. Accordingly, the class structure of contemporary societies is equally complex. In addition to owners and workers, there are considerable numbers who are neither: the self-employed (who Marx thought would be insignificant), the unemployed, those employed in public or quasi-public institutions, farmers, students, etc. Division *within* classes, or class fractions, can be as significant as the divisions *between* classes. Different segments of the business community have different needs and interests, above and beyond what they share in common. Similarly, workers of blue, white, and pink collars may be in as much competition and conflict with each other as with their bosses. An increasing **FRAGMENTATION** of the classes, considered structurally, puts impediments in the way of class politics. Sociologically, class is more likely to be considered today in terms of measures such as income, education, and status, or composites that combine several of these. To the extent that class becomes an academic construct, it is less likely to form the basis of an identity on which a politics will be based.

It is possible, then, that however real class may be, it remains latent as a cleavage, and there are several reasons for this. One is the growth of a so-called "middle-class" society in the affluent world, combined with the strength of those ideologies and cultural beliefs that ignore or minimize the significance of class in such societies. Studies show that many view themselves as members of the middle class (53 per cent of Americans self-identified as being somewhere in the middle class, according to the 2004 National Election Study, up from only 36 per cent who did so in 1956), which may reflect in part the increasing class structural fragmentation noted above as well as the increasing level of affluence in the postwar period. Viewing oneself as being "in the middle" of a potential line of social class cleavage means that these citizens are less likely to be mobilized on this basis. As with all cleavages, there must be a significant and relatively clearly defined "other" or the basis of identity does not become politicized. In societies where there are strong cultural beliefs that argue (contrary to all evidence) that individuals' social positions are the product of their hard work, intelligence, and initiative, to be disadvantaged in class terms can be a sign of failure. Certainly, in most European democracies, class is a significant cleavage, but it is much less so in North America, where political parties that campaign on behalf of a particular class are rare—and rarely successful. This is not to say that class is not an important variable in North American politics, only that it is not the primary identity that informs the political consciousness and action of large segments of society.

Any society will have a cleavage structure that will reflect some, but probably not all, of the cleavages discussed above. Across generations, the cleavages that matter politically may shift as technological, social, and demographic change work their effect. There may be other cleavages (like age) that remain latent but have the potential to manifest themselves at some future date. The constellation of cleavages operating in any given society has two significant relationships: one internal and one external. This latter is the relationship between the cleavages and the political organizations and institutions where behavior occurs. As noted, a cleavage may account both for the support given to a political party or an interest group and to the strength of an ideology within a political culture. Political parties, interest groups, and any other vehicles of representation will succeed or fail to obtain policies that respond to the needs of the segments of society they represent. In this way cleavages are accommodated within the polity or not. When a cleavage is most fully accommodated by responsive policies within a political community, the division represented by the cleavage ceases to be a basis for political mobilization. At worst, a cleavage that cannot be accommodated leads to civil war (see the former Yugoslavia), or partition (see the former Czechoslovakia), or other forms of extreme conflict. The ability of the society to accommodate or at least contain its cleavages will depend on features of the **PARTY SYSTEM** that we will be discussing below, in particular the electoral and party systems, which in turn shape the nature of party government. What also matters is the internal relationship, that of the cleavages to each other.

The crucial distinction here is between reinforcing and cross-cutting cleavages. In the former case, two or more bases of identity (or difference) are shared by the same population. This means, in effect, that on virtually every issue, the lines of opposition will separate the same groups from each other. In Austria, the Catholic population has tended to be more bourgeois; the working-class is generally anti-clerical. This division led to a brief civil war in the 1930s. Even more strikingly, in Belgium, the Flemish (Dutch) population is largely Catholic and generally more affluent than the Walloons (French), who are more secular. Tension between the two groups exists here on at least three levels, and the effect of such reinforcement in the Belgian case has been a steady decentralization

9.3
Reinforcing and Cross-Cutting Cleavages

of the political system. Generally speaking, we would expect **REINFORCING CLEAVAGES** to lead, all else being equal, to fragmentation of the polity, as happened in the former countries of Czechoslovakia and Yugoslavia. At the very least, reinforcing cleavages will require a special effort by all parties to avoid destabilizing consequences.

The situation is easier where cleavages do not coincide so neatly. Consider a situation where there is a strong religious cleavage and at the same time a strong class cleavage, but each class is divided equally among those who fall on either side of the religious divide. Here the cleavages offset each other perfectly: those who are united by religion are divided by economic class, and vice-versa. On different issues, then, the majority and minority groups will not be identical. The more cross-cutting cleavages there are, the more political majorities will be shifting and temporary, favoring or alienating no particular group on a regular basis. In this way, cross-cutting cleavages can be stabilizing in a pluralistic society.

Cleavages draw our attention to the fragmentation of identity and interest in modern societies. A central task for the political system of any such society is to contain or defuse the differences and contests of interest that emerge out of these various identities. This is perhaps the element of politics that is identified as the resolution of conflict, the engineering of consent, or the art of compromise. If one side of any division is always the "winner" in battles over policy, then the losing party will soon feel aggrieved, exploited, and alienated. The long-term consequences of such an outcome are rarely good for a political community. What will make a big difference in determining whether such outcomes are likely is the capacity of the political process to provide representation to the various segments of society and in so doing provide a share in government and/or a voice in the policy process. To explore this further means moving from cleavages to the representative vehicles such as parties, organized groups, etc. It is our contention, though, that the nature of parties is itself greatly effected by the **ELECTORAL SYSTEM** in which parties compete and by the party system that the electoral system in turn has a large part in shaping. It is these institutional systems, electoral and party, that we will now examine.

9.4 Electoral Systems: The Basics

In the modern age, most democracy is representative democracy, a term we have reserved for those systems in which citizens have the opportunity to vote for representatives in periodic competitive elections. In Chapter Seven we reflected on the significance of this kind of democracy; here we will extend that examination on the

basis of a closer look at the institutional machinery of the electoral process and its consequences for vehicles of representation in the political process. After examining some technical issues that must be addressed by all systems, we will turn to perhaps the most significant variable within any country's political process, namely, its electoral system. The electoral system in turn has enormous influence on the party system that operates in a country. The electoral and party system will determine the kind of **PARLIAMENTARY SYSTEM** that tends to prevail (as discussed in Chapter Seven) and also influence the other vehicles of representation to which citizens turn for political organization.

It is possible for officials from all three "branches" of government, or types of governmental institution, to be subject to periodic election. In practice, though, most electoral politics, particularly at the national level, concerns choosing representatives to sit in the legislature and, in some bicameral legislatures, in both houses of the parliament. The only other commonly elected post in national government is that of president, and this is true of strong presidents in systems characterized by what we called presidentialism and in some cases of presidents who serve as formal heads of state in parliamentary regimes. In the remainder of this chapter, our focus will be on the selection of representatives for the legislature and, in most cases, will remain with the lower or first chamber of the legislature (because of its role as the "confidence chamber" in parliamentary systems).

With regard to the last point, we should note that while different principles of representation exist, all (to our knowledge) first chambers in bicameral systems and all unitary legislatures are based on the principle of **REPRESENTATION BY POPULATION**. This is also known as the "one (hu)man, one vote, one value" principle, which requires that each citizen's vote carry (at least roughly) the same weight as that of every other citizen. In practice this means that each member of the legislature should ideally represent the same number of citizens (constituents). Thus, the territorial size of each representative's district or *constituency* should be determined by population, and each should contain the same population. We say "should" because populations do not remain static but shift through growth and migration. Periodically, constituency boundaries must change to keep the weight of each citizen's voice in the political process equal. This is one reason why in most (if not all) democracies, including the United States, a regular census is taken.

As we discussed briefly in Chapter Six, the expansion of the franchise to include all adult citizens in the United States was a long and complicated process. In the late 1700s, an estimated 23 per cent of the voting age population was eligible to cast a ballot. All property and religious requirements for the vote were dropped in all states except North Carolina and Virginia by 1829, resulting in universal white male suffrage by that time. American women, however, had to mount a long struggle and did not win the right to vote until 1920. The Fifteenth Amendment to the Constitution (1870) formally enfranchised African-Americans, following the abolition of slavery after the Civil War. However, a variety of restrictive practices (poll taxes, literacy tests, etc.) persisted in many parts of the American South until the 1960s. These practices effectively disenfranchised the African-American population in that region. By the beginning of the 1970s all adult American citizens (with the exception of convicted felons and those in mental institutions) enjoyed the right to vote.

FIGURE 9.1 Size of Legislature* / Constituency

COUNTRY	SEATS	MEAN CONSTITUENCY SIZE
Britain	646	93,000
Canada	308	105,000
France	577	105,000
Germany	614	134,000
Hungary	386	26,000
Italy	630	92,000
Netherlands	150	109,000
Poland	460	83,000
Spain	350	124,000
Sweden	349	26,000
United States	435	681,000

* Legislative seats are the number as of the most recent election, and in bicameral chambers represents the seats in the lower chamber. Constituency size is determined here by dividing the total population (2005 figures; <http://www.oecd.org/dataoecd/62/38/35267227.pdf>) by the number of seats, and thus represents total average constituency population, not average number of eligible electors.

We should also note that the redefinition of constituency (or electoral district) boundaries made necessary by demographic change provides an opportunity for any party that controls this process to maximize their own electoral chances in future elections. If in two adjacent constituencies the government won one electoral district by a two-to-one majority and lost the other by a slim margin, the temptation will be great to readjust the boundaries so that both electoral districts contain a simple majority of loyal supporters. Conversely, one might wish to concentrate as many of one's opponents' supporters in one electoral district as possible. These kinds of manipulations of electoral boundaries go by the name **GERRYMANDERING**, an activity that has much more potential in plurality than proportionate electoral systems. To avoid gerrymandering, the business of adjusting constituency boundaries is usually given to an all-party committee or to an (supposedly) impartial judicial panel.

The point behind electoral boundary commissions and the broader principle of representation by population is that of fairness. Several other features of democratic systems are designed to provide fairness to the parties contesting the election. One is rules about the **FINANCING** of election campaigns, rules that for the most part today are designed (not to say that they succeed) to minimize the influence of wealthy private or corporate donors and encourage broad public financing of political parties. The reasoning is that parties that are heavily reliant on support from narrow or particular interests cannot be expected to be fully responsive to the wishes of the broader public. So, too, no individual or group should be able to "buy an election." In some European countries and in Canada since 2004, there are severe restrictions on corporate or private contributions to political parties, but the latter receive monies from the public treasury, usually in proportion to the share vote received in the most recent election (Gallagher *et al.*, 2006: 327-30).

Just as there are rules about financing, there also are often restrictions concerning the use of the mass media and polling firms. In most European countries (excepting Germany, Italy, and Sweden), political parties cannot purchase **ADVERTISING** time on television, although in many cases they receive an allocation of free time for political broadcasts. In Canada, political parties can purchase advertising time, but they are limited to the share allocated each registered party from six-and-a-half hours of prime time in the last 39 days of the campaign. The allocation is determined largely (but not exclusively) on the basis of the party support received in the previous election and the number of seats held in the House of Commons. Parties also receive an amount of free time allocated in the same proportions. In the United States, however, there are no restrictions on the use of television. Another restriction altogether is the regulation of public opinion **POLLS**, usually in the very final stages of an election campaign. Once again, there are no restrictions on the release of poll data during American election campaigns. However, in Canada, for example, current regulations prohibit the publication of a poll or commissioned survey in the last three days of the campaign, a measure that the media companies have bitterly opposed but as yet have been unable to convince the courts to overturn. This regulation is similar to restrictions on polls in other democracies, where the period covered by the "gag law" may be as long as a week.

Last but not least, we should consider the extent of the democratic **FRANCHISE**, or the right to vote. Usually, but not always, the same rules determine who may or may not stand for election to office. Today, the franchise in the countries we have characterized as democratic is described as **UNIVERSAL ADULT SUFFRAGE**, meaning that—with a few exceptions such as those in prison or deemed to be mentally incapacitated—all citizens above a certain age (usually 18 to 21) have the right to participate in elections as voters or candidates. The universality of voting rights today obscures how recently, in many cases, this universality was obtained. Women did not receive the vote until just after World War I in many cases, following World War II in countries such as France and Italy, and in 1971 in Switzerland (see Figure 9.2). New Zealand deserves credit for having extended the vote to women at a time when some countries still restricted the male vote to those holding sufficient property. At many different times the franchise has been withheld from people on the basis of their race, their religion, or their ethnic origin. That voting is usually restricted to citizens and that citizenship is seen to be incomplete without the right to vote indicate the symbolic importance of elections, something which may be as significant as anything we can say about their representative characteristics.

FIGURE 9.2
Year Women Gained Vote

New Zealand	1893
Australia	1902
Canada	1918
Germany	1919
Sweden	1919
United States	1920
Britain	1928
Spain	1931
France	1944
Italy	1945
Japan	1945
Switzerland	1971

9.5 Electoral Systems: Main Variants

An electoral system is a mechanism for transforming the preferences of citizens (votes) into an allocation of the offices at stake (seats in the legislature, a presidency) among the competing candidates—a sorting out of the winners and losers. In some ways an electoral system is a very simple institution, not much more than some rules and mathematical formulas (although the latter may test the arithmetically challenged). On the other hand, the consequences of electoral systems are considerable for the party system, for the nature of representation that citizens receive, and for the nature of parliamentary government (discussed at greater length in Chapter Seven). Because these consequences are most clearly attached to the selection of representatives for the legislature, this will be our focus: the electoral system as a means of translating votes (v) for competing candidates and parties into seats (s).

As in Chapter Seven, we will make a distinction between those systems that tend (or are designed) to produce a majority outcome, hence **MAJORITARIAN ELECTORAL SYSTEMS**, and those systems which are designed to distribute seats proportionately among parties, hence **PROPORTIONATE ELECTORAL SYSTEMS**. Behind these distinctions (which are based on outcomes) are two variables that describe the basic features of an electoral system. One is the number of candidates elected in each of the constituencies (electoral districts), what is sometimes known as **DISTRICT MAGNITUDE** (D). The universe of electoral systems can be divided into those which have a D of 1, known as **SINGLE-MEMBER SYSTEMS**, and those where D > 1, **MULTI-MEMBER SYSTEMS**. Canada, the United States, and Britain each have single-member systems where citizens choose one candidate per electoral district; it may surprise students from these countries to learn that in most of the world's democracies, citizens either choose two or more candidates in each electoral district or cast separate votes for candidates and parties (a distinction explained below). The second variable is the **ELECTORAL FORMULA**, which is simply the rule by which the winner is (or winners are) determined. Three general types of electoral formula are used: **PLURALITY**, which indicates that the candidate (or candidates) with more votes than any other(s) is declared the winner; **MAJORITY**, which requires a winning candidate to secure a majority of the votes cast; and **PROPORTIONATE**, which distributes seats among parties in roughly the proportion that the votes were cast. As may seem obvious, the plurality and majority formulas are usually associated with single-member systems and the proportionate formula with multi-member systems. An overview of these variations is presented in Figure 9.3.

In comparing electoral system effects, again two broad variables can be noted. One is the amount of **DISPROPORTIONALITY**. In a perfectly proportionate system, the proportion of seats each party receives in the legislature is identical to the proportion of votes it received from the electorate; thus % s = % v. This is not simply a mathematical equation but represents what some would argue is the ideal of **ELECTORAL JUSTICE**: where there is strict **PROPORTIONALITY**, the legislature reflects most accurately citizens' preferences, and no party wins more or less seats than its share of the votes entitles it to. In this way, strict proportionality is extremely democratic. It is also something rarely achieved, although most proportionate systems come pretty close, and some come very close indeed.

The second outcome variable is called the **EFFECTIVE THRESHOLD**. This will determine how much support a party needs in order to gain seats in the legislature and, as a result, influence the number of parties in the legislature. In some proportionate systems there is a **LEGAL THRESHOLD**, a level of support that a party must receive in order to be allocated its share of legislature seats. In Germany, Italy, and New Zealand, for example, the threshold is (with exceptions) 5 per cent. Where there is no legal requirement, the features of the electoral system itself will determine the effective threshold. In the Netherlands, for example, there is one national constituency of 150 seats; this means that any party that can win more than 0.67 per cent of the vote will be guaranteed a seat in the legislature—this is a very low effective threshold. In a single-member plurality system like Canada's, Lijphart calculates the effective threshold to be 35 per cent (1994: 17). This doesn't mean a party must win 35 per cent of the vote to win seats but that

FIGURE 9.3 Electoral Formulas, District Magnitude, and Resulting System

ELECTORAL FORMULA	DISTRICT MAGNITUDE	
	SINGLE-MEMBER	MULTI-MEMBER
PLURALITY	**Majoritarian** Britain, Canada, New Zealand (pre-1996), United States	**Majoritarian** Japan (pre-1996): this system had multi-member constituencies in which citizens cast one vote
MAJORITY	**Majoritarian** France, Australia	None
PROPORTIONATE	**Proportionate** Germany, Italy, Japan (1996), New Zealand (1996): although there are single-member districts, a second vote cast for party is used to ensure proportionality	**Proportionate** Austria, Belgium, Denmark, Greece, Iceland, Ireland, Luxembourg, Malta, Netherlands, Norway, Portugal, Spain, Sweden, Switzerland, and most East European democracies

this level of support is required for a party to be reasonably assured of receiving a proportion of seats matching or exceeding its level of support. What matters here is that a high effective threshold will discourage or penalize new or small parties; a low threshold will have the opposite effect, all else being equal. Now let us consider the major types of systems a little more closely.

First and simplest are systems that elect a single member for each district, either by majority or plurality electoral formulae. Of these, the simplest system is **SINGLE-MEMBER PLURALITY** (SMP), which is common to the United States, Britain, and various other formerly British territories. The simplicity of the system is often presented as one of its virtues: citizens can understand it easily. In each constituency, eligible voters select one from a list of competing candidates, and the candidate receiving more votes than any other is the winner. If there are only two candidates, as was once often the case (and in some cases—particularly in the United States—may still be), the winner will also have a majority of votes. But as the number of candidates rises, the level of support with which it is possible to win decreases (for three candidates it is 33% + 1 vote, for four candidates it is 25% + 1 vote, for five candidates it is 20% + 1 vote, etc.), and it becomes more likely that the winner will have received less than a majority of votes cast in the electoral district (hence the designation as a plurality system). This system is quite accurately described as a "**WINNER TAKE ALL**" system; being a single-member

9.5.1
Single-Member Systems

FIGURE 9.4   A Hypothetical Example of Extreme Disproportionality in SMP Systems

	DISTRICT 1	DISTRICT 2	DISTRICT 3	DISTRICT 4	DISTRICT 5	TOTAL
Party A	1,500 v	1,200 v	800 v	750 v	668 v	4,918 v
Party B	400 v	750 v	750 v	700 v	666 v	3,266 v
Party C	100 v	50 v	450 v	550 v	666 v	1,816 v

TOTAL	%v	%s
Party A	49.18	100
Party B	32.66	0
Party C	18.16	0

constituency, there is just one "prize," which the winner receives no matter how large or small the margin of victory. The other candidates, no matter how close they were to the winning level of support, win nothing at all. This feature affects the outcome of SMP systems in several ways.

First of all, it contributes to the likelihood of disproportionality (%s ≠ %v); there is no necessary correspondence between the proportion of votes gained by each party, and its share of legislative seats. This is because in each electoral district one party wins 100 per cent of the seats with something less than 100 per cent of the vote. When these results are added up nationally there is considerable chance of distortion and no reason that these will somehow "balance out" among the parties. Figure 9.4 presents an extreme, but by no means impossible example for a very small parliament of five electoral districts.

As this hypothetical example shows, even though Party A wins every district seat by finishing ahead of its rivals, overall its share of the votes cast is actually less than 50 per cent. In such a situation, a majority of citizens voting expressed a preference for legislators from parties *other* than A, but receive no representation in the legislature. Figure 9.5 presents an hypothetical result for our five-seat parliament in which the party with the least support wins every seat but one, and the party with the most support is completely shut out.

The disproportionalities or distortions in outcome created by SMP systems are not random but follow regular patterns. Because of the "winner take all" feature of the system, the party that has the largest share of vote tends (the previous example notwithstanding)

FIGURE 9.5 Another Hypothetical Example of Disproportionality in SMP Systems

	DISTRICT 1	DISTRICT 2	DISTRICT 3	DISTRICT 4	DISTRICT 5	TOTAL
Party A	**700** v	100 v	**820** v	**730** v	**880** v	3230v
Party B	690 v	800 v	600 v	630 v	720 v	3440v
Party C	610 v	**1100** v	580 v	640 v	400 v	3330v

TOTAL	%v	%s
Party A	32.3	80
Party B	34.4	0
Party C	33.3	20

to be "overpaid" by the system, receiving a larger share of seats than its share of vote would warrant. Correspondingly, when one party is overpaid, another (or more) must be penalized: in a two-party system this will be the second-place party, but where there are several parties it may be some or all of these in varying degrees. This tendency to overcompensate the winning party at the expense of others is the feature that allows SMP systems to generate single-party majority governments, but these majorities are generally inflated and are often **MANUFACTURED MAJORITIES** (like the example in Figure 9.5). For example, Canada has had 11 (of a total of 18) majority governments since 1945; of these only two earned the support of more than 50 per cent of the electorate. Nine of the 11 majority governments were "manufactured," meaning that a majority of the electorate had actually voted against the government. A majority government based on minority support is in some respects a "false" victory produced by SMP. More rare are occasions when the party finishing second in voter support has received more seats in the legislature; this situation has occurred twice in Canadian history (1896, 1979). SMP is not necessarily responsive to changes in public opinion—parties can lose a little support and all their seats, or they can lose much support but few seats—and in some cases delivers a contrary result. At the very least, these kinds of results indicate that there is no necessary correspondence in this electoral system between inputs and outputs. If elections are to be a primary means for citizens to keep elites accountable, it seems curious to employ a system that fails to reflect accurately the public's expressed preferences.

The "winner take all" character of SMP is especially tough on new or small parties, and for this reason it supports or sustains two-party systems in most cases (the United States is an example confirming this generalization, while Canada is a notable exception). A new party can succeed only in electoral districts where it becomes *the* most popular party; by the same token a party that finishes second in every electoral district has no more to show for its effort than a party that finishes tenth in every electoral district. New or small parties with evenly distributed, weak to moderate support will win little or nothing while new or small parties with regionally concentrated support can succeed, or even flourish, for a time. In this way SMP encourages regionalism or sectionalism not only within the party system but within parties themselves, which may seek to concentrate on areas where they already have support rather than seeking to strengthen their appeal in more marginal areas. Finally, SMP encourages strategic voting. This occurs when voters anticipating a certain outcome vote for a party other than their first choice in an attempt to prevent that outcome. It may be difficult to find a reason to vote for a party that has no realistic chance (given available evidence) of winning the seat. In this way votes cast for any candidate other than the one who wins are "wasted" votes—they count for nothing in the outcome.

In France and Australia, different electoral formulas have been combined with single-member districts to produce results that are majoritarian, but in either case, a simple plurality of votes will not suffice to win the constituency. These are sometimes called **SINGLE-MEMBER MAJORITY** systems, but this is only partially (and not necessarily) true of the French legislative elections.

The distinctive feature of the French system is a second round of voting (or what is sometimes called a **RUN-OFF**) in constituencies where no candidate secures a majority of the votes cast in the initial round. The second vote occurs a week following the first. All candidates receiving less than 12.5 per cent of the vote in the first round are removed from the ballot for the second round. Whoever receives a plurality in the second round is the winner. In practice, this system encourages electoral cooperation between parties of the left and between parties of the right, parties within each group usually agreeing on whose candidate to support in the second round. This often has the result of reducing the number of effective candidates in the second round to two, which ensures that the winner has a majority of the votes cast. Nonetheless, this majority has also been manufactured: many will be forced to vote in the second round for a party that represents their second or third

FIGURE 9.6 Legislative Election: France, 2007

| PARTY | % VALID BALLOTS | | | |
	1ST ROUND	2ND ROUND	SEATS #	(%)
Communist	4.3	2.3	15	2.6%
Socialist	24.7	42.3	186	32.2%
Other Left	3.3	4.1	12	2.1%
UMP	39.5	46.4	313	54.3%
National Front	4.3	0.1	0	0.0%
Greens	3.3	0.5	4	0.6%
Other	20.6	4.8	44	7.6%

choice, or they do not vote at all. Similarly, there is no necessary correspondence between voter preferences and final party standings in the legislature. Figure 9.6 demonstrates some of these features of the French system in the context of the most recent legislative elections held in June 2007.

The effect of the run-off is clearly to draw support from the minor parties and concentrate it with the large parties within each ideological division. In terms of the final distribution of seats, the disproportionalities are considerable. The eventual winner of the election, Prime Minister François Fillon of the *Union pour un Mouvement Populaire* (UMP), won a higher proportion of the second ballot vote than he managed on the first. The UMP's 313 seats put them over the threshold of 289 seats required to form an absolute majority. The second place *Parti Socialiste* (PS), led by François Hollande (husband of the party's unsuccessful presidential candidate Ségolène Royal), increased its share of the popular vote by almost 18 per cent between the first and second rounds, but despite this dramatic improvement the party won only about a third of the seats in the National Assembly. By contrast, each of the traditionally smaller parties lost ground between the first and second ballots, since many of their candidates did not clear the 12.5 per cent threshold in the first round of balloting that would qualify them to compete in the second round.

The Australian single-member system employs what is called an alternative vote, by means of an **ORDINAL** or **PREFERENTIAL BALLOT**. This means that instead of choosing one among the available candidates, voters rank all the candidates in order of preference. If no candidate should secure a majority of first preference votes, then the candidate with the least number of first preference votes is eliminated, and her ballots redistributed among the remaining candidates on the basis of the second preferences indicated. This process continues until one candidate has a majority of accumulated preferences. Consider a hypothetical electoral district in which there are four parties (A,B,C, and D) and 100 voters. The standings of the candidates on the basis of the first preference on each ballot is

> *Party A*   40 votes   *Party C*   20 votes
> *Party B*   30 votes   *Party D*   10 votes

Since no one received a majority of first preferences, candidate D is eliminated and her ballots redistributed on the basis of the number of second preferences received. Suppose that of the ten ballots on which D received the first preference, it may be that the second choice went to Party A twice, Party B three times, and party C five times. The standing now is

> *Party A*   42 votes   *Party B*   33 votes
> *Party C*   25 votes

Since no one still has attained a majority, candidate C will be eliminated, and the 20 first preference votes cast for Party C will now be allocated among parties A and B on the basis of second preferences. Of these twenty ballots, suppose that nine second preferences went to Party A, three to Party B, and eight to party D (already eliminated). The standing is now

> *Party A*   50 votes   *Party B*   36 votes

Since candidate A now has a majority, she is the winner. In this particular example, Party A led from start to finish, as it were, through the adjustment process, but it could very well have turned out that Party B picked up more second preference votes and turned out the winner. Clearly, this is a potentially complicated system and one that becomes more cumbersome the more candidates are involved.

One is tempted to call the French and Australian systems idiosyncratic variations on the majoritarian theme, measuring marginally better than simple plurality systems with respect to disproportionality and effective threshold; as Figure 9.7 shows, they are also less likely to manufacture a parliamentary majority. The point is that majoritarian systems, whether resting on plurality rules or not, are increasingly idiosyncratic in the democratic world, where the virtues of proportionality seem increasingly to rule.

FIGURE 9.7 Effects of Electoral Formulas on Disproportionality and Party Systems

ELECTORAL FORMULA	DISPRO-PORTIONALITY (%)	EFFECTIVE NUMBER OF ELECTIVE PARTIES	EFFECTIVE NUMBER OF PARLIAMENTARY PARTIES	FREQUENCY OF PARLIAMENTARY MAJORITIES	FREQUENCY OF MANUFACTURED MAJORITIES
Plurality (5)	13.56	3.09	2.04	0.93	0.71
Other major-itarian (2)	10.88	3.58	2.77	0.52	0.52
PR (20)	4.27	4.07	3.56	0.20	0.12

Note: The number in brackets indicates the number of countries on which the numbers for each formula are based.
Source: Adapted from Lijphart (1994: 96)

The operation of plurality systems is easy to understand, but the results can be puzzling; the outcome of proportionate systems, by contrast, is fairly transparent, but the various means employed to achieve this result can be complicated and confusing. The entire rationale of proportionate representation (PR) systems is to distribute legislative seats among parties in proportions as true to their share of the vote as is possible. This can be seen in the contrast, presented in Figure 9.8, between the distribution of seats and votes in plurality and in proportionate systems. There are three sets of distinctions we need to examine in order to understand how proportionate systems actually work. First of all, we have noted that proportionate systems often employ a **MULTI-MEMBER CONSTITUENCY**. **CONSTITUENCY SIZE** can vary considerably, from three or four members up to a national constituency that effectively presents the whole legislature to each citizen (as in Israel and the Netherlands), but the normal range seems to be between five and 15 members returned to the legislature from each constituency. The larger the constituency the more easily a proportionate distribution of seats in the constituency will be. Consider an outcome like that noted above:

9.5.2
Proportionate Electoral Systems

Party A 40%	Party C 20%
Party B 30%	Party D 10%

If there are four seats at stake here, the division will (depending on the formula used) be one seat for each party, or two for party A and one each for B and C. Neither division is very close to the

FIGURE 9.8

A: Plurality Systems

CANADA 2006

PARTY	% V	# S	% S
Conservative	36.3	124	40.3
Liberal	30.2	103	33.4
New Democratic Party	17.5	29	9.4
Bloc Québécois	10.5	51	16.6
Green	4.5	0	0.0
Independent	0.5	1	0.3
Other	0.5	0	0.0
Total		308	

BRITAIN 2005

PARTY	% V	# S	% S
Labour	35.3	356	55.2
Conservative	32.3	198	30.7
Liberal Democrats	22.1	62	9.6
Referendum	2.6	–	–
Scottish National	1.5	6	0.9
Ulster Unionist	0.5	1	0.2
Social Democratic and Labour	0.5	3	0.5
Plaid Cymru/Party of Wales	0.6	3	0.5
Sinn Fein	0.6	5	0.8
Democratic Unionist	0.9	9	1.4
Other	2.0	3	0.5
Total		659	

B. Proportionate Systems

BELGIUM 2003

PARTY	% V	# S	% S
Flemish Liberals and Democrats	15.4	25	16.6
Socialists (Flemish)	14.9	23	15.3
Christian People's (Flemish)	13.3	21	14.0
Socialists (Walloon)	13.0	25	16.7
Flemish Block	11.6	18	12.0
Liberal Reformist	11.4	24	16.0
Francophone Ecologists (Ecolo)	3.1	4	2.7
Flemish Ecologists (Agalev)	2.5	0	0.0
Humanist Democratic Centre	5.5	8	5.3
New-Flemish Alliance	3.1	1	0.7
National Front	1.5	1	0.7
Other	3.1	–	0.0
Total		150	

CZECH REPUBLIC 2006

PARTY	% V	# S	% S
Civic Democratic Party	35.4	81	40.5
Social Democrats	32.3	74	37.0
Communists	12.8	26	13.0
Christian Democrats	7.2	13	6.5
Green	6.3	6	3.0
SNK – European Democrats	2.1	–	–
Total		200	

DENMARK 2005

PARTY	% V	# S	% S
Liberals	29.0	52	29.1
Social Democrats	25.9	47	26.3
Danish People's Party	13.2	24	13.4
Conservative People's Party	10.3	18	10.1
Social Liberals	9.2	17	9.5
Socialist People's Party	6.0	11	6.1
Red Green Alliance	3.4	6	3.4
Other	3.0	4	2.2
Total		179	

FINLAND 2003

PARTY	% V	# S	% S
Social Democrats	22.9	53	26.5
Centre Party	24.7	55	27.5
National Coalition Party	18.5	40	20.0
Left-Wing Alliance (Left Alliance)	9.9	19	9.5
Greens (Green League)	8.0	14	7.0
Finnish Christian League	5.3	7	3.5
Swedish People's Party	4.6	8	4.0
True Finns	1.6	3	1.5
For Aland in Parliament	0.2	1	0.5
Total		200	

GERMANY 2005

PARTY	% V	# S	% S
Christian Democrats/ Christian Social Union	35.2	226	36.8
Social Democrats	34.2	222	36.2
Free Democrats	9.8	61	9.9
The Left Party	8.7	54	8.8
Alliance 90 – The Greens	8.1	51	8.3
Other	4.0	0	0.0
Total		614	

GREECE 2004

PARTY	% V	# S	% S
Socialists	40.5	117	39.0
New Democracy	45.4	165	55.0
Communist Party of Greece	5.9	12	4.0
Left Coalition	3.3	6	2.0
Democratic Social Movement	1.8	0	0.0
Others	2.8	0	0.0
Total		300	

ITALY 2006

PARTY	% V	# S	% S
Olive Tree	31.2	220	34.9
Communist Refoundation	5.8	41	6.5
Rose in the Fist	2.6	18	2.9
Italy of Values	2.3	17	2.7
Parti Communist	2.3	16	2.5
Federation of the Greens	2.1	15	2.4
Popular UDEUR	1.4	10	1.6
Pensioners	0.9	0	0.0
South Tyrolean Peoples' Party	0.5	4	0.6
Autonomous Liberal Democrats	0.1	1	0.2
Other Left	0.6	0	0.0
Left (seats from abroad)	–	6	1.0
LEFT SUBTOTAL	49.8	348	55.2
Forza Italia	23.7	140	22.2
National Alliance	12.3	71	11.3
United Christian/ Centre Democrats	6.8	39	6.2
Northern League	4.6	26	4.1
Christian Democrats/ New PSI	0.8	4	0.6
Social Alternative	0.7	0	0.0
Tricolour Flame	0.6	0	0.0
Other Right	0.2	1	0.2
RIGHT SUBTOTAL	49.5	281	44.6
Others	0.7	1	0.2
Total		630	

NORWAY 2005

PARTY	% V	# S	% S
Labour	32.7	61	36.1
Progress	22.1	38	22.5
Conservatives	14.1	23	13.6
Socialist Left	8.8	15	8.8
Christian People's Party	6.8	11	6.5
Centre	6.5	11	6.5
Liberal	5.9	10	5.9
Others	2.9	0	0
Total		169	

NETHERLANDS 2003

PARTY	% V	# S	% S
Christian Democratic Appeal	28.6	44	29.3
Labour Party	27.3	42	28.0
People's Party	17.9	28	18.7
Socialists	6.3	9	6.0
List Pim Fortuyn	5.7	8	5.3
Green Left	5.1	8	5.3
Democrats 66	4.1	6	4.0
Reformation Political Federation (Christian Union)	2.1	3	2.0
Political Reformed Party	1.6	2	1.3
Total		150	

POLAND 2005

PARTY	% V	# S	% S
Law and Justice	27.0	155	33.7
Civic Platform	24.1	133	28.9
Self-Defense of the Republic of Poland	11.4	56	12.2
Democratic Left Alliance	11.3	55	11.9
League of Polish Families	8.0	34	7.4
Polish Peasant Party	7.0	25	5.4
German Minority Electoral Committee	0.3	2	0.4
Others	9.9	0.0	0.0
Total		460	

RUSSIA 2003

PARTY	% V	# S	% S
Communist Party of the Russian Federation	12.8	51	11.3
United Russia	38.0	222	49.3
Liberal Democratic Party Russia	11.7	37	8.2
Party Russian Regions	9.2	37	8.2
Union of Right Forces	4.0	3	0.6
Yabloko	4.4	4	0.9
Agrarian Party of Russia	3.7	3	0.6
Russian Pensioners' Party/ Russian Social Justice Party	3.1	1	0.2
People's Party of the Russian Federation	1.2	16	3.5
Party of Life/Rebirth	1.9	3	0.6
Unity	1.2	0	0.0
Others	8.8	74	16.4
Total		450	

FIGURE 9.8 (CONTINUED)

SPAIN 2004

PARTY	% V	# S	% S
Socialist Workers' Party	43.3	164	46.8
Popular Party	38.3	148	42.3
United Left	5.3	2	0.6
Democratic Convergence of Catalonia	3.3	10	2.8
Republican Left of Catalonia	2.5	8	2.3
Valencian Union (Entesa)	2.4	1	0.3
Basque Nationalist	1.6	7	2.0
Canarian Coalition	0.9	3	0.9
Galician Nationalist Bloc	0.8	2	0.6
Andalucista Party	0.7	0	0.0
Aragonese Council	0.4	1	0.3
Basque Solidarity	0.3	1	0.3
Naverra Yes	0.2	1	0.3
Total		350	

SWEDEN 2002

PARTY	% V	# S	% S
Social Democrats	39.9	144	41.3
Moderates	15.3	55	15.8
People's Party Liberals	13.4	48	13.7
Christian Democrats	9.2	33	9.4
Left-wing Party	8.4	30	8.6
Centre Party	6.2	22	6.3
Greens	4.7	17	4.9
Total		349	

SWITZERLAND 2003

PARTY	% V	# S	% S
Swiss People's Party	26.6	55	27.5
Social Democrats	23.4	52	26.0
Free Democrats	17.3	36	18.0
Christian Democratic People's Party	14.4	28	14.0
Green Party	7.4	13	6.5
Evangelical People's Party	2.3	3	1.5
Liberal Party	2.2	4	2.0
Others	6.4	9	4.5
Total		200	

actual proportions of support; with ten seats at stake, each party could receive exactly the proportion of seats warranted by its vote share: four for A, three for B, two for C, and one for D. The trade-off for greater proportionality is a more distant relationship between representatives on the one hand and citizens and localities on the other as constituencies become larger and more populous.

Given the number of parties that may be contesting the election, multi-member constituencies obviously involve a different balloting environment than that of single-member plurality systems. In two countries, Ireland and Malta, the voters employ a **SINGLE TRANSFERABLE VOTE** (STV), which is (like the Australian ballot) an ordinal ballot in which voters rank the candidates in order of preference. Unlike the Australian case, though, several candidates will be elected, so the ballot may be quite lengthy and counting procedures quite complicated. One virtue of STV is that it gives the voters a maximum freedom to choose among candidates of different parties and express their preferences for them.

Much more common in multi-member constituencies are **LIST SYSTEMS**, where voters choose between party lists. In a six-member constituency, each party contesting the election will present voters with a list of candidates for consideration (see Figure 9.9). List systems vary considerably with regard to the amount of choice they present to voters. In some cases, voters will simply have the choice of one party's list or another's. In other cases they are able to change the order of candidates, who appear on the ballot in an order determined by the party. Control over the ranking of candidates is clearly crucial to their electability (and it is also a very effective means of exercising party discipline). Obviously, in a six-member electoral district, given proportionality, it is extremely unlikely that a party will elect all of its candidates. Those at the top of the list will be the first elected; in the sample ballot shown, the party has attempted to increase the chances of electing its first candidate. Casting this ballot would give six votes to the Radical Party, two to B. Barker and one to each of the other candidates. The maximum amount of flexibility is perhaps exhibited in the degree of choice the Swiss system gives to voters. They may scratch names off a party ballot and write in names of individuals from other parties, thus indicating that while they wish to support a particular party, they also want to influence the determination of which representatives are elected from the other parties. In addition, the Swiss voter is given a blank ballot on which they may write the names of candidates from any of the party ballots supplied to them. As in so many other areas, Swiss practice is exceptional rather than typical.

Perhaps the most complicated aspect of proportionate systems, and one which is really only exciting to the specialist or the mathematically inclined, is the actual formula by which seats are allocated within the constituency. Various rules are applied to determine the allocation of seats within specific PR systems, and these differ in their overall tendency to favor small or large parties, but compared with the disproportionalities of SMP, these variations are normally small. Two types of formula are used: highest averages (the D'Hondt and modified Sainte-Laguë systems) and largest remainders (the Hare, Droop, and Imperiali quotas). The application of these systems is rather complicated and not something we need to explore further here, but Figure 9.10 illustrates the different allocation of seats that each method would make for the same results in an eight-member constituency with 100,000 votes cast.

The results in Figure 9.10 show that there is a slight difference within each type of formula in the outcomes generated. In the case shown, the D'Hondt system and the Droop and Imperiali quotas favor the largest party, and the Sainte-Laguë method and Hare quota favor the smaller parties, although here it is the middle party that benefits.

FIGURE 9.9
Radical Party: Radical List: #02

RADICAL
ballot October 21, 2007

ELECTION OF SIX MEMBERS OF PARLIAMENT
02.01 Barker, Brigitte
02.02 Dali, Georg
02.03 Feingold, Isaac
02.04 Lewis, Cynthia
02.05 Wilson, Deborah
02.06 Zubac, Jan

FIGURE 9.10 Proportional Electoral Formulas

| PARTY | VOTES | HIGHEST AVERAGES | | LARGEST REMAINDERS | | |
		D'HONDT	SAINTE-LAGUË	HARE	DROOP	IMPERIALI
Party A	32,000	3	2	2	3	3
Party B	24,000	2	2	2	2	2
Party C	20,000	1	2	2	1	1
Party D	13,500	1	1	1	1	1
Party E	10,500	1	1	1	1	1

As may be obvious, while these methods award seats in a much more proportional way than a plurality or majoritarian formula, strict proportionality is still not achieved on a constituency basis unless the constituency (or district magnitude = D) is very large. As Figure 9.8 demonstrates, results in the Netherlands, which has one national constituency, are extremely proportional. Since most systems employ smaller constituencies, they often also use what is called a **SECOND TIER**. This means that not all seats are allocated through the balloting for candidates in the constituencies; some are held back for a second round of allocation, the purpose of which—generally—is to adjust for any disproportionalities created by the constituency allocation of seats (i.e., the first round). Countries that employ a two-tier system include Austria, Belgium, Denmark, Germany, Greece, Iceland, Italy, Malta, Norway, and Sweden. For the second tier, district magnitude is usually much larger than for the first tier and often is a national constituency. The electoral formula is also usually different from that employed at the first tier. Depending on thresholds, legal or effective, the second tier may exclude smaller parties or ensure that they receive seats. The amount of disproportionality generated by the Greek system (see Figure 9.8) has a lot to do with the high threshold for participation in second-tier allocation of seats; this means the larger parties are rewarded. If, as is usually the case, the purpose of the second tier seats is to eliminate disproportionalities created in the first tier allocation, then the number of second-tier seats necessary will be determined by the level of disproportionality that the first tier generates. (The second-tier seats, for this reason, are often called **ADJUSTMENT SEATS**.) If the total discrepancy between share of votes and seats that parties ought to receive is small, then the second tier can be small also. As a general rule, the smaller the first-tier constituencies, the larger the possibility of disproportionality, and hence the larger the second tier will need to be.

This brings us to what seems to be emerging as one of the more popular forms of PR, a two-tier system that combines the virtue of single-member districts (e.g., attachment of a representative to a local constituency) with the justice of proportional outcomes. The model here is the German system, in which half (50 per cent) of the seats for the *Bundestag* are elected by voters choosing a candidate in single-member constituencies. Victory in the local constituency requires simply a plurality of votes cast. At the same time, German voters also cast a vote for the party of their choice, a vote that is quite separate from their vote for a local representative in parliament and that allows them to choose who they think is the best candidate without compromising their support for a national party. The "party vote" is used to determine the ultimate allocation of seats in the legislature. The seats not allocated through the single-member districts (i.e., the other 50 per cent) are used as adjustment seats in a national constituency and are allocated in such a way that the *total* seats in the *Bundestag* is proportionate to a party's support as registered by the party half of the ballot. The German system has a legal threshold; parties that do not receive at least 5 per cent of the party vote are ineligible for second-tier seats, except if they win at least three first-tier seats. In the latter case, they are entitled to a share of the second-tier seats that will deliver a proportionate result, even if their party vote was below the threshold. One remaining puzzle, perhaps, is how the second or upper tier seats are actually allocated among party members. In the German case, each party ranks all its candidates from party leader down. The upper tier seats will go in order to those on the party list who failed to win a lower tier seat. This is another case where party control over candidate ranking is a possibly powerful tool of party discipline.

In two other countries, a switch to a **GERMAN-STYLE MIXED-MEMBER SYSTEM** has been made in the attempt to address problems in the party system and parliament. In 1996, New Zealand held its first election under a new proportional system with 65 single-member seats and 55 proportional or adjustment seats. This is obviously very much like the German system and transforms one of the few remaining plurality system countries into the proportionate family. Significantly, this reform of the electoral system was approved by the people of New Zealand in a national referendum. The intent was to inject fairness and responsiveness into a system that tended to favor the two largest parties, which in turn were seen by many to be too much alike. Also at the end of 1996, Japan inaugurated a new electoral system with 300 single-member seats and 200 proportional seats chosen in 11 regional constituencies. The intent was to reform

9.5.3
Hybrid (Mixed-Member)
Systems

FIGURE 9.11 Elections in Japan and New Zealand, 1996

JAPAN		SEATS	% SEATS
Liberal Democratic Party		239	47.8
New Frontier		156	31.2
Democratic Party		52	10.4
Communists		26	5.2
Social-Democrats		15	3.0
New Harbinger Party		2	0.4
Others		10	2.0

NEW ZEALAND	%V	SEATS	% SEATS
National Party	34.1	44	36.6
Labour Party	28.3	37	30.8
Alliance	10.1	13	10.8
First Party	13.1	17	14.2
ACT	6.2	8	6.7
Christian Coalition	4.3	–	–
Others	2.3	1	0.8

a multi-member plurality system that had been dominated by the (often corrupt) Liberal Democratic Party. Japan, incidentally, is the only industrial democracy that requires voters to write in full the name of the candidate of their choice. The results of these two first elections in the new system are shown in Figure 9.11.

9.6
Party Systems

Electoral systems matter because of the outputs they deliver, which are first and foremost a party system and, out of that party system, a pattern of government formation. We discussed patterns of government formation in Chapter Seven, and in Chapter Ten we will examine political parties as vehicles (among others) of representation. To conclude this chapter, we need to make some observations about party systems, where a party system is a "set of political parties operating within a nation [polity] in an organized pattern, described by a number of party-system properties" (Lane and Ersson, 1991: 175). This system, most observers agree, is something larger than the sum of its parts, and the behavior and characteristics of individual parties are shaped by the systems within which they operate and, more specifically, by the properties of those systems. We will look at just three system properties: the size of the system, its ideological **POLARIZATION**, and its capacity to express distinct issue dimensions.

We have noted the principal features of plurality systems: their tendency to manufacture majorities by over-rewarding winning parties; their overcompensation of regionally concentrated parties; and the penalization of parties with diffuse but moderate to weak strength. The "winner take all" character of such systems also puts a very large hurdle in the way of new parties; to win a seat, a new party must finish ahead of all the established parties in the electoral district. To gain 15, 20, or even 30 per cent of the vote is something of an accomplishment for a new party, particularly if it can do this in several or many electoral districts and over the course of two or more elections. Nonetheless, this level of support is meaningless unless within specific electoral districts it means finishing first: there is no prize for finishing second, even if that has been 49.99 per cent of the votes cast. Not surprisingly, most plurality systems tend to sustain a two-party system.

Proportionate systems are almost uniformly associated with multi-party systems. The combination of several parties with more or less strict proportionality means that a one-party majority is unlikely and is almost never manufactured (see Figure 9.8). It is normal for the government in PR systems to be a coalition. Defenders of plurality systems are usually quick to associate coalition government with instability and point to Italy's series of short-lived governments since 1945 to demonstrate the undesirable side-effects of a proportionate system. There is, however, little conclusive evidence that PR (or coalition government) produces instability or that the "instability" of changing governments has detrimental consequences. In many cases the "new" government contains many of the same partners as the "old." Where governments are single-party majorities, by contrast, government change may well mean significantly new directions for public policy. For every Italy, there is a Switzerland *and* a Germany *and* a Luxembourg, where stability and coalition seem on intimate terms. What is beyond dispute is the responsiveness of PR systems to changes in public opinion; any increase or decline in a party's support is immediately and accurately reflected in its legislative standing, a feature that is bound to affect the way parties behave towards their supporters and others. If the existing parties are unsatisfactory to significant portions of the population, then new parties appealing to those sections of the electorate will form and are more likely to succeed under PR than SMP, the only barrier being the legal threshold (which may, of course, be a significant barrier). Regional parties are also unlikely to have a monopoly of representation in their region, as is often the case under plurality rules.

FIGURE 9.12 Effective Parties (N)

The number (N) of effective parties is calculated for various numbers of parties and distributions of support (either votes or seats).

TWO PARTIES

A: 50%	A: 65%	A: 85%	
B: 50% N = 2.0	B: 35% N = 1.83	B: 15% N = 1.34	

THREE PARTIES

A: 34%	A: 45%	A: 85%	
B: 33%	B: 45%	B: 10%	
C: 33% N = 3.0	C: 10% N = 2.41	C: 5% N = 1.36	

FOUR PARTIES

A: 25%	A: 40%	A: 45%	A: 85%
B: 25%	B: 30%	B: 40%	B: 5%
C: 25%	C: 20%	C: 10%	C: 5%
D: 25% N = 4.0	D: 10% N = 3.33	D: 5% N = 2.67	D: 5% N = 1.37

We have been referring to two-party and multi-party systems without defining our terms adequately. In fact, determining the "size" of a party system is not the same as simply counting the number of parties. In the case of the American Congress, where there are in fact only two parties, the judgment that we are talking about two-party systems is rather obvious. But what about the situation where a third party emerges and wins a few seats; how does this change the picture? To say that the picture is unchanged until the third party becomes sufficiently large enough just begs the further question: what is sufficiently large enough? These kinds of questions have prompted political scientists to generate an index that measures the **EFFECTIVE NUMBER OF PARTIES** based on a combination of their numbers *and* their relative strength. Thus the British Parliament (see Figure 9.8) contains what is virtually a two-party system, even though more than half-a-dozen parties have some representation, because the Labour and Conservative parties control a disproportionate share of the seats in the House of Commons (for example, after the 2005 election they combined for almost 86 per cent of the 646 seats). Figure 9.12 shows how different distributions of support between parties affect the number of effective parties and how distribution of support between parties rather than number of parties is the key variable.

Additionally, we should note the difference between **ELECTIVE PARTIES** and **LEGISLATIVE PARTIES**. In virtually every election there is a difference between the number of parties that contest the election and the number of parties that actually win seats in the legislature. The former are elective parties, the latter are legislative parties. As Figure 9.8 and other data we have presented indicate, the electoral system has a large effect on the difference between the number of elective and legislative parties. Generally speaking, the electoral system presents more hurdles to elective parties in a plurality system than in a proportionate system (this is known as Duverger's "mechanical effect"). At the same time this effect is compounding: voters who know that minor parties will not receive their share of seats in plurality systems will consider votes for these parties "wasted" and vote strategically for other parties they may in fact prefer less (this is known as Duverger's "psychological effect"). Figure 9.13 shows the effective numbers of elective and legislative parties for a variety of countries in the early to mid-1990s. Depending on legal thresholds, proportionate systems will admit a larger portion of the elective parties into the legislature (thus Greece with its large threshold has a low number of legislative parties). In some cases, however, there is very little difference at all between the number of elective and legislative parties, and generally the proportionate systems produce multi-party systems.

Perhaps even more significant than the number of parties in the system (but much more difficult to measure) is the degree of choice it presents to the voters. It hardly matters if there are two or 12 parties if the policy choices they present to the voters are pretty much indistinguishable. Conceptually, determining the degree of polarization entails plotting the position of parties on a right-left ideological scale and observing the patterns that result. Consider two very different situations within a two-party system:

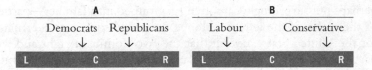

Clearly situation A is very unpolarized, while B presents an extremely polarized scenario. It is not unfair to suggest that American politics has often resembled A, and B has at various times been true of British party politics (particularly at the start of Margaret Thatcher's tenure in office in 1979). Situation B offers a much clearer choice to voters than A, but a single party government in B will be extremely distasteful to its non-supporters, while one could argue that it doesn't make much difference in A which party governs.

FIGURE 9.13 Size of Legislature and Average Constituency (lower chamber in bicameral legislatures), July 2006

COUNTRY	SEATS	POPULATION (MILLIONS)	CONSTITUENCY SIZE (POPULATION/SEAT)
Ireland	166	4.0	24,000
Finland	200	5.2	26,000
Hungary	386	10.2	26,000
Sweden	349	9.0	26,000
Norway	169	4.6	27,000
Denmark	179	5.4	30,000
New Zealand	120	4.0	31,000
Greece	300	10.7	36,000
Switzerland	200	7.5	37,500
Portugal	230	10.6	43,000
Austria	183	8.2	44,000
Israel	120	6.3	48,000
Czech Republic	200	10.3	51,000
Belgium	150	10.4	68,000
Poland	460	38.6	84,000
Italy	630	58.1	90,000
United Kingdom	646	60.6	90,000
France	577	60.8	102,000
Canada	308	33.0	103,000
Netherlands	150	16.5	105,000
Spain	350	30.4	112,000
Australia	150	20.2	127,000
Germany	614	82.4	134,000
Japan	480	127.5	252,000
Russia	450	142.8	325,000
United States	435	298.5	627,000
India	545	1,095.4	1,836,000

Similar patterns are common in multi-party systems, which, perhaps not surprisingly, can often be grouped into families—parties of the right, of the left, etc. Hence we could substitute Germany for the United States, noting that the two dominant right and left parties tend to converge on the center, and for Britain substitute Italy, with parties ranged across the ideological spectrum from the refounded Communists on the left to the neo-fascists on the right. Here, too, is a contrast between political competition played out at the center and a contest covering a broader ideological range. It could be argued that all else being equal, a party system that provides a range of ideological positions presents clearer choices to citizens and offers the conditions for a more meaningful political discourse about policy issues. Parties competing at the center are more likely to craft platforms that do not differ greatly in substance, shifting attention to issues of character and personality of candidates and leaders.

We should perhaps point out that not all competition is evenly balanced on either side of a "neutral" center. By definition, whichever party controls the median voter is "at the center" of the country's political culture. Hence in Sweden, ranging the parties ideologically from left to right results in the following:

LEFT PARTY	SOCIAL DEMOCRATS	GREENS	CENTRE	LIBERALS	CHRISTIAN DEMOCRATS	MODERATES
22	162	18	27	26	14	80

Interestingly, while the Center party is in one sense centrally located—three parties sit to its left, three to its right—the median vote in the legislature (the halfway point starting from right or left) is controlled by the Social Democrats, which means they are "in the center." At the same time the strength of the Social Democrats and the distance between them and the second place Moderates at the far end of the spectrum suggests a fair degree of polarization in this party system. On a polarization index that generates an average for 16 European democracies of 3.1 in the period between 1945–89, Lane and Ersson report a high of 5.1 for France and a low of 0.9 for Ireland (1991: 185).

It is also the case that the center is not fixed but moves in one direction or another as the political culture changes. There are differences between countries (in both the United States and Germany, the major parties converge on the center, but the American center is much to the right of the German center) but also within countries over time. American parties have (almost) always competed at the center for the middle-class voter, but most observers would probably agree that this center has shifted considerably to the right in the last two decades—as, indeed, it has in most industrial democracies. To what degree this is a temporary reaction to the accumulated deficits that governments have faced in this period or a real shift in principle remains to be seen.

Finally, we may note that the right-left classification of parties is itself suspect. On the one hand, the assessment of where a party falls on this scale is always a judgment call and not a matter of exact science. In addition, most right-left scales are largely concerned with party policy positions concerning socio-economic policy, issues that deal with what has been discussed as the class cleavage. As Lijphart (1994) argues, there are at least six other **ISSUE DIMENSIONS** that play a role in at least some of the stable democracies we have been considering: the religious, cultural-ethnic, urban-rural, regime support, foreign policy, and post-materialist issue dimensions. Parties

Key Terms

adjustment seats
advertising
class
constituency size
cross-cutting cleavages
disproportionality
district magnitude
effective number of parties
effective threshold
elective parties
electoral formula
electoral justice
electoral system
ethno-linguistic cleavage
financing
fragmentation
franchise
German-style mixed-
  member system
gerrymandering
hinterland
identities
interest
issue dimensions
latent cleavage
legal threshold
legislative parties
list system
majoritarian electoral system
majority
manufactured majority
metropole
mixed-member system
multi-member constituency
multi-member system
ordinal ballot
parliamentary system
party system
periphery
plurality
polarization
polls
preferential ballot
proportionality
proportionate
proportionate electoral
  system
race
regionalism

reinforcing cleavages
religion
representation by population
run-off
second tier
single transferable vote
single-member majority
single-member plurality
single-member system
universal adult suffrage
"winner take all"

that may be poles apart on questions of socio-economic policy may be close allies on the religious dimension, while a third set of allies links up on foreign policy questions. The presence of different issue dimensions poses intriguing challenges for government formation and explains many of the sources of internal division between coalition partners. Lijphart has calculated the number of relevant issue dimensions for 22 democracies in the 1945-80 period, ranging from a low of 1.0 in Ireland, New Zealand, and the United States to a high of 3.5 in France, Norway, and Finland (1994: 130). Perhaps more striking is the fairly strong correlation he finds between the number of issue dimensions present and the number of effective parties. The higher the number of effective parties, the more issue dimensions a party system seems able to accommodate. This implies that multi-party systems will be better able to accommodate multiple issue dimensions (and thus, conceivably, accommodate social cleavages) than two-party (duopolistic) systems. This again, suggests an advantage to proportional systems compared with SMP electoral machinery.

9.7 Conclusion

To summarize, electoral systems determine the distribution of legislative seats among the competing political parties and do so in a great variety of manners. The electoral and legislative party systems created by the electoral system are significant outputs that are at the heart of democratic politics. The legislative party system will determine the government of the day, and distinct types of party systems lead to significantly different kinds of government, as discussed in Chapter Seven. At the same time, the nature of the electoral party system and the degree to which popular preferences for political parties are reflected in the legislature will have a great influence on the organization and strategy of political parties, considered as actors in the drama of democracy. In the next chapter we will examine this aspect of political parties, namely, their competence as vehicles of representation, as well as some of the alternatives to political parties.

It has no doubt also become obvious that the author of this text has a clear preference for proportionate systems over the SMP systems that have dominated the Anglo-American world. To put the argument most simply, the plurality system emerged in a time that was much simpler, in social, political, and technological terms, but it has little to recommend it to today's complex, pluralistic societies. The principal virtue of plurality is its ability to return a majority government to parliament, but the degree to which this is in fact a virtue needs critical examination, particularly considered against the costs of manufacturing such a majority through a system that is by no means consistently responsive to the preferences of voters.

References and Suggested Readings

Bennett, W. Lance. 1992. *The Governing Crisis*. New York: St. Martin's Press.

Bogdanor, Vernon, and David Butler. 1983. *Democracy and Elections*. Cambridge: Cambridge University Press.

Crewe, Ivor, and David Denver. 1985. *Electoral Change in Western Democracies*. London: Croom Helm.

Duverger, Maurice. 1963. *Political Parties*. New York: Wiley.

Farrell, David. 2001. *Electoral Systems: A Comparative Introduction*. London: Palgrave Macmillan.

Gallagher, Michael, Michael Laver, and Peter Mair, eds. 2006. *Representative Government in Western Europe*, 4th ed. New York: McGraw-Hill.

Katz, Richard S. 1997. *Democracy and Elections*. Oxford: Oxford University Press.

Kelley, Stanley. 1983. *Interpreting Elections*. Princeton, NJ: Princeton University Press.

Lakeman, Enid. 1974. *How Democracies Vote*, 4th ed. London: Faber and Faber.

Lane, Jan-Erik, and Svante O. Ersson. 1991. *Politics and Society in Western Europe*. London: Sage Publications.

Lijphart, Arend. 1994. *Electoral Systems and Party Systems: A Study of Twenty-Seven Democracies, 1945–1990*. Oxford: Oxford University Press.

Lipset, Seymour M., and Stein Rokkan. 1967. "Cleavage Structures, Party Systems and Voter Alignments: An Introduction" in Lipset, S.M., and S. Rokkan, eds., *Party Systems and Voter Alignments: Cross-National Perspectives*. New York: The Free Press.

Penniman, Howard, and Austin Ranney, eds. 1981. *Democracy at the Polls: A Comparative Study of Competitive National Elections*. Washington, DC: American Enterprise Institute.

Shugart, Matthew Soberg, and Martin P. Wattenberg, eds. 2001. *Mixed-Member Electoral Systems: The Best of Both Worlds?* Oxford: Oxford University Press.

TEN | Parties, Organized Groups, and Direct Democracy

"A party is a group whose members propose to act in concert in the competitive struggle for political power. If that were not so it would be impossible for different parties to adopt exactly or almost exactly the same program. Yet this happens as everyone knows. Party and machine politician are simply the response to the fact that the electoral mass is incapable of action other than a stampede, and they constitute an attempt to regulate competition exactly similar to the corresponding practices of a trade association. The psycho-technics of party management and party advertising, slogans and marching tunes, are not accessories. They are the essence of politics."
—Joseph Schumpeter, *Capitalism, Socialism and Democracy*, 1942

"Political parties and party systems are among the most important institutions of twentieth century societies ... popular government in all its distinctive patterns has seemed to require parties to mobilize people and to articulate their needs."
—Peter Merkl, *Western European Party Systems: Trends and Prospects*, 1980

We have encountered various bits of evidence of something that a few moments reflection will confirm: that democracy in the age of mass society is necessarily representative. There is very little that you or I or anyone else can accomplish individually in today's political world; even if we have the inclination, and the time, we lack the ability to go it alone and succeed. Behind each successful individual stands an organization or network of organizations providing expertise, financial backing, communications, transportation, etc. Interestingly, in this sense, the candidate we elect is not simply representing us—the voters and "our interests"—but represents *to us* the whole organization of supporters, staff, and others whose passion, wit, and labor has sustained this candidacy. Ironically, this is increasingly true even as the predominance of television obscures to us anything except the images of the candidate.

In this chapter we will examine a few of the central questions surrounding some of the principal vehicles of representation upon which the political process of modern democracy depends. For simplicity's sake we will make four contrasts:

1. between **POLITICAL PARTIES** and **INTEREST GROUPS** as organized vehicles of representation;

**10.1
Introduction**

2. within political parties, between those that primarily serve their leaders and those that primarily serve the electorate;
3. within **ORGANIZED INTERESTS**, between those that have an institutionalized role in the policy process (neo-corporatism) and those that compete for policy influence (pluralism); and
4. by contrast to the foregoing, the operation of **DIRECT DEMOCRACY** as an alternative to representative institutions.

Our approach in this chapter is more macro-political than micro-political. That is to say, we want to understand first and foremost the significance of political parties to the political process of democracies and will examine the internal working of parties, their strategies, problems, etc., only (or mainly) to the extent that they illuminate the former for us.

10.2
Political Parties

If democracy in the contemporary age is necessarily representative, then so, too, the politics of democratic (and some non-democratic) nation-states depends on the functioning of political parties. The observation that political parties are *institutionalized* within modern democratic systems is another way of saying the same thing. One reason parties have become so indispensable is that they perform a variety of functions central to the political process; some of these functions they perform consciously, and some are accomplished as byproducts of the activity parties deliberately engage in. For example, parties consciously seek to organize the electorate by recruiting candidates, organizing campaigns, assisting voters with registration, arranging child care on polling day, etc. Less effectively, parties help to stimulate policy development through conventions, workshops, and debates. In the effort to construct broad bases of public support, parties may build bridges between disparate communities within society and help to balance competing interests. These are examples of activities that parties engage in more or less self-consciously in their pursuit of their own objectives; in the process they may accomplish much more for the political system. By engaging citizens within the political process and organizing opportunities for activity, debate, and dissent, parties may increase citizen feelings of efficacy and enhance the legitimacy of the political system. In a similar way, parties can be agents of socialization for the broader population and organizations that recruit and groom future political leaders. As important, perhaps, as any of these, parties are said to simplify to a manageable level the range of issues and options presented to the public—the critic might well argue today that, collectively, parties have gone too far in this simplification of the political agenda.

It is important to grasp that political parties serve many masters or, for the sake of argument, at least three: their leaders, their members, and the broader public. This is reflected in the different ways that political parties are described, defined, and evaluated. Consider the definitions in Figure 10.1 (and the opening quote from Joseph Schumpeter). The overwhelming emphasis here is upon parties as means of securing scarce positions of authority and power. This puts the emphasis on the service(s) that parties can provide for their leaders, what we might call their **MOBILIZATION FUNCTION**. This is an important part of the picture, for certainly the modern political campaign requires an extensive machinery to support it, to mobilize supporters, and to collect the financial support required to finance television advertising, jet travel, professional pollsters, image consultants, etc. On the other hand, we should not expect leaders to be the only beneficiaries of party politics. The following discussion of parties by G. Bingham Powell emphasizes what parties can do for the political system at large and for citizens generally:

> Political parties are the institutions that link the voting choices of individual citizens with aggregate electoral outcomes in the competitive democracies. The parties set the alternatives offered to the citizens in elections and their organized activities can encourage both registration and election-day turnout. The relationships between party systems and national cleavage structures should play a major role in shaping voting participation levels. (Powell 1982: 115)

This description indicates clearly how, in performing the mobilization function for leaders, parties perform what we might call an *administration* function for the political process or the electorate, considered collectively. In between the party leaders and the broad public at large, though, stands the party membership: those individuals who actually join a party and sustain it with their labor, time, and money. The relationship of the party to its members is not included in any of the definitions we have provided so far! In this respect we might define parties as *voluntary organizations that seek to further the interests and principles of their members through gaining elected office.* Like all the other definitions we have seen, this one is incomplete, but it presents a dimension lacking in the others, what

---

FIGURE 10.1 Parties Defined

"Party is a body of men united for promoting by their joint endeavors the national interest upon some principle in which they are all agreed." (Edmund Burke, 1770)

"... structured, articulated, and hierarchical groups adapted to the struggle for power." (Duverger, 1954)

"... a political party is a coalition of men seeking to control the governmental apparatus by legal means." (Downs, 1957)

"A political party is an institution that (a) seeks influence in a state, often by attempting to occupy positions in government, and (b) usually consists of more than a single interest in the society and so to some degree attempts to 'aggregate interests.'" (Ware, 1996)

we will call the **REPRESENTATIVE FUNCTION** of political parties. As organizations within the political process of democracies, political parties perform a mobilization function for leaders, a representative function for members, and an **ADMINISTRATIVE FUNCTION** for the political process at large.

It is possible to approach any of the issues relevant to the discussion of political parties in terms of the three functions we have just identified, whether it be the process by which party leaders are selected, the rules of party finance, or whatever. For our discussion here, we will focus on the possible tension between the mobilization function and the representative function. In other words, parties can operate primarily as **ELECTORAL VEHICLES**, in which case their primary purpose is to elect candidates or generate support for their leaders, *or* they can operate primarily as **AGENTS OF REPRESENTATION**, when their primary activities focus on furthering their members' interests. The immediate objection may be that this is an unnecessary dichotomy—that parties surely can be *both*! Indeed they can, but while this is possible, and maybe even desirable, it is not automatic. In the best of possible worlds, parties will succeed in electing their candidates *because* they are good agents of representation, but in the real world, it is quite possible that electoral success may hinge upon practices or strategies that are contrary to good representation. Many observers have noted, for example, that the modern television campaign puts a stress on images of leadership and the politics of "character" rather than on issues of policy or favors 15-second "sound bites" over detailed explanation or debate of policy positions. It is hard to see how these media-driven strategies enhance the party's ability to represent members' concerns or interests. Similarly, while parties cultivate members to provide organizational resources and financial support, they may also turn to pollsters for advice on how to pitch their campaign to the larger, less active public; the demands and ideas of party members in this context become a nuisance or a handicap. By the same token, it is also true that parties that cannot elect members to official positions will not be very effective in representing their members' concerns. This can also be a matter of degree; in some settings—e.g., minority or coalition government—parties may very well be able to influence public policy without controlling, or even participating in, the government. In short, while it is ideal that the party's mobilization and representative functions be complementary, it is also possible for them to be in tension.

Another way to approach the question of political parties is to consider their relationship to the cleavages within a society, as Bingham Powell notes in the passage quoted above and as we remarked earlier. The challenge in democracy is to mobilize the support of a majority of citizens for public policy, and within contemporary pluralistic societies this will involve building coalitions of diverse interests and identities. A key question is whether this coalition or majority-building takes place between parties (as in coalition government formation), or within parties. Where parties closely correspond to the cleavage structure of a society (i.e., their basis of support corresponds to class identities, or ethnic solidarities, or religious affiliations), it may be necessary and appropriate for majorities to be built through negotiation and bargaining between the elected representatives of the various communities represented by political parties. In such cases, it would appear that the representative function of parties is primary and the mobilization function limited by the constraints of the government formation process. The role of the electoral system will also be a key ingredient here, as we will explain shortly.

Parties are adaptive organizations, and their organization, structure, and functioning is in large measure a product of the larger social and political context. As such, parties have evolved over time in relation to larger developmental shifts in societies. In the 1950s Maurice Duverger (1954) made a distinction about party organization between **CADRE** and **MASS PARTIES**. At the risk of oversimplification, cadre parties were the first type of parties to emerge, appearing in the nineteenth century as a result of the organizational efforts of legislators who had already been elected from the small, elitist electorate. Initially, these were extremely weak organizations, consisting essentially of interpersonal networks among parliamentarians and their chief supporters. As the right to vote was extended, the organizations remained under the control of their parliamentary representatives who used their resources to mobilize support at election time. In return, supporters received patronage from elected officials. Outside of campaign periods, the organizations lay largely dormant, and representatives were not expected to be bound by their constituents in their legislative voting. (See Figure 10.2 for summary characteristics of this and other party types.)

Mass parties by contrast depend on a large, loyal membership that remains active in the period between elections, employ a full-time secretariat of professional workers and organizers, and keep their parliamentary wing accountable to the broader membership. For a variety of social, economic, and historical reasons, Duverger associated cadre organization with conservative parties rooted in the *status quo* and mass parties with left-wing political movements.

These oppositional parties could not be assured of access to the established institutions of bourgeois democracy and could not rely on the financial contributions of wealthy individuals. They therefore developed their own internal party instruments for education, mobilization, membership dues collection, and communication or, in some cases, relied upon the organizational resources of trade unions. These circumstances led to stronger party organizations than were found in cadre parties and contributed to an expectation that the party's elected representatives would regularly consult with, and be bound by, the wishes of the larger party organization.

Duverger's typology of political parties has undergone refinement as social and economic conditions changed in the post-World War II period. In particular, the spread of mass media, the expansion of postwar economies, and an expanded ideological consensus on the need for a strong welfare state combined to transform the larger socio-political context within which parties operated. Such developments in a number of European liberal democracies led Otto Kircheimer (1966) to argue that a new form of "catch-all" party had emerged. **CATCH-ALL PARTIES** developed out of more ideologically coherent political organizations as the latter strove to broaden their electoral appeals and attract voters from across the political spectrum. Such parties were characterized by five features: a weakening of their ideological appeal, a down-grading of the role of the individual party member to the status of cheerleader for a party leadership, an attempt to distance the organization from any particular social cleavage or groups, an attempt to gain access to a variety of interest groups, and an effort to appeal to voters from the population at large. According to Kircheimer, American parties were archetypal catch-all parties, and his interpretation of the transition made during the post-World War II period was that any European parties were becoming "Americanized." Both the transformation of the German Social Democrats (SPD) and changes within the British Labour Party in the 1950s and 1960s were often pointed to as evidence that parties of the left had made such a transition to the status of catch-all parties.

Catch-all parties seek to build coalitions across social groups, providing a brokerage function. When parties can bridge societal cleavages successfully, they can play an important unifying or integrating function within the political system. Not surprisingly, building such bridges may mean downplaying ideology; being flexible about policy solutions to potentially divisive issues; and placing the emphasis on leaders, because the bridge between different segments of society is built in part by assuring each segment that

FIGURE 10.2 Characteristics of Types of Parties

	CADRE PARTY	MASS PARTY	CATCH-ALL PARTY	CARTEL PARTY
TIME PERIOD	nineteenth century	1880–1960	1960–	1970–
PRINCIPAL GOALS	distribution of privileges	social reform	social improvement	politics as a profession
CAMPAIGN STYLE	irrelevant, due to small electorates	mobilization—labor intensive	both labor and capital intensive	capital intensive
PRINCIPAL FUNDING SOURCE	personal contacts	large number of memberships and fees	varied sources (individuals, groups, and corporate)	state subventions
COMMUNICATIONS	interpersonal networks	party provides its own	parties compete for access to mass media	parties gain privileged access to state-regulated media
PARTY-SOCIETY RELATIONSHIP	unclear boundary between state and political segment of society	party belongs to cleavage group in society	parties act as brokers between state and society	party absorbed by the state
REPRESENTATIVE STYLE	trustee	delegate	political entrepreneur	agent of state

Source: adapted from Mair, 1997: Table 5.1.

they will have strong spokesmen in the government and therein lies their guarantee that policy will not compromise their interest(s).

Parties continue to evolve in terms of their organization, structure, and functioning. Richard Katz and Peter Mair have argued that since the 1970s catch-all parties in liberal democracies have undergone a further transformation, becoming what they label "**CARTEL PARTIES**" (Katz and Mair, 1995). This latest twist in the evolution of party organization and functioning is largely a response to the recognition that regular alternation of major parties in government is probably necessary and inevitable. As a result, parties have established collusive relations that serve to mitigate the negative consequences of electoral defeat and to share control of (and insofar as possible limit access to) the electoral process. Cartel parties, according to these authors, are similar to catch-all parties in their highly professionalized and capital-intensive campaigns, shrinking memberships, and ideological blandness. Cartel parties differ, however, in that they are heavily dependent upon public (state-provided) funding sources and on their privileged access to state-provided channels of communication. The interpenetration of party and state, then, is the defining feature of political life in the era of cartel parties. As the label "cartel" suggests, parties fitting this description are aware of their status and work together both to control and constrain their electoral competitors and to mitigate the negative effects of political defeat.

In recent decades, as parties have diluted their substantive or ideological appeals and adopted a more professionalized, power-seeking approach, voters have responded to the changing party environment by weakening their traditional allegiances or identification with parties. The result was a general increase in the level of partisan volatility by the mid-1970s, with more voters switching their party allegiances between elections (see Figure 10.3). Students of parties in many countries noted a general weakening of voter identification with parties, and some argued that parties were failing (Wattenberg, 1991; Dalton, 2002; Dalton and Wattenberg, 2000). As parties increasingly became de-aligned from their traditional social bases, new parties sometimes emerged to appeal to voters on different bases (e.g., Evans, 1999). In Britain, for example, the Social Democratic Party (which later merged with the Liberal Party to form the Liberal Democrats) formed in the early 1980s from disaffected Labour members of Parliament (MPs) and, according to opinion polls taken shortly after its formation, appeared on the verge of "breaking the mold" of party competition in that country. The emergence of "Green" parties in many European party systems, "reform" parties in Canada, and growing regionalist parties or leagues in many countries were other developments that contributed to the impression that voters were in the process of rethinking their partisan allegiances to the traditional major party alternatives. As yet, however, constant monitoring of voter opinions and partisanship has failed to turn up any evidence of a new, stable pattern in the relationship between parties and social groups.

The refusal of parties to distinguish themselves in terms of ideology or long-term policy commitments forces the attention of both strategists and voters elsewhere, and in the age of **ELECTRONIC POLITICS**, this means the focus falls on leaders. Parties are thus only as popular as their leaders (or as popular as the images associated with their leaders), and because parties change leaders or their leaders' public image changes, their popularity is inevitable volatile. This means that the attachment of voters to any party is weak; their vote is essentially "up for grabs." Instead of addressing the concerns

FIGURE 10.3 Partisan Instability

A relatively simple measure of **PARTISAN INSTABILITY**, or volatility in the party system, is found by summing the absolute values of the changes in party support from one election to the next, and dividing by two (because one party's gain is another's loss).

CANADA (1988-93)

Progressive Conservative Party	41 − 16	=	27
Liberal Party	41 − 32	=	8
New Democratic Party	20 − 7	=	13
Reform Party	19 − 0	=	19
Bloc Québécois	14 − 0	=	14

Total: 78 ÷ 2 = 39% or 7.8% per party.

This average of 7.8% per party represents one of the largest shifts in voter support between two elections ever recorded. Compare this level with that arising in the following countries (calculated using all parties with 3 per cent or more of the popular vote):

Britain (1992-97)	=	3.45 (3 parties)
Canada (1997-2000)	=	1.75 (5 parties)
Czech Republic (1996-98)	=	1.39 (7 parties)
Germany (1994-98)	=	1.29 (5 parties)
Netherlands (1994-98)	=	2.12 (7 parties)
Spain (1993-96)	=	0.79 (4 parties)
Sweden (1994-98)	=	2.04 (7 parties)

(i.e., representing the interests) of a stable long-term following, parties seek the approval of the flexible electorate.

At the same time, we may expect the electoral system to play a role here. In pluralistic societies, brokerage or catch-all parties succeed by building a coalition of supporters drawn from diverse segments of society, segments with often diverging interests. All else being equal, we would expect members of a particular societal interest (say labor, or agriculture, or small business) to receive better representation from a party of their own than from a party representing them and several other interests. In other words, why would a party that claims to represent everyone be more attractive than a party that just represents you? One reason might be that it stands a better chance of forming the government, which is certainly true in plurality systems with their tendency to manufacture majorities. The brokerage party needs only seek the support of a coalition comprising some 40 to 44 per cent of the vote to secure a majority government in a plurality system. In a proportionate system, though, the brokerage party will not be assured of a place in government and certainly will not have a majority government, unless it can secure the support of 50 per cent of the electorate or more. Such a level of support for one party in a multi-party system is very rare. If, as in most proportionate systems, the norm is a coalition government, then a party that represents a narrower segment of society may be just as likely to participate in government, but more likely to provide good representation, than the brokerage party.

Consider the position of farmers, whose interests may clash with those of consumers, food processors, wholesalers and retailers, bankers, etc. Are they better represented by a party of their own or by throwing their support behind a party that also claims to represent bankers, consumers, retailers, etc.? In a plurality system, a focused agrarian party is likely to win few seats and those only in areas where the farm vote is concentrated. At best they will be a minor party within the opposition, with little voice in public policy. By supporting the brokerage party at least they may have a spokesman within the government who is committed to their cause and will argue for it when it is threatened by policies favoring other interests. In a proportionate system, the share of seats won by the agrarian party will correspond to the share of the vote the agrarian party can draw. This party may be one of the partners in a coalition government formed after the election, and in that event in all likelihood the agrarian party's share of cabinet will be (or include) the agriculture ministry and thus considerable control over agricultural policy. This kind of opportunity in proportionate systems for small, focused parties presents a challenge to (and perhaps limits) the success of parties trying to practice brokerage politics in such systems.

Parties practice electoral politics within the rules or constraints of a particular electoral system. In the background also are the political culture, the patterns of socialization, the tools of influence for shaping public opinion, parties' and leaders' performances, and many other variables. In short, at several points in this book we have touched upon the variables that feed into the modern electoral campaign. Any further detailed examination is beyond our scope here, but there is no shortage of good and accessible material on this topic. A few summarizing observations must suffice.

First, the modern campaign has become increasingly sophisticated and professional as it has become increasingly focused on the use of mass communications technology, in particular of public opinion polling, and of television. This has meant several things:

- A focus on leadership and images associated with the personality of the leader rather than a clear, detailed articulation of policy (McAllister, 1996; Mughan, 2000).
- Increasingly centralized campaigns run from party headquarters, essentially by professional consultants who are specialists in polling, advertising, marketing, media management, and image creation (Dalton and Wattenberg, 2000).
- A corresponding need for considerable sums of money to finance such professional, technology-intensive campaigns; hence, mass-mailing and telephone solicitation efforts.
- An increasingly superficial politics—superficial in the desire to avoid commitment to long-term positions and in the poverty of detailed information actually shared about likely policy outcomes.
- In the absence of anything positive to offer, a negative style of campaigning that seeks to demonstrate the weakness of opponents rather than one's own strengths.

This kind of politics must share at least some—if not the largest portion—of the blame for some of the features of our political process:

- Voters are cynical, distrustful of politicians, and of government generally.
- Journalists practice judgmental journalism and become participants in the political campaign rather than conduits by which political candidates speak to voters.
- Partisan attachments are weak and highly flexible.
- Politics becomes less a matter of public discourse about means and ends and more a matter of mass psychology and attempted manipulation of public opinion.

What is perhaps most troubling about this situation is the difficulty of imagining what might happen to change things for the better. To the extent that campaigning has focused on party leaders and has come to rely on television advertising and opinion sampling, this means a centralization of control over the campaign in the hands of the party elite and the paid professionals who provide modern communication and public relations expertise. Direct mail approaches, together with state subsidies to parties in many systems, enable parties to finance these campaigns. These enable them to build a base of mass support without the nuisance of an actively participating mass membership. Parties want to be free of the actual demands of loyal members in order to pursue the more flexible demands of the uncommitted larger public. In short, parties want support (financial and political) on the order of a mass party, but they seek to centralize control of agenda-formation and policy direction on the order of a cadre party.

It is difficult to escape Schumpeter's conclusion (expressed in the introductory quote to this chapter) that parties continue to perfect their techniques as electoral vehicles while stagnating or deteriorating as agents of representation. It is not surprising that citizens have sometimes looked for alternative agents of representation, such as interest groups, or to participate directly without mediation, as in some of the instruments of direct democracy.

10.3
Organized Interests

An alternative to the political party, and one with potentially great significance, is the interest group, or organized interest. Like parties, organized interests are voluntary organizations that seek to further the interests of their members, but unlike parties they seek to accomplish this not by winning election to political office but by influencing policy-makers (this influence, as we shall see, may be exerted in a number of ways). This small but critical difference between political party and organized interest leads to several others. For the most part, interest groups are not as institutionalized as political parties, and where they are institutionalized it is in different ways (see the discussion of neo-corporatism below). While many political parties gear up for elections and all but disappear in the between times, organized interests engage in a more regular calendar of activity and may mobilize most intensely at any point in the political cycle, since they are driven by policy considerations. Whereas citizens are unlikely to belong to more than one political party and at election time are forced to choose between parties, there is no limitation to their membership in, activity on behalf of, or support for organized interests. Multiple membership may mean that citizens simultaneously support groups that are competing or in conflict, as well as those that are more obviously complementary. The flip-side is that the claim of groups to represent a particular constituency in society may often be a very partial representation.

The validity of these observations may depend on the types of organized groups with which we are dealing. One distinction is between groups that organize around an issue (e.g., saving wetlands, opposing political imprisonment and torture, either side of the abortion issue, etc.) and those that are institutional or structural, that is, representing an interest determined by the structure

Providing testimony

or organization of society or the economy (e.g., labor federations, chambers of commerce, professional associations, etc.). But apart from subject matter, does this distinction stand for anything else? The idea that **ISSUE GROUPS** will be temporary and loose collections of a mobilized public while institutionalized groups are permanent structures organized and served by a bureaucracy just doesn't wash;

issue groups are often as permanent and as bureaucratized as any structural associations.

On the other hand, when it comes to the functions organized interests perform, there may be real differences between issue and **STRUCTURAL GROUPS**. By definition, as it were, all groups have the role of trying to influence policy-makers, seeking government action on a problem experienced by or of interest to members, or trying to block or modify policies perceived as contrary to members' interests. In addition—and this we suggest is more likely to be true of the structural group than the issue group—organized interests may provide support and information to members, offer training and educational programs, provide access to a variety of professional services, and in some cases regulate and discipline members. This last point indicates that, like other institutions, the functions performed by organized interests may not affect just these groups and their members; in particular, organized groups can be very useful for policy-makers and administrators. The resources that groups command and employ to influence public policy can in turn be tapped into by policy-makers looking for alternative sources of expertise, for reaction to policy proposals, or for means of mobilizing a particular segment of the population. In the case of self-regulating professional associations, actual governmental authority has been delegated from the state to recognized organizations.

While organized interests serve a variety of purposes, what still interests us most, politically speaking, is their activity to influence public policy; this is where we must assess their significance as vehicles of political representation. Here too the strategies of groups are various, and the activity of any particular group is less likely to be a choice between these strategies than a calculated mix of each of them. One set of strategies concerns offering or threatening to withhold from policy-makers certain scarce resources that groups have at their disposal. These resources may be the votes of the group's members, or financial contributions, or cooperation in the implementation or enforcement of particular policies. If policy-makers are not influenced directly by the incentives or disincentives that groups can put before them, they may be more influenced by the larger public, and a second set of strategies concerns spreading the group's concerns to society at large through information or advertising campaigns, demonstrations, or even acts of civil disobedience. Perhaps more effective than either of these avenues is to have an "inside track," that is, to be able, through a good working relationship with policy-makers, to exercise influence through consultation. This may be the pay-off, as it were, for being a source of information, advice, feedback, and support to policy-makers: the group's interests are taken into consideration as a key variable in policy formulation. This is why policy communities and policy networks have become so important within public policy literature today (see Chapter Eleven).

The activity of trying to influence politicians generally, and policy-makers more specifically, is often indicated by the term **LOBBYING**, which involves making a representation to political officials (elected or otherwise) on behalf of a group, interest, or company. Lobbying can be an important part of the job of the officers or paid employees of interest groups, and organized interests with sufficient resources will employ their own full-time lobbyists, who are called "in-house lobbyists." On the other hand, there are professional lobbyists not committed to any particular cause but who sell their expertise and their political connections as a professional service. It is this last aspect of the lobbyists' activity that worries outside observers and critics of the political and policy process: in using their connections to provide privileged access to the viewpoints of their paying clients, lobbyists are subverting the democratic process. Consequently, the greater the apparent influence of lobbyists, the greater the calls for regulation that requires the public registration of lobbyists and disclosure of their clients and of the issue for which they have been hired. In the United States, the first serious effort to regulate the activities of organized interests took the form of the *Regulation of Lobbying Act* of 1946. In 1995 the *Lobbying Disclosure Act (LDA) 5* was passed to tighten up provisions, and in 2007 Congress is considering further legislation to regulate the activities of lobbyists and their relationships to lawmakers.

Other countries have been slower to adopt a regulatory approach to lobbying. For example, in Canada legislation was passed in 1989 requiring both in-house and professional lobbyists to register and file returns disclosing their clients and their concerns. As of March 31, 2006, a total of 4,847 lobbyists or organizations whose senior officers are active in the policy process were registered. After a scandalous public inquiry reported on widespread fraud and kickbacks involving public relations firms and the Liberal Party in Quebec, this framework was tightened up in a variety of ways, including the appointment of a Commissioner of Lobbying to investigate possible breaches of the regulations. By contrast, however, Britain and the EU have favored self-regulation of the lobby industry (though Scotland has adopted a registry for lobbyists operating in that political setting).

Part of the reason for the American lead in regulating lobbyists is because lobbying plays a much larger role in American politics and has been prominent for a longer time. The difference between lobbying in the United States and Britain or Canada reflects an important dimension to this whole issue, namely, the environment within which organized interests are active. Since groups seek to influence policy, it is important to distinguish the number and nature of the **ACCESS POINTS** where influence can be exerted. A system of separated powers, such as in the United States with weak (undisciplined) parties and no responsible government requirements, has many more access points, and they are found at a lower "level" in the hierarchy of elected officials than is the case in a parliamentary system such as Canada's, particularly when this entails a one-party majority government. In the United States, for example, because party discipline is weak, the vote of any senator or congressman is to some degree "up for grabs," and there is no member of Congress who is not important enough to lobby. In Britain or Canada, by contrast, policy is made in the cabinet, and unless one hopes to engineer a rare caucus revolt, there is not much to be gained by lobbying backbench MPs. On the other hand, those who cannot get a hearing from cabinet ministers, officials in the Prime Minister's Office, or senior public servants will be forced to lobby MPs. In these majoritarian parliamentary regimes access points for lobbyists are fewer and higher up in the system, and in this sense they represent fairly closed systems for organized interests. In Britain and Canada, if organized interests cannot ultimately gain the ear of cabinet level decision-makers (by whatever path), their chance of influencing policy is slight. By contrast, the United States is a very open system in which there are many more targets of influence. However, since this applies for all groups, it will be easier to stop a policy from going ahead than to get a new policy implemented—all those access points are also potential **VETO POINTS**.

For a variety of reasons there is a growing concern in American politics directed towards interest group and lobbying activity and any party or legislator who is seen to be in the pocket of "special interests"—however these might be defined. In part this reflects the enormous sums of money that are involved in influencing policy. The Center for Responsive Politics places the total spent on lobbying activities in 2006 at more than $2.5 billion, and most of this money comes from corporate and business interests (see Figure 10.4 for a list of the biggest spenders). Public concerns about how the lobbying industry operates were also inflamed by

FIGURE 10.4   Lobbying in Washington—Top Spenders, 1998–2006

CLIENT	TOTAL
US Chamber of Commerce	$317,164,680
American Medical Association	$156,375,500
General Electric	$137,770,000
American Hospital Association	$129,114,026
Edison Electric Institute	$105,642,628
AARP (American Association of Retired Persons)	$105,332,064
Pharmaceutical Research and Manufacturers of America	$104,302,000
National Association of Realtors	$97,530,000
Business Roundtable	$97,060,000
Northrop Grumman	$95,682,374
Blue Cross/Blue Shield	$84,156,418
Freddie Mac	$81,884,048
Lockheed Martin	$80,206,965
Boeing Co.	$77,898,310
Verizon Communications	$75,836,522
Philip Morris	$75,500,000
General Motors	$71,158,483
Fannie Mae	$70,957,000
Ford Motor Co.	$67,670,808
US Telecom Association	$65,280,000

Lobbyists have to file semi-annual reports with the Secretary of the Senate and the Clerk of the House identifying their clients, the lobbyists working for each client, and the amount of income they receive. Companies have to report their overall lobbying expenditures and the names of any lobbyists employed as part of an in-house lobbying effort. Data are periodically updated to reflect late filings and amendments. Expenses indirectly aimed at influencing policy are not included.

Source: <http://www.opensecrets.org/lobbyists/index.asp>.

the recent scandal involving lobbyist Jack Abramoff and several of his colleagues. Abramoff and his colleagues worked on behalf of Indian casino interests and received approximately $85 million for their efforts. The lobbyists were accused of a wide variety of abuses, including overcharging their clients and illegally giving gifts to lawmakers in return for the latter's support. In January 2006 Abramoff pleaded guilty to three felony counts—conspiracy, fraud, and tax evasion. It is in this climate that the Senate and House are contemplating enacting tougher regulatory measures.

Finally, the Abramoff affair raises questions about the accountability of organized interests. How democratic are these organizations? How well do they represent their constituents? There is considerable difference among organized interests; some may indeed demonstrate a leadership clearly representative of and accountable to the membership, but others may simply solicit members' money and support without inviting or indeed allowing any input over decisions about the issues that supposedly unite them. In other words, interest groups are no worse or better than other organizations. On this dimension, it may well be that structural or professional groups are more democratic than issue groups, the bulk of whose members often remain anonymous individuals on the other side of a mailing list and who may never meet one another.

10.4
Pluralism versus
Neo-corporatism

The degree to which organized interests are able to influence policy is not only an empirical, but also a normative question. The discussion of groups in the previous section made reference only to settings where their participation in policy is informal and the product of competition with other groups for influence on the policy process. This is the reality described by (and usually advocated by) *pluralists*.

PLURALISM presents group activity in the political process as a competition of multiple elites. There are numerous groups of various and varying strength, whose leaders bargain, compete, and compromise in the effort to shape public policy. By and large, pluralists have no difficulty regarding the competition of organized groups as legitimate. The only normative question they consider important is one of fairness: are the terms on which such groups compete balanced? If so, then no one interest or set of interests will be able to dominate, and policy outputs generally, over time, will represent a compromise between the favored positions of different interests. In the minds of some, this is as close to the "will of the majority" or the "common good" as any other mechanism is likely to produce in today's complex societies. Pluralism takes a *laissez-faire* approach to the competition of groups for influence in the political system. It is not surprising, then, that pluralism has been championed most strongly in the United States, where its roots are traced back to the early Federalists, in particular to James Madison. Critics argue, of course, that the playing field of organized interests is *not* level, that interest group activities—whether lobbying or mobilizing public opinion—are expensive, and the advantage will also be with those who have resources (e.g., Lindblom, 1977).

In **NEO-CORPORATISM** (called "neo-" or "new" corporatism to distinguish it from the original variant that is associated with fascist techniques of labor control during the interwar period), the place of organized interests is not left to haphazard competition but is institutionalized. In other words, what distinguishes neo-corporatism is the regular, official participation of organized interests in the formation of public policy. (Obviously the degree of neo-corporatism can vary, depending on the degree to which interest group participation in policy formation is formalized.) Most of the countries ranked medium to high in neo-corporatism are found in Western Europe (especially Switzerland, Norway, Sweden, Austria, the Netherlands, and Belgium). Typically, neo-corporatism involves trilateral negotiation and consensus between representatives of the state, the business community, and organized labor. It is possible for other actors such as farmers or consumers to be involved also. In any case, the non-state actors are agents of **PEAK ASSOCIATIONS** that are granted a representational monopoly. This means that interest groups are organized hierarchically on the basis of functional interests (like labor, business, etc.), and **UMBRELLA ORGANIZATIONS** covering each functional group are accorded status by the state in the policy process. This usually means there is an extra-parliamentary institution or forum (a council, or chamber, etc.) where these interests meet, negotiate, and come to decisions. The aim of neo-corporatism is clearly to ensure that all major interests are involved in the formation of a social consensus on policy—which should also increase the likelihood that that policy will be acceptable to the public at large. Those interests that fall outside the functional or institutionally recognized categories will obviously not be included here.

In countries where neo-corporatism is weak or non-existent, the term has a bad reputation, being linked to fascism or to authoritative one-party states. This is called state neo-corporatism, and should be distinguished from the societal neo-corporatism of Western Europe, which is entirely compatible with political pluralism. Also, and not surprisingly, in countries where organized labor is weak and business interests are strong, like the United States, neo-corporatism is not seen to be an attractive option.[1]

What distinguishes pluralism and neo-corporatism is the nature of the interaction among competing non-state elites and the nature of the interaction between non-state and state actors. Both, though, are essentially about the role of elites in the policy process. Regardless of their concern with consensus, or a fair representation of social diversity, or balanced competition, neither is fundamentally democratic in the sense of inviting or requiring participation by non-elites.

1 Note that neo-corporatism is not a system dominated by the business corporation. Rather it attempts to treat the entire society as a "corporation," i.e., as a single, united body.

A uniquely American variant of these two general models of the interest representation process has been identified as arising when a private interest group (usually a business or business trade organization) forms an alliance with a bureaucratic agency and some committee or subcommittee of Congress. The goal is to promote policies and programs that serve the interests of all members of the alliance. A common example of an **IRON TRIANGLE** is the alliance that has formed among defense industry contractors, the Pentagon, and the armed services committees of Congress. In this case, the government agency, ostensibly responsible to regulate and otherwise oversee a policy sector or area, is seen to be "captured" by politicians and private interests alike.

If democracy is not possible in the longer term in our changing world, or if the degree of democracy possible will always be constrained by other factors, then pluralism or neo-corporatism (or something in between?) may be important alternatives. In either case the organized group provides an alternative mode of representation to that provided by the political party. Another, less traveled route, is to bypass representation and involve the citizenry directly in decision-making.

10.5
Direct Democracy

Among Western democracies, only the United States and the Netherlands have not held a national referendum, but few countries use this device regularly and only four (France, Denmark, Australia, and Switzerland) have held more than ten. Direct democracy is known but not trusted or, if you like, is common but infrequent. Direct democracy refers to instruments that involve direct citizen participation or input on questions of policy. The device of direct democracy most commonly employed is the **REFERENDUM**, but some important distinctions are often collapsed by applying this term to all instances of popular voting on questions rather than for candidates. Referendums are opportunities for citizens to propose legislation and subsequently vote to adopt it (or not).

First of all, it is useful to distinguish between those votes that are binding upon the state and those that are only consultative. Those that compel the government to act, or by a negative vote veto a government action, are properly *referendums*; those votes that the government may legally ignore (whether positive or negative) are more properly called **PLEBISCITES**. To a large degree, a plebiscite today probably carries as much force as a referendum in countries with a democratic tradition. Another difference is that while the decision to hold a plebiscite is always at the discretion of the government (since it is consultative), referendums are often mandatory, particularly in countries where constitutional change requires popular ratification (e.g., Australia, Switzerland).

Secondly, it is important to distinguish those cases where the question originates with the state—most referendums or plebiscites—from those where the question emerges from the public—an *initiative*. An initiative is a device allowing a segment of the public to force a question to be placed before the wider population. At the very least, it usually requires collecting a specified number or proportion of signatures within a limited time period (say, 150,000 signatures in 90 days, or 50,000 signatures in 45 days, etc.). In addition, there may be procedures to ensure that the question put before the public is constitutional, and in some jurisdictions (e.g., Switzerland) the government may also present the public with a counter-proposal. While **INITIATIVES** are popular in many American states (some two dozen states, mostly in the west, have mechanisms for referendums or initiatives; see Figure 10.5), Switzerland is the only country that employs them with any frequency on a national level, and there they are limited to proposals for revision of the constitution. Popular initiative has placed a matter on the national ballot three times in Italy and once in Austria.

Similar to the initiative is the **ABROGATIVE REFERENDUM** (or popular veto), where a petition gathered in much the same manner as an initiative forces an act of parliamentary legislation to face popular ratification (or defeat) in a referendum. This is usually possible only in a limited period of time after the passage of legislation and obviously will be resorted to by opponents of the law in question. In Denmark, such a vote may be requested by one-third of the members of the legislature except for laws concerning finance and international law. The very existence of this device might well cause governments to avoid passing legislation which it knows is unpopular—it is difficult to imagine a measure such as the Canadian GST (Goods and Services Tax, a federal tax on virtually all goods and services consumed in the country) being passed in a country with an abrogative referendum. In short, the abrogative referendum is like the initiative except that it seeks to negate a governmental action, while the initiative seeks to force governmental action (or inaction).

There are any number of reasons why people choose to bypass the representation and employ direct instruments, although we should note that in all cases this is supplementary or complementary to the processes of representative government, not replacing them. Referendums seem, most commonly, to meet one of two needs. The first is to give legitimacy to a decision, the scope or status of which is too large or too important to be decided on the people's behalf by representatives. Hence the common use of referendums to ratify constitutional changes, and in some countries constitutional change *must* be ratified in a referendum—in Australia and Switzerland, which are federal countries, the referendum must win a majority nationally *and* a majority in a majority of the states/cantons. Similarly, entry into the European Economic Community (now known as the EU) has required a successful referendum on the question in each country; in the expansion that saw the admission of Austria, Finland, and Sweden, the people of Norway rejected membership in a binding referendum.

A second basis for direct democracy is to locate responsibility for deciding questions of a politically sensitive or potentially divisive nature squarely with the public; in this way parties can avoid internal division over an issue or being forever identified with a decision that might be unacceptable to a significant segment of the population. Questions that deal with moral issues have often been decided directly; in Italy and Ireland, abortion and divorce have been addressed by referendum. Switzerland's politics present special conditions that provide a compelling basis for direct democracy, and thus it is no accident that this country leads the world in the variety and frequency of its use of direct instruments. Simply put, Switzerland has been governed for many years by a grand coalition of the four leading parties in parliament. Every election returns the same four parties to office. This means that there is no effective parliamentary opposition to the government. The referendum and initiative thus place the people themselves in the oppositional role of providing a check on the government through these direct instruments.

Of course it is also possible that the Swiss have just come to believe in the value of direct democracy, and principle is another reason for advocating non-representative decision-making. Depending on your ideological perspective, the conservative character of direct democracy (and Switzerland is famously conservative) can be seen as a virtue or a defect. A variety of other concerns are raised about the feasibility or desirability of direct democracy. Clearly, there are practical limits to the type of issue that can be addressed by referendum; only some matters are capable of being addressed by a question that permits only "yes" or "no" responses. In forcing categorical responses, the referendum also forces decisions and thereby may exclude the possibility of compromise or consensus. As in all situations where the majority has clear control

FIGURE 10.5 Direct Democracy in the United States, 2006

On Election Day, November 7, 2006, American voters cast their ballots on 204 statewide ballot propositions, up from 162 such ballot measures in 2004. Voters approved 137 (67 per cent) of these measures, and rejected 67.

Of the measures, 76 were initiatives involving new laws qualified for the ballot by petition, four were referendums (proposals to repeal existing laws; one was placed on the ballot by a commission, and the rest were legislative measures). In addition, three initiatives were voted on in the summer. The total of 79 initiatives was the third largest total of such actions that have been recorded since the initiative was first used in 1902.

Issues receiving approval in multiple states were eminent domain restrictions (nine), bans on same sex marriage (seven), and minimum wage increases (six).

Source: *Ballotwatch Election Results 2006, November, Number 5*, Initiative and Referendum Institute, <http://www.iandrinstitute.org/BW%202006-5%20(Election%20results-update).pdf>.

of the outcome, minorities may feel threatened by direct democracy. A different issue concerns the expertise or competence of the general public; if referendums appeal to common sense, how informed or educated is that common sense? This critique may rest on the possibly dubious assumption that the decisions of representatives are always well-informed. At any rate, it seems to us that the onus of educating citizens on the pros and cons of the issue at stake falls to the groups campaigning on either side of the issue. This last point directs us to perhaps a more serious set of issues, namely, the rules governing direct democracy campaigns and whether or not some interests are advantaged here. If there are no rules, then the referendum campaign becomes a free-for-all in which those with the most influence are advantaged, and in all likelihood this will be those with the most resources to spend on advertising, polling, and the other tools of mass communication. In many jurisdictions, referendum legislation requires the establishment and registration of "umbrella" organizations for both sides of the question, and these organizations in turn are subject to regulations concerning financing, expenditures, advertising, etc. The effectiveness of these rules in creating an open, fair, and informative campaign varies considerably.

In short, in addition to the principled belief that "the people should decide," there are many practical reasons why referendums or initiatives may be desirable and provide important enhancement to the processes of representative government. At the same time, there are clear limitations to the feasibility of such mass instruments, and they are always likely to be supplementary rather than the basis of modern democracy. The ability of such instruments to provide citizens with "good government" will ultimately depend on the citizens themselves and their preparation for sound decision-making. Here, no less than in voting for representatives, what will matter is the quality of information on which citizens depend, the activity of the mass media, the distribution of resources among competing actors, and the susceptibility or immunity of the public to manipulation.

10.6 Conclusion

Just as we all have become used to the fact that our governments are several, that the state exists at several levels, so too in modern society it is probably good that we have many vehicles of representation at our disposal. Although they may sometimes compete among themselves, these vehicles ultimately serve us in different ways, in different contexts. We are not in a position of having to choose between political parties, organized interests, or direct instruments of decision-making, but ideally we live in a polity where we have the opportunity to employ each as the context and issues seem to require. None of these will serve us perfectly; the point, perhaps, is to recognize how the ways in which they do serve us can bear improvement and seek to generate the will to make such improvements.

It should also be clear that in contemporary society political activity is organized activity. Whether we are talking about parties, interest groups, or the campaign organizations that support one side of a referendum question, organization is critical to the marshaling and employment of the resources that are necessary to communicate and persuade a mass public. This is the inevitable consequence of the size and complexity of the communities in which we live today. The challenge is to ensure that the representative organizations remain responsive and accountable to those they claim to represent.

References and Suggested Readings

Bingham Powell, G. 1982. *Contemporary Democracies: Participation, Stability, and Violence*. Cambridge, MA: Harvard University Press.

Butler, David and Austin Ranney. 1978. *Referendums*. Washington, DC: American Enterprise Institute.

Dalton, Russell J. 2002. *Citizen Politics in Western Democracies: Public Opinion and Political Parties in the United States, Great Britain, West Germany, and France*, 3rd ed. Chatham, NJ: Chatham House Publishers.

Dalton, Russell J., and Martin P. Wattenberg, eds. 2000. *Parties Without Partisans: Political Change in Advanced Industrial Democracies*. Oxford: Oxford University Press.

Downs, Anthony. 1957. *An Economic Theory of Democracy*. New York: Harper and Row.

Duverger, Maurice. 1954. *Political Parties*. London: Methuen.

Evans, Geoffrey, ed. 1999. *The End of Class Politics? Class Voting in Comparative Perspective*. Oxford: Oxford University Press.

Katz, Richard, and Peter Mair. 1995. "Changing Models of Party Organization and Party Democracy: The Emergence of the Cartel Party." *Party Politics* 1: 5-28.

Kircheimer, Otto. 1966. "The Transformation of West European Party Systems," in Joseph LaPalombara and Myron Weiner, eds., *Political Parties and Political Development*. Princeton, NJ: Princeton University Press. 177-200.

Lehmbruch, Gerhard, and Phillip Schmitter. 1982. *Patterns of Corporatist Policy Making*. Beverly Hills, CA: Sage Publications.

Lindblom, Charles. 1977. *Politics and Markets*. New York: Basic Books.

Mair, Peter, ed. 1990. *The West European Party System*. Oxford: Oxford University Press.

Mair, Peter. 1997. *Party System Change: Approaches and Interpretations*. Oxford: Oxford University Press.

McAllister, Ian. 1996. "Leaders," in Lawrence LeDuc, Richard G. Niemi, and Pippa Norris, eds., *Comparing Democracies: Elections and Voting in Global Perspective*. Thousand Oaks, CA: Sage. 280-98.

Merkl, Peter, ed. 1980. *Western European Party Systems: Trends and Prospects*. New York: Free Press.

Mughan, Anthony. 2000. *Media and the Presidentialization of Parliamentary Elections*. New York: Palgrave.

Pross, Paul. 1986. *Groups Politics and Public Policy*. Toronto: Oxford University Press.

Schumpeter, Joseph. 1942, 1976. *Capitalism, Socialism and Democracy*, 3rd edition. New York: Harper and Row.

Ware, Alan. 1996. *Political Parties and Party Systems*. Oxford: Oxford University Press.

Wattenberg, Martin P. 1991. *The Rise of Candidate-Centered Politics: Presidential Elections of the 1980s*. Cambridge, MA: Harvard University Press.

Wilson, Graham K. 1981. *Interest Groups in the United States*. Oxford: Clarendon Press.

Key Terms

abrogative referendum
access points
administrative function
agents of representation
cartel parties
cadre parties
catch-all parties
direct democracy
electoral vehicles
electronic politics
initiatives
interest groups
iron triangles
issue groups
lobbying
mass parties
mobilization function
neo-corporatism
organized interests
partisan instability
peak associations
plebiscite
pluralism
political parties
referendum
representative function
structural groups
umbrella organization
veto points

PART SIX | governing

ELEVEN | Public Policy, Legislation, and the Bureaucracy

"Not summer's bloom lies ahead of us,
but rather a polar night of icy darkness
and hardness, no matter which group may
triumph externally now."
— Max Weber, "Politics as a
Vocation," 1919 (Weber, 1958)

"I do not rule Russia; 10,000 clerks do."
— Czar Nicholas I

People look to the state to solve problems, or to take action on issues that are pressing; this is what we mean when we say that the political process delivers "demands" to the state. A considerable area of ideological debate concerns what kinds of demands should be made of the state or what kinds of tasks the state should be set to do. In a variety of ways, and for several purposes, it is useful to think of the state as an ensemble of resources organized for solving problems. In recent decades an increasing focus has been on this problem-solving activity of the state, its organization for doing so, its efficacy and efficiency, its coordination and rationales. This focus constitutes the study of public policy.

Leslie Pal has defined policy as "a course of action or inaction chosen by public authorities to address a given problem or set of problems" (1992: 2). Several aspects of this definition are worth highlighting, and some of them are more problematic than might first appear obvious. First, there is the idea that policy can involve action *or* the decision *not* to act; there may indeed be problems that decision-makers consider but are unable or unwilling to tackle. The obvious difficulty is in determining when inaction is the result of a deliberate decision, and for this reason most policy studies focus on the actions rather than the inactions of the state. As an example of policy as inaction, consider a government that, when pressured to

11.1
Public Policy Defined

"do something" about unemployment, announces that it will leave job creation to the private sector forces of the marketplace.

Secondly, where action *is* chosen, it is "a course" of action, implying a relatively coherent or coordinated set of different interventions. As noted, policy is in response to problems in the environment of the policy actors, and it will involve decisions at various levels. At its most basic, a policy decision is about whether or not to become involved, and the decision to address a particular problem will in all likelihood involve identification of some goal or purpose, however vaguely it might be articulated (e.g., reduce health care costs). Policy, then, is a commitment to certain ends, and at the next level will involve identification and selection of various means for achieving these purposes. To describe policy as a "course of action" presents the reality that the means governments employ to achieve their purposes are usually several, ideally coordinated into a coherent strategy of action. Much of what governments do in the modern world, whether it involves providing services, transferring resources, facilitating private actions, or delivering public goods, is captured by the term **PROGRAMS**. Student loans, legal aid, and employee retraining schemes are examples of government programs. Policy is broader and more fundamental: it is the decision to have programs (or not), the decision about what kind and mix of programs to have, the selection of the goals and objectives that programs should meet, and often the decision to change or abandon existing programs. Programs are the means or instruments by means of which governments implement policy.

What students of public policy are (and, we would argue, all citizens should be) interested in is how and by what means specific policies come to be chosen and implemented. It is in this context that there has come to be talk of a **POLICY PROCESS**, a set of stages linking the behavior of individuals within various institutional structures and producing as an outcome some identifiable public policies. Obviously, within any state such a process will depend on the institutional structure, the political culture, the experience of political actors, the resources available, and any number of other relevant factors.

The definition of public policy, the designation of a policy process, and indeed much of the study and literature on public policy rests on the notion that governmental outputs are deliberately

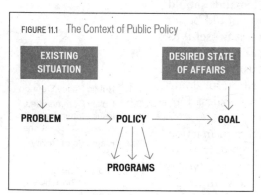

FIGURE 11.1 The Context of Public Policy

chosen, that someone is "in charge," that there is control over what emerges. Simply put, this is less certain than it appears, depending on a variety of circumstances, and it may be more accurate to say that the degree of control implied by the discussion of public policy is more or less so rather than absolutely so. To give just one example of why this assumption is problematic, consider the number of actors and institutions involved in deciding, designing, and delivering policy; the more diffuse the authority involved, the less control will rest anywhere identifiable within the whole. In this respect, policy may often be a byproduct of the activity of any number of actors rather than the product of a dedicated, coherent process.

While students of the policy process differ in the terms they use to describe the universe of "players," they are all in agreement that the cast of characters in the policy game involves a broader cross-section of actors than merely politicians and public employees. In fact, so broad have conceptualizations of the policy process become that distinguishing policy relevant actors from their environments is increasingly difficult. Three terms that have emerged to define the setting of policy-making and the most relevant set of actors are **POLICY COMMUNITY**, **ISSUE NETWORK**, and **ADVOCACY COALITIONS**. A policy community refers to all those actors, governmental and private, who "have a continuing stake in, and knowledge about, any given policy field or issue" (Doern and Phidd, 1992: 76-77). In other words, for any **POLICY SECTOR**— such as health care, education, defense, etc.—there will be a cluster of institutions, associations, and individuals who/which have an ongoing interest in whatever policy is made in this sector. This community is sometimes referred to as the **ATTENTIVE PUBLIC** for any policy area. The most important segment of the attentive public will usually be the organized interests concerned. These may be issue groups, professional associations, and corporate interests. Academics, private institution scholars, and journalists will be another key component. Officials of other governments (domestic or foreign), opposition politicians, and interested individuals with no institutional affiliation may round out the policy community. What they all have in common is their interest in the policy sector, of course, but also their willingness, if not eagerness, to influence policy outcomes. Importantly, though, many of these segments of the policy community will have opposing perspectives or be seeking very different and incompatible solutions to their problems. A key determinant of any policy will be which voices within the

11.2
Policy Communities, Issue Networks, and Advocacy Coalitions

attentive public succeed in gaining the attention and the sympathy of those who matter within the policy community.

Some critics of the policy process have emphasized the extent to which particular actors have come to dominate the entire policy process and successfully close out their competitors. Theodore Lowi (1969), for example, has argued that interest groups have largely taken over large parts of the federal policy process in the United States. He has coined the phrase "**INTEREST GROUP LIBERALISM**" to describe a system of interest group (primarily business corporations)-government relations in which the **PUBLIC AGENDA**, and hence **PUBLIC POLICY**, is largely determined by private interests. Other scholars point to the existence of "**IRON TRIANGLES**" (as discussed in Chapter 10) or "**SUBGOVERNMENTS**," which are the alliances based on common interests shared by powerful corporations or interest groups, an agency of the executive branch, and key congressional committees or sub-committees that have come to dominate the federal policy process. Each leg of the triangle supports the others, and while the arrangement may be mutually beneficial for each player, the sense of what is good for the public gets overlooked. An example of an iron triangle commonly referred to during the 1970s and 1980s was the alliance among the Pentagon, defense contractors, and the armed services committees of Congress. A contractor may contribute heavily to the re-election campaigns of key members of congressional committees, hire retiring Pentagon officials at high salaries, and in turn receive lucrative defense contracts. For this reason, defense expenditures and programs may reflect a variety of considerations apart from those of defense strategy.

As the downsizing in the armed forces following the collapse of the Soviet Union suggests, however, iron triangles are not necessarily permanent features of the policy-making landscape. More recent conceptualizations of the policy process have tended to stress the openness, multiplicity, and fluidity of policy influence. Two such conceptualizations of policy-making and policy change focus on the role of issue networks and advocacy coalitions. Hugh Heclo (1978: 103) has defined issue networks as: "... a shared knowledge group having to do with some aspect (or, as defined by the network, some problem) of public policy." Broader still is the "advocacy coalition framework." Advocacy coalitions consist of "... actors from a variety of public and private institutions at all levels of government who share a set of basic beliefs (policy goals plus causal and other perceptions) and who seek to manipulate the rules, budgets, and personnel of governmental institutions in order to achieve these goals over time" (Sabatier and Jenkins-Smith, 1993: 5). We have

Closing a deal

noted that many within the attentive public will bring opposing interests to the table, so to speak. Because these networks are determined only in part by the institutional structure of the state, they will vary from policy community to policy community depending also a great deal on the make-up of the particular attentive publics involved. Ultimately, mapping these networks or advocacy coalitions is useful in explaining, in part, how some segments within society succeed in exerting influence on the formation of public policy and, perhaps, why some are not so successful.

Consider a policy community such as health care policy. Interested actors in the policy community's attentive public will include doctors' associations, nurses' associations, and various unions representing health care workers. For example, among the key contributors to the demise of the Clinton health care reforms in the mid-1990s were the American Medical Association and the American Dental Association, both of which lobbied hard against the package. Other members of the health policy attentive public will include pharmaceutical companies, and there has been a bitter division and battle for control over public policy between brand–name and generic drug producers. One of the issues raised by this rivalry is the cost of medication, and this may bring into the policy community actors normally found elsewhere, such as anti-poverty groups or seniors' associations, etc. The size of the attentive public within a policy community will fluctuate in part in response to the level of activity within that sector. Some groups are always there; others will become involved only when the fate of a particular policy in which they have taken an interest is still being determined.

11.3
Elements of Policy-Making

It follows from what we have said above, that there is not *one* policy process but many. Indeed, some observers argue that policy is the product of essentially uncoordinated, unstructured activities. Nonetheless, we believe that whether the policy process is structured or unstructured, coherent or chaotic, there remain five stages that may be distinguished analytically in the emergence of policy.

11.3.1
Agenda Formation

We have employed the notion at several points of the state as a problem-solving mechanism and of policy as deliberate decisions to act (or not) in response to societal problems. A basic issue is the matter of *whose* problems catch the attention of policy-makers and receive their response. This stage of the policy process is often identified as the business of **AGENDA FORMATION**. An agenda is a list of things to be done; in public policy we want to know who controls that list, whose problems get on that list (and whose don't), how the order of items for action is determined and by whom, and even whose view of the problem is reflected by its formulation on the agenda and the responses considered. Various approaches have been taken to these questions, and we can only touch upon a couple of these briefly. One is to distinguish between the public agenda (the problem is highly visible and the public is interested) and the **FORMAL AGENDA** (policy makers have noticed the problem and included it for consideration) and to examine the relationship between the two. Clearly, policy requires that an issue reach the formal agenda, and it may or may not do so by first becoming an important item on the public agenda (see Cobb and Elder, 1983).

The idea of the policy community may be useful here, particularly if we consider that most issues that are candidates for policy consideration are probably identified and articulated first either within the attentive public by an interested group or within the subgovernment. Consider an issue initiated by an organized group within the attentive public of a policy community, say the demand of childcare advocates for the conversion of commercial daycare into non-profit care. The nature of the **POLICY NETWORK**(s) within this community (i.e., the links with the subgovernment) may determine whether this group is able to place its issue on the formal agenda. If the association of commercial childcare operators has sufficient influence, it may be able to block this issue from proceeding any further. At this point childcare advocates opposed to commercial care may resort to a public awareness campaign to generate broader support for their position and, by placing the issue on the public agenda, hope to obtain the attention of policy-makers. Some groups may succeed at influencing policy-makers only by influencing the broader public first and mobilizing public demand for policy action. Other groups may wish to influence policy-makers without arousing the attention of other interested parties in the public. Various strategies of moving issues from the public to the formal agenda, or onto the formal agenda by bypassing the public agenda, will be involved here.

Some issues will originate with state actors, who may be able to use their privileged access to the subgovernment to place their concerns on the formal agenda. Assuming that these issues receive a policy response, policy-makers must also decide whether the policies in question require public support for their successful resolution. If so, the challenge will be to move the issue from the formal to the public agenda and build support for it there. If not, the issue may be dealt with without ever achieving prominence on the public agenda.

As we saw in the last chapter, a central premise of pluralism as an approach to politics was the belief that all groups in society have access to some resources that they can use to influence the policy agenda. However, studies have shown that the issues that receive entrance to the formal agenda, and the prominence they receive on that agenda, will vary according to a variety of factors. Obviously, the ideology of those in government and of those who advise them is one important aspect (there is no point lobbying for increased spending on social programs from a government committed to downsizing and rolling back the welfare state), but there are others also. In most societies and political systems, the agenda of the rich and powerful receives careful attention, in part simply because of the strategic power within capitalist economies of those whose investment and employment decisions will impact on the popularity of governments judged for the state of the economy over which they preside. As E.E. Schattschneider (1960: 35) once observed, the flaw in the pluralist heaven, premised as it is on a relative parity of interest group forces and the possession of resources by all groups, is "... that the heavenly chorus sings with a strong upper class accent." Changing demographics (the structure of the population) can also be significant, as are the constraints placed on policy-makers by the health of the economy, the degree of government indebtedness, and the amount of time remaining before the next election.

Finally, we should note that succeeding in placing one's concern or issue on the formal agenda is no guarantee (1) that the government will take action or (2) that choosing to take action, it will implement the solutions preferred by those who originally sought the response. Entrance onto the broader public agenda or the formal agenda may be the precise moment where the group responsible for initiating and specifying an issue loses control of it.

11.3.2
Decision-making

The placing of an issue on the formal agenda entails a commitment eventually to decide its fate or, more indeterminately, the arrival of a problem on the official agenda means ultimately a policy decision concerning its resolution (and such a decision may well be to take no action and to leave the problem unsolved). A point of some debate among students of public policy concerns the model of **DECISION-MAKING** that most accurately depicts the policy-making reality. At one end is the **RATIONALIST** model, which proposes an orderly process of identifying, evaluating, and matching ends in a "rational" manner that satisfies criteria such as efficiency, efficacy, etc. In this model, the goal of policy-makers is to identify and implement the best possible solution to the problem at hand. In contrast is the **INCREMENTALIST** or **PLURALIST EXCHANGE** model, according to which policy is a byproduct of competition among interested parties, emerging as a result of conflict, bargaining, and trade-offs. What results here is a compromise between competing ideas of what is best or, indeed, between the opposing positions of self-interested actors; rather than the "best" policy, this model generates what is the most practical or feasible given the circumstances that constrain policy-makers.

The difference between these models is sometimes presented as the ideal versus the real: the rationalist model describing how policy should be made and the incrementalist model describing how it in fact *is* made. However, the supporters of the incrementalist model point not only to its empirical accuracy but argue that it is actually preferable to the rationalist model. For one thing, the rationalist model rests on various assumptions about information, knowledge, and resources that policy-makers are unlikely to find met in the real world. Above all, rationalist decision-making implies a degree of control that is incompatible with most policy environments—consider the complexity and potential fragmentation of not only the policy community but also the subgovernment. If rationalist decision-making were possible, it would certainly create the possibility of very radical change, unconstrained by anything but the desire to implement the "best" solution. The very constrained nature of actual policy-making, which makes the incrementalist model more empirically attractive, is also a reason why its adherents argue its superiority: we cannot predict the success or failure of our policies with any great accuracy, radical changes are unnecessarily disruptive and potentially destabilizing, and policy-making that proceeds in small ("incremental") steps from existing practices is more prudent and likely to produce long-term successes. Clearly the incrementalist model has a "conservative" element, while the rationalist model has the potential to be radical.

Interestingly, the incrementalist model has been most closely associated with Charles Lindblom (1980), and it is arguable that this model is particularly applicable to policy-making in the United States given the fragmentation and dispersion of power within the American system. In other institutional environments where policy-making is more concentrated, some degree of rationalist decision-making may be feasible. Certainly, radical and deliberate shifts in policy *do* occur in regimes and should not surprise us in majoritarian parliamentary systems. In Britain, Margaret Thatcher's so-called "revolution" in public policy in the 1980s and Tony Blair's more recent "New Labour" agenda for constitutional reform and political renewal illustrate quite significant policy shifts associated with determined prime ministers.

As noted, forced to choose between these two models of decision-making, most observers would probably agree that the incrementalist model depicts actual policy-making more realistically. Many, though, have looked for other models, some of which fall somewhere between the extremes presented by the rationalist and incrementalist variations. An alternative is provided by Herbert Simon's (1957) notion of "**SATISFICING**," which is in some ways a less ambitious or more realistic application of the rationalist decision-making process. Instead of arriving at *the best* solution, policy-makers aim for something *satisfactory*, an adjective which implies a compromise between what is ideal and what is practical.

Whatever the model that applies, policy requires decision-making, and this involves a variety of types of decisions. Most generally, there is a decision to consider a problem as a candidate for attempted solution and, secondly, a decision whether or not to commit the government to action in response to this issue. Where the decision is a "go" for action, at some level, in some way, certain objectives or *ends* will be specified or stated as the justification for or intent of the government's policy. The next stage, perhaps the most crucial, will be deciding what particular means will be used to achieve the policy goals.

11.3.3
Instrument Choice

In choosing to act or not, policy-makers consider specific actions and in doing so evaluate a variety of possible instruments for achieving their goals. Most simply, **INSTRUMENTS** are the various kinds of exercise of authority that governments have at their disposal—from regulations and laws, to penalties like imprisonment or fines, to taxation, to the provision of public goods like education or services like postal delivery, etc. In the policy process, instrument choice presupposes that ends have been identified and that it is a matter of choosing the means best suited to their achievement; in practice the distinction may not be so clear, and choosing between means may in fact be a way of choosing different ends. Any number of factors may determine the choice of instruments that is made. Ideology will dispose some political parties towards certain instruments and against others: socialists have traditionally been comfortable with public enterprises, while neo-conservatives would privatize as much of government as is feasible. Cost or difficulty of implementation may be key considerations. The rationalist view of decision-making would place the emphasis in instrument choice on efficiency, that is, on the instrument or combination of instruments that will most closely achieve the desired objectives while incurring the least cost. It is possible to distinguish between **TECHNICAL EFFICIENCY** and **POLITICAL EFFICIENCY**.

Technical efficiency is fairly straightforward: the ability of an instrument to achieve objectives without an undue or unreasonable expenditure of resources. If the goal of childcare policy is to increase the number of available spaces, then the technical efficiency of promoting commercial versus not-for-profit establishments will simply come down to which strategy creates more new spaces. If, in addition, the policy goal is to improve the quality of care provided, then the tendency of profit or non-profit care to deliver high staff-to-child ratios, or to employ staff with early childhood education training, etc., must also be measured. Political efficiency, by contrast, has to do with the benefits or costs of the policy instrument for the policy-makers: will the use of an instrument create goodwill among a particular constituency that will come in handy down the road, or will it cost the governing party key votes in the next election? In almost any policy environment, the political efficiency of instruments will be as much a part of the calculation as their technical efficiency, if not more so. It is also worth noting that instrument choice may be constrained by matters of law, tradition, or resources.

There are almost as many catalogues of the kinds of instruments available to policy-makers as there are writers on the topic, but typical categories include **EXHORTATION** (e.g., advertised guidelines), **TAXATION** (extracting resources to finance public policy), **EXPENDITURE** (e.g., government money for subway construction), **REGULATION** (e.g., an anti-noise bylaw), **SUBSIDY** (e.g., free prescriptions for seniors), **GRANT** (e.g., arts funding), **SELF-REGULATION** (e.g., delegation to professional associations), and **DIRECT PROVISION** (e.g., national parks). These instruments differ in the way they employ resources; some—like regulation—tend to be less expensive than others—like expenditure. They also vary in terms of the amount of coercion or force involved; exhortation is low in its coercive content, taxation and regulation are high. These are the ingredients in designing programs to fulfill the policy objectives identified.

It should also be clear that in most cases a policy does not involve choosing *an* instrument but a bundle or mix of various instruments; this is one reason why we define a policy as a *course* of action, involving moving on several fronts at once. A government wishing to reduce the public health costs associated with smoking could simultaneously employ a public education campaign (exhortation), restrictions on the sale of products to minors and on advertising (regulation), punitive taxes (taxation), and subsidies to farmers who shift production from tobacco to other crops (expenditure/ subsidy).

At some point, the decision-making and the design of policy must give way to the delivery and **IMPLEMENTATION** of these decisions. Here policy is turned over from its designers and architects to the administrators who execute policy in their exercise of bureaucratic power. The results, as Pressman and Wildavsky (1973) have shown, may not correspond strictly to what was intended. A variety of theories and approaches are employed to examine the actual

11.3.4
Implementation

experience of policy administration, and some common themes recur. One is that the distinction between policy-making and policy administration is somewhat artificial; policy administrators are not only frequently involved in the design and decision stages, but policy is also effectively made by administrators in the ways they choose to implement the program entrusted to them. Some observers use the term "**SLIPPAGE**" to describe the difference between the intentions of policy-makers and the actual results brought about by policy administrators. Others note that "perfect implementation" depends on a variety of conditions not likely to be found in the real world; this alerts us to the possibility that slippage need not be the result of deliberate decisions by public servants to sabotage policy-makers' intentions but may simply be an inevitable consequence of the complexity of policy in today's world. Again, knowledge by policy-makers of the ways in which policy is likely (or not) to be changed by administrators in the process of implementation may in turn influence instrument choice or other design considerations.

We noted above that policy will involve a variety of decisions, beginning with the most general and becoming increasingly specific and concrete. We should acknowledge in this regard that the policy/administration distinction is something of a fiction. The more general and fundamental the decision, the more we expect it to be made by elected officials—i.e., cabinet ministers—keeping in mind that these decisions will in all likelihood have benefited from consultation with and advice provided by senior administrators in the ministers' departments. At some level of decision-making, as we move from principles to the details, the bulk of discretion will pass to the public servants whose expertise and experience provides them with the resources to solve the practical problems of implementation. In other words, some decisions are clearly the business of policy-making, and some are clearly the nitty-gritty of implementation; to pretend there is a neat line that can be drawn between them is just that, a pretense.

11.3.5 Evaluation

Finally, it is suggested that the policy process is incomplete without a stage for follow-up, where the degree to which the policy has met expectations or goals can be formally assessed. This stage of **EVALUATION** is not without controversy. On the one hand are debates concerning the methods of evaluation: what are the criteria with which policies should be assessed? What quantitative or qualitative methods are most useful? Is evaluation best done by experts or by the general public? A second set of issues concerns the value of conducting formal evaluation of policy: does evaluation lead to revision? Do policy-makers pay attention to the results of evaluation? Generally, skepticism about evaluation is closely associated with adherence to the incrementalist view of policy as the product of pluralist exchange. On the other hand, for the rationalist paradigm of policy-making, evaluation is necessary to allow policy-makers to receive feedback and from there consider policy revision or redesign. If policy-making is a form of problem solving, then evaluation is intended to provide information about how well problems have in fact been solved by the adoption of policies, information that might well be useful for other similar situations. As in many areas, so too in policy there is also a powerful disincentive for evaluation: it may draw attention to failures, mistakes, or miscalculations, an attention that will not be appreciated by those to whom any lines of responsibility can be drawn.

The impression we do *not* want to leave is that policy is made according to a simple five-step process; on the contrary we have been discussing five elements or dimensions of public policy, dimensions that will be present in one fashion or another in most policy environments. At the same time, the actual "process" by which policy is made will vary by country, by policy sector, and even by specific policy cases—no two instances of policy are alike. This is one reason why many treatments of public policy are case studies.

In countries where the rule of law has become a firmly entrenched constitutional norm, all policy will ultimately rest on some authority that is grounded in law. In cases where the legislative authority for policy is already clear and complete, policy-makers will transmit instructions to departmental or agency officials to fulfill the policy's intentions; this is the move from decisions about instruments to their implementation (as described above). Institutionally, within a parliamentary context, this means that the cabinet, or ministers individually, deliver instructions to public servants to change operating procedures, rules, etc. In many cases, though, policy decisions require a change in the law that authorizes public officials to act or requires new legislative authority altogether. Institutionally this means that between decisions about policy and their implementation by the **BUREAUCRACY**, they must receive legislative authorization, which momentarily at least puts the fate of policy in the hands of the legislature.

The degree to which the legislature plays an active role in determining policy outcomes, or is largely reduced to giving ratification to decisions reached elsewhere, depends for the most part on the type of constitutional system. In the United States, not only the fate of policy, but the very shape and details of policy are often determined on the floor of the legislature or in its committees. In most parliamentary systems, particularly when the executive (single party *or* coalition) controls a majority in the legislature, policy decisions are made by cabinet and presented when necessary to the legislature for approval. It is not normally expected that the legislature will defeat government policy nor modify it in any significant way in the **LEGISLATIVE PROCESS**. Nonetheless, the principles of the rule of law, representation, and democracy combine to place significance on the activity of the legislature in formulating and legitimizing the laws that are a primary instrument of authority and power.

Our first observation must be that the legislative process depends very much upon the constitutional model involved; legislating is very different in a system with separated powers and weak parties than it is in a system with fused powers and strong parties. At the same time, there are many elements common to legislative processes regardless of constitutional model. A legislative process is a set of decisions concerning a proposal for a new law or a proposal to amend an existing law or laws. Such proposals are often known as "bills."

The constitutional model defines who can introduce legislation; in parliamentary systems legislation can be introduced by individual members of parliament ("private members' bills"), or by members of the government (i.e., the cabinet). Government bills occupy the greatest part of the parliamentary legislature's time and attention and are usually the only bills passed (in Britain and Canada, *only* government bills can involve the expenditure of public monies). In a separated powers system, there are no "government" members: all legislators may introduce bills, and every legislator will do so.

Once introduced, a bill will go through a variety of stages whose mix will differ from legislature to legislature; nonetheless, there are some common ingredients involved. These amount to various opportunities for careful examination of the contents of legislation, discussion and debate over its merits or weaknesses, change to its contents through **AMENDMENT**, and decision over its fate through votes. These opportunities are governed by strict procedural rules and take place in public so that formal lawmaking at least can be witnessed by the people. Cable television channels that telecast such proceedings make this true today as never before (although, ironically, this is an age in which the mass media generally pay less and less attention to the substance of legislative debate). As indicated, the specific order and arrangement of the stages of the legislative process differs from country to country. We will discuss some of the common stages that are found, and then briefly contrast the Canadian and American processes as examples of legislating within parliamentary and separated powers systems, respectively.

1. PRESENTATION   Before anything can happen, a legislative proposal must be put before the members of the legislature. In the British parliamentary tradition this involves a series of *readings*, which originally were quite literally that; in an age before general literacy, proposals would be read aloud for the benefit of all members. Obviously, today it is not necessary to read bills to the members, but the stages called "readings" persist. The first stage in a legislative process is typically *introduction*, in which a bill is presented, printed, and distributed to members of the legislature. Normally the bill will not proceed to the next stage of the process until some later point in the parliamentary calendar in order that members may have time to acquaint themselves with the bill's substance.

2. DEBATE   It is regarded as an essential part of rational decision-making that there be a chance for people to speak for or against a proposal. In this way the strengths and weaknesses of the proposal have the best chance of being uncovered, and presumably their illumination can lead to better decisions. Debate is significant not only so that legislators have a chance to discuss and argue the relative merits and demerits, but also so that the public has the opportunity to learn of the bill and hear from its supporters and critics.

3. SCRUTINY AND TESTIMONY   For the same set of reasons that debate is important, so too is the opportunity for **SCRUTINY** and **TESTIMONY**, scrutiny being the close examination of the bill in all its details and testimony being the opportunity for legislators to hear the views of others with an interest in the bill, such as those who would be affected by it, or those who might have to administer it, or experts in the subject area the bill concerns. This stage of the consideration of a bill is normally done in committee and thus not on the floor of the legislature. The committee is better situated than the whole legislature to perform detailed examination of the contents of the bill, and committee hearings provide an opportunity for non-parliamentarians to speak about a proposal.

4. AMENDMENT   One result of the debate and scrutiny that a proposal receives may well be ideas about improvement or second thoughts by the sponsors about what will achieve their purposes; in either case, or for other reasons, there is often a need to change or amend a proposal. Opportunity for amendment suggests that the legislature is really engaged in taking a proposal and making law from it. As we have implied, and will see further below, this is more true in some legislatures than others. At any rate, even though amendments may fail, the opportunity for opponents of a bill to propose amendments is important, because it allows the public to judge their representatives not only on the basis of what is done but on what was proposed and ignored or defeated.

5. DECISION   Ultimately, it is clear that there will have to be a time of decision and a determination of whether the bill lives or dies. In fact, there are usually several stages of decision in the legislative process, and this is something that enhances the legitimacy of the bill by demonstrating that its passage was not the result of a coincidence or accident of fate. Depending on the system and on the nature of bills, it may be desirable that some proposals be rejected sooner rather than later, and in this way the finite time of the legislature is not consumed by unnecessary labor. In some systems there is an "approval in principle," which indicates consent to the idea behind the bill but as yet no commitment to the specifics of the bill. In theory, this is simply asking "is this a good idea?" and should streamline the process by weeding out those ideas not receiving adequate support and allowing the legislature to concentrate on the "good" ideas. In practice, as we shall see, this is not always the case.

6. PROCEDURE   In addition to the above elements of a legislative process, there are some common procedural devices or issues involved. One is the use of committees for performing one or more of the stages in the legislative process, in particular that of scrutiny and testimony. Such committees are drawn from the legislature and meet separately; their composition usually reflects proportionally the balance of parties within the legislature as a whole. A second procedural point concerns bicameral legislatures and whether or not a bill proceeds through both chambers concurrently (as in the United States) or consecutively (as in Canada and most parliamentary systems). A further set of questions concerns whether each chamber has equal weight in the legislative process. In some systems, certain types of bills must originate in a specific chamber (i.e., in Canada, bills that involve government expenditure—money bills—must be introduced in the House of Commons, the "lower" chamber). In most bicameral systems the approval of both chambers is necessary for a bill's passage, but there are cases where one house (the Canadian Senate, for example) can only delay legislation from its counterpart in what is called a suspensive veto. Where both chambers approve a bill, they may nonetheless in the process of amending it have produced different versions that require reconciliation, something that usually involves the activity of a committee drawn from both chambers.

Once a bill has passed through all the stages of approval by the legislature, it may require a further consent by the formal executive—the head of state in a parliamentary system, the chief political executive in a system of separated powers. In the former case, such **EXECUTIVE ASSENT** is more or less automatic; in the United States, the president has the ability to **VETO** legislation, and the legislature in turn may overturn a presidential veto with a two-thirds majority. Usually with the granting of executive assent, the bill has become law; however, it may be necessary to indicate further when the law will come into effect (and there can be very good reasons for delaying this final step). In Britain or Canada, this last step is called *proclamation* and is made by the head of state on the advice of the government. There have been instances where the legislature has passed legislation, and it has received assent, but it has never been proclaimed into force as law. Once proclaimed, or brought into effect, a law is no longer the object of the legislature (unless there are subsequent proposals to amend the law) but passes to the executive for administration and enforcement or to the courts for interpretation or judicial review. In addition to these post-legislative stages, in some systems direct democracy may allow citizens to challenge the law through an initiative.

Because of strong party discipline and the majority position of the government, most bills introduced into the legislature in a parliamentary system become law. Further it is unusual for more than one bill on the same subject to be introduced at any one time, and bills in bicameral systems tend to go through the two houses in sequence, proceeding from the lower to the upper chamber. The picture is very different in the American system. It may be useful to consider the American legislative process as something of an obstacle course; a large number of bills (often several on the same topic) are introduced into Congress, but a small fraction of these succeed in surmounting all the obstacles. The legislative process is characterized by a series of veto points which filter out or select which bills will proceed to the next stage. Thus, while the two

FIGURE 11.2 The Legislative Process

CANADA		UNITED STATES	
LEGISLATIVE STAGE	**FUNCTION**	**LEGISLATIVE STAGE**	**FUNCTION**
First Reading	Introduction	Introduction	Introduction
Second Reading	Debate/Approval in Principle	Subcommittee	Scrutiny and Testimony
Committee Stage	Scrutiny and Testimony	Committee	Debate/Amendment/ Decision
Report Stage	Amendment/Decision	*(House Rules Committee)*★	
Third Reading	Decision	House/Senate	Debate/Amendment/ Decision
(Process repeated in other house of Parliament)		Conference Committee	Harmonization
Royal Assent	Executive Assent	Full House/Senate	Decision
Proclamation	Inform and Put Into Effect	Executive Signature/Veto	Executive Assent

★ In the House of Representatives only, the Rules Committee sets the parameters of debate and amendment concerning the bill when it is considered by the full House.

processes can look not dissimilar (see Figure 11.2) the reality of the processes is very different. It is worthwhile to stress again the essential points of this difference.

The most dominant feature of the parliamentary legislative process is its dominance by the executive (the cabinet) and its subjection to party discipline. This means that given a majority government, the legislature has a very limited role in determining the content of legislation, and there are few impediments to the passage of government bills. This is why parliamentary systems are identified with strong government; the only obstacle in the way of the fulfillment of the government's legislative agenda is time. In a majority situation, given party discipline, the parliamentary opposition will never succeed in defeating government legislation or in forcing its amendments to government bills. The most that the opposition can do is delay the passage of bills by using as much of the scarce time on the parliamentary calendar, maximizing the length of debate, proposing amendments that the government must take time to defeat, and employing any other procedural maneuvers. As party discipline becomes stronger in legislatures, minority opposition is more and more reduced to obstructionist tactics, and the debate and decision of the legislature is less and less a matter of constructive lawmaking. For a government in power, there are two ways around the delaying tactics of the opposition. One is to employ procedural weapons such as strict rules governing debate (time allocation) or even closure (which ends debate and brings immediate decision); a second is to make concessions such as accepting an amendment or two, or dropping a controversial clause, in order to secure the opposition's cooperation. By and large then, a majority government in a parliamentary system is assured of the passage of its legislative program and of the passage of legislation in essentially the same form that the cabinet minister responsible originally presented it to the legislature.

By contrast, the legislature in a system with separated powers and weak parties is much more chaotic and fluid. Here the legislature actually does legislate and is not simply legitimizing proposals approved by the executive. As we noted above, in this system each legislator may introduce legislation, and virtually each one will do so, some prodigiously. The passage of none of these proposals is assured, and defeat is a real possibility at each point of decision along the legislative path. In contrast to the parliamentary model, where the greatest portion of legislation introduced will also be passed, here most bills will be defeated at one or another point in the legislative process. Thus, while the two models differ considerably regarding the number of bills introduced, they are much more alike in terms of their legislative output. Instead of resting upon party discipline, bills in the United States often command a consensus that cuts across party lines. Bargaining and compromise is the name of the game, as is the collection and expenditures of favors or debts owed for past support. It is also worth noting the different roles played in each model by committees and by the head of state. In both cases, committees do the work of detailed scrutiny and of hearing testimony concerning bills. In the parliamentary model this occurs *after* the legislature has given approval in principle, meaning commitment to some sort of action on the bill has been made. In practice, and given that committees are very much creatures of party discipline also, bills are reported back to the legislature much as they were when sent to committee. In the American legislature, the committee, and sometimes first the subcommittee, serves as an important gatekeeper, censor, or editor: eliminating bills, consolidating bills of similar intent into one, or rewriting bills to suit the committee's own views on the subject. Committees play a most important role here, and the chairmanship of such committees (and subcommittees) is a position of considerable influence.

A similar distinction between systems concerns the head of state. In the parliamentary model, legislation that passes the legislature requires approval by the head of state, but this approval is a formality: it is always given. Failure to give such consent would create a constitutional crisis and is virtually unthinkable. In the United States, by contrast, bills passing the legislature come to the president for approval, but here nothing is automatic. The president may sign the bill into law, or refuse to sign and have the bill become law without executive approval, or veto the bill. In reply, the legislature may override the presidential veto by repassing the bill by a two-thirds majority in each chamber. Here we see the operation of the checks and balances associated with separated branches of government.

In the end, the significance of the legislative process will depend greatly on the system in which it operates. At one extreme a very active legislature subject to a minimum of executive control may have a relatively free hand to make policy through the legislative process; at the other extreme a legislature dominated by the executive will do little more than ratify the legislative proposals of that executive. In both cases, though, the legislature's most important function is to make the authorization of policy a public act, which proceeds by means of procedures that allow for scrutiny, criticism, and opposition. These procedures may seem often to be mere formalities, but they are at the heart of our legal-rational notions of legitimacy. To some degree also, the legislative process is as significant not for what it does but for what it prevents, namely, the arbitrary unopposable implementation of policy through secret means. However much our governments control the policy and legislative processes, they are forced to do their business in public, where a vigilant opposition and mass media (assuming these are vigilant) are able to hold the government to the judgment of public opinion.

11.5 The Bureaucracy

After the political executive and legislature have issued legislation, or on the basis of instructions issued directly by the cabinet, policy comes to the bureaucracy for implementation. The contact that most of us have with government is in respect to one of the many programs or services it provides, and the human dimension of that contact is with our interaction with public servants, the employees of the state. The terms "bureaucracy," "civil service," and "**PUBLIC SERVICE**" have become somewhat interchangeable: all represent that veritable army of full and part-time employees of the state who staff its various departments, agencies, enterprises, etc. Although the term "bureaucracy" is sometimes used by people pejoratively, implying needless layers of staffing and closely associated with the infamous "red tape," it needn't carry this connotation. In fact, the term originates from the French word for "office"—"le bureau." Its use to describe a form of organization stems from the work of Max Weber, who defined it as a structure of authority (an hierarchical, rule-governed system in which individuals perform specialized tasks) that is common to all modern organizations, from the corporation to the university to the trade union (see Figure 11.3).

As Weber predicted, the twentieth century was the century of public sector bureaucracy: Mény (1990: 277) reports that the Italian civil service grew from 50,000 at the end of the nineteenth century to almost 2 million by 1992 and Britain's from 20,000 in the early nineteenth century to 500,000 in the early 1990s. In the United States in the 1990s, federal civil servants numbered almost 3 million (about the same number as in the early 1970s) and the state and local officials another 13 million. In Canada, the federal bureaucracy numbered over 550,000 in 1993, with a total of 2.4 million government employees in the country at all levels of government. Obviously, the size of the bureaucracy reflects the growth in governmental activity in the twentieth century, particularly the development of the postwar welfare state. At the same time, the last two decades have been a time in which many governments have attempted to scale back the state, sometimes for ideological reasons, often because of the pressures of mounting government debt. Clearly one target for downsizing has been the public payroll, but to date in most countries while the public service has not grown in recent years, neither has it shrunk much.

One trend that is apparent across virtually all liberal democracies is the professionalization of public service that has accompanied the emergence of the modern state. Once upon a time, most government jobs were **PATRONAGE** appointments, which is to say that one of the great benefits of winning elections and forming governments was the ability to give employment to one's supporters, friends, family, etc. Known in the nineteenth-century United States as "the **SPOILS SYSTEM**," a change in governing party often meant a wholesale change in the public service from supporters and friends of one party to the supporters and friends of the newly triumphant party. As the American Civil War drew attention to the administrative weakness of the federal government, industrialization in the latter decades of the 1800s also led to demands

> FIGURE 11.3 Weber's Ideal Type of Bureaucracy
>
> - Fixed and official jurisdictional areas ordered by rules.
> - Official duties governed by rules and methodically carried out.
> - Hierarchically organized and integrated.
> - Management based on "files" or written documents.
> - Office-holders are full-time professionals, who are trained to separate public from private roles.
> - Rules provide for orderly, predictable treatment of clients.
>
> Source: Weber, 1958: Chapter 8.

for more efficient, predictable administration. By the turn of the century civil service reform became a top priority. Along with the growing role of government and the growing complexity and specialization of the tasks of government, there was an increasing need—increasingly recognized—for permanence, the development of expertise, and promotion on the basis of merit—in short, for a *professional* public service. All advanced democracies today employ a professional public service, a distinction that involves several components. First of all, entrance to the public service, and promotion within ranks is based on the **MERIT PRINCIPLE**, that is, demonstrated ability and accomplishment, not personal connections or political ties. The degree to which, and the means by which, this is enforced vary from country to country. Usually, entrance to the public service is gained on the basis of competitive public examinations. In some countries (e.g., France, Italy, and Germany) the examinations favor those with specialized knowledge, often those with particular legal training; in other countries (e.g., Britain, Canada) generalists are more commonly sought.

Establishing a non-partisan recruitment procedure based on merit did not happen overnight. Spurred on by the murder of President James Garfield by a dissatisfied office-seeker, the *Pendleton Civil Service Act* (1883) established the federal civil service in the United States. Today, the Office of Personnel Management (OPM) is in charge of recruitment for most federal agencies. Even today, however, there remain positions for which some measure of patronage and connections remain important for recruitment. Hugh Heclo (1977: 94) estimates that there are approximately 300 top policy-making positions and several thousand lower level positions in the federal government that are filled by presidential appointment, often combined with senatorial confirmation. Ranging from cabinet secretaries through bureau chiefs to ambassadors, those appointed to these positions do not expect a long tenure in office. Similarly, in parliamentary systems any number of senior administrative posts are still filled by appointment by the prime minister and cabinet, including deputy ministers, heads and members of agencies, and boards and commissions.

A second principle is that the public service should be **NON-PARTISAN** or politically neutral. This is based in part on the notion that a clear distinction can be made between decisions of policy (which are political and should be left to elected, publicly accountable officials), and implementation (which is non-political and should be carried out in a disinterested, efficient manner by career professionals). In practice this has often meant clear rules or even laws restricting public servants from engaging in partisan political activity, but interesting variations exist. In the United States, the *Hatch Act*, originally passed in 1939, aimed to ensure this by prohibiting active partisan politics by bureaucrats while they were on duty. In Canada, restrictions on the partisan activity of public servants were challenged successfully on the basis of the *Charter of Rights and Freedoms*, except for senior bureaucrats, whom the Court ruled should continue to be seen to have no partisan attachments. On the other hand, it is precisely at the senior levels of the bureaucracy where politicization of the bureaucracy matters most, and politicization may mean other things than partisan attachment. As a consequence, it is often the top-ranking public servants in parliamentary systems—that is, deputy ministers—who are replaced by incoming governments who suspect these deputies may be too closely aligned with the previous government or, more importantly, its policies.

If public servants adequately perform their duties in an impartial disinterested manner, then they should be secure in their employment, not subject to the whims of political superiors. A professional public servant is a career public servant, and just as in other walks of life, loyal, competent performance of duties should be rewarded with secure employment. On the other hand, in all sectors of society in recent years, employment has not been secure; for various reasons downsizing has been attractive in both private and public sectors. Public sector cuts often involve eliminating public sector jobs, eliminating bureaucracies, salary freezes, etc. One consequence has been increasing activity by public sector unions and an increased level of political activity from public servants who find themselves on the receiving end of the negative effects of policy decisions made by their political masters.

The model of a professional public service is, of course, just that: an ideal, which is realized in different settings and under different governments to a greater or lesser degree. Each country has its own traditions and expectations about public sector management and performance. In any country the model probably works less well when the state itself is the object of public policy, because public servants have a real abiding interest in the state, a set of interests that they cannot be expected to set aside easily, if indeed at all.

O ur concern in this chapter has been with the processes of governing, which ultimately can be subsumed under the heading of public policy. We have tried to outline the role of the various

**11.6
Conclusion**

institutions in the making and implementation of policy, and on many topics we have barely scratched the surface. The emphasis here has been on personnel and procedure, on the "who" and the "how." An altogether different approach, and perhaps the most popular today, focuses on the substance of public policy. In some cases this involves tracing the career of particular policies through the process from genesis to implementation and realization; in other cases it is a comparative look at policies n a particular sector across different jurisdictions. Some people become specialists in a particular area of public policy—social policy, economic policy, defense policy, etc. Our look at the substance of public policy in Chapter Thirteen focuses on the complex of policies associated with the emergence, expansion, and (lately) contraction of the welfare state in advanced industrial democracies. In doing so, we combine a concern with the substance of public policy with an introduction to some of the concepts and questions of *political economy*.

There remains one institution or "branch" of the state that we have not considered in our discussion of policy so far, the courts. This is in part reflective of an important distinction, namely, that the determination of public policy is indeed a political act—indeed, it is the essence of what democratic politics is about—but the courts are supposed to be apolitical, independent of and removed from the political fray. Nonetheless, as a result of the liberal notions of justice that underlie Western democratic practice, in particular the principle of *constitutionalism*, the courts are asked from time to time to rule on the constitutionality of the legislation that authorizes the activity of the state. In delivering such judgments, the courts become active in the policy process. It is to this dimension we now turn in Chapter Twelve.

References and Suggested Readings

Cobb, Roger W., and Charles D. Elder. 1983. *Participation in American Politics: The Dynamics of Agenda-Building*, 2nd ed. Baltimore, MD: Johns Hopkins University Press.

Doern, G. Bruce, and Richard W. Phidd. 1992. *Canadian Public Policy: Ideas, Structure, Process*, 2nd ed. Toronto: Nelson Canada.

Heclo, Hugh. 1977. *A Government of Strangers: Executive Politics in Washington.* Washington, DC: The Brookings Institution.

——. 1978. "Issue Networks and the Executive Establishment," in Anthony King, ed., *The New American Political System*. Washington, DC: The American Enterprise Institute. 87-124.

Heidenheimer, Arnold J., Hugh Heclo, and Carolyn Teich Adams. 1990. *Comparative Public Policy: The Politics of Social Choice in Europe and America*, 3rd ed. New York: St. Martin's Press.

Lindblom, Charles. 1980. *The Policy Making Process*. Englewood Cliffs, NJ: Prentice-Hall.

Lowi, Theodore. 1969. *The End of Liberalism*. New York: Norton.

Mény, Yves. 1990. *Government and Politics in Western Europe: Britain, France, Italy, West Germany*, trans. Janet Lloyd. New York: Oxford University Press.

Pal, Leslie A. 1992. *Public Policy Analysis: An Introduction*, 2nd ed. Toronto: Nelson Canada.

Pressman, Jeffrey L., and Aaron B. Wildavsky. 1973. *Implementation: How Great Expectations in Washington Are Dashed in Oakland or Why It's Amazing that Federal Programs Work at All*. Berkeley, CA: University of California Press.

Sabatier, Paul A., and Hank C. Jenkins-Smith. 1993. *Policy Change and Learning: An Advocacy Coalition Approach*. Boulder, CO: Westview Press.

Schattschneider, E.E. 1960. *The Semi-Sovereign People*. Glencoe, IL: Holt, Rinehart and Winston.

Simon, H.A. 1957. *Models of Man: Social and Rational*. New York: John Wiley and Sons.

Weber, Max. 1958. *From Max Weber: Essays in Sociology*, trans. and ed. Hans Gerth and C.W. Mills. New York: Oxford University Press.

Key Terms

advocacy coalitions
agenda formation
amendment
attentive public
bureaucracy
decision-making
direct provision
evaluation
executive assent
exhortation
expenditure
formal agenda
grant
implementation
incrementalism
instruments
"interest group liberalism"
"iron triangle"
issue networks
legislative process
merit principle
non-partisan
patronage
pluralist exchange
policy community
policy network
policy process
policy sector
political efficiency
programs
public agenda
public policy
public service
rationalism
regulation
satisficing
scrutiny
self-regulation
slippage
spoils system
subgovernment
subsidy
taxation
technical efficiency
testimony
veto

TWELVE | Justice, Law, and Politics

"Justice without force is powerless; force
without justice is tyrannical."
— Blaise Pascal, *Pensées*, 1660

"Nobody has a more sacred obligation to obey
the law than those who make the law."
— Sophocles, *Antigone*, 442 BC

JUSTICE is one of the oldest concepts in political discourse. Plato's
Republic, which is essentially concerned with the question "what
is justice?," is still taught as the first great text of the Western political tradition. In the modern age, justice has become a central
standard by which policies of governments are judged and very
often is something on which the legitimacy of states rests. Our political tradition is rich in terms of the understandings of justice that
have been presented, acted upon, or put forward for consideration.
Is there something that these diverse conceptions of justice share,
something that is basic to justice, however conceived?

There are two elements common to our conceptions of justice: a normative element and a specifically political dimension. The
normative dimension means that we intend our statements about
justice to be evaluative, to provide standards by which we measure
the appropriateness of actions and behaviors, policies and programs.
Where there is a consensus about the claims of justice, they are not
merely evaluative but regulative: measures will be taken to ensure
adherence to the standards provided by justice. Justice is also political. Loosely stated, justice is *a set of normative principles concerning both
the relationship between the state and its individuals and those relationships
between individuals in which the state or society at large has taken an interest.* Thus, much of the content of justice deals with the exercise of

12.1
Justice Defined

FIGURE 12.1 The Vendetta: Rough Justice?

We may note, recalling our anthropological discussion in Chapter Two, that in less complex societies where the state has not emerged, binding decisions are reached and enforced by means other than government. In such communities, justice will be concerned with these alternative means and the types of matters with which they deal.

An example to consider is the **VENDETTA**: the customary response in certain societies or cultures to an act such as murder is not apprehension and punishment of the murderer by the state but rather a restitution that involves taking the life of the murderer or of one of his family by a member of the victim's family. In societies where this is the accepted and expected response to murder, is the vendetta a concept of justice or not? According to our definition, it might not be seen as a matter of justice, since the authority of the state (or whatever process or institution that makes and enforces decisions) is not actively involved. It is not unusual, however, to view customs such as the vendetta as culturally and historically specific acts of justice. One way to accept this view and remain consistent to our definition, is to say that in the case of vendetta the community has delegated to injured individuals the authority to punish or sanction the offending party. Standing in the background behind the individual act of vengeance in this case is the approval and indeed the expectation of the community for this response. This makes the case vastly different from those individual actions to which society is indifferent. It may very well be that in pre-state cultures, much of the enforcement of societal or public norms is in a similar way delegated to individuals who occupy no "official" capacity. With the development of the state and its monopoly on coercive sanctions, the responsibility for maintaining community standards of justice is no longer delegated but executed directly by state officials.

authority or power by the state and with what individuals have a right to claim or expect from the state. In virtually any society, justice is also concerned with certain kinds of relations between individuals. Criminal and civil law each concern a separate class of actions between individuals. It is entirely possible that what is an issue of private morality in one society, such as adultery or personal insult, may be regarded as a public issue subject to authoritative sanctions in another society. In the latter case, this may indicate a moral consensus that the state has been entrusted with enforcing or which the state has taken upon itself to enforce. Whichever is the case, the involvement of the power or authority of the state makes the matter one of justice.

As the example of the vendetta shows (see Figure 12.1), it may be difficult to draw the line between public morality and justice. This is in part because notions of justice are often informed or governed by the moral and/or religious doctrines prevailing in the community. Students in Western societies may very well take for granted the notion that justice is distinct from religious or moral beliefs, but this distinction (like the distinction between religion and morality) is a product of the historical development that distinguishes and explains Western culture. In other cultures, it may be difficult, if not impossible, to distinguish clearly between religious and moral beliefs, public and private morality, issues that concern justice and those that do not. However, operating within the context of Western liberal society, we will use the term justice to refer to normative principles concerning the exercise of authority and power.

In saying this, we have answered the question in only the broadest and most general sense. More commonly, discussions of justice concern specific principles. Should rewards be distributed on the basis of merit or of need? Should discriminations be made on the basis of race, language, or creed? Is ignorance of the law an excuse from its sanctions? Should individuals accused of crime be required to prove their innocence, or should the accusers be required to prove the guilt of the accused? Answers to these questions assume or draw upon specific principles of justice, and each is susceptible to various formulations. In what follows, we will examine three concepts that have become central for modern liberal society: the **RULE OF LAW**, **RIGHTS**, and **EQUALITY**. This is the historical order in which these three principles were articulated and received recognition, something reflected in the degree of consensus that has been achieved about their suitability. While it is rare in our society to hear the rule of law disputed as a valid regulative principle, it is still possible to find rights skeptics, and there is yet considerable disagreement about the validity of equality as a principle of justice or, among those who believe in equality, much uncertainty about what it requires. In this second sense then, the question "what is justice?" is really asking "what are the correct principles of justice?"

Finally, even with consensus obtained about the principles of justice, there may yet be debate about whether or not policies or laws or actions conform to those principles. It is one thing to articulate the elements contained in the principle of the rule of law, another still to determine whether or not specific legal practices or legislative procedures meet these standards. People who agree that justice demands equality may disagree completely on whether affirmative action is consistent with or contrary to the principle of equality. At this third level, the question "what is justice?" concerns the application of the principles in concrete, everyday situations. This certainly complicates things, for the applications of justice principles will be as numerous as the concrete situations or problems that arise in a society and in which the state or the community has taken an interest. One of the differences underlying civil law versus codified law, for example, is different assumptions or propositions concerning the application of abstract principles to empirical cases.

Our normative discourse concerning justice, then, may not be about the principles of justice but their proper application or, even, about their applicability. In any given situation, how do we know which principle of justice to apply? Should individual rights be our prime consideration, even when the exercise of those rights leads to inequality, or should the claims of equality justify setting aside or overlooking individual rights? Should restitution or deterrence be the principle guiding criminal sanctions? Should welfare be treated as a matter of individual right or as a question of the proper distribution of societal goods? It is not our concern here to provide the answers to such questions, but to stress the complexity of what is involved in that familiar concept—justice.

To summarize, then, we can consider the question "what is justice?" to be meaningful in at least three distinct but related ways, moving from the most general and abstract to the more concrete and empirical. At any or all three levels, in any given society, there may be considerable consensus, or vigorous debate, or a combination of the two. Thus justice is:

1. *normative conceptions* concerning the political realm, most commonly addressing the proper exercise of authority, and the proper objects of authority;
2. *specific principles* indicating how authority should be exercised and with what it should or should not be concerned (i.e., rule of law, rights, fairness, equity, equality, etc.); and
3. *concrete applications* of specific principles to particular situations, problems, policies, laws, procedures, actions, behavior, etc.

12.2 The Rule of Law

The rule of law, as we know it today, emerges as a principle of justice in liberal society, although law itself has of course been with us for many more centuries than liberal society. The *Concise Oxford English Dictionary* describes law as "[the] body of enacted or customary rules recognized by a community as binding," or "one of these rules" (1982: 568); on this basis, we might observe that all political communities or societies possess law. Even if, like Hobbes, we reserve the term "law" for those rules that are made binding through the enforcement of coercive sanctions, we will have to admit that there has been law as long as there have been states (since the state is distinguished by the centralization of authority necessary to make and enforce rules or decisions upon the community). The rule of law, then, has nothing to do with the presence or absence of law and everything to do with the nature or use of law. The rule of law places certain requirements upon lawmakers and demands certain qualities of law itself.

Discussion of the rule of law in our philosophic tradition goes back to Aristotle, who asks the old question, "Which is preferable, the rule of the best man or the rule of the best law?" (Book III, Ch.16).[1] Aristotle's answer is both—government by the best men *and* the best laws—but the issue then breaks down into at least three questions: who are the best men to rule? What are the best laws with which to govern? In which cases should men rather than laws govern? Behind these questions stands Aristotle's observation that laws or rules are relatively inflexible; this is their advantage in that they provide us with a standard or procedure to follow in cases that are alike, and by acting in accordance with them we are able to be consistent. The inflexibility of rules is also their disadvantage when they do not permit us to take into account different circumstances or considerations. The law against theft, for example, does not distinguish between the single mother in a society with inadequate social assistance who steals to feed her children and the well-paid bank employee who steals to cover his gambling debts. Aristotle's concern is that justice sometimes requires a distinction and a flexibility that is not given by the law: "Among the matters which cannot be included in laws are all those which are generally decided by deliberation" (Book III, Ch. 16). (In our own society, flexibility is not achieved by allowing officials to set aside the law and decide according to the situation but rather in the allowance given to magistrates in sentencing to take into account particular circumstances and individual conditions.) Thus, Aristotle indicates the need for laws *and* for individuals able to make proper decisions when the law is inappropriate or too rigid:

> ... it is obvious that to rule by the letter of the law or out of a book is not the best method. On the other hand, rulers cannot do without a general principle to guide them; it provides something which, being without personal feelings, is better than that which by its nature does feel.... It seems clear then that there must be a lawgiver—the ruler himself, but also that laws must be

1 Any reference to Aristotle's *Politics* is to the T.A. Sinclair translation (1962).

laid down, which shall be binding in all cases, except those in which they fail to meet the situation. (Book III, Ch. 15)

We should stress that Aristotle would only set aside the rule of law for the rule of the *best* men, who are those with wisdom, good judgment, moderation, and a variety of other virtues. This rule of the best men is never something that can be done by one man: "it is preferable that law should rule than any single one of the citizens" (Book III, Ch.16). The best form of government and the one most consistent with justice is the "rule of the best men, true aristocracy," a government by "the majority who are all good" (Book III, Ch. 15).

By the time of the liberal revolution, experience and history had come to place the distinction between rule of men and rule of law in a different light. The feudal system had established rule by a class of nobility, and the rise of the nation state brought government by absolute, hereditary monarchy. It was obvious that rulers were determined by chance, by tradition, by war or intrigue, and by accidents of birth and death, but it was by no means necessarily on the basis of their enlightenment, their virtue, or their judgment. Lunatics, idiots, and children at various times inherited the office of sovereign, and even the most enlightened monarch remained just one individual whose word (reflecting his/her whims, passions, and prejudices) became law for a nation and its people. The "rule of men," which Aristotle had seen as the exercise of judgment by wise and virtuous men in situations not best dealt with by inflexible rules, had by Hobbes's day frequently come to mean a simply personal authority. Authority was viewed by medieval rulers as their own personal property, as something belonging to them (or to their family), sanctioned by tradition, or by God's blessing (the "divine right" of kings).

Through much of the Middle Ages and the Renaissance, a rudimentary framework of law prescribed penalties for particular harms and means for establishing innocence or guilt. By modern standards this framework was extremely narrow in scope, and its dictates could be—and frequently were—overridden on the authority of a nobleman or monarch. The fact that such rulers used the instrument of law did not hide the fact that their decisions often reflected purely personal criteria and dispositions. The rule of men was in this way personal, irregular, particular, and arbitrary. Because it was a product often of only personal criteria, it was also very unpredictable.

In contrast to such arbitrary rule or government, the ideal of a rule of law came to represent something impersonal, regular, universal, rule-governed, and (because based on public criteria) more predictable. In the background here stands the Enlightenment, with its call to set aside tradition and establish rational institutions and processes, and also the emerging market economy, with its need for rational, predictable, and uniform rules and policies. While the rule of men had not turned out in practice to match the ideal Aristotle had called for, contemporary notions of the rule of law match his expectations: "[i]n law you have the intellect without the passions" (Book III, Ch 16). "Laws ... prescribe the rules by which the rulers shall rule and shall restrain those that transgress the laws" (Book IV, Ch. 1).

The rule of law is the principle that obliges everyone, including those in power, to obey formal, public, neutral rules of behavior. In theory, the rule of law requires that citizens be governed by consistent, publicly known, impartial rules *and* that those who exercise authority do so by publicly known, impartial, and consistent rules. In practice, implementing the principle of the rule of law means establishing procedures by which authority is exercised. Consequently we can identify the "rule of law" as a principle of **PROCEDURAL JUSTICE**, one that has come to command general consensus within Western political culture. There are at least five elements that we can identify as requirements of the rule of law:

1. **LEGAL CULPABILITY**   One is punished only for breaking a law—that is, for what one has done or failed to do—and is subject to uniform, known sanctions. Simply displeasing or annoying those in authority should not be grounds for action.
2. **PUBLIC LAW**   The law must be publicly known, in that it would be unjust to find one responsible for breaking a rule of which one was ignorant. This places two obligations— one on the state, to publish all laws, and another on the citizen, to inform herself of the laws that apply to her. This lies behind the idea that "ignorance of the law is no excuse from its penalties."
3. **VALID LAW**   Hobbes argued that it is not enough for the law to be published; there must be a sign that indicates it is actually the Sovereign's will, a real enough concern in a day before mass media of communication. This sign could be the use of a royal seal or stamp or today the use of official state letterhead, but in the final analysis we know the law is

genuine and not counterfeit when it is made according to known and accepted procedures. This is one function performed by the legislative stages through which all legislative proposals must pass (see Chapter 11).

4. **UNIVERSALITY** It must be possible to enforce or apply the law to everyone, including those who exercise power and/or authority. Our lawmakers and law-enforcers must be no less subject to the law than ordinary citizens; indeed, as the opening quote from Sophocles suggests, they are especially bound by them.

5. **IMPARTIALITY** All individuals stand equal before the law, and on this basis only relevant criteria such as guilt or innocence are applied. The personal prejudices or interests of judges should never play a role in proceedings, nor should individuals be judged on the basis of their personal attributes. This is the idea that lies behind the image that "justice is blind." That is to say, if justice is impartial, it takes no notice of irrelevant differences such as race, religious creed, age, gender, etc., but rather it treats all individuals as identical abstract legal personalities. In this sense it might be said that the state does not need to know *who* we are, only *that* we are. Before the state, all stand equally as abstract legal entities or persons.

If these five elements seem extremely obvious, this is in part because they have become so imbedded in our legal and political practice and in part because we have lost acquaintance with states where the exercise of authority conforms to different criteria. This dominance of the rule of law as a regulative principle of procedural justice is part of what it means to say that we live in a society with legal-rational legitimacy.

There are also at least four institutional conditions that seem necessary accessories to the rule of law:

1. A *constitution*. As we note in Chapter Seven, a constitution is a body of fundamental laws concerning the exercise of authority and the relation between the state and the people. Some such body of rules is necessary if the requirement of universality is to be met.

2. An *independent judiciary*. It is essential, if impartiality is to be maintained and if rulers are also to be subject to the law, that judges be free from the influence or power wielded by officials of the state. Judges must be able to decide cases on the

The US Supreme Court

basis of the issues at hand, not out of concern for the wishes of third parties who take an interest. Neither should the state nor its officials be able to influence proceedings to which they are a party, either as accused or defendant.

3. A *public legislature*. For Aristotle, the virtue of law is that it is dispassionate, not distracted by personal passions and feeling. For this very reason, though, he thought it necessary that law emerge from a consensus of the wise and just individuals in a society. On the other hand, one of the weaknesses in Hobbes's theory is that it would leave the law to the judgment and reason (let alone arbitrary passions and whims) of only one individual, the absolute monarch. The practical solution of this problem in Hobbes's England was the transfer of legislative power from the monarch to a legislative assembly (Parliament). Law became the product of the collective effort of legislators, operating within a set of rules or procedures. The advantages of a group here are important. A group needs rules and procedures to operate effectively, and such rules can provide for greater fairness, openness,

and even flexibility than might otherwise be the case. The establishment of such rules and procedures also allows for debate, reflection, and reconsideration of proposed laws. In short, quality of law is enhanced—all else being equal—by the procedural requirements practically entailed by delegating legislative power to a group rather than an individual. In order to meet the requirements of validity and publicity, it is necessary that lawmaking itself occur in public. Only in this way can citizens have any certainty that good and correct procedures have in fact been followed.

4. *Civilian control of the police and military.* The state is commonly identified as that body which has a monopoly of coercion; that is, only the state may legally force behavior or actions, and only the state may use force to punish violations of the law. The body that employs force to uphold the law within the state is the police, and the body that employs force to defend the state against foreign aggression or encroachment is the military. It is noteworthy that two cases where the rule of law is violated are captured by the terms "police state" and "military dictatorship." What has happened in these situations is the collapse of the distinction between lawmakers and law-enforcers. There are many reasons why it is generally accepted in liberal cultures that those who enforce the law should not make the law but rather serve or be answerable to those who do make the law. Some of these reasons have to do with democracy or our notion of rights (i.e., the concern that there should be limits on the legitimate use of force), and some have to do with our notions of law as impartial, public, and predictable.

In summary, then, the rule of law involves the articulation and establishment of legal-rational principles governing the exercise of authority and power and the development of procedures and rules conforming to those principles. The rule of law is thus a set of regulative concepts, existing as standards by which we can measure the performance of the state and its officials, and providing a basis for increasing the likelihood that citizens will receive a fair, impartial, and consistent treatment whenever authority is exercised. At the same time, we might recall Aristotle's concern that authorities possess the flexibility to deal with individual cases as they merit and not be hampered in this fashion by rigid rules. We see this concern addressed in the discretion given to magistrates in sentencing, to executives to pardon or commute sentences, and in other ways in which officials are granted discretion in the exercise of their power. Most often though, this leeway or flexibility is itself today something prescribed and confined by laws.

T he rule of law is a *procedural* rather than a *substantive* principle. That is to say it deals with *how* the law is made rather than with *what* the law concerns. The rule of law is concerned with the recipe but not the meal that emerges, with the grading practices of a course rather than its curriculum, with the rules of a sport but not with the game itself. This is why we said that the rule of law only "provides a basis for increasing the likelihood" that citizens receive justice; it is, in and of itself, no guarantee. It is still quite possible to make bad laws using proper procedures. Establishing correct procedures may lessen the likelihood that we will be governed arbitrarily or unfairly, but it says nothing about what kind of laws should or should not be made, only that they be made according to a certain set of rules.[2] For the most part, the rule of law is silent concerning the *content* of the law. Does the law ban all abortions or permit all abortions? Does it forbid religious practice or allow the private ownership of semi-automatic weapons? Does it permit pollution of the environment or limit public nudity? None of these questions, or an infinite number of others, can be answered on the basis of the principle of the rule of law.

Rights, however, are very much about the content of the law. They are **ENTITLEMENTS** *that citizens can claim against the state and other individuals* and that therefore confine the content of the law within certain established limits. Rights are an attempt to remove or at least reduce the possibility that the government will make unjust laws or exercise power legally but unjustly. Rights state that there are certain subjects about which the government may not legislate, certain freedoms which the government may not abridge, or certain actions that the state may not take. If nothing else, the story of justice in the twentieth century and today narrates the triumph of rights. Almost every issue that receives attention is presented by at least one of the interested parties as a question of rights. We live in an age in which people speak seriously about rights for animals, an age in which governments have legislated such rights. The discourse on rights has become so ingrained that to challenge the notion of animal rights, let alone the sense of speaking about individual rights, is for many people unthinkable.[3]

As often happens when a term becomes extremely commonplace, "rights" is used by people to mean many different things, but

12.3 Rights

2 By analogy, elections are also procedures by which citizens determine who will gain positions of authority, and it has been argued that elections are a better procedure for determining the ruling class than other alternatives that have been used. Elections, however, do not guarantee good government.

3 Nonetheless, there are some very good arguments that invite us to rethink what we are doing in employing the language of rights, arguments challenging some of the assumptions and notions underlying that language. See especially Andrew, 1988; and MacIntyre, 1984.

some key elements are clear. Most generally, the centrality of rights to modern political discourse represents a triumph of certain kinds of individualism on one hand and the decline of community on the other. The concept of rights is a specifically modern notion, the liberal counterpart to **MEDIEVAL RIGHT**, and it is a central product of the liberal revolution that replaced the feudal community with modern civil society.

In feudal communities, individuals enjoyed rights and could claim redress for entitlements denied. But in such communities your right or my right would be legitimate because of its agreement with "*the Right*," the objective moral order upon which the community was agreed and which governed its relations. "Rights," then, in this context, were not properties of individuals but were enjoyed by individuals by virtue of their membership in a moral community, their collective participation in "what is right." An individual who was not of the community could not be said to have rights; for this reason, there was no difficulty with the idea of foreigners as slaves. At the same time, rights were particular. Because feudal communities were inegalitarian, highly differentiated structures, rights would depend on one's "station," i.e., as peasant, soldier, nobleman, or priest. Rights were thus derived from *right* and served as part of the glue binding together the social whole. Just as rights served to properly establish the place of the individual within the community, so too did duties. If my right here is what I am morally entitled to as peasant, king, etc., then my duty is what I am obliged to do as peasant, king, or artisan. Individuals' rights and duties were inseparable halves of the communal whole embodied in the notion of *Right*.

In liberal society, by contrast, individuals have rights (or claim redress for denied entitlements) that are understood to be inalienable individual properties. Rights are claims that you or I make and that some other party, such as the state or another individual, is required to respect. What justifies these claims is no longer a shared notion of "what is right," for none may exist, but rather legal definition. Rights are legal entities, embodied in law, whether statute or common, or in the device of an entrenched constitutional code.[4] Regardless of the different moral beliefs that citizens may have, their rights are recognized through the legal rules that govern the society. Because these rights are the property of individuals *per se*, and not as members of a community, they are universal rather than particular, at least in theory. The abstract individual created by the notion of an impartial rule of law is also the bearer of rights. This separation of rights from community is what informs declarations

4 Rights are commonly enumerated in a "code." When such a code is placed in the constitution it is said to be "entrenched," because amendment is thereby made more difficult. A rights code may also be embodied in ordinary statute, but then it is easily amended, repealed, or added to by subsequent legislative activity. An entrenched rights code (like those defined by the first 10 amendments to the American Constitution), however, is constitutionally enshrined and can therefore be used to overturn ordinary statutes or laws that contravene its provisions.

of the "Rights of Man," the United Nations' universal declaration of human rights. Finally, because rights have become legal (and political) rather than moral claims, they are no longer seen to be contingent upon or tied to the performance of duties.

The distinction between medieval Right and liberal rights is not simply philosophical but characterizes two different ways in which individuals are reconciled within the social whole. *Right* has to do with the shared moral vision of a community, while *rights* is a legal-political means of establishing relations between both state and individual and between individual and individual in a secular, often pluralistic society. We will not debate the relative merits of Right versus rights here, but we simply suggest that Right is only relevant to members of a community, and community in the strict sense (discussed in Chapter One) is not a feature of contemporary liberal societies. Elsewhere in this text we have referred to groups as aggregates of individuals united by interest. Most groups are intent on securing rights for their members; some justify this by claims about "what is right."[5]

Together the liberal argument that rights are inalienable properties of individuals that other parties (including the state) must respect and the enshrinement of individual rights in entrenched codes tend to obscure the political nature of rights. Consider the question, "to what rights are you entitled?" One answer is to talk about what you *should* receive, that is, what is yours by *right*, and this returns us to notions about "what is right"; in this way of talking, rights are moral entitlements. It is also possible to talk about what each of us is entitled to in fact, which requires reference to the law that defines or entrenches entitlements. This will vary from polity to polity, each with its own definition of legal entitlements. For example, the American Constitution appears to give citizens the right to bear arms; Canadians know they have no such entitlement, though many resent the government's requirement that their firearms be officially registered (note that neither position is the same as saying that citizens should bear arms, that it is not right for citizens to bear arms, etc.). The rights actually enjoyed are defined by law, and law is itself a political act, the result of humans legislating. As such, rights exist only so long as the legislation that defines them remains in force, and even entrenched **RIGHTS CODES** can be changed through subsequent political actions. In this way, you and I enjoy rights not as individuals possessing inalienable properties but in our capacity as members of a polity. The status of the rights we enjoy will ultimately depend upon the political decisions made within our state and thus upon the distribution of the power to make such decisions.

5 Most organized groups (see Chapter Ten) are groups in the sense used here: aggregates of individuals united by a common interest. Some groups are also communities, when the members share a set of fundamental values, norms, and practices; the interests pursued by such groups may in fact be collective or community interests.

We will subsequently consider rights to be legal entitlements enjoyed by individuals with respect to other parties, i.e., other individuals or the state. The objects of rights are of basically three kinds:

1. **FREEDOMS**   These are negative entitlements, which require the other party to refrain from interference with individual action or behavior. Examples: freedom of expression, freedom of association, etc.
2. **PROTECTIONS**   These too are negative entitlements, which require some party (usually the state) to protect us from harm that others might inflict, intentionally or otherwise. Examples: human rights codes, environmental protection legislation, labor laws.
3. **BENEFITS**   Positive entitlement to specific goods, services, or resources. Examples: minority language services, medical care, employment, social assistance payments, alimony.

Although the actual distribution of freedoms, protections, and benefits within societies is of interest to us, we are more concerned here with the means by which citizens acquire rights and the institutions that define and enforce rights. In fact, the way(s) in which these latter issues are addressed is more likely than anything to determine the claims, both negative and positive, which citizens may successfully make (see below, also).

**12.4
Equality**

In our look at ideology (Chapter Four), we noted the spread—however unevenly and incomplete—of the idea of equality within liberal democracy in the nineteenth century. This has involved the movement from a naïve belief among early liberals in an equality of opportunity that required no state assistance to the recognition that anything approaching a "level playing field" requires the activity of the government as a leveling agent. Eventually, liberalism moved from focusing on individuals as abstract units to considering them collectively and to considering the distribution of values or goods within the community or society as a whole. Most generally we talk about *wealth*, *power* (or authority), and *status* as the usual values with which distributional justice is concerned. Perhaps in our own society we could also include specific public goods such as education and health care. In short, attention within liberal democracies has increasingly turned to principles of **SOCIAL JUSTICE**, one of which is equality. Concern within liberal democracies for social

FIGURE 12.2 Blind Justice

One liberal who has contributed greatly to the debate concerning social justice is John Rawls (see *A Theory of Justice*, 1971). Like many of his predecessors, Rawls asks us to imagine social arrangements as the result of a contract that we enter into with other individuals. However, we determine the nature of this contract behind a "veil of ignorance" concerning where we will be situated in that society.

At present, most of us are well aware of our social position or standing, and could imagine social arrangements by which our position or standing would be improved. Rawls's question is "what set of arrangements would we construct if we didn't know where we might end up, or if it was entirely up to chance which position we came to occupy?" Rawls concludes that our self-interest would lead us to establish arrangements consistent with equality. In other words, if equality is the principle of justice governing our social arrangements, it does not matter which social position we occupy; we are left no better or worse off than others. The one exception to equality that this argument allows is that any inequality must tend to the benefit of those currently least-advantaged. In other words, any unequal employment of authority must work to improve the positions of those who are disadvantaged by the current working of the social arrangements. For Rawls, then, justice consists of initial conditions of equality and action to correct or compensate for any inequalities that arise.

justice has found concrete expression in a wide variety of measures, from progressive income tax, to selective grants for post-secondary education, to affirmative action hiring programs.

Behind the concern for social justice stands the observation that individuals are not by and large the authors of their own fate but determine their own outcomes only within the opportunities and with the advantages that the particular circumstances of their birth and life afford them. The distribution of these opportunities and advantages is in large part the outcome of social arrangements and forces ultimately resting on the exercise or abstention of authority. On this argument, then, it is not enough that authority be exercised within the rule of law and in respect of rights but that the state do all that it can to ensure a just distribution of social goods and benefits. What then constitutes a just distribution? About this there is considerable debate. It is not at all obvious to everyone that an equal distribution is the most just distribution, nor do those who endorse equality agree about what it means.

We should also observe that, in reality, patterns of distribution are largely the result of social customs and individual transactions in which competing interests and judgments of utility are worked out. Justice is not primarily or often a central consideration. Moreover, patterns of distribution are reinforced and maintained by institutions and social structures that individuals come to inhabit, having little say or control over these institutions or structures. Inequalities are passed on from generation to generation, and it is simply not true to say that at any moment in time, the people of a society have freely chosen the patterns of distribution that prevail. It is possible to argue, however, that only such consent could make these patterns of distribution "right" or "just." On this view, social justice requires democracy, whether in order to preserve or maintain a condition of equality, whether to work towards the transformation of an inegalitarian society into one more consistent with equality, or whether simply to ensure that the inegalitarian distributions in society are the product not of custom, coercion, or ignorance, but rather of universal, informed consent.

Of the three principles of justice that have emerged since the liberal revolution, equality is the most recent and the one to which allegiance is yet most tenuous. It may be premature still to judge whether or not equality is a practical or desirable option for humanity, or in what shape it is such.

12.5
Justice and Institutions

Justice does not simply consist in defining and reaching a consensus about principles; it also concerns the application and embodiment of principles within institutions and processes of the state. A good illustration of this is the question of the articulation and defense of rights within liberal democracies. Consideration of who should define and defend rights generally falls upon two alternatives: legislators in their capacity as lawmakers, or judges in their role of interpreting the law. Within the parliamentary tradition, this is a distinction between elected representatives and non-elected officials appointed by the political executive. To put the definition and protection of rights into the hands of one or the other of these is to choose between *parliamentary supremacy* and *judicial review*.

12.5.1
Parliamentary Supremacy

PARLIAMENTARY SUPREMACY (or **"PARLIAMENTARY SOVEREIGNTY"**) (discussed briefly in Chapter Seven) is best reflected by the British Constitution, for it lies at the heart of the model of parliamentary government created by the Whig revolution of 1688. As the second Earl of Pembroke is supposed to have said, "A parliament can do any thing but make a man a woman, and a woman a man." This means that the legislature is supreme, in two senses: (1) there is no other institution that can overturn its decisions, and (2) there is

FIGURE 12.3 Excerpt from the United Kingdom "Charter '88's" Original Charter

The following charter has been signed by 82,657 people (as of July 15, 2002):

We have had less freedom than we believed. That which we have enjoyed has been too dependent on the benevolence of our rulers.

Our freedoms have remained their possession, rationed out to us as subjects rather than being our own inalienable possession as citizens.

To make real the freedoms we once took for granted means for the first time to take them for ourselves.

The time has come to demand political, civil and human rights in the United Kingdom. We call, therefore, for a new constitutional settlement which will:

Enshrine, by means of a Bill of Rights, such civil liberties as the right to peaceful assembly, to freedom of association, to freedom from discrimination, to freedom from detention without trial, to trial by jury, to privacy and to freedom of expression.

Subject Executive powers and prerogatives, by whomsoever exercised, to the rule of law.

Establish freedom of information and open government.

Create a fair electoral system of proportional representation.

Reform the Upper House to establish a democratic, non-hereditary Second Chamber.

Place the Executive under the power of a democratically renewed Parliament and all agencies of the state under the rule of law.

Ensure the independence of a reformed judiciary.

Provide legal remedies for all abuses of power by the state and by officials of central and local government.

Guarantee an equitable distribution of power between the nations of the United Kingdom and between local, regional and central government.

Draw up a written constitution anchored in the ideal of universal citizenship, that incorporates these reforms.

Source: <http://www.charter88.org.uk/politics/charter88.html>.

no fundamental body of law or precepts to which the legislature's decisions must conform. Anything that is possible falls within the legislative competence of Parliament. The role of the judiciary in this context is to interpret the meaning of the law it receives from Parliament and apply it to relevant cases. If Parliament should disagree with the interpretation that the courts give to the law as it stands, it need only amend the law to match its intentions less ambiguously. Ultimately, then, the rights of citizens depend upon the political activity of legislators; their security is the degree to which lawmakers must consider the possibility of a withdrawal of support in the next election. Rights are secured through the political process, and those who dominate the political process will be more successful in ensuring that the law protects their rights. If the political process favors those with economic power, then they will be more secure in their rights than those whose rights require the limitation of economic power (i.e., labor, the unemployed, etc.). In a truly democratic system, whoever constitutes the majority should be most adept at securing protection in law for their rights, and in a majoritarian democracy, minorities may have no such protections. As the excerpt from the original charter of "Charter '88" (a group in Britain that advocated a constitutional bill of rights and other "modernizing" reforms to the legal and electoral system for that country) in Figure 12.3 suggests, not all agree that the political process offers adequate protection for individual rights.[6]

12.5.2
Judicial Review

JUDICIAL REVIEW involves two elements: (1) a written constitution, including an entrenched rights code (e.g., the American *Bill of Rights*, the Canadian *Charter of Rights and Freedoms*) and (2) a Supreme Court empowered to reject legislation that it judges to be contrary to the constitution. In this system the court acts as a check on the legislature, protecting the rights of citizens as defined within the constitutional document. The status of rights will thus depend not only on their original articulation in the written document but also on the patterns of interpretation taken by the court.

Where there is judicial review (and to the extent that judicial review is possible), parliamentary supremacy has been eliminated; the courts have the ability to second-guess policy-makers by subjecting their acts to scrutiny on the basis of the written constitution. Judicial review means a replacement of parliamentary supremacy with constitutional sovereignty. In theory the final word (in a democracy) remains with the people; if the constitution becomes a roadblock to popular or necessary legislation, it is always possible to amend the constitution. In practice, though, this is often difficult, and this is precisely why rights that are defined by the written constitution are said to be *entrenched*.

We have noted that with parliamentary sovereignty there is the danger of a legislative majority oppressing a minority. The entrenchment of rights and the provision of judicial review allows an independent institution (i.e., the courts) to protect minorities against the actions of a legislatively represented majority. It is not, though, a guarantee of such protection, nor does it ensure that those minorities who receive the protection afforded by judicial review are those who actually need it. Just as securing rights through the political process requires having the resources on which political success rests, so too, securing rights through the courts (i.e., successfully challenging the constitutionality of a law) requires legal resources, namely, legal expertise and the ability to fund a sustained legal challenge. We need to remember that in common law systems at least (the Anglo-American world), a constitutional challenge is not really won or lost until the high or supreme court has delivered its judgment (which binds all lower courts). The possibility that a successful challenge might involve three separate trials (court of first instance, court of appeal, supreme court) means that the protection of rights through a written constitutional document may favor those with resources—either wealthy individuals or corporations or organized groups which pool the more meager resources of their members.

One concern with judicial review is the unaccountability of the judges who finally rule on the constitutionality of legislation. Although in the United States many judges are elected (and therefore politically accountable), this is not true of the Supreme Court justices, who are appointed for life by the president. In Canada, similarly, the prime minister appoints justices who serve until age 75. To a certain degree this unaccountability is a necessary byproduct of the principle of **JUDICIAL INDEPENDENCE**, which requires that courts be free from political influence (particularly by the government of the day). In the United States, the president's nominees to the court face hearings and approval by the Senate, an example of the checks and balances in this system. The consequence, though, has been to politicize the appointment process. In 1987 Ronald Reagan's nomination of Judge Robert Bork was rejected by the Senate on the basis of what were perceived to be extremely conservative positions held by the candidate. Subsequently, Reagan's nomination of Douglas H. Ginsburg was withdrawn as a result of a different kind of controversy, this one following disclosures that he had used marijuana as a law professor at Harvard. In the early 1990s, one of George Bush Senior's nominations, Judge Clarence Thomas, was ratified by the Senate only after much controversy and hearings investigating claims of sexual harassment. It may seem appropriate that if justices are to be making political decisions, they should be chosen at least partly on political grounds, but then why not simply leave the definition and protection of rights with properly political bodies (the legislature and executive)? The length of tenure that judges may hold means that political opinions consistent with public values at the time of appointment may increasingly fall out of step; appointment for life to the court often saddles subsequent generations with the political values of a preceding era.

None of this would matter if the decisions the court makes were simply (as many citizens seem to regard them) findings of fact and, as legal questions, merely "objective," "scientific" matters for which nothing else is relevant but legal expertise and judicial experience. As countless observers—particularly legal scholars—have noted, in performing judicial review the courts are making political decisions. They may be hearing legal arguments and rendering legal decisions on the basis of legal precedents, but the content of what is being decided through these legal means is very often extremely political. The simple reason for this is that the phrases contained in any constitutional code of rights are often so vague as to require considerable interpretation by the courts before they can be applied to particular cases. Judges individually, and courts collectively, gain a reputation for the styles of interpretation that they favor. One common distinction is between **JUDICIAL ACTIVISM** and **JUDICIAL RESTRAINT**. Proponents of judicial activism support bold, constitutionally path-breaking decisions by judges, on the grounds that the courts enjoy the freedom from public pressures that is often necessary to take "tough" decisions. Supporters of judicial restraint, on the other hand, argue that the judicial branch ought not to be a policy-making body. Such matters are best left to elected and democratically accountable legislatures and executives. Instead, judges ought to be closely guided by past legal precedents in their decisions and aim to avoid controversial or politically "hot" issues, such as abortion rights or school prayer.

Certainly in some circumstances, a narrow (restrained) interpretation could lead to support for governmental actions (e.g., ruling that "freedom of peaceful assembly" does not entail the right of public servants to picket courthouses), while in other circumstances it could lead to judicial review of legislation (e.g., the "right to the enjoyment of property" is improperly infringed by environmental regulations). Similarly, a broad, "between the lines" interpretation could, depending on circumstances, enlarge the legislative competence of the state or limit it on behalf of individuals. At any rate, what either set of distinctions should make clear is that there is no neutral, objective middle ground that we should expect the courts to be in a position to articulate simply because they contain judges not elected politicians.

The language and concerns of justice occupy a large part of the political terrain in liberal democracies. Competing conceptions articulate notions of what is right when it comes to the exercise of power and authority, and various institutions make concrete the mechanisms and procedures for realizing and securing these notions. Common to the rule of law, rights, and equality as notions of justice is the depersonalization of authority that, we argued, accompanied the transformation from feudalism to liberal modernity in Western Europe. Particularly in the case of the rule of law and rights, but perhaps in the ways that equality is embodied in rights and other legal instruments, there is a tendency in liberal notions of justice to look for a procedure, a formula, or a process that by being followed or invoked will ensure that justice ensues. This reflects the concern with the bias, discrimination, or prejudice that can result when too much discretion is given to those in positions of authority. At the same time, we may do well at times to recall Aristotle's teaching that justice is never wholly a matter of applying the rules but is sometimes something that also calls for our wisdom and judgment applied to the particularities or circumstances before us.

Perhaps related to the search for an impersonal, impartial justice but also connected to the broad degree of public consensus (or lack of dispute) over their essential aptness, the rule of law and rights have largely departed from the political realm, almost entirely with the former and increasingly with rights as they are further judicialized. As we argued above, this should not obscure to us that political decisions continue to be made, particularly when it comes to rights, even though the forum for decision-making (i.e., the courts) is not generally seen to be political. It is also worth noting that there remain important subjects that, even though understood as rights questions, are *not* constitutionalized, but are left to legislatures to determine and define, and are thus still understood to be legitimate political questions. For example, however much the *Charter of Rights and Freedoms* has transformed justice and politics in Canada since 1982, we do well to remember that it only applies to the activities of the two constitutionally protected levels of government. The rights of Canadians with respect to each other, of employees with respect to employers, of consumers with respect to corporations—all these are rights (insofar as they are rights) defined in ordinary legislation. Entrenched rights codes such as the American Bill of Rights or the Canadian *Charter of Rights and Freedoms* put limits on the power of the state, but we do well to remember that there are significant sources of private power in our world also. One legitimate concern with entrenching rights is that it has the

Key Terms

benefits
entitlement
equality
freedoms
impartiality
judicial activism
judicial independence
judicial restraint
judicial review
justice
legal culpability
medieval Right
parliamentary sovereignty
parliamentary supremacy
procedural justice
protections
public law
rights
rights code
rule of law
social justice
universality
valid law
vendetta

potential to limit the state from making policies that shift the balance of private power in society—which, obviously, is also why some are very pleased to constitutionalize rights. At the beginning of the twenty-first century, the role of the state in society and the relationship of public power to private power have come very much into question as a result of shifting political and economic realities. It is this relationship that we explore in the next chapter.

References and Suggested Readings

Andrew, Edward. 1988. *Shylock's Rights*. Toronto: University of Toronto Press.
Aristotle. [350 BC] 1962. *The Politics*. Trans. T.A. Sinclair. New York: Penguin Putnam.
Benn, S.I. and R.S. Peters. 1959. *Social Principles and the Democratic State*. London: Unwin.
Dworkin, Ronald. 1977. *Taking Rights Seriously*. London: Duckworth.
Green, Phillip. 1981. *The Pursuit of Inequality*. New York: Pantheon.
MacIntyre, Alasdair. 1984. *After Virtue*, 2nd ed. Notre Dame, IN: Notre Dame Press.
Rawls, John. 1971. *A Theory of Justice*. Cambridge, MA: Harvard University Press.
Russell, Peter. 1987. *The Judiciary in Canada: The Third Branch of Government*. Toronto: McGraw-Hill Ryerson.
Woodward, Bob, and Scott Armstrong. 1979. *The Brethren: Inside the Supreme Court*. New York: Simon and Schuster.

THIRTEEN | The Rise (and Fall?) of the Welfare State

"All shall equal be.
The Earl, the Marquis, and the Dook,
The Groom, the Butler, and the Cook,
The Aristocrat who banks with Coutts,
The Aristocrat who cleans the boots."
—Gilbert, *The Gondoliers*

A variety of themes we have examined in earlier chapters converge here. In the last chapter we noted that questions of justice sometimes turn upon the notion of equality (or inequality), and one factor determining the **DISTRIBUTION** of material resources in society is the relative weight of the market economy and of the state, respectively, in allocation. In our treatment of ideology in Chapter Four, we observed the convergence of the mainstream ideologies around the notion of a **PRIVATE PROPERTY** market economy. Economic policy, or the particular relationship between the state and the market, remains a fundamental dimension on which ideologies distinguish themselves, but it has become abundantly clear in the modern age that citizens expect the state to take responsibility for the management of the economy and in a democratic polity will give expression to their preferences through the political process. Rival positions concerning the economic management function of the state remain crucial to contemporary politics.

To approach the subject from another angle, we have suggested that democracy can be viewed as a means to procure or enhance justice in modern societies. By the same token, democracy can also be a means by which citizens enhance their security—that is, their continued assurance of the means of life, if not of material well-being—by requiring particular social and economic policies

13.1
Introduction

in return for their political support. While disagreement may be widespread about the proper role of the state in the economy, all expect it to do something.

It is also clear that the ways in which the state performs its function (limited or extensive) of economic management are very much influenced by the presence or absence of democracy. It is only in the twentieth century as democracy has taken root that the modern state has acknowledged responsibility for management of the economy, only in the age of democracy that the extensive level of activity associated with the term "welfare state" has arisen. Charles Lindblom has noted that while **MARKET SOCIETY** has arisen in non-democratic regimes, liberal democracy has survived only in market societies; something which in itself invites exploration of the linkages between politics and economics (Lindblom, 1977: 5).

Finally, we should note that a distinct approach to the study of politics, namely **POLITICAL ECONOMY**, explores the links between politics and economics. A stronger sense of the term implies a conviction that *politics is essentially about economic questions*, or that *politics cannot be understood without reference to economic variables*, or even *that political issues not immediately perceived to be economic are often determined by economic considerations*. Within economics, the term "political economy" denotes a specific tradition in economic theory that held that the source of all value is human labor. Adam Smith, David Ricardo, James Mill, and Karl Marx were classical political economy theorists, but contemporary economics focuses instead on the nature of **MARKETS** and the values assigned to things by markets (see Howlett and Ramesh, 2003).

Not surprisingly, political scientists and economists often have very different views of the relationship between politics and economics. Some (but by no means all) political scientists argue that the economy should be subordinate to political purposes or goals. Supporters of tariff protection of industries reflect a belief in the primacy of politics over economics, that market forces should be subject to political decisions and interests. In some cases, the justification for protecting industries hinges on their supposed strategic importance for the country. Most (but not all) economists argue instead that economics should be autonomous from political direction, that market forces should be given free reign to determine outcomes. There are three fundamental questions at stake here in modern market societies:

1. What is the proper role of the state with respect to the market?

2. Who benefits most from a regulated or unregulated market? and

3. Is the "efficient use of resources" (as the economist defines "efficient") the most appropriate criteria for judging public policies?

The context of our discussion is the predominance of a private property market economy, which indicates two dimensions of economic life: how resources are allocated and who owns the principal means of economic production. In market societies resources are primarily allocated in one of two ways: by **PRIVATE TRANSACTIONS**, in which individuals purchase goods or services from others, or by the **AUTHORITATIVE TRANSFER** of these by the state. In other words, resources are largely allocated either by the market or by the authority of government. What we call "the market" is simply the aggregation of individual transactions or the purchase and sale by individuals of goods, services, and labor. In a completely "free" or unregulated market, resource allocation occurs through non-authoritative relations, that is, private exchanges governed only by the "natural" laws of the market (i.e., supply and demand). Almost all societies beyond a minimal level of development have had a market (i.e., private exchanges), but a market economy exists only where the bulk of production occurs for the purpose of market activity (as opposed, for example, to economies where production occurs for immediate consumption or for **AUTHORITATIVE ALLOCATION**).

Beyond the allocation of resources, political economy is concerned with the way in which goods are produced in a society. How, for example, are the materials of nature cultivated or transformed to produce what humans can use, consume, or possess? Agriculture is one or, more accurately, a set of such processes; industry is another. Both rely upon the progressive development of technology, that is, new ways of accomplishing the practical tasks of humanity. The kinds and levels of production are as important in characterizing an economy as the allocation of resources, and here too the policies and laws implemented by the state can be crucial. The National Policy, a program of tariffs on goods imported to Canada that was introduced by Canada's first prime minister, John A. Macdonald, was designed to provide protection from foreign competition for Canadian manufacturers. Critics of this policy argue that it was an uneconomical allocation of resources, artificially inflating the costs of goods to support a non-competitive

**13.2
Market Society**

manufacturing sector. Supporters point to the jobs created by such industry and argue that these justify the higher prices. At any rate, modern market economies are characterized by technologically intensive manufacturing processes and an increasingly large "service" sector, including activities developing and employing "information" technology.

A related but separate issue is the matter of ownership in an economy; is it something vested in individuals, somehow shared as in a cooperative, or held by citizens in common through the state? Ownership is twofold: it reflects the title to possession of the goods, services, and labor that are exchanged (or not) in the marketplace. In this respect almost everyone owns something. More crucial, though, is *who* owns the processes of production by which the objects of exchange are created. The usual distinction here is between private property, where the **MEANS OF PRODUCTION** are owned by (some of) the individuals in society, and **PUBLIC PROPERTY**, where ownership is held by the state on behalf of the people. (There remain other possibilities, such as cooperatives.)

In contemporary Western societies that rely on markets for allocation, the production of goods is generally associated with private property. Modern market economies are consumer societies in which most individuals procure the means of life through purchases. (And, as levels of disposable income have risen, the quantity and quality of goods consumed has become concerned with much more than the provision of mere necessities.) In addition, most individuals in a modern market economy are also employees who sell their labor to a corporation, a government institution, or other individuals. There is thus a modern market in labor as well as in goods, products, or raw materials. In this way the market is central to the life of virtually everyone in modern society.

The modern market economy servicing a consumer society and organizing the largest part of socially productive labor did not come about all at once. It is the result of several centuries of development; of the emergence and development of technology; of the organization and employment of labor by capital; and of many other processes and techniques that have had to be invented, learned, used, and perfected. Moreover, all this was not spontaneous but rather was the result of countless laws, policies, and programs implemented by governments, and it was often secured after much struggle among competing interests over the shape of these policies or laws.

The growth and dominance of the market required a revolutionary transformation of the economic system that had governed medieval society, an economic revolution that had profound political consequences. In brief, the new market economy required two developments: (1) that individuals be removed from the structures of medieval society in order to be "free" to be active in the market (consumers and/or buyers or sellers of labor); and (2) that political authority be exercised in ways consistent with, and supportive of, the needs of the market. These correspond with the two ideological themes stressed by supporters of the market ever since the seventeenth century: (1) that government *respect the autonomy of the market*; and (2) that government *provide market interests with the structure of law, services, and incentives* deemed optimal for market activity, that is, with *support*.

MARKET AUTONOMY is the demand that the primary (if not only) allocation of resources be done through the market (private voluntary transactions between individuals) and that the laws and **REGULATIONS** made by the state interfere as little as possible with the operation of market forces (such as the determination of price through "supply" and "demand"). The second theme, **MARKET SUPPORT**, is the demand that the state provide the conditions or infrastructure necessary for individuals to be able to produce, buy, and sell in the market, conditions such as a stable currency, enforcement of contracts, freedom from theft or extortion, etc. While the exchanges that characterize market economies are private voluntary transactions, these rely in turn on a public system of involuntary laws that enforce contracts, protect property from theft, and settle disputes over title. The state has a very important role in establishing the framework of law in which market activity can occur and in establishing thereby how this market activity will occur. It would certainly be possible to have a market without a supportive state but not the extensive economic activity we recognize as a market society. The question put properly is not *whether* the state should make policies that affect the market but rather *how* the state's policies should affect the market. This is where matters become controversial, not least because of differing evaluations of the market and of who benefits most from its operation.

Liberalism was the original ideology of market society, embracing new economic developments and arguing for the conditions of rational government and economic (social) liberty conducive to the progressive development of market forces. Liberalism was also flexible enough to demand of the state policies corresponding to the nature of the market and the needs of its dominant producers. In

**13.3
Liberalism and
Laissez-faire**

the works of some of the early liberals, it is possible to see demands for market support and for the creation of a rational government under the rule of law that would provide the framework of order and appropriate policies for an emerging market economy. As the liberal state replaced the absolutist monarchy of feudalism and as the market became more securely established, liberal thinkers turned their emphasis to policies stressing the need for market autonomy.

By the end of the eighteenth century these policies were most eloquently summed up in Adam Smith's landmark treatise *The Wealth of Nations*; the doctrine of economic liberalism represented by this work came to be known as **LAISSEZ-FAIRE**. As this term suggests, the emphasis was on leaving the market as unfettered by regulation and state interference as possible, and the reason for this was to maximize competition among producers, consumers, and laborers. This competition, it was argued, would result in the most efficient and, at the same time, productive use of resources, an economy by which the interests of all would best be served.

According to the model, markets are not only efficient but progressive: competition improves the standard of living of all by lowering prices that consumers pay for goods, by improving the quality of products, by encouraging research that produces beneficial goods and byproducts, by productively employing the resources of society, and by increasing the level of wages paid to workers. All this is the unintended consequence of rational self-interested activity in the marketplace; such results were said by Smith to be the product of "an **INVISIBLE HAND**." According to Smith the beneficial social effects of individual actions will not be produced if governments interfere in the market or artificially determine its outcomes. Therefore, this ideal model seeks what has been called a **MINIMAL STATE**, one that interferes least with the supposed "free" nature of markets. This model works because of the assumptions made about competition and the incentives or penalties imposed by competition between producers and buyers and sellers. Anything that inhibits this competition is deemed harmful and likely to reduce efficiency. The policy that would remove or resist restrictions on trade and thereby completely open markets to competition was called *laissez-faire*, a term which is often employed, and which we shall employ, to refer to the political economic doctrine of a maximum amount of market autonomy and, correspondingly, of a minimal state.

While the *laissez-faire* doctrine calls for a minimal state, it nonetheless relies upon this state to perform some important roles and to perform them in ways that benefit entrepreneurs or producers. For Adam Smith, these functions were as follows: the administration of justice, provision of defense, provision of public works (necessary to facilitate economic activity), and reform of a variety of traditional legal and institutional threats to natural liberty.

By the nineteenth century, *laissez-faire* had become the dominant economic theory of liberalism and was to become the effective economic policy of the British government, managing what was then the world's most advanced market economy. This last point is important: *laissez-faire* was adopted in Britain when this nation had the most efficient and developed industrial economy in the world and therefore could compete with any state on favorable terms. Where industry is less efficient, or must cope with higher production costs, the commitment to *laissez-faire* will be less strong and tariffs or other forms of protectionism more popular. *Laissez-faire* was originally the doctrine of successful industrial **CAPITALISM**; it is therefore not necessarily the optimal policy for less competitive industrial economies or for other segments of the economy, such as merchant capital, finance capital, farmers, or (especially) workers. Thus while *laissez-faire* became the economic theory of classical liberalism, we should not be surprised that other ideologies were critical of this policy and its effects.

M arket society has been criticized from any number of directions for its effects on collective and individual human existence. At the risk of caricature, we might summarize some of these critiques as follows:

13.4
Critiques of Market Society

- the conservative ("tory" variety) identifies market society with progress (or vice-versa) and progress as corrosive of what is eternal, valuable, and worthy of respect;
- the socialist by contrast believes in progress and that progress demands proceeding beyond market society in our social and political–economic development;
- the feminist identifies the market with the perpetuation of patriarchal structures and attitudes, arguing for a radically different organization of production and a correspondingly revised set of attitudes about production; and
- the environmentalist identifies market society with the destruction of the planetary biosphere.

Other objections are raised against market society, often with compelling force, although critics may not be clear about a possible alternative. For example, modern market societies are sometimes criticized for their narrow view of "the good life," with their stress on consumption and pleasure rather than on the development of abilities or on creative human activity. In this view, market society is not just a means of organizing economic life, it organizes our entire life, determining our priorities and values in a narrow fashion. These are important issues and difficult questions, some of which take us beyond the sphere of political economy.

Tories who supported the agrarian feudal economy of the medieval period tended to view the new market economy as disruptive of established relations and practices. This was not simply a matter of disrupting feudal relations but also of displacing the landed aristocracy with a new class of capitalists. In some nations the opposition between tory and liberal reflected a distinction between country and city. Market society was associated with urbanization, secularization, commercialism, materialism, and anything else that challenged traditional ways and institutions. Nonetheless, eventually many, if not most tories came to accept (and often prosper in) the market economy.

The rise of industrial capitalism in the nineteenth century and its operation within the bounds of the minimal state had a dramatic effect on the class of industrial workers that it brought into being. It is no accident that the nineteenth century saw the rise of the rival political economic doctrine of socialism. The most formidable socialist critic of the market system or capitalism was Karl Marx.

Marx regarded his work as consistent with the tradition of political economy that included such orthodox market advocates as Adam Smith, David Ricardo, and John Stuart Mill. More than any socialist before him, Marx's critique was based on a close acquaintance with the workings of capitalism and an appreciation of the productive powers it had developed. His critique consisted of roughly five main points.

1. Instead of the liberal approach of treating market society as simply an association of individuals entering into private economic transactions, Marx analyzed it in terms of **CLASSES**, where class is determined by the position occupied by individuals within the productive process. Marx argued that industrial capitalism creates a two-class society, divided between the proletariat (workers) and the **BOURGEOISIE** (owners). The latter own or control the means of production and hire labor power for a wage payment; the **PROLETARIAT** consists of those who sell their labor to the owners (who are owners of capital, hence *capitalists*). The capitalist and the wage laborer stand at opposite ends of the capitalist mode of production. In time, Marx believed, all other classes in society would disappear, and social life would be dominated by the **CLASS CONFLICT** between these two remaining classes.

2. Marx also argued that the relationship between the bourgeoisie and proletariat is exploitative; that is, the worker is paid less than full value for his/her labor by the capitalist, and this surplus extracted from the worker is the source of profits and capital. At various points, Marx also suggested that the capitalist treatment of labor in the effort to maximize profits is dehumanizing, alienating individuals from the full expression of their humanity in creative, self-directed activity.

3. As capitalism progressed, Marx believed, the proletariat would become conscious of itself as an oppressed class, that is, become aware of its collective exploitation by the

capitalist class. This would lead to a revolution—which Marx thought might even occur by democratic means (the election of a proletarian party)—which would replace class-divided society with a classless community that would organize the economic machinery created by capitalism on socialist principles.

4. Politically, Marx believed that the chief impediment to socialism was the existence of the state operating as an instrument of the bourgeoisie. That is to say, the government in capitalist societies not only creates the conditions necessary for capitalism to flourish but supports and promotes the ideas and ideology that support that economic system. This helps prevent workers from gaining revolutionary **CLASS CONSCIOUSNESS**; instead, they accept the legitimacy of the very system that exploits them.

5. From his analysis of capitalism, Marx concluded that capitalism would self-destruct because of its own internal contradictions; the product of this would be a socialist revolution led by a class–conscious proletariat. These contradictions within capitalism have to do largely with the business cycle (a somewhat cyclical pattern of growth and decline) which in Marx's lifetime had regularly brought market economies into periods of economic depression that seemed increasingly acute and protracted. Marx believed the revolution could very well occur in the most developed industrial societies, like Britain or Germany.

Marx's critique (which is much more complicated than what has been presented above), like the models of orthodox economists, was based not only on a variety of assumptions but also on the social and economic realities of the time when Marx was writing, in the middle of the nineteenth century. Industrial capitalism had created an urban working class of factory laborers dependent upon market activity for their existence. Nineteenth-century capitalism *was* exploitative: real wages were lower after the Industrial Revolution than before, urban laborers had much less security than peasants had enjoyed, and the working conditions imposed by industrial capitalism were generally abominable. At one point it was normal for every man, woman, and child over the age of four or five to work a 12- to 14-hour day for a subsistence wage (the minimum necessary to feed and clothe workers). The state could very well be seen as an instrument for the preservation and support of the interests of the economic elite, especially as long as the government continued to rest on a property franchise. The nineteenth century gave evidence of increasing class-consciousness on the part of laborers, who attempted to organize to protect their interests, forming Working Men's Associations, unions, working-class political parties, etc. Capitalism also regularly exhibited the swings of the business cycle, in which periods of expansion and prosperity were regularly followed by periods of contraction and poverty.

There is little of substance in Marx's critique of British industrial society to illuminate what alternative economic system he thought could take its place. Clearly the private ownership of the productive processes would be replaced with collective ownership by (or in the name of) the people (workers). Marx also seemed to believe that the state should play a transitional role in managing the change from a market economy to a socialist system and that when this transition was complete, the state would "wither away," having become redundant. The basic point for Marx was that socialism would inherit the tremendous productive forces created by the market system, but it would organize productive labor in a way so as to eliminate class division and the effects of class exploitation.

The economic systems established in the former Soviet Union and East European countries in the guise of Marxist-Leninism replaced private ownership of production with centralized state ownership, where the state was monopolized by the Communist Party (ostensibly on behalf of the proletariat). It is these **COMMAND ECONOMIES** that collapsed in the last decade of the twentieth century and that are being reformed in the direction of market systems at present. The failure of these Marxist-Leninist regimes owes little if anything to Marx and does nothing to invalidate his analysis of nineteenth-century capitalism or discredit his reflections on the nature of human creative activity. As with Adam Smith, the limits of Marx's insights into market society are found in his theory, not in the deeds of his disciples.

Whatever the strengths of Marx's analysis of the mature developed industrial capitalism, his prognosis regarding its future health and development was flawed in two principal respects. First, Marx overestimated the revolutionary potential of the working class, whose members generally seem more concerned with improving their own living conditions *within* the existing social framework than with embarking upon a grand social experiment. Second, Marx underestimated the ability of capitalism to reform itself without abandoning its basic commitment to private property or to the market as the principle means of allocating resources and values.

The reform of capitalism, which Marx could not have foreseen, entailed moving away from the ideal of *laissez-faire* and, from the middle of the nineteenth century, increasingly involved the state in economic affairs, something that accelerated dramatically after the Depression of the 1930s. While the existence in socialism of a rival economic ideology no doubt influenced liberal theory, the reform of *laissez-faire* was largely the result of pressures internal to developed market economies.

One consequence of economic liberalism and its emphasis on market autonomy is to suggest that politics must take second place to economics. Some conservatives, by contrast, will argue that economics should take second place to politics. Thus, even while embracing a private property market economy, it is possible for conservatives to argue that the state has a role in directing and shaping the activities of the market for the larger good of the community. One economist who argued this point, and who has largely been ignored in the English-speaking world, was Friedrich List.

List's fundamental point was to argue that the unorganized individual pursuit of self-interest will not necessarily lead to the greater good of all. Rather, it is requisite for the state to encourage, regulate, and erect tariffs if necessary—in short, the state should play an active role in shaping the economy. As List wrote in *The National System of Political Economy* (1837):

> The cosmopolitan theorists [e.g., Smith, Ricardo] do not question the importance of industrial expansion. They assume, however, that this can be achieved by adopting the policy of free trade and by leaving individuals to pursue their own private interests. They believe that in such circumstances a country will automatically secure the development of those branches of manufacture which are best suited to its own particular situation. They consider that government action to stimulate the establishment of industries does more harm than good ...
>
> The lessons of history justify our opposition to the assertion that states reach economic maturity most rapidly if left to their own devices ... the growth of industries is a process that may take hundreds of years to complete and one should not ascribe to sheer chance what a nation has achieved through its laws and institutions. In England Edward III created the manufacture of woolen cloth and Elizabeth founded the mercantile marine and foreign trade. In France Colbert was

responsible for all that a great power needs to develop its economy. Following these examples every responsible government should strive to remove those obstacles that hinder the progress of civilization and should stimulate the growth of those economic forces that a nation carries in its bosom.

As this passage indicates, List was an **ECONOMIC NATIONALIST**, in contrast to the internationalist (free trade) policies of economic liberalism (*laissez-faire*). James Fallows (1993) has pointed out that in Japan the economic ideology of List has been much more influential than the work of Adam Smith. Written in 1837, List's *The National System of Political Economy* is a non-socialist counterpoint to Adam Smith's *The Wealth of Nations*. In most Western nations, and certainly in the English-speaking democracies, conservatives have remained economic liberals, that is to say, have continued to support the minimal state of *laissez-faire*. By contrast liberalism, in reforming itself, abandoned *laissez-faire* economics. It did so in part because *laissez-faire* turned out in practice to work less well than in theory and in part because the coming of political democracy forced liberalism to accommodate the interests of those least well served by *laissez-faire*.

The political economic position of *laissez-faire* rests on an economic model, and as a model it necessarily abstracts from real life to postulate ideal conditions that may never actually be found and that may in many cases or respects be impossible to obtain. Few (if any) participants in the market ever have perfect information, nor is perfect competition realized, nor are completely rational decisions always made, nor do participants come to the market equal in resources or having benefited from equal opportunities. This divergence should not surprise us: the point of models is to make abstractions from real conditions for the purpose of comparison, manipulation, or other study. What became problematic for liberals was that the divergences between the real experience of *laissez-faire* and its ideal operation made it difficult to justify the minimal state, particularly from a liberal perspective. Most importantly, the divergence between how markets operate ideally and how they work in practice is a cost that is usually borne by the least advantaged members of market society. Not surprisingly, this is why advocates of *laissez-faire* economics in the nineteenth century were often very suspicious of democracy, fearing it would deliver political power to those least advantaged, if not actually disadvantaged, by market society, who might use the state to replace or regulate market mechanisms.

TABLE 13.1 Government Sector, 2004

	TOTAL GENERAL GOVERNMENT REVENUE % OF GDP	TOTAL GENERAL GOVERNMENT EXPENDITURE % OF GDP	GENERAL GOVERNMENT FINAL CONSUMPTION EXPENDITURE % OF GDP	SOCIAL SECURITY TRANSFERS % OF GDP
Australia★	36.6	36.2	17.9	9.2
Belgium	49.3	49.3	22.6	19.2
Canada★	41.7	41.1	19.7	10.4
Czech Republic	41.5	44.6	22.9	11.8
Denmark	58.9	56.3	26.7	16.9
France	49.8	53.4	23.9	17.7
Germany	43.2	46.8	18.4	19.2
Hungary	44.6	48.9	22.6	14.2
Ireland	35.6	34.2	16.0	9.2
Italy	45.3	48.5	19.2	17.3
Japan★★	30.3	38.2	17.7	10.9
Netherlands	46.2	48.6	25.0	12.3
New Zealand	41.2	37.0	17.5	10.5
Norway	57.9	46.4	22.0	15.0
Spain	38.4	38.6	17.4	11.7
Sweden	58.3	57.3	27.7	11.7
Switzerland	35.6	35.5	11.8	11.3
United Kingdom	40.8	43.9	21.2	13.4
United States★	31.9	36.5	15.6	12.0

Source: OECD.   ★ = 2003   ★★ = 2002

For example, the economic model accepts that inequality accompanies a capitalist market economy, an inequality rationalized on two grounds. One is the claim that a market economy will generate prosperity for all and that it is better to be unequal and secure than equal and poor. The second is that "the invisible hand" of the unregulated market will improve the position of the least advantaged by providing for full employment and by constantly increasing the cost of labor while decreasing the margins of profit. In this way inequality is diminished over time. Both these arguments, which rest on certain theoretical assumptions, are not confirmed by experience. Full employment and an increasing price for labor are conditions that *laissez-faire* meets only occasionally, if at all. Very often, there is considerable unemployment and periods of low or diminishing wages. The claim that policies increasing or sustaining market autonomy will benefit everyone needs always to be examined critically in light of the possibility that only some interests will benefit or will benefit disproportionately (*and* that these interests

TABLE 13.2 Taxation, 2002

	TOTAL TAX RECEIPTS % OF GDP	TAX STRUCTURES AS % OF TOTAL TAX RECEIPTS				
		PERSONAL INCOME TAX	CORPORATE INCOME TAX	SOCIAL SECURITY CONTRIBUTIONS	TAXES ON GOODS AND SERVICES	OTHER TAXES
Australia	31.5	38.5	16.8	0.0	30.3	14.4
Belgium	46.4	31.7	7.6	28.9	24.6	7.1
Canada	33.9	35.0	10.1	14.7	26.3	13.9
Czech Republic	39.3	12.8	11.8	38.3	29.7	7.3
Denmark	48.9	53.2	5.8	3.4	33.1	4.5
France	44.0	17.3	6.6	34.6	25.4	16.2
Germany	36.0	25.1	2.9	37.4	29.2	5.5
Hungary	38.3	20.3	6.2	30.0	37.4	6.1
Ireland	28.4	26.2	13.1	14.1	39.5	7.1
Italy	42.6	25.5	7.6	26.0	26.9	14.0
Japan	25.8	18.4	12.2	33.9	20.1	15.4
Netherlands	39.2	18.3	8.8	18.3	30.8	13.8
New Zealand	34.9	42.3	12.1	0.0	35.2	10.4
Norway	43.5	24.8	18.9	21.4	31.2	3.7
Spain	35.6	19.4	9.1	30.5	28.6	12.4
Sweden	50.2	30.4	4.8	30.1	26.4	8.3
Switzerland	30.3	34.4	8.8	23.8	22.6	10.4
United Kingdom	35.8	29.8	8.1	16.4	32.7	13.0
United States	26.4	37.7	6.7	24.7	17.6	13.2

Source: OECD.

will not be those most in need of benefit). These are considerations to which liberalism is particularly vulnerable, since it claims not to discriminate between individuals but to give all equal regard. If liberalism is indifferent to the treatment by the market of the poor and working classes, then it risks justifying Marx's claim that it is simply the ideology of the owning classes passing itself off as something more universal.

Market society is the best alternative for the poor and the lesser advantaged only under certain conditions, and it appears that unregulated markets cannot sustain these conditions indefinitely. The supposed benefits that accrue from the efficiency that a market system promotes are accompanied by the costs of weeding out inefficient or outmoded production: competition produces losers as well as winners. It may be true that "in the long run" everyone is better off and that conditions are improved for all. But who pays the short-term costs? How short is that short term? How temporary are the human costs of paying that short-term economic cost? Consider for example an economic downturn—what is today called a "recession" and what used to be experienced as a "depression." Someone must pay the costs of this economic contraction as firms declare bankruptcy and close their doors, as unemployment grows and welfare rolls swell. It may be, as the economist observes, that inefficient producers are being eliminated, that surviving producers and new firms will be forced to be more efficient, and that in this way eventually all will benefit—but who pays this cost of restructuring? Clearly, the owners of the firms that close or are put into receivership lose their investment, but that is generally all they lose. At the very least they will retreat from their investments before their own survival is threatened. The employee, however, is likely to have no surplus; the wage is all that stands between her and the food bank or the unemployment line. The greater economic cost may well be borne by the employer or owner, but the more immediate and human cost is often borne by the worker. Increasing efficiency (the epitome of market rationality) may well, if it involves improving technology or automation, mean less jobs, and there is no reason that this improved efficiency will somehow necessarily result in job creation that sustains those displaced by this rationalization.

The nineteenth century offered considerable real world experience of *laissez-faire*, and it was obvious that often the condition of the working classes was not progressively improving and that often it was the poor and working classes who were most devastated by the periodic economic contractions and restructurings of the market economy. During the latter half of this same century, **TRADE UNIONS**, working men's (and women's) associations, and socialist parties began to form and grow. In the late nineteenth century and first decades of the twentieth century, the franchise was extended to all (or almost all) adults. In 1917, the Bolshevik Revolution put a government in power in Russia dedicated to creating the communist utopia of a classless society, and it would not be clear for some time that this effort would eventually fail. It is not surprising, then, that reform liberalism abandoned *laissez-faire* economics in search of a political economic policy that might plausibly benefit all members of society. The pragmatic argument that moved them was something like the following.

The kind of market society that can be justified as the best available system for all will be one that can minimize the imposition of the costs of its restructurings, downturns, or modernizations on those who are least advantaged within that system under the best of conditions. This will involve action by the state and will therefore not be true to *laissez-faire* policy with maximal market autonomy and a minimal state. Something more than the minimal state may not be in the interest of producers, entrepreneurs, or investors (although it can be argued that it is), but that is a question of their economic interest, and politically these individuals are only one set of voices seeking policies conducive to their interest. From a political rather than economic standpoint and from the perspective of democracy, it is only reasonable to demand that if those least advantaged in a market society are to be expected to pay the short-term economic costs (which may entail long-term human costs) for the purported long-term benefits of improved efficiency, their consent to this payment should first be obtained. If they should have the opportunity for input on political economic questions, we would not be surprised if they support a state that manages changes in the market economy for the benefit of all, if not primarily for the least advantaged groups. In fact, in the twentieth century, in almost every advanced market economy, *laissez-faire* economic policy was exchanged for something called the **WELFARE STATE**.

The distance traveled in the transition from *laissez-faire* capitalism to the contemporary welfare state is enormous (although not all countries have taken the same path or taken it so far), but it has not challenged *primary* reliance on the market as the allocator of resources. Nor has it challenged the private ownership of productive property or the dependence of the majority of individuals on the wage they receive for their labor. A strong argument can be made, and has been made by supporters and critics of the welfare state alike, that the welfare state has done much to preserve and strengthen the market economy in this century. The reform of capitalism entailed by the welfare state has undermined the appeal of those who would replace private property capitalism with a collectivist alternative.

Most generally, the welfare state is an **ACTIVIST STATE,** a state intentionally involved in the economic life of the nation, a state that performs economic management functions with specific social and political goals in mind. Ringen (1987) emphasizes the redistributive character of the welfare state: its attempt to eliminate poverty and create equality through a system of taxes and transfers. (A transfer is a payment from government to individuals or corporations, and as such it has the potential to be strongly redistributive if the class of individuals receiving transfers is largely distinct from the class of individuals paying for them through taxes and

13.5
Ideological Compromise:
The Welfare State

other levies. In practice, though, many transfers are universal, eliminating much of their redistributive impact.) By contrast, Mishra (1990: 18) talks about the welfare state as a "three-pronged attack on want and dependency," involving (1) a government commitment to **FULL EMPLOYMENT**, (2) the delivery of **UNIVERSAL SOCIAL PROGRAMS**—like health care and education—and (3) the provision of a "**SAFETY NET**" of assistance for those in need, or what others have referred to as **INCOME MAINTENANCE** schemes.

Mishra sees the welfare state as the result of a postwar consensus between the interests of business, labor, and government; others—like Ringen—claim that such a consensus never existed, that business interests always resisted the elements of the welfare state. The truth may well be somewhere in between: a balance of political forces in the postwar period coupled with a prolonged period of sustained economic growth made the welfare state "affordable." Part of the difficulty here may be that the welfare state was not so much one conscious aim of policy but rather the result of countless different policy decisions, sometimes only loosely connected or coordinated with each other. Finally, we should note that the welfare state comes in many varieties, ranging from small welfare states in countries like the United States and Switzerland to large welfare states in countries like the Netherlands and Sweden. The "size" of welfare states is simply the share of a nation's economy that can be accounted for by government activity (spending or revenue). Regardless of size, though, in all advanced industrial democracies in the last century the role played by the state with respect to the private property market economy has changed significantly. The "welfare state" is a product of these various departures from *laissez-faire* capitalism.

One of the earliest liberal strategies was to reform the market economy through regulations. Some regulation is designed to correct the worst abuses of the capital-labor relationship or to compensate for other consequences of market activity; it does not replace that relationship or alter the fundamental nature of that activity. Many such regulations would be taken for granted today, such as the elimination of child labor, minimum wage laws, health and safety regulations, and limits on the length of the working day. More recent (and often controversial) regulations concern subjects such as pay equity or smoke-free work environments.

A second significant reform was recognition of the legitimacy of trade unions, formed by workers beginning in the nineteenth century in an effort to improve their conditions within *laissez-faire* capitalism. The union of workers aggregates the minimal power of individual laborers so that they can bargain collectively on more equitable terms with producers. The trade union does not threaten or change the capitalist wage-labor relationship but accepts it as legitimate and, in fact, strengthens it insofar as organization provides a route for grievance within the structure of market society. Unions (like market society) do not "just happen" but require legislation and enforcement by the state of rights of organization, the legitimization and regulation of the collective bargaining process, and a variety of other possible supports from the state. Labor law varies greatly from country to country, reflecting in part differences in the strength of the working classes and in part differences in political culture. In many countries, the rise of trade unions and their eventual legal recognition occurred only after considerable struggle, sometimes violent.

The welfare state is also a child of democracy. In the last quarter of the nineteenth century and the first quarter of the twentieth century, most societies with a developed market economy became representative democracies with full adult suffrage. A political party that advocates *laissez-faire* in a representative democracy with full adult suffrage must convince a sufficient portion of the working class that the minimal state is in their best interest. In the latter half of the nineteenth century or early in the twentieth, many members of the working and middle classes did not have fond experiences of the minimal state. Again, not surprisingly, extending the vote to members of the working and middle classes not only made it possible for there to be middle- or working-class political parties but made it more likely that all parties would begin to support regulation of the market economy.

At least in part, if not in large part, in response to pressures generated by representative democracy, the state has grown enormously in market societies in the twentieth century. There are many circumstances and factors involved here: the role of the state in fighting and then rebuilding after two world wars, the response of the state to the Depression of the 1930s, the demand for services and the need for infrastructure created by social and technological change—which seems to have proceeded at an accelerating pace—and, as important as any of these, the adoption of Keynesian fiscal policy.

Keynes was an economist whose major work—*General Theory of Employment, Interest, and Money*—was published in 1936. Following the war and in the attempt to avoid more periods of pronounced stagnation like the Depression of the 1930s, governments in market societies adopted the fiscal policy Keynes recommended. Keynes argued that the periodic slumps experienced by capitalism arise from a combination of overproduction and insufficient demand—there is not enough money to keep the exchange of goods and labor in equilibrium. What he proposed was the concept of **DEMAND MANAGEMENT**, whereby governments would stimulate consumer demand in slow times and put a brake on its acceleration in good times, thereby evening out the cycle. Governments could accomplish both strategies by unbalancing their books. Until this time, government practice had been that accounts should "balance"—government expenditures should always equal government revenues. Keynes proposed that when the economy slows down, the government should spend more money than it collects and accumulate a deficit on its books—go into debt. By putting more money into the economy than is taken out, the government would stimulate flagging demand and production. Conversely, when the economy is booming, the government should collect more money than it spends, thus removing demand from the system and slowing down economic expansion. The surplus accumulated in good years should erase the **DEFICITS** accumulated in lean times. Western industrial nations adopted Keynes's strategy of demand management, although they found that it was always easier to accumulate deficits than surpluses.

The growth of the state with regard to the economy takes many forms. Public works programs (building highways, bridges, hydro-electric dams, etc.) are one way; assuming ownership of companies, for strategic or political reasons, is another. The increase in the size of the state has its own impact by increasing the number of employees, the scale of government purchases in the economy, and so on. A fourth area of economic influence by the state is the transfers it makes to citizens—payments or entitlement to goods like health care or education for which the state must pay. These payments are central to the welfare state, and they are made for several reasons. One is to provide relief to those disadvantaged, often through no fault of their own, because of the inability of the market economy to sustain them. Another is to alleviate some of the inequality that the market system tends to reproduce. These payments are also a means by which governments can inject money into the economy when it stagnates. They take many forms and have come about over many decades. Like other phenomena, the welfare state is not uniform, but varies from one advanced industrial country to another under the influence of history, political culture, and economic circumstance. The net effect of all of these developments was the creation of a significant **PUBLIC SECTOR**, which characterizes all modern welfare states.

Now whether or not Mishra is accurate in describing the welfare state as a compromise between the interests of business, labor, and the state, it is clear that in many ways the welfare state represented a compromise or even consensus among ideologies. Reform liberals, social democrats, and even market tories (or European Christian Democrats) could find reason to agree on the continued justification of the welfare state, even though they might disagree on its optimal size or on the particular programs it should encompass. Standing outside this consensus would be those economic liberals (i.e., conservatives) who advocate a return to the minimal state and, on the other side, those radical socialists (i.e., communists) who still believe that a private property market economy can and should be overthrown. Such socialists are difficult to find today in any great number, but economic liberalism has made a significant comeback, so much so that many see the contemporary welfare state as a state in crisis. As is so often the case in ideology, what has shifted is the context, and the result is that a question that seemed more or less settled a few decades ago—the proper role of the state in the economy—has once again become central to ideological debate.

For a considerable period after World War II, the Keynesian welfare state seemed to work; market economies were able to achieve relatively stable economic growth in conditions of relatively full employment and low **INFLATION**. At the same time government services and transfers continued to be introduced and enriched. After 1970, for a variety of reasons, the Keynesian strategy seemed to fail. While previously there had been a trade-off between unemployment and inflation, so that governments could tackle at least one of these conditions at the expense of the other, after 1970 both inflation and unemployment persisted (what was called "stagflation"). This and other factors led to a prolonged period of government deficits, which led to ever-larger levels of accumulated indebtedness. Keynesian economics fell out of favor with economists and was replaced by **MONETARISM**: instead of practicing demand management, governments should attempt to influence the rate of economic growth through their control of the money supply (hence "supply-side economics") and the use of instruments such as interest rate policy. This meant the end of the commitment to full employment in favor of policies focusing on fighting inflation; in most advanced economies, unemployment remains high, often in double-digit rates.

**13.6
Rolling Back
the Welfare State**

Industrial Production

While governments were no longer committed to Keynesian policies, they continued to spend more than they were raising in revenue. There is considerable debate about why deficits have seemed so irreversible. Certainly, the fact that demand for government spending on social welfare programs is highest at times when the economy is stagnant or in recession will make it difficult for governments to always balance their budgets. The end of a full employment economy means there are more people eligible and/or requiring income maintenance, either unemployment insurance or general social assistance. At the same time, it is difficult to raise more revenue to match continued spending commitments. In an age of transnational corporations and increasingly free trade, it is relatively easy for wealthy individuals and corporations to move investments away from regimes that impose higher taxes (or their threats to do so seem more plausible). The middle class has borne an increasingly higher proportion of the tax burden but has also shown its willingness to punish governments that tax too highly. While the debate about the causes and the cures of government deficits continues, the seriousness of the mounting debt-load is increasingly recognized by left and right alike. Not so long ago, one could distinguish adherents of ideologies by their attitude towards deficits, fiscal conservatives (economic liberals) abhorring them and reform liberals and social democrats dismissing them as a short-term expedient that could be paid down at some point in the future (presumably once the economy turned around). The practical problem is that governments must at least meet interest payments on the debt they have accumulated over the years. As the level of this debt has risen, the interest payments have consumed an ever larger portion of government expenditure, inhibiting the ability of governments to implement the policies to which they are committed. More and more government revenue goes to pay bondholders and other investors from whom governments have borrowed, and proportionately less is spent on services or transfers to the public. This is a situation that compels even reform liberals and democratic socialists who still might be committed to **KEYNESIANISM** in principle to question the ability of governments to continue to finance deficits.

Given the difficulty governments experience in trying to increase revenues, deficit reduction or elimination appears to require reductions in government spending. This means reducing the size of the public sector, cutting back or eliminating government programs, or reducing government transfers. Clearly then, the fiscal crisis that many states have experienced has placed the continued shape (if not existence) of the welfare state in question. In the debate about how to downsize government and about the impact of this exercise on the welfare state, competing ideologies are at work.

Fiscal conservatives (who are economic liberals) have found in the mounting debt of market economy governments confirmation of their argument that the welfare state ought to be dismantled. The so-called neo-conservative revolution of the Thatcher and Reagan decade (the 1980s) was premised on this basis (although government deficits rose under the Reagan Administration, largely because of military outlays). Liberals who once participated in the design and expansion of the welfare state discussed the need to reform the welfare state, to redesign programs, to "do more with less." Ultimately, the only defense of the welfare state as we have known it comes today from the left, from democratic socialists or social democrats, who a generation ago would have argued that the welfare state does not go far enough in redressing inequalities created by a market economy. It is also the case today that even socialists, when in power, have found themselves holding the line on, or even limiting, government expenditures. Tony Blair's 1997 victory for the British

Labour Party demonstrates that a leftist party could even campaign on a platform of fiscal responsibility and win. To a large degree the questions that dominated most of the twentieth century—"how large the state?"—has become "how small the state?"

At the beginning of the twenty-first century, in light of the collapse of East European and Soviet non-market command economies, the political economic question appears to be not "whether markets?" but "whither markets?" In which directions is market society heading, and in particular, how will the relationship of the state to the economy be defined? Conservatives and conservative liberals will argue for more market autonomy. This is not necessarily the demand for a classic *laissez-faire* economy with a minimal state; in the present realities this may not even be feasible, let alone desirable, and many (but not all) supporters of market autonomy recognize this. Their concern is rather to generate more autonomy, less government activity, less regulation, and less extensive or expensive social programs; as a result of all these reductions in the role of the state, greater investment and greater opportunities for investors will be created. The justification for this increase in market autonomy continues to hinge upon the claim that all will benefit from this autonomy, if not equally, then at least in ways substantial enough in the long term to justify hardship in the short term. The evidence to support this claim is, at the least, rather thin. Moreover, while the current economic orthodoxy appears to be for a less rather than more active state, signaled particularly by the commitment to "free" or "unmanaged" trade and the creation of larger common markets, there does remain (particularly outside the English-speaking world) a belief among some supporters of market capitalism in the continued viability (if not necessity) of promoting a national economy through an active sympathetic state. Here the emphasis is not on market autonomy but on market support.

For another group, too, the solution is not less government activity but an activist focus by the state in economic management. This may mean a greater role in job creation through public works, or increased regulation of the economy, or expanding the network of social services, or even government ownership of key sectors of the economy. The justification is the belief that in this way the power of the state can provide economic opportunity, if not equality, for everyone and only in this expanded role counter the tendencies of the market to generate inequality and frustrate opportunities.

Finally, there are those who do not call for an expansion of the state's activity but a refinement or redefinition of that role with respect to the market. This may mean neither abandoning nor expanding social programs but redesigning them to meet the double end of serving those in need without needlessly expending resources. For a country like Canada, the future may involve drawing on the experience of countries like Germany or Japan, where the role of the state is much more closely linked to participation by both business and labor interests in shaping policy goals and in implementing programs to meet the challenges of a changing world. There seems to be little impetus, however, for such a development in the United States. The ultimate question will be: who benefits from the shape of the state that comes after the welfare state?

For most of the 1980s and the early-to-mid 1990s in North America and also in parts of Europe and Australasia, the political climate favored those who would roll back the welfare state. In part this occurred because of the general acceptance that continued deficit financing and increasing accumulated debt was unacceptable, in part also because politicians were able to capitalize on "tax fatigue," and in part because of a resentment of the disadvantaged or non-working poor by the working middle class. These last two are related and require some further explanation.

13.7
After the Welfare State?

As noted, a large portion of the tax burden shifted in recent decades from wealthy individuals and corporations to the middle class. Tax cuts have been a common strategy of neo-conservative politicians and a populist plank for election campaigns. While such cuts appeal to the tax-paying working and middle classes, the irony is that, in many cases, the bulk of the benefit has been enjoyed by the upper-middle and upper classes. One rationale for this upward **REDISTRIBUTION** of wealth is that it puts more money in the hands of those likely to invest it productively and thereby stimulate economic growth, higher employment, etc. There is little evidence that this has happened and much to the contrary. There is every reason to believe that the real reason for tax cuts is not to put money in the hands of taxpayers but to force the state to shrink and make it difficult for it to grow in the future. A tax cut in an age weary of deficits *forces* government downsizing, in particular of the government spending programs associated with the welfare state.

In most welfare states, these spending programs can be divided into the two categories we appropriated from Mishra (see above): universal social services, which by definition benefit all or which all can claim; and income maintenance programs, targeted at those least advantaged within society. In most cases, and contrary to what seems elementary fairness or justice, the immediate target for spending reductions has been the income maintenance programs that support the most disadvantaged within society. It is difficult to escape the conclusion that this segment is targeted because it is the most politically marginal portion of the electorate, less likely to vote, and in all likelihood less likely to vote for the party that is cutting their supports. The rationalization of this strategy takes many forms: arguing that the need of this segment is exaggerated, or that their benefits are too generous, or that high numbers of the poor are simply "taking advantage of the system" in one way or another. While the evidence for all these claims is slight (or non-existent), it is often compelling enough to those working- and middle-class taxpayers who resent the apparent existence of a lazy or undeserving underclass supported by state transfers. Interestingly, those who believe that those on welfare should be put to work are often those who share a concern for child poverty and profess the belief that children should be raised by their mothers; in most jurisdictions the majority of social assistance recipients are children under 18, a large proportion of whom are being raised by a single parent who is usually the mother.

In many cases, though, the demand for smaller government has moved on from income maintenance to the universal social services at the heart of the welfare state and from which all have benefited in the past, education and health care being the two largest areas of such expenditure. These areas are more politically sensitive and hence difficult to cut; the constituency that benefits from and identifies with these programs is much broader and better organized than the disadvantaged on social assistance. Here a tax cut may provide the sugar coating that will make the bitter pills of cutbacks more palatable.

As noted earlier, Ringen (1987) suggested that the purpose of the welfare state was redistribution, which, along with eliminating poverty, would create greater economic equality. It is not accidental that Ringen is a Swede, for it is the Swedish welfare state as the world's most extensive welfare state that came closest to meeting this characterization. In most other welfare states, while poverty may have been diminished, there is little evidence that equality was created. Interestingly, though, in every country in which the welfare state has been rolled back through tax and spending reductions, thus moving back in the direction of the minimal state, there has been an increase in inequality, a polarization with important political implications.

As the pendulum has swung since the mid-1970s towards neo-conservatism, the elimination of Keynesian policies, and the downsizing of the postwar welfare state, the very "successes" of this shift to the right may lead eventually to a swing in the other direction. The return of the Democrats to the presidency in America in 1992 and 1996; of the centrist Liberal Party to government in Canada in elections in 1993, 1997, and 2000; of Tony Blair's Labour Party to government in Britain in 1997 and again in 2000 and 2005—all might be taken as evidence that the full frontal attack on the welfare state might have abated after years of conservative control—although the elections of Republican George W. Bush in 2000 and 2004, Christian Democrat Angela Merkel in Germany as the first woman chancellor in Germany in 2005, Stephen Harper's Conservative Party in Canada in 2006, and Gaullist Nicolas Sarkozy to the presidency in France in 2007 all point to the need to be cautious when drawing such conclusions. Indeed, the possibility arises that in the very near future governments will no longer be as constrained by deficits and debt in the way they have been for the last two decades. This also creates the possibility that the question "how small the state?" can become "how small *or large* the state?" The debate is already being engaged between those who call for tax reductions and those who advocate renewed government activity (see Figure 13.1).

There is no reason to think that the state of tomorrow will look, or even that it should look, like the postwar welfare state. It is possible, though, to consider that in an age where governments are not constrained by fiscal realities, they will be constrained more by the political forces at work within their environment. It is not unreasonable to expect that those who have been disadvantaged or inconvenienced by government cutbacks and the reduction in programs will agitate for more rather than less government activity. If the economy continues to be unable to re-employ the 10 per cent who remained chronically unemployed in the 1980s and 1990s, it will be harder to ignore calls for job creation programs, or increased levels of income support, once the deficit is no longer there as an excuse for inaction.

It may be that many citizens will prefer to pay less taxes to government than receive more services. On the other hand, the public goods that citizens have valued—such as health care and education—address real needs, and it may not be so obvious to many that these services can be provided for privately in an adequate fashion. A very real consideration is the reality that we live in community with others. We may well judge that a community in

Key Terms

activist state
authoritative allocation
authoritative transfer
bourgeoisie
capitalism
class conflict
class consciousness
classes
command economy
deficits
demand management
distribution
economic nationalism
full employment
income maintenance
inflation
invisible hand
Keynesianism
laissez-faire
market autonomy
markets
market society
market support
means of production
minimal state
monetarism
political economy
private property
private transactions
proletariat
public property
public sector
redistribution
regulation
safety net
trade unions
universal social programs
welfare state

FIGURE 13.1 Is There a Third Way? Tony Blair's "New Labour"

Tony Blair's victory in the British general election in 1997 brought the Labour Party back to power for the first time since 1979. He had taken over as party leader in 1994, promising a wide range of reforms designed to moderate the party's social democratic ideology. One of his first acts of reform was to revise "Clause Four" of the party's constitution, replacing the commitment to the "common ownership of the means of production" with a more generic statement of the party's commitment to a tolerant, free, and just society. Blair's "New Labour" advances a centrist ideological agenda that combines support for market discipline in the economy, respect for traditional family values, and an emphasis on law and order, with more traditional left-wing values of welfare, openness and social inclusion, and educational opportunity. Blair's energy and image as a "modernizer" (both of the party and of the unwritten British constitution) resonated positively with many baby-boomers, particularly those who are liberal on social issues while conservative on fiscal questions. It remains to be seen if Blair's successor, Prime Minister Gordon Brown, will continue Blair's search for a viable third way.

which all are whole, healthy, and have an adequate opportunity at happiness is preferable to one in which some have these basic goods at the expense of others. In a democracy, it is always legitimate for the people to turn to the government to solve those problems for which there appears no private solution. In the "age of deficits," economics managed to assert its primacy over politics; in the time after deficits it may well be that politics will return to the driver's seat and that the level of government activity, minimal *or* extensive, will reflect the collective judgment of that polity's citizens.

References and Suggested Readings

Publishing information is not provided for texts in political thought that are either out of print or widely available in contemporary editions.

Fallows, James. 1993. "How the World Works." *Atlantic Monthly* (December).

Friedman, Milton. 1963. *Capitalism and Freedom.* Chicago, IL: University of Chicago Press.

Galbraith, John Kenneth. 1973. *Economics and the Public Purpose.* Boston, MA: Houghton Mifflin.

Giddens, Anthony. 2000. *The Third Way and its Critics.* Malden, MA: Blackwell Publishers.

Heilbroner, Robert L. 1970. *Between Capitalism and Socialism.* New York: Random House.

Howe, Irving, ed. 1970. *Beyond the Welfare State.* New York: Schocken Books.

Howlett, Michael and M. Ramesh. 2003. *Studying Public Policy: Policy Cycles and Policy Subsystems,* 2nd ed. New York: Oxford University Press.

Keynes, John Maynard. 1936. *The General Theory of Employment, Interest and Money.* Cambridge: Cambridge University Press.

Lindblom, Charles. 1977. *Politics and Markets.* New York: Basic Books.

List, Friedrich. 1837. *The National System of Political Economy.*

Marx, Karl. 1849. *Wage Labor and Capital.*

Mishra, Ramesh. 1990. *The Welfare State in Capitalist Society.* Toronto: University of Toronto Press.

——. 1999. *Globalization and the Welfare State.* Cheltenham, UK: Edward Elgar Publishing.

Ringen, Stein. 1987. *The Possibility of Politics.* Oxford: Clarendon Press.

Schumpeter, Joseph A. 1962. *Capitalism, Socialism, and Democracy.* New York: Harper and Row.

Smith, Adam. 1776. *The Wealth of Nations.*

FOURTEEN | Politics and the International System

Christopher Holoman

"But though there had never been any time wherein particular men were in a condition of war one against another, yet *in all times* kings and persons of sovereign authority, because of their independency, are in *continual jealousies*, and in the state and posture of gladiators, having their weapons pointing, and their eyes fixed on one another; that is, their forts, garrisons, and guns upon the frontiers of their kingdoms, and continual spies upon their neighbours, which is *a posture of war*."

—Thomas Hobbes, *Leviathan*, 1660 [emphasis added]

"Today's globalization system significantly raises the costs of countries using war as a means to pursue honor, react to fears or advance their interests ... Today's version of globalization ... makes for a much stronger web of constraints on the foreign policy behavior of those nations which are plugged into the system. It increases the incentives for not making war and increases the costs of going to war in more ways than in any previous era in modern history."

—Thomas Friedman, *The Lexus and the Olive Tree*, 2000

The field of International Relations occupies an unusual position in our introduction to politics. On one hand, it is an old and well-recognized subdiscipline of Political Science. Many of the great scholars of the past who were discussed in Chapter Three, especially Hobbes and Machiavelli, gave substantial attention to how countries interact. And if we are attempting to understand the forces that affect our daily lives, the international system *must* concern us. Indeed, one of the most significant political developments of recent decades has been the growing interconnectedness of the world, a process that has been called **GLOBALIZATION**. Neither countries nor individuals can afford to ignore the actions and decisions made in other countries. The increasing speed and declining costs of transportation, communication, and commerce guarantee that the lives and welfare of the earth's inhabitants are intertwined.

On the other hand, international politics does not look much like the politics we have been studying in the rest of this book. We have been discussing politics as the way societies make decisions for themselves and how they give authority to some people or institutions to carry out those decisions. But even that simple definition does not seem to be much help in looking at the international system. Almost every component of it can be questioned: what is the society? Is it all nations, a group of some nations, the

14.1
Introduction

individual citizens of the world, or something else? Whatever the answer is, can that group be called a society in any meaningful sense? Who makes the decisions? Where is the state or government structure? Politics *between* states is surely very different than politics *within* states.

Does this mean that we cannot use our understandings of politics to make sense of the international system? No, although obviously some of our findings only have limited applicability at the international level. One of the defining features of the international system is that there is no over-arching international government. States in the system are said to be sovereign—no other nation or institution has legitimate authority to tell a state what to do.[1] There may be international treaties, or groups such as the United Nations (UN), which states might agree to abide by, but if, at some point the state chooses not to, there is no international equivalent of the police or court system to force them to change their actions. (There is an International Court of Justice, usually referred to as the World Court, but it has little or no power to compel compliance.) You might recall the brief discussion in Chapter Three of **ANARCHY** when we noted that Hobbes asked his readers to envision the hypothetical state of nature, when individuals were in "a constant state of warre." We argued there that the state of nature was indeed hypothetical—it is almost impossible to imagine a human not existing in *some* sort of society. But also recall that Hobbes suggested that the easiest way to imagine this was to look at the way *states* interact; the idea of a society of nations, in whatever form, is not nearly as "automatic" as a society of humans. International relations, according to this view, is very close to the "state of nature." The result is that many of the questions we ask as we study international relations are ones that we usually consider settled at the domestic level.

This points us to the fundamental puzzle that has fascinated scholars of international relations for centuries: how can order be maintained in the absence of any legitimate authority to enforce agreements? Although we will refine our definitions further, at this point we can distinguish between two general answers to this question. One approach argues that nation-states, like individuals in Hobbes's state of nature, are in a state of conflict. They cannot rely on any outside help and so must constantly be on their guard. If other states gain power, it endangers one's own survival. Although under certain circumstances, states might find it in their interest to cooperate with one another, such agreements will always be fragile, and nations will readily break agreements if they conflict with

1 This system of sovereign states evolved in Europe and is often dated from the end of the Thirty Years War in 1648 when German principalities no longer recognized the supremacy of the Holy Roman Empire. The war ended in the Treaty of Westphalia, and so the system which is still in place is sometimes referred to as the *Westphalian* system.

national interest. This approach has been labeled **REALISM**. The traditional alternative, labeled **IDEALISM**, suggests that states might enter into agreements that *can* bring order to the anarchy of the international system. In the same way that individuals can escape the "state of nature" by establishing a government, nation-states might agree to abide by the rule of international law. Scholars and diplomats have been exploring this idea for centuries. Individuals give up some of their liberty to some higher authority in order to escape the state of nature. Could there be an international parallel: that nation-states give up some of their **SOVEREIGNTY**—their freedom to pursue whatever policies they deem reasonable—so that there is *some* international order?

But this brings us quickly to a related question: even if such agreements could be reached, who would enforce that law? After the unprecedented carnage of World War I, the League of Nations was established to provide a legal framework for an international community so that states would not have to resort to war to settle their differences. The American president at the time, Woodrow Wilson, was a great believer in this idealist vision. However, the League was doomed from the start because states were unwilling to give up their sovereignty in any meaningful sense: all votes had to be unanimous, virtually guaranteeing inaction; the United States was unwilling to join the League because of concerns about becoming involved in the quarrels of other nations; the traditional "great powers" were unwilling to give newer or weaker states a voice in governing the international system equal to their own; and so on. Nation-states did not find Hobbes's logic so compelling— perhaps the state of nature *was* preferable to the alternative.

This reveals a major problem in applying models of politics drawn from individuals to the international system. When we deal with individuals, it is reasonable to start from a premise that "all men are created equal" and to construct a political system in which all individuals have equal rights and responsibilities. Now, obviously, all "men" are *not* created equal; some of us are taller, stronger, smarter, and so forth, than others. But in political terms, those differences are not important—no matter what our physical or mental attributes, we all, by virtue of being humans (or citizens) have equal political rights.

Nations are different. Although we might speak about countries as if they were individuals—"the United States took action against ...," "the French announced a new policy towards ..."—that is just a simplification. Obviously, nations are not individuals for whom it makes sense to argue that, at some fundamental level, all are equal. In what meaningful sense is the United States, with its population of more than 300 million, an economy measured in the trillions of dollars, and the most powerful military in the world, equal to a country like Tuvalu in the South Pacific, with a population of 12,000, an area of 10 square miles, a gross national product of around $11 million, and no military? They are both members of the United Nations, and in that international legislature have an equal vote. In fact, the structure of the UN gives the appearance of offering equality to all states while in fact reserving substantial privileges to the "great powers"—in particular, those nations who were on the winning side in World War II. But the only sense in which they are equal is their status as sovereign states. However, this notion of sovereignty as conferring equal rights to all states regardless of their size or power is a relatively recent development, and one whose importance has been exaggerated. Boutrous Boutrous-Ghali, former secretary-general of the UN, has written: "The time of absolute and exclusive sovereignty has passed. Its theory was never matched by reality" (1992).

Unlike individuals, when dealing with nations, the conventional wisdom is that the differences are more important than the similarities. It is hard to imagine powerful states giving equal voice in, say, arms control or trade negotiations to weak states who might have little or no vested interest in the subject of the talks, simply because the weaker parties are also sovereign countries. That may not seem fair, but the concept of fairness is another example of an idea that we can make sense of between individuals but not necessarily between countries. The Greek historian Thucydides recounts an episode during the Peloponnesian War when the mighty Athenians were attempting to compel the tiny island of Melos to surrender. When the Melians protested the unfairness of the situation, the Athenians responded "You know as well as we do that right, as the world goes, is only in question between *equals* in power, while the strong do what they can and the weak suffer what they must."[2] The Melians continued to protest, but the Athenians surrounded them and eventually conquered them, killing all the men and selling the women and children into slavery. The Athenians themselves, often lauded as the founders of democracy, seemed to view international relations as a very different situation.

This chapter can touch on only a few of the issues in the field of International Relations. As alluded to above, one of the fascinating things about this area is that there are some questions that seem to endure across the centuries and others that reflect the uniqueness of our particular historical circumstances. We suggest that there are

2 This "Melian dialogue" is one of the fundamental documents in the realist tradition; realists sometimes point to it as evidence that the basic shape of international relations persists across the centuries. It is also worth noting that Hobbes's ideas about international relations were probably profoundly influenced by Thucydides, since Hobbes was among the first to translate *The Peloponnesian War* into English.

UN

three questions that are both old and new and help us organize our investigation of politics between nations: who are the actors? Is the world basically conflictual or cooperative? What does the future look like?

F or most of history, international relations have been about the interaction of political units. Although there are some notable differences between the city-states of ancient Greece, the empires of the first millennium AD, and the nation-states of the last 400 years, in every case there is a political unit that is supreme, or sovereign. And since, until relatively recently, those states were not democracies, the leaders could engage in foreign policy without much oversight. Even after the emergence of democracy, leaders were able to pursue their international interests largely unchecked by the voters, since foreign affairs had so little impact on their day-to-day lives. With only a few exceptions, commodities traded locally, so markets were smaller than the governments who had jurisdiction over them. Scholars sometimes refer to the "billiard ball" model—the

14.2
The Actors

international system was made up of nations, and only nations, who acted on their own interests, sometimes colliding with one another to change their directions. There were no other significant types of actors, and there was no reason to examine the internal politics of the countries.

Many scholars (but certainly not all) believe this is changing now. We cannot understand the international system without taking account of actors other than nation-states, since nations interact on so many more dimensions than they did in the past, and economies are so much more closely tied together. New actors have emerged in response to these new circumstances. The two new types of actors on the scene most frequently thought to be important are **MULTINATIONAL CORPORATIONS** (MNCs) and **INTERNATIONAL ORGANIZATIONS** (IOs). In addition, recent events suggest that international terrorist organizations such as al-Qaeda may be very influential. Now, obviously, there can be no question that these other actors exist—we can all observe them. The question is whether or not they influence the actions of nation-states enough to alter the course of international relations.

MNCs and IOs are both relative newcomers to the international stage. Although we can find isolated examples of both in earlier historical periods, they only emerge in an important way after 1900 and explode after World War II. And while we will develop these points a bit more fully below, we can say now that both of these new actors gain in importance from the decline in the costs of transportation and communication that mean that nations and their economies are more closely tied than at any time in history.

In some respects, these two new actors are mirror images of one another. MNCs are huge, sprawling economic forces, apparently *beyond the control* of any country. International organizations, on the other hand, are important for understanding international relations only to the extent that they *constrain* the actions of nation-states. What they have in common is that they change the nature of the international system *away* from simply the interaction of sovereign countries.

At this point, by "international organizations" we mean those groups whose members are governments, such as the UN or the World Trade Organization. These are more specifically known as "intergovernmental organizations," or IGOs, and are distinguished from those groups who, although internationally oriented, are made up of individuals, local chapters, etc. These are referred to as "non-governmental organizations," or NGOs. Examples include Greenpeace, Amnesty International, and the Red Cross. These groups, of which there are thousands, are important for a variety of reasons, but their impact on international relations varies wildly from group to group and issue to issue. They are certainly an important part of the process of globalization, but an attempt to say anything systematic about their influence is beyond the scope of this text.

Terrorist organizations targeting more than one country are also a recent development (depending on what groups are included in the definition). It should be stressed that "terrorism" and related terms have been used inappropriately at times to label as illegitimate one's political adversaries; it has been said that "one person's terrorist is another person's freedom fighter." At some point, however, most people would agree that some actions are unacceptable, no matter the desired goal, although there would be disagreement on where that line is crossed. The presence and activities of such terrorist organizations raise a number of questions about the nature of war as well as actors in the system.

Companies have been investing in foreign markets for centuries. In fact, much of the "New World" was explored and settled by agents of private enterprises looking for new sources of raw materials and customers. This process accelerated with the Industrial Revolution and again after World War II with what has been called the transportation and communication revolution. However, what really made the explosive growth of MNCs possible was the relaxation of rules limiting the movement of investment capital across borders. Many casual observers do not understand or perhaps remember this important point. Prior to World War II it was difficult and expensive for companies in most nations to invest overseas, due to regulations imposed by their own governments. One of the central goals of the international economic system constructed largely by the United States after World War II was to reduce or eliminate these barriers. This allowed corporations to move beyond merely buying or selling overseas to actually investing in their own productive capacity in other nations—factories, mines, wells, distribution networks, and so forth. By the late 1960s, a number of these firms, most of which had started out as very large companies in their own countries, had become global giants. Some people began to worry that these new actors were moving beyond the ability of governments to control them, an idea captured succinctly in the title of one of the first books to analyze this phenomenon, *Sovereignty at Bay.* (The author of this book, Raymond Vernon, has been careful

14.2.1
Multinational Corporations

to emphasize that he was not predicting the *end* of sovereignty, although some people who only looked at the book's title did not understand that.) By the mid-1970s, this fear seemed exaggerated when the oil-producing countries, having formed their cartel, the Organization of Petroleum Exporting Countries (OPEC), had some success in coercing the large oil companies, then as now some of the largest MNCs in the world. Other nations were able to close some of the loopholes that had allowed countries to shift money to avoid taxes and other regulations. The caricature of MNCs as able to do whatever they wanted unchecked was clearly overstated.

As with all caricatures, however, there was also some truth in the picture. Multinational corporations do indeed have qualities that give them some advantages and increase their ability to affect international relations. Concerns about MNCs usually relate to two characteristics of these firms: their size and their ability to move faster than attempts to regulate them.

1. *Size*. Multinational corporations are defined as firms that exert managerial control (as opposed to simply owning stock) over operations in more than one country. By that simple definition, a hot dog stand in San Diego, California that sets up a stand a mile away in Tijuana, Mexico is an MNC. But most of the time we are concerned with the firms at the other end of the spectrum--those with billions of dollars under their control. Such corporations are bigger than many nations. Table 14.1 combines a ranking of nations and MNCs to generate a list of the 100 largest economic actors in the world. Note that while the top 22 places are held by nation-states, after we get beyond this top tier, most of the biggest players are corporations. While only 14 (28 per cent) of the first 50 are MNCs, 37 of the second 50 (74 per cent) are private enterprises.[3] Even for large countries, the size of these firms is significant. Leaders must be sensitive to the welfare of those companies based in, or even simply operating in, their territory. The old saying "what's good for General Motors is good for the United States" is clearly based in fact. There are numerous historical examples of countries taking foreign policy, even military, action to protect the interests of "their" corporations. The economic importance of these firms may tempt even large countries to interfere inappropriately in the internal affairs of another country.

The situation is even more difficult when MNCs deal with developing countries. These nations desperately need

3 This ranking uses Gross Domestic Product to measure nations' size and annual sales for MNCs. These have been criticized as not the correct measures or not comparable. However, some critics believe this ranking overstates the importance of MNCs, and others think it understates it. Thus, we will take it as a reasonable estimate.

TABLE 14.1 The Size of Multinational Corporations

COUNTRY/CORPORATION	GDP/SALES ($MIL)	COUNTRY/CORPORATION	GDP/SALES ($MIL)
1 United States	8,708,870.0	51 Colombia	88,596.0
2 Japan	4,395,083.0	52 AXA	87,645.7
3 Germany	2,081,202.0	53 IBM	87,548.0
4 France	1,410,262.0	54 Singapore	84,945.0
5 United Kingdom	1,373,612.0	55 Ireland	84,861.0
6 Italy	1,149,958.0	56 BP Amoco	83,556.0
7 China	1,149,814.0	57 Citigroup	82,005.0
8 Brazil	760,345.0	58 Volkswagen	80,072.7
9 Canada	612,049.0	59 Nippon Life Insurance	78,515.1
10 Spain	562,245.0	60 Philippines	75,350.0
11 Mexico	474,951.0	61 Siemens	75,337.0
12 India	459,765.0	62 Malaysia	74,634.0
13 Korea, Rep.	406,940.0	63 Allianz	74,178.2
14 Australia	389,691.0	64 Hitachi	71,858.5
15 Netherlands	384,766.0	65 Chile	71,092.0
16 Russian Federation	375,345.0	66 Matsushita Electric Ind.	65,555.6
17 Argentina	281,942.0	67 Nissho Iwai	65,393.2
18 Switzerland	260,299.0	68 ING Group	62,492.4
19 Belgium	245,706.0	69 AT&T	62,391.0
20 Sweden	226,388.0	70 Philip Morris	61,751.0
21 Austria	208,949.0	71 Sony	60,052.7
22 Turkey	188,374.0	72 Pakistan	59,880.0
23 General Motors	176,558.0	73 Deutsche Bank	58,585.1
24 Denmark	174,363.0	74 Boeing	57,993.0
25 Wal-Mart	166,809.0	75 Peru	57,318.0
26 Exxon Mobil	163,881.0	76 Czech Republic	56,379.0
27 Ford Motor	162,558.0	77 Dai-Ichi Mutual Life Ins.	55,104.7
28 Daimler Chrysler	159,985.7	78 Honda Motor	54,773.5
29 Poland	154,146.0	79 Assicurazioni Generali	53,723.2
30 Norway	145,449.0	80 Nissan Motor	53,679.9
31 Indonesia	140,964.0	81 New Zealand	53,622.0
32 South Africa	131,127.0	82 E. On	52,227.7
33 Saudi Arabia	128,892.0	83 Toshiba	51,634.9
34 Finland	126,130.0	84 Bank of America	51,392.0
35 Greece	123,934.0	85 Fiat	51,331.7
36 Thailand	123,887.0	86 Nestle	49,694.1
37 Mitsui	118,555.2	87 SBC Communications	49,489.0
38 Mitsubishi	117,765.6	88 Credit Suisse	49,362.0
39 Toyota Motor	115,670.9	89 Hungary	48,355.0
40 General Electric	111,630.0	90 Hewlett-Packard	48,253.0
41 Itochu	109,068.9	91 Fujitsu	47,195.9
42 Portugal	107,716.0	92 Algeria	47,015.0
43 Royal Dutch/Shell	105,366.0	93 Metro	46,663.6
44 Venezuela	103,918.0	94 Sumitomo Life Insur.	46,445.1
45 Iran, Islamic rep.	101,073.0	95 Bangladesh	45,779.0
46 Israel	99,068.0	96 Tokyo Electric Power	45,727.7
47 Sumitomo	95,701.6	97 Kroger	45,351.6
48 Nippon Tel & Tel	93,591.7	98 Total Fina Elf	44,990.3
49 Egypt	92,413.0	99 NEC	44,828.0
50 Marubeni	91,807.4	100 State Farm Insurance	44,637.2

Sources: Sales: *Fortune*, July 31, 2000. GDP: World Bank, *World Development Report 2000*.

the financial resources offered by the corporations; however, these funds frequently come with strings attached: tax breaks, relaxation of environmental regulations, perhaps even illegal bribes and kickbacks. An economically weak nation may have very little leverage in negotiating with its much larger "partners." It is true that these nations remain the sovereign power and have tools of law that they can attempt to use, but in doing so they risk losing the needed investment. In any bargaining situation, the player who needs the deal the least holds the power. In most cases, MNCs can site their factories in any of a number of countries, while the potential host nation may not have many other alternatives for getting investment dollars. The MNC can afford to drive a hard bargain. Even when these poorer nations attempt to control the MNCs, they frequently lack the manpower to enforce any regulations they put in place. Sometimes, these conditions combine in tragic human cost. In 1984, a Union Carbide chemical plant in Bhopal, India leaked poison gas that killed 4,000 people in the first few hours and has been responsible for another 10,000 deaths in subsequent months and years. The plant had been put in India in part to avoid stricter environmental controls in more developed countries. There are many other less dramatic examples of the inability and, sometimes, unwillingness of poor countries to regulate the actions of large corporations acting within their borders.

2. *Agility.* Even large countries can find it difficult to regulate MNCs effectively. Big corporations may not be the speediest decision-makers, but they can still move more quickly than governments. As we have discussed in previous chapters, a policy outcome from government is usually the result of a laborious political process. By the time the government has identified, studied, and addressed a problem of "corporate abuse," the corporations have long since moved on to other ways of reaching the same end. To be successful in business, these corporations have learned to move resources quickly to respond to changing economic or political conditions. And since corporations are an important part of the economies of these nations, the governments have an interest in not overly restricting them.

This combination—size, agility, and economic importance—make MNCs actors that both policy-makers and scholars must take into account in their analysis of international relations.

As a general rule, nations have joined together in international organizations when they have been confronted by problems they could not solve by individual action. One of the oldest international bodies, for example, was formed to address navigation on the Rhine River, since it flows through and between so many countries. In the past, such problems were relatively rare. The world wars and the Depression demonstrated to nations that this range of shared problems was much greater than in the past. In response, as World War II was winding down, the Allied powers, led by the United States, began a process to organize the international system around international organizations. The UN is the one we probably think of first, but as it developed it became paralyzed by the Cold War stalemate between the United States and the Soviet Union. In terms of outcomes, other organizations have been more significant. The World Health Organization, for instance, by coordinating the sharing of science and resources, completely eradicated smallpox from the globe and has made significant progress against many other diseases that formerly killed millions.

14.2.2
International Organizations

Most important have been the organizations designed to manage the international economic system. In response to the Depression, nations had pursued competitive "beggar-thy-neighbor" policies that served to make everyone, themselves included, worse off. The economic problems of the 1930s taught policy-makers that markets, while normally efficient and beneficial, needed oversight and management. (Recall the discussion in the last chapter on the rise of the welfare state.) Even before the war was over, the Allies had begun meeting to organize the postwar economy. In June 1944, these nations met at a resort in Bretton Woods, NH and formed two of the three institutional pillars of the new system— the International Monetary Fund (IMF) and the World Bank. The resulting international monetary system was thus known as the **BRETTON WOODS SYSTEM**. Without going into detail, these institutions were designed to structure and manage (with the least amount of interference as possible) a global free market system of money and investment. The third pillar, the International Trade Organization (ITO), was set aside in separate negotiations since the actors recognized that trade negotiations were going to be particularly difficult. In fact, the United States refused to ratify the treaty that would have formed the ITO and what was to be a temporary measure, the General Agreement on Tariffs and Trade (GATT), became the *de facto* international trade institution. Over time, that organization was changed and strengthened to such an extent that it was renamed in 1999 as the World Trade Organization (WTO). It now has significant powers to enforce free trade measures on its members, which include the vast majority of the world's nations.

All three of these institutions, in fact, have real leverage they can use to change the policies of their member nations. In that sense, they represent important challenges to sovereignty and are significant actors in the international system. And they are not alone. The number of IGOs has mushroomed since World War II, and this was an explicit goal of the United States in designing the postwar world. The United States recognized that it had the power to design the system but also knew that that power would not last forever. By resting the international system on institutions, the United States hoped to erect a structure that would still stand, even if that country was no longer able (or willing) to support it fully. For better or worse, that is what has happened. The present arrangement of international organizations reflects an American view of a desirable world that is focused on free market capitalism and democracy.

When combined with the dominant American position in the world since the collapse of the Soviet Union, this American-centric view has caused resentment in many areas. The United States argues that nations join these groups voluntarily and can leave them at their own discretion. They can be thought of as a type of club—as long as the benefits to membership outweigh the costs, you will stay in and pay your dues. But if the costs begin to outweigh the benefits, you are free to leave. Other countries would suggest that these organizations are more like gangs than clubs. You are coerced to join and once you are in, you are threatened with dire consequences if you think about leaving. The powerful states in the international system have put their support behind these organizations. If you choose not to be a part, you are rejecting their view of what constitutes the best international system. From their perspective, the strong states are simply trying to implement what both history and theory demonstrates is the optimal system—free markets only interfered with in extreme circumstances. But weaker states see a system designed to further the interests of the powerful—the rich getting richer and the poor, if not getting poorer, certainly not becoming rich. These new international actors are part of a larger pattern of domination.

This question of new actors may seem like a rather abstract theoretical question, but it is not. A world in which nation-states must take account of not just their sovereign peers but all manner of other actors is less predictable and thus, at least potentially, more dangerous. James Rosenau (1990) has written extensively on how this "turbulence" in world affairs itself helps undermine the importance of nation-states: they are being pushed together into international organizations to try to deal with problems they can no longer solve on their own, but they are also being pulled apart by "sub-groupism" as individuals identify not with their nations but with more local religious, ethnic, or cultural groups. This in turn can lead to other types of international actors and issues.

Terrorism can be defined in a number of different ways, but the basic common elements involve the killing or injuring of civilians outside of the context of warfare in an attempt to cause fear among the broader population and thus bring about some policy change on the part of a nation-state or international organization. Furthermore, we often confine the use of the word to activities carried out by forces not officially connected to a national government.[4] As such, we need to ask whether or not these groups are significant actors in the international system.

14.2.3
Terrorist Groups

4 There is a grey area of "state-sponsored terrorism" in which a government covertly supports terrorist activities. The state-sponsored aspect does not affect the comments below. If the support becomes too overt, the sponsor risks becoming the target of retaliation.

On the one hand, one might suggest that although highly visible, terrorist groups and their activities are not of a magnitude to require taking account of them in a model of the international system. Of course, we do not want to minimize any human loss, but even a large-scale attack such as the destruction of the World Trade Center results in smaller losses of life than traffic accidents or the daily deaths due to poverty. And the economic impact was minimal compared to natural disasters such as Hurricane Katrina in Louisiana or the tsunami in South Asia in 2004. So we could reasonably conclude that terrorist acts either *should not* be included in our model given their relatively small scale or *cannot* be included because, like natural disasters, they are unpredictable.

On the other hand, however, terrorist acts can, at least in some instances, affect the policies of nations. Obviously, wars in Afghanistan and Iraq were precipitated by 9/11, although there were other forces at play as well. In other cases, determining the effects of terrorism is difficult, because no country would admit that their policies were influenced by the illegal actions of a small number of people. However, it does appear, at least to many observers, that, in Northern Ireland and the Basque regions, for example, the governments of Britain and Spain, respectively, altered their policies in response to protracted campaigns of terrorism.

These cases also represent another facet of the issue: as groups achieve recognition and legitimacy in the political arena, they tend to cease their more violent activities. Terrorist acts are not ends in and of themselves, and groups do not pursue this extreme strategy simply for the destruction caused. Instead, terrorism is a last resort for those who feel shut out of the political process. Sometimes they have been excluded because their views are too extreme. But we must also recognize that, as abhorrent as we may find their tactics, in some cases these groups have legitimate causes for their dissatisfaction. Addressing the problem of terrorism requires attention to the causes, not simply trying to stave off planned attacks.

In the future, the major concern for many people is that a terrorist group will acquire the means to inflict much greater harm through the use of weapons of mass destruction—chemical, biological, or nuclear. Experts disagree about how great a threat this is: are these weapons as easily acquired as is feared? Would they really inflict dramatically greater damage than conventional attacks? One factor is a significant cause for concern. Since terrorist groups rarely possess physical "home territory," they are not subject to deterrence in the same way that nation-states are. Since World War II, there have been no nuclear attacks and only very limited uses of chemical or biological weapons, even when possessed by nations that seem to be pursuing confrontational or irrational foreign policies. Even leaders of so-called "rogue states" understand that crossing the line in the use of such weapons runs the risk that their territory will be the target of a devastating retaliatory blow. (It is impossible to prove, of course, what caused an event *not* to happen, but deterrence is generally believed to be an effective check on aggression in a wide range of situations.)

Terrorist groups do not face such a threat. How does one retaliate against such a shadowy, stateless opponent? How was al-Qaeda directly punished for the 9/11 attacks? If deterrence is what has prevented the routine use of weapons of mass destruction, we might very well fear that terrorist groups are, in fact, significant new actors on the international stage. However, we return to the questions posed before: are terrorist attacks a common enough and significant enough phenomenon that states can or should try to factor them into decision-making? Consistent with the issues raised above, perhaps the funds spent on trying to prevent terrorist attacks would be better spent to alleviate the root causes of terrorism, such as poverty and alienation.

We cannot have complete confidence in any conclusions we draw at this point in history. Certainly, governments will continue to take precautions against terrorist attacks, and those precautions might entail simple inconveniences such as metal detectors in doorways or losses of what had been thought to be fundamental liberties or expectations of privacy. There will undoubtedly continue to be groups to whom violence seems the only effective strategy to gain attention for their grievances. And, as we will take up in the following sections, the causes that lie at the root of much of the current terrorist activity will likely persist for some time. The unanswerable question currently is whether or not terrorist attacks will become markedly more frequent or more destructive.

Recall our discussion in Chapter Two of paradigms and the work of Thomas Kuhn. One way of summarizing his ideas is that as scholars study any particular field, the questions they ask and the answers they find are largely shaped by their image of the field of inquiry they start with. In international relations, many of the debates of both analysts and policy-makers can be traced to fundamentally different preconceptions about the international system. Is it basically hostile and conflictual, or is it generally benign and cooperative? For most of its history, the answer has been the former, and the field of International Relations has been the study of war. Nations fought when it seemed likely to offer some gain, and that was often. Cooperation was seen only as the absence of conflict. War was a natural part of the way countries interacted. This sentiment is most famously captured in the dictum of Carl von Clausewitz, a German who spent much of his career observing the world and war in the period dominated by Napoleon Bonaparte. In his often-assigned (but not often finished) book *On War*, von Clausewitz wrote that "war is the continuation [or extension] of diplomacy [or politics] by other means." The resort to deadly force was just another tool that statesmen could, and should, use. Even if this focus on war was unfortunate, it was necessary, since only wars threatened the fundamental security of a country. And if a nation's security was at risk, all other matters—economic, social, and so forth—were unimportant. This is the perspective of the realists discussed above.

This view of the world is sometimes referred to as **ZERO-SUM**. International relations is like a game of poker: anything one player wins is balanced by the loss of another player. This must be the case, in this world-view, since military might is the sole, or at least

14.3
Conflict or Cooperation?

5 This is the situation the United States faced for most of the post-World War II period: it was growing, but other nations were growing faster. Of course, this was inevitable. The United States had built up a huge industrial capacity, which was untouched by the war's destruction. It possessed, on many measures, one-half of the world's productive resources. Other countries, starting from such a low base, could hardly help from growing faster.

decidedly most important, component of national power, and the effectiveness of any given level of military might can only be determined by comparing it to what other actors have. If you have to defend your home from your neighbor and you have an old-fashioned musket, are you powerful? There is no way of knowing, since the only way in which this question makes sense is: are you more powerful *than your neighbor*? And the answer to that depends not just on your own capabilities but on those of your neighbor: does he have a sharp stick, a musket, or a machine gun? Put more formally, nations are (and must be) primarily concerned with **RELATIVE POWER**: how much more or less powerful are you than other countries? Even if your power is increasing, if another nation's power is increasing *faster*, you are losing—becoming less secure.[5] The result is a world defined by conflict.

Beginning some time after World War II, some scholars began to recognize that perhaps this was not the only possible picture. This change in perspective involves comprehending both a changed nature of war and the potential of significant gains from states working together. Each of these deserves attention on its own.

14.3.1 War

There can be no doubt that war is an important part, perhaps, even today, the *most* important part of international relations. Losing a war, unlike any other event, can endanger the very existence of a country. (Although it must be noted that this extreme outcome—a country *disappearing* after losing a war—has rarely actually happened.) Recall our discussion from Chapter One about power, authority, and legitimacy. In a system of sovereign nation-states, there is no authority for one state to legitimately tell another what to do. If one country desires to get another country to do its bidding, war may be an appropriate way to do that. Power and the use of force are, for all practical purposes, unchecked, at least in any legal sense.

However, the nature of modern war may make this use of force difficult or impossible. In fact, one scholar, John Mueller (1989), has argued that total war between developed nations is obsolete, a part of society that, while important for many years, no longer serves any useful purpose. Even if we do not accept this sweeping conclusion, we can still recognize that there are many aspects of modern war that contribute to this change. The easiest to see are the changes in its destructiveness. The long history of war is almost a steady march of increased killing power. As with other activities driven by technology, however, the *rate* of change has increased dramatically since the Industrial Revolution. Machine guns, tanks, aircraft, and so forth have made the battlefield a much more deadly place than in the past. Indeed, World War II was the first war in history where more soldiers died of battle wounds than died from illness. But the battlefield itself may not be as relevant anymore. The development of long-range bombers and missiles, especially when combined with nuclear weapons, makes it possible to devastate a nation's population and economy without defeating its army on the battlefield. The result of these changes is to raise the stakes of going to war. A leader, calculating whether the risk of going to war is worth the cost, will now have to take account of the very real possibility of sustaining heavy losses not just among the armed forces but also to the civilian population and the industrial and economic capacity of the nation. In its most extreme version, this dynamic produced the stability of the Cold War between the United States and the Soviet Union. Even though each side possessed enough firepower to destroy the other (and presumably conquer it), each side also recognized that it could not stop its adversary from similar destruction. This relationship—known as Mutual Assured Destruction, an extreme form of deterrence—kept both sides from using their awesome military strength. In addition, not only were the two sides deterred from a nuclear exchange, they were also deterred from attacking one another with conventional weapons. George and Smoke (1974) provide numerous examples of how the deterrent relationship kept potentially volatile situations, such as the Cuban Missile Crisis or the Berlin Blockade, from sparking a shooting war. It is, however, true that during the Cold War the superpowers sponsored opposing sides in several "proxy wars."

Not all war, however, is great-power, all-out war, and violence will continue in many times and places. Governments should clearly continue to maintain defenses consistent with reasonable dangers. As wars, defined as armed conflict between nation-states, becomes less frequent, however, the necessary actions of governments become less like military functions and more like police roles.

Furthermore, what would cause a leader to embark on war in any circumstances? A second change in the nature of war is the goals pursued. Although nations have gone to war for many reasons, historically it is usually argued that they fought in order to add to their own strength and, especially, their territory. More land equaled more power: you could grow more crops to support a larger population, the new land may have important resources, etc. Also note that, in the terms used above, a dispute over land is zero-sum: any land gained by one side must be lost by another. In the modern world, however, this direct link between territory and national power has weakened. The conquest of land is not so clearly a quick way to become stronger. National boundaries are still important, of course, and there are a number of border disputes that have lingered for decades and occasionally break out into shooting, but the importance of territory there is largely symbolic. Similarly, many of the most direct threats to peace are separatist movements where one group wants territory for its own. Current examples are the Tamils in Sri Lanka; the Kurds in Iraq, Iran, and Turkey; and the Palestinians in Israel. The territory is symbolic of self-determination rather than conferring power *per se*. What would nations go to war for, then? In the Cold War, the answer was ideology—to stop the spread of Communism, for example. But that ideological struggle has ended and not been replaced, and even at the time it was not, apparently, cause enough for either side to engage in direct confrontation and risk nuclear annihilation. Perhaps the answer is cultural or religious conflict; we take up this possibility below. Perhaps this combination of the way war is fought and what wars are fought for has made it unlikely that nations will resort to war as they have in the past. Wars of some sort will still take place, but focusing on war as the dominant force in international relations will cause us to ignore much of what is going on in the international system. This draws our attention not only to other types of interactions, such as economic affairs, but also to the possibility of cooperation as something more than just what happens when nations are not at war.

14.3.2
Gains from Cooperation

A second avenue of challenge to the realist world-view questions the zero-sum nature of international relations. Certainly there must be *some* areas where nations can recognize the ability to work together for mutual gains. Perhaps countries are concerned with **ABSOLUTE POWER** rather than (or in addition to) relative power. If so, one nation's gains would not necessarily represent a threat or loss to another. The metaphor to be drawn on is not the poker game but the market, where individuals, each looking out for his or her own best interest, manage to cooperate so that all are better off.

We need to emphasize several points here. First, this is a different argument from the idealist view covered above, although they both share a more optimistic outlook than the realist perspective. Idealism, recall, draws a parallel between individuals and nations: as

FIGURE 14.1 War and Democracy

The relationship between democracy and war is complex. Note these three avenues of inquiry:

- It has long been hypothesized that democracies are less likely to go to war than autocratic governments. This certainly makes sense intuitively. One of the themes of this book is the need for democracies to maintain public support and war is, at least in principle, not very popular since the costs of war are high, both in money and in lives. So democratic leaders, who should be reluctant to risk popularity, should be less willing to go to war than dictators who answer to no one. However, the historical data do not support this hypothesis. Democracies seem to go to war at about the same rate as other forms of government. Under many circumstances, democratically elected leaders seem to be able to convince their constituents that war is, if not desirable, at least necessary. (And in the extreme case, as in the movie *Wag the Dog*, elected leaders have been accused of starting wars to divert attention from domestic problems, since citizens tend to "rally around the flag" in times of international trouble.) You should be able to think of several real-world examples.

- One of the most discussed findings in recent years has been that, so far, there have been no wars between industrialized democracies. While this fact is generally agreed upon, there is no consensus on why it is so. As noted above, democracies are not necessarily less war-like than other forms of government. Certainly, there is no obvious relationship between industrial development and reluctance to go to war. (If anything it is the reverse: an obvious material superiority might well tempt a nation into attacking a disadvantaged opponent.) Perhaps there are shared values between industrialized (capitalist) democracies that make war less likely. Perhaps this is a by-product of globalization: nations cannot attack each other because they own so many assets in each other's territory and their economies are too closely linked. Or perhaps the world has just been lucky so far that these types of countries have not fought each other. It could be just an historical accident. After all, democracy in its modern form is only a little more than 200 years old and is still absent in many places. Industrialization is neither as old nor as widely practiced. In the long sweep of history, we shouldn't have too much confidence in findings based on such a short period.

- On a somewhat different note, there may be a link between democracy and the *conduct* of war. Victor Davis Hanson (1989), originally a scholar of classical Greek language and civilization, has now become well-known in the field of military history. His study of how the Greek city-states (where democracy was developed) waged war has led him to argue that the nature of democracy affects the way war is fought. In particular, democracies (or perhaps "Western" countries, the inheritors of Greek civilization) emphasize total war: citizens fully mobilized fighting all out, hoping for a single decisive battle. But war doesn't have to be this way. Other cultures have developed very different forms of war that are smaller in scale, less final, and often concluding in a negotiated end rather than unconditional surrender. In the war against the Taliban in Afghanistan in 2001-02, many analysts noted the problems caused for the United States by the tradition of Afghan fighters to surrender or change sides before a "decisive" end was reached in anticipation of a compromise settlement. In the "Western way of war" (to use Hanson's term) this type of war and outcome is hard to understand.

6 Astute readers will note a weakness in the metaphor. Markets of any significant size probably require some minimal government to do things like enforce property rights, contracts, and so forth. But it is easy enough to find examples of mutual self-interested cooperation without a government.

individuals give up some liberty to a domestic government, so nations should give up some sovereignty to an international government, or something like it. But the market model seems to indicate that the possibility of mutual gains can bring about cooperation between actors even *without* a government.[6] This means that we can think about an international system that is less conflictual than the Hobbesian state of nature without getting bogged down, as scholars had for centuries, in questions of the possibility of international law and government.

Second, this argument should also not be confused with a weaker version that realists would subscribe to. It has long been recognized that under some circumstances even very competitive rival nations will find it worthwhile to forego war. One of the enduring lines of research within the realist tradition attempts to discover what arrangement of power among nations leads to stability or conflict. Is the world safer when there is one dominant country, two competitive super-powers, a multi-state balance of power, or something else? Whatever the answer, there is the possibility of something besides a "constant state of warre." (This idea is reflected in the title of one of the classics of realist thought, Hedley Bull's *The Anarchical Society* (1995); order might emerge even under circumstances of anarchy.) But these cooperative arrangements will always be fragile. States cannot afford to let their guard down nor allow other states to gain much, since others' gains are your losses.

This newer perspective, which unfortunately has not yet acquired a succinct label, makes a stronger argument. Nations will find it in their interest to cooperate in certain areas to achieve gains that they all enjoy. The clearest example is probably international trade. It has been known since the 1800s that, overall, national wealth increases for all nations when they specialize in producing those goods and services that give them an advantage and trading with other nations for those products they produce less well. If they choose instead to raise trade barriers in an effort to protect their inefficient industries, any gains in the protected domestic industry will be outweighed (for the country as a whole) by the higher prices everyone pays now that the cheaper imports are no longer available. The problem is that protecting inefficient industries is politically attractive: even though for the nation as a whole higher textile prices, for example, are costly, those of us who pay $1 extra for our shirts are less likely to complain to our representative than the worker who loses his or her $20,000 per year job sewing those shirts. Policy-makers end up protecting inefficient industries because the economic costs are easier to bear than the political costs.

But if all nations succumb to this political temptation, the free trade system, best for all when considered as a whole, will unravel. In order to safeguard the gains from cooperation—in essence, protecting themselves from political temptation—states will establish institutions or rules, sometimes formal, sometimes informal, that limit their own ability to make choices that are attractive but ultimately self-defeating. The economic institutions discussed above, especially the WTO, reflect this understanding.

This argument takes on additional strength in the next step. Not only will nations cooperate for mutual benefits, as they enjoy those gains the cooperation will strengthen their ties and make them less likely to break off relations, much less go to war. This can be the case even in times of fairly deep conflict. The Uruguay Round of international trade negotiations in the 1990s was stalled for years as the various parties were unable to agree on the next steps towards freer trade. Each side believed that the other had unfair trade barriers, and the diplomatic rhetoric frequently became heated, but there were no calls to simply give up negotiating. Even if nations, for a time, did not think that the international trade system was working and they would not have success expanding cooperation, they were still unwilling to endanger not just the current gains but also the possibility of future benefits.

That is not all. Once nations are cooperating in one area, they may find it possible to cooperate in others as well. This can occur in many ways, such as by borrowing institutional arrangements, by sharing necessary technical information, even just by added trust through more regular interaction. This dynamic was the rationale driving the cooperation between European countries after World War II. Having suffered two devastating wars in the space of 30 years, but with no background of cooperation to draw on, six nations, including the old rivals, France and Germany, began working together in limited areas where their interests clearly intersected, starting with the European Coal and Steel Community. Over the next 60 years, the European Community (now known as the EU) has spread both to 27 nations (with three more in the process of joining) and to a wide range of political and economic issues, culminating, so far, in a common currency in use in many member states. This is a truly striking development, since minting and controlling money has historically been one of the hallmarks of sovereignty. The emergence and growth of cooperation has fundamentally changed politics, both international and domestic, in Europe. Globally, of course, the process is not nearly so advanced, and there in no widespread interest in the level of integration that

7 It is regrettably beyond the scope of this text to pursue this idea much further. One of the most important concepts in social science is the "Prisoners' Dilemma"—a situation where all the actors in a situation pursue their own best interest and wind up making everyone, including themselves, worse off. Commercial fishermen, for example, have no incentive to not catch as many fish as they can individually. The result is less, or no, fish for all. Even though the benefits of cooperation—a stable supply of fish, in this case—are clear, cooperation is difficult or impossible.

14.4
The Future

is taking place in Europe. But we can certainly observe the broad strokes—cooperation leading to closer relations in other areas and a reduction in conflict.

Two qualifications are necessary. First, the possibility of gains from cooperation does not imply that cooperation will, in fact, take place. There might be any number of reasons that countries might choose not to cooperate or find it difficult to do so. Under some circumstances, actors might even recognize the potential of substantial benefits but be unable to cooperate to reach them.[7] It is an important area of research to determine the conditions under which cooperation will or will not emerge. This is particularly true in international relations, where cooperative arrangements must be, in the jargon, self-enforcing. Since there is no international enforcer, the structure of the system itself must induce nations to cooperate.

Finally, this perspective does not attempt to completely displace realism. Most adherents would admit that the competitive zero-sum world view probably is more appropriate to studying war and military matters. Again, the argument is that that is only a part, and probably a shrinking part, of international relations.

The view of the world that emerges is one where the likelihood of war, at least all-out war, is seriously limited. Nations find themselves enmeshed in a "web of cooperation" that grows larger and stronger. There will be conflicts, but they will be largely over how to divide the gains from cooperation. States will be reluctant to take their disagreements so far as to endanger these gains. Capitalism and democracy are both spreading, and since, as noted above, industrialized democracies fight each other rarely, if ever, this too will lead to a more stable and secure international system.

This essentially optimistic perspective is not universally held, however. A traditional realist would simply respond that this view wildly overstates the willingness of nations to enter into agreements that threaten sovereignty and allow potential rivals to grow in strength. In the absence of some international security arrangement, the system remains one of "self-help." If the world has been more peaceful in recent years, it is a product of either the dominance of the United States in the wake of the fall of the Soviet Union, a condition that is probably temporary, or perhaps just luck. But there are observers who see threats to international stability on other fronts. Even if relations between the major powers are less likely to end in war than in any time in history, that is only part of the story of international relations.

The most tragic issue that international relations scholars deal with is the plight of the poorest countries in the world. Since these nations as a rule do not have the military or economic power to directly influence world events, they have frequently been ignored by international analysts. However, the statistics tell a story of a large portion of the world suffering in ways that should not be ignored. Almost half the world's population lives on less than $2 per day. But that raw statistic does not capture the human tragedy.

14.4.1
Haves vs. Have-nots

- In developing countries, 91 children out of 1,000 will die before their fifth birthday. In the United States, the number is eight.
- Most of those—over 30,000 children *every day* in the developing world—die from preventable diseases such as diarrhea, breathing difficulties, or malaria.
- Malnutrition weakens many of these children (and adults), thus allowing diseases to become life-threatening. More than 800 million people around the world—that is, roughly two-and-a-half times the population of the United States—are malnourished. About 80 per cent of these are in the developing world. This is despite the fact that the world grows more than enough food to feed everyone.
- Life expectancy in the wealthiest countries is about 78 years. In the poorest countries, it is about 59 years, and in sub-Saharan Africa, it is only 46.5 years and has been falling, largely due to the rapid spread of HIV/AIDS.
- Roughly 50 per cent of the adult population in the developing world cannot read or write at a minimal level. When combined with poverty and persistent disease problems, it is difficult to see how these countries will improve in the foreseeable future.

This is a situation that has not been encountered before in history. Although poverty has always been present, the gap between rich and poor nations is bigger than it has ever been and shows no real sign of decreasing. What makes this so disturbing and a potential threat to the international system is that to those at the bottom it looks like a broken promise. The developed capitalist countries, led by the United States, have constructed an international economic system based on free market ideas with the promise that if countries would just play by the rules, they would get better. After all, free markets manifestly distribute resources efficiently. But after 60 years or so, the poorest countries are by and large not much better off than they ever have been.[8] Where are all the gains that these countries have been promised by opening their borders to international trade?

There are dozens of answers, all true to some extent. Some of the gains were squandered on bad projects, some were stolen by corrupt leaders, some were lost by not fully implementing market-based policies. However, some of the gains were lost when the *developed* states refused to follow their own rules, persistently discriminating against goods produced in developing countries. Developing countries will often begin industrializing by producing those products that are most appropriate for their situation, such as relatively low technology industries—textiles, shoes, some types of appliances, and basic electronics—that do not need very large capital investments and use many workers, thereby capitalizing on their lower wage rates. And developed nations should, in theory, be willing to give up manufacturing these items. Their advantages lie elsewhere in those products and services that require large amounts of capital, cutting-edge technology, and so on. But the threatened industries have often been able to persuade their government to keep out the imports from the developing world.

As time has gone on, and alternatives to a capitalist world economy have fallen by the wayside (for good reason, generally), attention is now turning to methods to cushion the poorest nations from the worst blows of the market. This should not seem too radical; nations have recognized since the Depression in the 1930s that markets create winners and losers, and within their own countries governments have a responsibility for helping out those who, through no fault of their own, are harmed by the functioning and expansion of free markets, even if this means stepping back from purely free markets. However, the United States and other developed nations have been very reluctant to allow similar movements away from free markets at the international level. Where is the international equivalent of the welfare "safety net"?

This issue takes on even more importance when we observe that virtually all the population growth in the world today is taking place in these poorest parts of the world. Not only does this pose the threat of a growing pool of poor, dissatisfied people, it also magnifies the problems associated with growing populations, especially environmental degradation and the spread of diseases, many of which are exacerbated by population pressures. For example, population growth will frequently outpace the supply of clean drinking water. Tainted water bears many diseases that cause diarrhea, which in turn leads to dehydration and the consumption

8   There are exceptions, of course. But several of those countries most often pointed to as models of development were badly set back by the Asian financial crisis of 1999. Sustained success stories outside of Asia are hard to find.

of more tainted water. As noted above, most of the children who die in the developing world die from diseases easily preventable by access to safe water. Tuberculosis, a disease largely wiped out in the developed world, has made a comeback in the poorer parts of the world. It is transmitted by air, especially in closed spaces. Growing populations lead to more people living in overcrowded housing with subsequent higher rates of disease transmission. How long will the poor peoples of the world be content with promises? They view their current plight as no fault of their own. Why should they accept it? Specific scenarios for this kind of "revolution from below" are not always easy to envision, but the demographic facts—more and more desperately poor people looking up at a group of privileged wealthy—should raise concern.

In 1993, a very different view of the future was outlined by Samuel Huntington, a pre-eminent American political scientists. That year, he published an article in *Foreign Affairs*, a journal unusual in that it is read by both academic scholars and policy-makers. His article, titled "The Clash of Civilizations" and the book published in 1996 in which he expanded his ideas, have generated a great deal of discussion. For a few years, the dialogue was largely among international relations specialists. Since the terrorist attacks of 9/11, Huntington's ideas have been revisited by the popular media and government officials.

14.4.2
Clash of Civilizations

His point is straightforward, although its surface simplicity has led some to ignore the nuances of his argument. The central idea is that the divisions in the world today—what Huntington calls the "fault lines"—are no longer ideological, capitalist versus communist in particular, nor are they economic, as the view discussed above stressed. Instead, they are cultural. The metaphor of geology is not accidental; in the same way that the presence of tectonic plates was discovered by plotting the occurrence of earthquakes and volcanoes, we can find splits between cultures in world history by plotting where wars occurred. They have largely been along the divides between European, Islamic, and Asian cultures. The Balkans is one of the clearest examples; in this area where the Christian and Islamic worlds come into physical contact, they have fought wars for centuries. Huntington's broadest point is that, contrary to the more optimistic view outlined above, the spread of capitalist democracy is not particularly encouraging and is unlikely to sweep across the globe. Other cultures, he argues, simply do not share the values that Western culture celebrate—individualism, liberalism, constitutionalism, profit, etc.

This is a particularly grim view of the future, since these divides are based not on empirical measurements of wealth or other "facts" but on questions of faith. Cultures and religions believe they are right about issues that are not subject to proof and that others are wrong. They thus do not tolerate opposing views easily. The **POSITIVE-SUM** gains from trade spelled out above no longer exist. They are only part of a larger, zero-sum game where Western capitalism is trying to overwhelm any and all challenging ideologies.

Huntington's views have been criticized as overly simplistic; his "cultures" are not as monolithic as he suggests as there are substantial differences within these groups. The most protracted war since World War II was fought between Iran and Iraq, adherents of two different sects of Islam. The difference in Huntington's work between culture and religion is not always clear, especially since some of his hypothesized cultures have religious labels, such as "Islamic." This is helpful, in some ways. Remember our discussion of cleavages from Chapter Nine: cleavages become destabilizing when they reinforce one another. Huntington's study can be read as an international version of this argument. The clash of civilizations is dangerous because nationality, culture, religion, and ethnicity overlap to create a volatile environment. And these cleavages are much older than the capitalist/communist divide. If anything, the Cold War kept a lid on these historical splits. Now, for many of the reasons we have addressed in this chapter, these cleavages are more apparent and more sensitive. This is the dark side of **GLOBALISM**. As nation-states become less important, individuals look to other sources for their identities, and those sources may be more inherently in conflict.

14.5 Conclusion

In this chapter, we have tried to give an overview of both the field of International Relations and the current state of the international system. As with the other topics we have covered in this text, political scientists attempt to balance accurate descriptions with helpful generalizations and theories. Unless we can draw lessons from history to apply to other circumstances, we cannot be helpful in trying to find solutions to current problems. This is a particularly difficult task in international relations where there are so many possible explanations for any given phenomenon and so many different opinions on what the important issues are. Furthermore, as we have touched on several times, the stakes—war and peace, depression and prosperity—are so high.

The question lurking behind most of this chapter is whether the international system is changing to such an extent that the tools we have used to understand it—our theories—need to be seriously revised or even discarded. The interconnected nature of the world represented by the shorthand "globalism" is clearly new. Although openness of trade has ebbed and flowed over time, the presence of instantaneous, virtually free global communication is unprecedented and has staggering consequences. Indeed, it makes possible the kinds of financial transactions, long-distance management, sharing of resources, and transmission of cultures that drive, for better or worse, the other, more specific types of globalism. The age of relatively isolated nation-states that has been in place for the last 350 years may be ending. We need to be careful not to get trapped into thinking that just because we've only lived in one sort of system, that system will last forever.

We must also exercise caution in making predictions about the demise of the **WESTPHALIAN SYSTEM**. Early in the twentieth century, Sir Norman Angell, a British scholar and member of Parliament, argued that the spread of international commerce made war unthinkable. Within five years, Europe was embroiled in "the war to end all wars," followed by another great war 20 years later. Observers have been looking for the end of the nation-state for decades. Sovereign countries possess resources that other types of actors in the system, no matter how important, cannot equal. What seems most likely is that nation-states will remain the most important actors internationally, but they will operate in a system with other types of players that can dramatically affect them and that they must, therefore, take account of. The terrorist attacks of 9/11 are a dramatic example of how groups that on virtually any traditional measure would be considered insignificant can profoundly affect the strongest nation on earth. The globalizing international system clearly offers the possibility of greatly increased wealth, knowledge, and human welfare. It is also clearly a more complex place. Living in, understanding, and managing this new environment will require sophisticated, knowledgeable observers of international politics.

Key Terms

absolute power
anarchy
Bretton Woods System
globalism
globalization
idealism
international organization
  (IO)
multinational corporation
  (MNC)
positive-sum
realism
relative power
sovereignty
Westphalian system
zero-sum

References and Suggested Readings

Publishing information is not provided for texts that are either out of print or widely available in contemporary editions.

Angell, Norman. 1909. *The Great Illusion*.

Boutrous-Ghali, Boutrous. 1992. *An Agenda for Peace*. New York: UN Publications.

Bull, Hedley. 1995. *The Anarchical Society*, 3rd ed. New York: Columbia University Press.

Clausewitz, Carl von. 1873. *On War*.

Friedman, Thomas. 2000. *The Lexus and the Olive Tree: Understanding Globalization*. New York: Farrar, Straus and Giroux.

George, Alexander, and Richard Smoke. 1974. *Deterrence in American Foreign Policy*. New York: Columbia University Press.

Hanson, Victor Davis. 1989. *The Western Way of War: Infantry Battle in Classical Greece*. New York: Knopf.

———. 2001. *Carnage and Culture: Landmark Battles in the Rise of Western Power*. New York: Doubleday

Hobbes, Thomas. 1660. *Leviathan*.

Huntington, Samuel. 1993. "The Clash of Civilizations?" *Foreign Affairs*, Summer.

———. 1996. *The Clash of Civilizations and the Remaking of World Order*. New York: Simon and Schuster.

Mueller, John. 1989. *Retreat From Doomsday: The Obsolescence of Major War*. New York: Basic Books.

Rosenau, James N. 1990 *Turbulence in World Politics: A Theory of Continuity and Change*. Princeton, NJ: Princeton University Press.

Thucydides. 431 BC. *The Peloponnesian War*.

Vernon, Raymond. 1971. *Sovereignty at Bay*. New York: Basic Books.

Zacher, Mark. 1992. "The Decaying Pillars of the Westphalian Temple: Implications for International Order and Governance," in J. Rosenau and E.O. Czempiel, eds., *Governance without Government*. Cambridge: Cambridge University Press.

APPENDICES

APPENDIX A | The Constitution of the United States

We the People of the United States, in Order to form a more perfect Union, establish Justice, insure domestic Tranquility, provide for the common defence, promote the general Welfare, and secure the Blessings of Liberty to ourselves and our Posterity, do ordain and establish this Constitution for the United States of America.

Preamble

§ 1 All legislative Powers herein granted shall be vested in a Congress of the United States, which shall consist of a Senate and House of Representatives.

Article I

§ 2 **CLAUSE 1:** The House of Representatives shall be composed of Members chosen every second Year by the People of the several States, and the Electors in each State shall have the Qualifications requisite for Electors of the most numerous Branch of the State Legislature.

CLAUSE 2: No Person shall be a Representative who shall not have attained to the Age of twenty five Years, and been seven Years a Citizen of the United States, and who shall not, when elected, be an Inhabitant of that State in which he shall be chosen.

Article I

CLAUSE 3: Representatives and direct Taxes shall be apportioned among the several States which may be included within this Union, according to their respective Numbers, which shall be determined by adding to the whole Number of free Persons, including those bound to Service for a Term of Years, and excluding Indians not taxed, three fifths of all other Persons. The actual Enumeration shall be made within three Years after the first Meeting of the Congress of the United States, and within every subsequent Term of ten Years, in such Manner as they shall by Law direct. The Number of Representatives shall not exceed one for every thirty Thousand, but each State shall have at Least one Representative; and until such enumeration shall be made, the State of New Hampshire shall be entitled to chuse three, Massachusetts eight, Rhode Island and Providence Plantations one, Connecticut five, New York six, New Jersey four, Pennsylvania eight, Delaware one, Maryland six, Virginia ten, North Carolina five, South Carolina five, and Georgia three.

CLAUSE 4: When vacancies happen in the Representation from any State, the Executive Authority thereof shall issue Writs of Election to fill such Vacancies.

CLAUSE 5: The House of Representatives shall chuse their Speaker and other Officers; and shall have the sole Power of Impeachment.

§ 3 CLAUSE 1: The Senate of the United States shall be composed of two Senators from each State, chosen by the Legislature thereof, for six Years; and each Senator shall have one Vote.

CLAUSE 2: Immediately after they shall be assembled in Consequence of the first Election, they shall be divided as equally as may be into three Classes. The Seats of the Senators of the first Class shall be vacated at the Expiration of the second Year, of the second Class at the Expiration of the fourth Year, and of the third Class at the Expiration of the sixth Year, so that one third may be chosen every second Year; and if Vacancies happen by Resignation, or otherwise, during the Recess of the Legislature of any State, the Executive thereof may make temporary Appointments until the next Meeting of the Legislature, which shall then fill such Vacancies.

CLAUSE 3: No Person shall be a Senator who shall not have attained to the Age of thirty Years, and been nine Years a Citizen of the United

States, and who shall not, when elected, be an Inhabitant of that State for which he shall be chosen.

CLAUSE 4: The Vice President of the United States shall be President of the Senate, but shall have no Vote, unless they be equally divided.

CLAUSE 5: The Senate shall chuse their other Officers, and also a President pro tempore, in the Absence of the Vice President, or when he shall exercise the Office of President of the United States.

CLAUSE 6: The Senate shall have the sole Power to try all Impeachments. When sitting for that Purpose, they shall be on Oath or Affirmation. When the President of the United States is tried, the Chief Justice shall preside: And no Person shall be convicted without the Concurrence of two thirds of the Members present.

CLAUSE 7: Judgment in Cases of Impeachment shall not extend further than to removal from Office, and disqualification to hold and enjoy any Office of honor, Trust or Profit under the United States: but the Party convicted shall nevertheless be liable and subject to Indictment, Trial, Judgment and Punishment, according to Law.

§ 4 CLAUSE 1: The Times, Places and Manner of holding Elections for Senators and Representatives, shall be prescribed in each State by the Legislature thereof; but the Congress may at any time by Law make or alter such Regulations, except as to the Places of chusing Senators.

CLAUSE 2: The Congress shall assemble at least once in every Year, and such Meeting shall be on the first Monday in December, unless they shall by Law appoint a different Day.

§ 5 CLAUSE 1: Each House shall be the Judge of the Elections, Returns and Qualifications of its own Members, and a Majority of each shall constitute a Quorum to do Business; but a smaller Number may adjourn from day to day, and may be authorized to compel the Attendance of absent Members, in such Manner, and under such Penalties as each House may provide.

Article I

CLAUSE 2: Each House may determine the Rules of its Proceedings, punish its Members for disorderly Behaviour, and, with the Concurrence of two thirds, expel a Member.

CLAUSE 3: Each House shall keep a Journal of its Proceedings, and from time to time publish the same, excepting such Parts as may in their Judgment require Secrecy; and the Yeas and Nays of the Members of either House on any question shall, at the Desire of one fifth of those Present, be entered on the Journal.

CLAUSE 4: Neither House, during the Session of Congress, shall, without the Consent of the other, adjourn for more than three days, nor to any other Place than that in which the two Houses shall be sitting.

§ 6 CLAUSE 1: The Senators and Representatives shall receive a Compensation for their Services, to be ascertained by Law, and paid out of the Treasury of the United States. They shall in all Cases, except Treason, Felony and Breach of the Peace, be privileged from Arrest during their Attendance at the Session of their respective Houses, and in going to and returning from the same; and for any Speech or Debate in either House, they shall not be questioned in any other Place.

CLAUSE 2: No Senator or Representative shall, during the Time for which he was elected, be appointed to any civil Office under the Authority of the United States, which shall have been created, or the Emoluments whereof shall have been encreased during such time; and no Person holding any Office under the United States, shall be a Member of either House during his Continuance in Office.

§ 7 CLAUSE 1: All Bills for raising Revenue shall originate in the House of Representatives; but the Senate may propose or concur with Amendments as on other Bills.

CLAUSE 2: Every Bill which shall have passed the House of Representatives and the Senate, shall, before it become a Law, be presented to the President of the United States; If he approve he shall sign it, but if not he shall return it, with his Objections to that House in which it shall have originated, who shall enter the Objections at large on their Journal, and proceed to reconsider it. If after such Reconsideration two thirds of that House shall agree to pass the Bill, it shall be sent, together with the Objections, to the other House, by which it shall likewise be reconsidered, and if approved by two thirds of that House, it shall become a Law. But in all such Cases the Votes of both Houses shall be determined by yeas and Nays, and the Names of the Persons voting for and against the Bill shall be entered on the Journal of each House respectively. If any Bill shall not be returned by the President within ten Days (Sundays excepted) after it shall have been presented to him, the Same shall be a Law, in like Manner as if he had signed it, unless the Congress by their Adjournment prevent its Return, in which Case it shall not be a Law.

CLAUSE 3: Every Order, Resolution, or Vote to which the Concurrence of the Senate and House of Representatives may be necessary (except on a question of Adjournment) shall be presented to the President of the United States; and before the Same shall take Effect, shall be approved by him, or being disapproved by him, shall be repassed by two thirds of the Senate and House of Representatives, according to the Rules and Limitations prescribed in the Case of a Bill.

§ 8 CLAUSE 1: The Congress shall have Power to lay and collect Taxes, Duties, Imposts and Excises, to pay the Debts and provide for the common Defence and general Welfare of the United States; but all Duties, Imposts and Excises shall be uniform throughout the United States;

CLAUSE 2: To borrow Money on the credit of the United States;

CLAUSE 3: To regulate Commerce with foreign Nations, and among the several States, and with the Indian Tribes;

CLAUSE 4: To establish an uniform Rule of Naturalization, and uniform Laws on the subject of Bankruptcies throughout the United States;

CLAUSE 5: To coin Money, regulate the Value thereof, and of foreign Coin, and fix the Standard of Weights and Measures;

CLAUSE 6: To provide for the Punishment of counterfeiting the Securities and current Coin of the United States;

Article I

CLAUSE 7: To establish Post Offices and post Roads;

CLAUSE 8: To promote the Progress of Science and useful Arts, by securing for limited Times to Authors and Inventors the exclusive Right to their respective Writings and Discoveries;

CLAUSE 9: To constitute Tribunals inferior to the supreme Court;

CLAUSE 10: To define and punish Piracies and Felonies committed on the high Seas, and Offences against the Law of Nations;

CLAUSE 11: To declare War, grant Letters of Marque and Reprisal, and make Rules concerning Captures on Land and Water;

CLAUSE 12: To raise and support Armies, but no Appropriation of Money to that Use shall be for a longer Term than two Years;

CLAUSE 13: To provide and maintain a Navy;

CLAUSE 14: To make Rules for the Government and Regulation of the land and naval Forces;

CLAUSE 15: To provide for calling forth the Militia to execute the Laws of the Union, suppress Insurrections and repel Invasions;

CLAUSE 16: To provide for organizing, arming, and disciplining, the Militia, and for governing such Part of them as may be employed in the Service of the United States, reserving to the States respectively, the Appointment of the Officers, and the Authority of training the Militia according to the discipline prescribed by Congress;

CLAUSE 17: To exercise exclusive Legislation in all Cases whatsoever, over such District (not exceeding ten Miles square) as may, by Cession of particular States, and the Acceptance of Congress, become the Seat of the Government of the United States, and to exercise like Authority over all Places purchased by the Consent of the Legislature of the State in which the Same shall be, for the Erection of Forts, Magazines, Arsenals, dock-Yards, and other needful Buildings;—And

CLAUSE 18: To make all Laws which shall be necessary and proper for carrying into Execution the foregoing Powers, and all other Powers vested by this Constitution in the Government of the United States, or in any Department or Officer thereof.

Article I

§ 9 CLAUSE 1: The Migration or Importation of such Persons as any of the States now existing shall think proper to admit, shall not be prohibited by the Congress prior to the Year one thousand eight hundred and eight, but a Tax or duty may be imposed on such Importation, not exceeding ten dollars for each Person.

CLAUSE 2: The Privilege of the Writ of Habeas Corpus shall not be suspended, unless when in Cases of Rebellion or Invasion the public Safety may require it.

CLAUSE 3: No Bill of Attainder or ex post facto Law shall be passed.

CLAUSE 4: No Capitation, or other direct, Tax shall be laid, unless in Proportion to the Census or Enumeration herein before directed to be taken.

CLAUSE 5: No Tax or Duty shall be laid on Articles exported from any State.

CLAUSE 6: No Preference shall be given by any Regulation of Commerce or Revenue to the Ports of one State over those of another: nor shall Vessels bound to, or from, one State, be obliged to enter, clear, or pay Duties in another.

CLAUSE 7: No Money shall be drawn from the Treasury, but in Consequence of Appropriations made by Law; and a regular Statement and Account of the Receipts and Expenditures of all public Money shall be published from time to time.

CLAUSE 8: No Title of Nobility shall be granted by the United States: And no Person holding any Office of Profit or Trust under them, shall, without the Consent of the Congress, accept of any present, Emolument, Office, or Title, of any kind whatever, from any King, Prince, or foreign State.

§ 10 CLAUSE 1: No State shall enter into any Treaty, Alliance, or Confederation; grant Letters of Marque and Reprisal; coin Money; emit Bills of Credit; make any Thing but gold and silver Coin a Tender

Article I

in Payment of Debts; pass any Bill of Attainder, ex post facto Law, or Law impairing the Obligation of Contracts, or grant any Title of Nobility.

CLAUSE 2: No State shall, without the Consent of the Congress, lay any Imposts or Duties on Imports or Exports, except what may be absolutely necessary for executing its inspection Laws: and the net Produce of all Duties and Imposts, laid by any State on Imports or Exports, shall be for the Use of the Treasury of the United States; and all such Laws shall be subject to the Revision and Controul of the Congress.

CLAUSE 3: No State shall, without the Consent of Congress, lay any Duty of Tonnage, keep Troops, or Ships of War in time of Peace, enter into any Agreement or Compact with another State, or with a foreign Power, or engage in War, unless actually invaded, or in such imminent Danger as will not admit of delay.

Article II

§ 1 CLAUSE 1: The executive Power shall be vested in a President of the United States of America. He shall hold his Office during the Term of four Years, and, together with the Vice President, chosen for the same Term, be elected, as follows:

CLAUSE 2: Each State shall appoint, in such Manner as the Legislature thereof may direct, a Number of Electors, equal to the whole Number of Senators and Representatives to which the State may be entitled in the Congress: but no Senator or Representative, or Person holding an Office of Trust or Profit under the United States, shall be appointed an Elector.

CLAUSE 3: The Electors shall meet in their respective States, and vote by Ballot for two Persons, of whom one at least shall not be an Inhabitant of the same State with themselves. And they shall make a List of all the Persons voted for, and of the Number of Votes for each; which List they shall sign and certify, and transmit sealed to the Seat of the Government of the United States, directed to the President of the Senate. The President of the Senate shall, in the Presence of the Senate and House of Representatives, open all the Certificates, and the Votes shall then be counted. The Person having the greatest Number of Votes shall be the President, if such Number be a Majority of the whole Number of Electors appointed; and if there be more than one who have such Majority, and have an equal Number of Votes, then the House of Representatives shall immediately chuse by Ballot one of them for President; and if no Person have a Majority, then from the five highest on the List the said House shall in like Manner chuse the President. But in choosing the President, the Votes shall be taken by States, the Representation from each State having one Vote; A quorum for this Purpose shall consist of a Member or Members from two thirds of the States, and a Majority of all the States shall be necessary to a Choice. In every Case, after the Choice of the President, the Person having the greatest Number of Votes of the Electors shall be the Vice President. But if there should remain two or more who have equal Votes, the Senate shall choose from them by Ballot the Vice President.

CLAUSE 4: The Congress may determine the Time of chusing the Electors, and the Day on which they shall give their Votes; which Day shall be the same throughout the United States.

CLAUSE 5: No Person except a natural born Citizen, or a Citizen of the United States, at the time of the Adoption of this Constitution, shall be eligible to the Office of President; neither shall any Person be eligible to that Office who shall not have attained to the Age of thirty five Years, and been fourteen Years a Resident within the United States.

CLAUSE 6: In Case of the Removal of the President from Office, or of his Death, Resignation, or Inability to discharge the Powers and Duties of the said Office, the Same shall devolve on the Vice President, and the Congress may by Law provide for the Case of Removal, Death, Resignation or Inability, both of the President and Vice President, declaring what Officer shall then act as President, and such Officer shall act accordingly, until the Disability be removed, or a President shall be elected.

CLAUSE 7: The President shall, at stated Times, receive for his Services, a Compensation, which shall neither be encreased nor diminished during the Period for which he shall have been elected, and he shall not receive within that Period any other Emolument from the United States, or any of them.

CLAUSE 8: Before he enter on the Execution of his Office, he shall take the following Oath or Affirmation:— "I do solemnly swear (or affirm) that I will faithfully execute the Office of President of the

Article II

United States, and will to the best of my Ability, preserve, protect and defend the Constitution of the United States."

§ 2 **CLAUSE 1:** The President shall be Commander in Chief of the Army and Navy of the United States, and of the Militia of the several States, when called into the actual Service of the United States; he may require the Opinion, in writing, of the principal Officer in each of the executive Departments, upon any Subject relating to the Duties of their respective Offices, and he shall have Power to grant Reprieves and Pardons for Offences against the United States, except in Cases of Impeachment.

CLAUSE 2: He shall have Power, by and with the Advice and Consent of the Senate, to make Treaties, provided two thirds of the Senators present concur; and he shall nominate, and by and with the Advice and Consent of the Senate, shall appoint Ambassadors, other public Ministers and Consuls, Judges of the supreme Court, and all other Officers of the United States, whose Appointments are not herein otherwise provided for, and which shall be established by Law: but the Congress may by Law vest the Appointment of such inferior Officers, as they think proper, in the President alone, in the Courts of Law, or in the Heads of Departments.

CLAUSE 3: The President shall have Power to fill up all Vacancies that may happen during the Recess of the Senate, by granting Commissions which shall expire at the End of their next Session.

§ 3 He shall from time to time give to the Congress Information of the State of the Union, and recommend to their Consideration such Measures as he shall judge necessary and expedient; he may, on extraordinary Occasions, convene both Houses, or either of them, and in Case of Disagreement between them, with Respect to the Time of Adjournment, he may adjourn them to such Time as he shall think proper; he shall receive Ambassadors and other public Ministers; he shall take Care that the Laws be faithfully executed, and shall Commission all the Officers of the United States.

§ 4 The President, Vice President and all civil Officers of the United States, shall be removed from Office on Impeachment for, and Conviction of, Treason, Bribery, or other high Crimes and Misdemeanors.

§ 1 The judicial Power of the United States, shall be vested in one supreme Court, and in such inferior Courts as the Congress may from time to time ordain and establish. The Judges, both of the supreme and inferior Courts, shall hold their Offices during good Behaviour, and shall, at stated Times, receive for their Services, a Compensation, which shall not be diminished during their Continuance in Office.

Article III

§ 2 CLAUSE 1: The judicial Power shall extend to all Cases, in Law and Equity, arising under this Constitution, the Laws of the United States, and Treaties made, or which shall be made, under their Authority;—to all Cases affecting Ambassadors, other public Ministers and Consuls;—to all Cases of admiralty and maritime Jurisdiction;—to Controversies to which the United States shall be a Party;—to Controversies between two or more States;—between a State and Citizens of another State;— between Citizens of different States;— between Citizens of the same State claiming Lands under Grants of different States, and between a State, or the Citizens thereof, and foreign States, Citizens or Subjects.

CLAUSE 2: In all Cases affecting Ambassadors, other public Ministers and Consuls, and those in which a State shall be Party, the supreme Court shall have original Jurisdiction. In all the other Cases before mentioned, the supreme Court shall have appellate Jurisdiction, both as to Law and Fact, with such Exceptions, and under such Regulations as the Congress shall make.

CLAUSE 3: The Trial of all Crimes, except in Cases of Impeachment, shall be by Jury; and such Trial shall be held in the State where the said Crimes shall have been committed; but when not committed within any State, the Trial shall be at such Place or Places as the Congress may by Law have directed.

§ 3 CLAUSE 1: Treason against the United States, shall consist only in levying War against them, or in adhering to their Enemies, giving them Aid and Comfort. No Person shall be convicted of Treason unless on the Testimony of two Witnesses to the same overt Act, or on Confession in open Court.

Article III

CLAUSE 2: The Congress shall have Power to declare the Punishment of Treason, but no Attainder of Treason shall work Corruption of Blood, or Forfeiture except during the Life of the Person attainted.

Article IV

§ 1 Full Faith and Credit shall be given in each State to the public Acts, Records, and judicial Proceedings of every other State. And the Congress may by general Laws prescribe the Manner in which such Acts, Records and Proceedings shall be proved, and the Effect thereof.

§ 2 CLAUSE 1: The Citizens of each State shall be entitled to all Privileges and Immunities of Citizens in the several States.

CLAUSE 2: A Person charged in any State with Treason, Felony, or other Crime, who shall flee from Justice, and be found in another State, shall on Demand of the executive Authority of the State from which he fled, be delivered up, to be removed to the State having Jurisdiction of the Crime.

CLAUSE 3: No Person held to Service or Labour in one State, under the Laws thereof, escaping into another, shall, in Consequence of any Law or Regulation therein, be discharged from such Service or Labour, but shall be delivered up on Claim of the Party to whom such Service or Labour may be due.

§ 3 CLAUSE 1: New States may be admitted by the Congress into this Union; but no new State shall be formed or erected within the Jurisdiction of any other State; nor any State be formed by the Junction of two or more States, or Parts of States, without the Consent of the Legislatures of the States concerned as well as of the Congress.

CLAUSE 2: The Congress shall have Power to dispose of and make all needful Rules and Regulations respecting the Territory or other Property belonging to the United States; and nothing in this Constitution shall be so construed as to Prejudice any Claims of the United States, or of any particular State.

§ 4 The United States shall guarantee to every State in this Union a Republican Form of Government, and shall protect each of them against Invasion; and on Application of the Legislature, or of the Executive (when the Legislature cannot be convened) against domestic Violence.

The Congress, whenever two thirds of both Houses shall deem **Article V** it necessary, shall propose Amendments to this Constitution, or, on the Application of the Legislatures of two thirds of the several States, shall call a Convention for proposing Amendments, which, in either Case, shall be valid to all Intents and Purposes, as Part of this Constitution, when ratified by the Legislatures of three fourths of the several States, or by Conventions in three fourths thereof, as the one or the other Mode of Ratification may be proposed by the Congress; Provided that no Amendment which may be made prior to the Year One thousand eight hundred and eight shall in any Manner affect the first and fourth Clauses in the Ninth Section of the first Article; and that no State, without its Consent, shall be deprived of its equal Suffrage in the Senate.

CLAUSE 1: All Debts contracted and Engagements entered into, before **Article VI** the Adoption of this Constitution, shall be as valid against the United States under this Constitution, as under the Confederation.

CLAUSE 2: This Constitution, and the Laws of the United States which shall be made in Pursuance thereof; and all Treaties made, or which shall be made, under the Authority of the United States, shall be the supreme Law of the Land; and the Judges in every State shall be bound thereby, any Thing in the Constitution or Laws of any State to the Contrary notwithstanding.

CLAUSE 3: The Senators and Representatives before mentioned, and the Members of the several State Legislatures, and all executive and judicial Officers, both of the United States and of the several States, shall be bound by Oath or Affirmation, to support this Constitution; but no religious Test shall ever be required as a Qualification to any Office or public Trust under the United States.

The Ratification of the Conventions of nine States, shall be suffi- **Article VII** cient for the Establishment of this Constitution between the States so ratifying the Same.

Article VII

Done in Convention by the Unanimous Consent of the States present the Seventeenth Day of September in the Year of our Lord one thousand seven hundred and Eighty seven and of the Independence of the United States of America the Twelfth In witness whereof We have hereunto subscribed our Names.

George Washington, President, and Deputy from Virginia

Delaware
George Read
Gunning Bedford, jr.
John Dickinson
Richard Bassett
Jacob Broom

Maryland
James M'Henry
Daniel Jenifer, of St. Thomas
Daniel Carroll

Virginia
John Blair
James Madison Jr.

North Carolina
William Blount
Richard Dobbs Spaight
Hugh Williamson

South Carolina
John Rutledge
Charles Cotesworth Pinckney
Charles Pinckney
Pierce Butler

Georgia
William Few
Abr Baldwin

New Hampshire
John Langdon
Nicholas Gilman

Massachusetts
Nathaniel Gorham
Rufus King

Connecticut
William Samuel Johnson
Roger Sherman

New York
Alexander Hamilton

New Jersey
William Livingston
David Brearley
William Paterson
Jonathan Dayton

Pennsylvania
Benjamin Franklin
Thomas Mifflin
Robert Morris
George Clymer
Thomas Fitzsimons
Jared Ingersoll
James Wilson
Gouverneur Morris

Attest
William Jackson
   Secretary

APPENDIX B | Amendments to the Constitution

Congress shall make no law respecting an establishment of religion, or prohibiting the free exercise thereof; or abridging the freedom of speech, or of the press; or the right of the people peaceably to assemble, and to petition the Government for a redress of grievances.

Article I

A well regulated Militia, being necessary to the security of a free State, the right of the people to keep and bear Arms, shall not be infringed.

Article II

No Soldier shall, in time of peace be quartered in any house, without the consent of the Owner, nor in time of war, but in a manner to be prescribed by law.

Article III

The right of the people to be secure in their persons, houses, papers, and effects, against unreasonable searches and seizures, shall not be violated, and no Warrants shall issue, but upon probable cause, supported by Oath or affirmation, and particularly describing the place to be searched, and the persons or things to be seized.

Article IV

Article V   No person shall be held to answer for a capital, or otherwise infamous crime, unless on a presentment or indictment of a Grand Jury, except in cases arising in the land or naval forces, or in the Militia, when in actual service in time of War or public danger; nor shall any person be subject for the same offence to be twice put in jeopardy of life or limb; nor shall be compelled in any criminal case to be a witness against himself, nor be deprived of life, liberty, or property, without due process of law; nor shall private property be taken for public use, without just compensation.

Article VI   In all criminal prosecutions, the accused shall enjoy the right to a speedy and public trial, by an impartial jury of the State and district wherein the crime shall have been committed, which district shall have been previously ascertained by law, and to be informed of the nature and cause of the accusation; to be confronted with the witnesses against him; to have compulsory process for obtaining witnesses in his favor, and to have the Assistance of Counsel for his defence.

Article VII   In Suits at common law, where the value in controversy shall exceed twenty dollars, the right of trial by jury shall be preserved, and no fact tried by a jury, shall be otherwise re-examined in any Court of the United States, than according to the rules of the common law.

Article VIII   Excessive bail shall not be required, nor excessive fines imposed, nor cruel and unusual punishments inflicted.

Article IX   The enumeration in the Constitution, of certain rights, shall not be construed to deny or disparage others retained by the people.

Article X   The powers not delegated to the United States by the Constitution, nor prohibited by it to the States, are reserved to the States respectively, or to the people.

Article XI   The Judicial power of the United States shall not be construed to extend to any suit in law or equity, commenced or prosecuted against one of the United States by Citizens of another State, or by Citizens or Subjects of any Foreign State.

The Electors shall meet in their respective states, and vote by ballot for President and Vice-President, one of whom, at least, shall not be an inhabitant of the same state with themselves; they shall name in their ballots the person voted for as President, and in distinct ballots the person voted for as Vice-President, and they shall make distinct lists of all persons voted for as President, and of all persons voted for as Vice-President, and of the number of votes for each, which lists they shall sign and certify, and transmit sealed to the seat of the government of the United States, directed to the President of the Senate;—The President of the Senate shall, in the presence of the Senate and House of Representatives, open all the certificates and the votes shall then be counted;—The person having the greatest number of votes for President, shall be the President, if such number be a majority of the whole number of Electors appointed; and if no person have such majority, then from the persons having the highest numbers not exceeding three on the list of those voted for as President, the House of Representatives shall choose immediately, by ballot, the President. But in choosing the President, the votes shall be taken by states, the representation from each state having one vote; a quorum for this purpose shall consist of a member or members from two-thirds of the states, and a majority of all the states shall be necessary to a choice. And if the House of Representatives shall not choose a President whenever the right of choice shall devolve upon them, before the fourth day of March next following, then the Vice-President shall act as President, as in the case of the death or other constitutional disability of the President. The person having the greatest number of votes as Vice-President, shall be the Vice-President, if such number be a majority of the whole number of Electors appointed, and if no person have a majority, then from the two highest numbers on the list, the Senate shall choose the Vice-President; a quorum for the purpose shall consist of two-thirds of the whole number of Senators, and a majority of the whole number shall be necessary to a choice. But no person constitutionally ineligible to the office of President shall be eligible to that of Vice-President of the United States.

Article XII

1 Neither slavery nor involuntary servitude, except as a punishment for crime whereof the party shall have been duly convicted, shall exist within the United States, or any place subject to their jurisdiction.

Article XIII

Article XIII   **2** Congress shall have power to enforce this article by appropriate legislation.

Article XIV   **1** All persons born or naturalized in the United States, and subject to the jurisdiction thereof, are citizens of the United States and of the State wherein they reside. No State shall make or enforce any law which shall abridge the privileges or immunities of citizens of the United States; nor shall any State deprive any person of life, liberty, or property, without due process of law; nor deny to any person within its jurisdiction the equal protection of the laws.

2 Representatives shall be apportioned among the several States according to their respective numbers, counting the whole number of persons in each State, excluding Indians not taxed. But when the right to vote at any election for the choice of electors for President and Vice President of the United States, Representatives in Congress, the Executive and Judicial officers of a State, or the members of the Legislature thereof, is denied to any of the male inhabitants of such State, being twenty-one years of age, and citizens of the United States, or in any way abridged, except for participation in rebellion, or other crime, the basis of representation therein shall be reduced in the proportion which the number of such male citizens shall bear to the whole number of male citizens twenty-one years of age in such State.

3 No person shall be a Senator or Representative in Congress, or elector of President and Vice President, or hold any office, civil or military, under the United States, or under any State, who, having previously taken an oath, as a member of Congress, or as an officer of the United States, or as a member of any State legislature, or as an executive or judicial officer of any State, to support the Constitution of the United States, shall have engaged in insurrection or rebellion against the same, or given aid or comfort to the enemies thereof. But Congress may by a vote of two-thirds of each House, remove such disability.

4 The validity of the public debt of the United States, authorized by law, including debts incurred for payment of pensions and bounties for services in suppressing insurrection or rebellion, shall not be questioned. But neither the United States nor any State shall assume or pay any debt or obligation incurred in aid of insurrection or rebellion against the United States, or any claim for the loss or emancipation of any slave; but all such debts, obligations and claims shall be held illegal and void.

5 The Congress shall have power to enforce, by appropriate legislation, the provisions of this article.

Article XIV

1 The right of citizens of the United States to vote shall not be denied or abridged by the United States or by any State on account of race, color, or previous condition of servitude.

2 The Congress shall have power to enforce this article by appropriate legislation.

Article XV

The Congress shall have power to lay and collect taxes on incomes, from whatever source derived, without apportionment among the several States, and without regard to any census or enumeration.

Article XVI

1 The Senate of the United States shall be composed of two Senators from each State, elected by the people thereof, for six years; and each Senator shall have one vote. The electors in each State shall have the qualifications requisite for electors of the most numerous branch of the State legislatures.

2 When vacancies happen in the representation of any State in the Senate, the executive authority of such State shall issue writs of election to fill such vacancies: Provided, That the legislature of any State may empower the executive thereof to make temporary appointments until the people fill the vacancies by election as the legislature may direct.

3 This amendment shall not be so construed as to affect the election or term of any Senator chosen before it becomes valid as part of the Constitution.

Article XVII

1 After one year from the ratification of this article the manufacture, sale, or transportation of intoxicating liquors within, the importation thereof into, or the exportation thereof from the United States and all territory subject to the jurisdiction thereof for beverage purposes is hereby prohibited.

Article XVIII

Article XVIII

2 The Congress and the several States shall have concurrent power to enforce this article by appropriate legislation.

3 This article shall be inoperative unless it shall have been ratified as an amendment to the Constitution by the legislatures of the several States, as provided in the Constitution, within seven years from the date of the submission hereof to the States by the Congress.

Article XIX

1 The right of citizens of the United States to vote shall not be denied or abridged by the United States or by any State on account of sex.

2 Congress shall have power to enforce this article by appropriate legislation.

Article XX

1 The terms of the President and Vice President shall end at noon on the 20th day of January, and the terms of Senators and Representatives at noon on the 3d day of January, of the years in which such terms would have ended if this article had not been ratified; and the terms of their successors shall then begin.

2 The Congress shall assemble at least once in every year, and such meeting shall begin at noon on the 3d day of January, unless they shall by law appoint a different day.

3 If, at the time fixed for the beginning of the term of the President, the President elect shall have died, the Vice President elect shall become President. If a President shall not have been chosen before the time fixed for the beginning of his term, or if the President elect shall have failed to qualify, then the Vice President elect shall act as President until a President shall have qualified; and the Congress may by law provide for the case wherein neither a President elect nor a Vice President elect shall have qualified, declaring who shall then act as President, or the manner in which one who is to act shall be selected, and such person shall act accordingly until a President or Vice President shall have qualified.

4 The Congress may by law provide for the case of the death of any of the persons from whom the House of Representatives may choose a President whenever the right of choice shall have devolved upon them, and for the case of the death of any of the persons from whom the Senate may choose a Vice President whenever the right of choice shall have devolved upon them.

5 Sections 1 and 2 shall take effect on the 15th day of October following the ratification of this article.

6 This article shall be inoperative unless it shall have been ratified as an amendment to the Constitution by the legislatures of three-fourths of the several States within seven years from the date of its submission.

1 The eighteenth article of amendment to the Constitution of the United States is hereby repealed.

2 The transportation or importation into any State, Territory, or possession of the United States for delivery or use therein of intoxicating liquors, in violation of the laws thereof, is hereby prohibited.

3 This article shall be inoperative unless it shall have been ratified as an amendment to the Constitution by conventions in the several States, as provided in the Constitution, within seven years from the date of the submission hereof to the States by the Congress.

1 No person shall be elected to the office of the President more than twice, and no person who has held the office of President, or acted as President, for more than two years of a term to which some other person was elected President shall be elected to the office of the President more than once. But this article shall not apply to any person holding the office of President when this article was proposed by the Congress, and shall not prevent any person who may be holding the office of President, or acting as President, during the term within which this article becomes operative from holding the office of President or acting as President during the remainder of such term.

2 This article shall be inoperative unless it shall have been ratified as an amendment to the Constitution by the legislatures of three-fourths of the several states within seven years from the date of its submission to the states by the Congress.

Article XXIII   **1** The District constituting the seat of government of the United States shall appoint in such manner as the Congress may direct: A number of electors of President and Vice President equal to the whole number of Senators and Representatives in Congress to which the District would be entitled if it were a state, but in no event more than the least populous state; they shall be in addition to those appointed by the states, but they shall be considered, for the purposes of the election of President and Vice President, to be electors appointed by a state; and they shall meet in the District and perform such duties as provided by the twelfth article of amendment.

2 The Congress shall have power to enforce this article by appropriate legislation.

Article XXIV   **1** The right of citizens of the United States to vote in any primary or other election for President or Vice President, for electors for President or Vice President, or for Senator or Representative in Congress, shall not be denied or abridged by the United States or any state by reason of failure to pay any poll tax or other tax.

2 The Congress shall have power to enforce this article by appropriate legislation.

Article XXV   **1** In case of the removal of the President from office or of his death or resignation, the Vice President shall become President.

2 Whenever there is a vacancy in the office of the Vice President, the President shall nominate a Vice President who shall take office upon confirmation by a majority vote of both Houses of Congress.

3 Whenever the President transmits to the President pro tempore of the Senate and the Speaker of the House of Representatives his written declaration that he is unable to discharge the powers and duties of his office, and until he transmits to them a written declaration to the contrary, such powers and duties shall be discharged by the Vice President as Acting President.

4 Whenever the Vice President and a majority of either the principal officers of the executive departments or of such other body as Congress may by law provide, transmit to the President pro tempore of the Senate and the Speaker of the House of Representatives their written declaration that the President is unable to discharge the powers and duties of his office, the Vice President shall immediately assume the powers and duties of the office as Acting President.

Thereafter, when the President transmits to the President pro tempore of the Senate and the Speaker of the House of Representatives his written declaration that no inability exists, he shall resume the powers and duties of his office unless the Vice President and a majority of either the principal officers of the executive department or of such other body as Congress may by law provide, transmit within four days to the President pro tempore of the Senate and the Speaker of the House of Representatives their written declaration that the President is unable to discharge the powers and duties of his office. Thereupon Congress shall decide the issue, assembling within forty-eight hours for that purpose if not in session. If the Congress, within twenty-one days after receipt of the latter written declaration, or, if Congress is not in session, within twenty-one days after Congress is required to assemble, determines by two-thirds vote of both Houses that the President is unable to discharge the powers and duties of his office, the Vice President shall continue to discharge the same as Acting President; otherwise, the President shall resume the powers and duties of his office.

Article XXV

1 The right of citizens of the United States, who are 18 years of age or older, to vote, shall not be denied or abridged by the United States or any state on account of age.

2 The Congress shall have the power to enforce this article by appropriate legislation.

Article XXVI

No law varying the compensation for the services of the Senators and Representatives shall take effect until an election of Representatives shall have intervened.

Article XXVII

INDEX